HISTORY IN A GLASS

HISTORY IN A GLASS

SIXTY YEARS OF WINE WRITING FROM *GOURMET*

*Edited and with an Introduction
by Ruth Reichl*

THE MODERN LIBRARY

NEW YORK

LIBRARY OF CONGRESS CATALOGING-IN-PUBLICATION DATA
History in a glass: sixty years of wine writing from
Gourmet/edited and with an introduction by Ruth Reichl.
p. cm.—(Modern Library food series)
ISBN 0-679-64312-5
1. Wine and wine making—History—20th century.
2. Wine writers—History—20th century.   I. Reichl, Ruth.
II. Gourmet.   III. Modern Library food.

TP549.H57 2006
641.2'2'0904—dc22   2005050500

Printed in the United States of America on acid-free paper

www. modernlibrary.com

2 4 6 8 9 7 5 3 1

First Edition

CONTENTS

THE AMERICAN REVOLUTION

SALUT!

A WORLD OF WINE

VINTAGE YEARS

INTRODUCTION

Ruth Reichl

Gourmet was born into a nearly wineless world. It was 1941, and although America had not yet joined the war, crossing the ocean had become far too dangerous for any cargo so frivolous as wine. Before long, supplies of older French and German wines—at the time, virtually the only wines being imported—began to dry up. Even if the shipping lanes had remained open, there was little to import: The vineyards of Europe had turned into battlegrounds, and producing wine was no longer a priority.

It should have been a fine time for the American wine industry. But Prohibition was less than ten years behind us; most of the vineyards had been torn up, and replanting proceeded slowly. Reading *Gourmet*'s coverage, sixty-five years later, makes you realize what a precious window of opportunity this was. The fact that American winemakers wasted it makes you want to weep.

I don't say that lightly: Putting this book together turned out to be a remarkably emotional experience. Although I knew, intellectually, about the enormous changes that had taken place in the world of wine over the relatively short period since *Gourmet* began, reading these dispatches from the past gave me the opportunity to live right through them.

And so I found myself celebrating the repeal of Prohibition while listening to Frank Schoonmaker—perhaps my favorite wine writer of all time—excoriating American winegrowers for not doing a better job. When he is infuriated by the way American vintners insist on making endlessly mediocre copies of great French wines instead of drawing on their native strengths, I'm angry too. Why not, he argues, produce good, drinkable American wines? From the vantage point of history, you can't help wondering how different things might have been had they taken his advice.

Then the war ends and all the wine writers hurry over to France to see if the vineyards are still intact. They're hoping that a few wily winemakers have managed to hide their bottles from the invading *boches*. We celebrate each time an unheralded stash is discovered, jubilant that the German occupiers have left some for us. It's a halcyon time—great wine is still affordable—and as *Gourmet*'s writers drink more than their share, we're standing right there with them. Then James Beard is dispatched on a truly epic tour of France, inhaling, ingesting, and imbibing enough to feed a few small villages. It's quite a performance—where did he get the stamina?—but you can't help wishing that you'd been at his side, matching him swallow for swallow.

When the fifties and sixties roll around, Americans broaden their wine horizons. As writers like Hugh Johnson, Frederick Wildman, Jr., and Lillian Langseth-Christensen head off to Austria, Spain, and Italy on assignment for the magazine, we find ourselves wandering through the vineyards enjoying a kind of simplicity that will never come again. We stand in the fields picking grapes, we eat in charming little inns, and we stroll through the Viennese countryside enjoying our first taste of new wine.

There's wonderful history here too, forgotten lore like America's long love affair with Madeira. There is passion as well, for the people who wrote about wine in those early years were a lonely lot, and they were eager to swell their ranks. Their mission was clear: They wanted all the Americans who were not wine drinkers (and they were legion) to discover what they were missing.

And finally we share the enormous excitement as Americans, at last, discover wine and the world starts to change. *Gourmet* watches wine come into the culture, and rejoices as the industry matures and prospers. We witness Italian wine, once despised as negligible stuff in straw-covered bottles, begin to get respect. Before long we're paying attention to Australia, Spain, and Chile.

But this is much more than a long look backward. What makes *History in a Glass* so thrilling is that we are watching history as it happens. America's appreciation for wine grows, and we get to join the action.

Gourmet was, from the very beginning, committed to covering wine. In the early days, few other publications had much interest in the subject, and every expert was eager to contribute. Over the years the magazine published thousands of pages on wine, written by the very best writers in the language at the top of their form.

I think they would be amazed at the way things have turned out. I like to imagine telling Frank Schoonmaker or Frederick Wildman that America has become a country of wine connoisseurs. I'd like to be able to take them into one of our great wine stores and show them how impressive our native wines have become. But more than anything I'd like to be able to raise a glass of something very, very good and thank them for their eloquence as I toast them for leading the way.

CELEBRATING THE REPEAL

THE VINE DIES HARD

Frank Schoonmaker

It could hardly be expected that a part of the United States which has had as fantastic and extraordinary a history as California, would be anything but extraordinary as far as the history of its viticulture is concerned. A state in which a Mexican general, born a Spaniard, received as his guest a Russian princess who had arrived in America by way of Siberia and Alaska, and protected this Russian princess from the amorous advances of an Indian chief, is no ordinary state. The treatment which the vine has received in California has been exactly as fantastic and as extraordinary as that story, and involves an even greater array of nationalities and events tragic and comic.

In California was planted the largest vineyard in the world, 3,060,000 vines that never produced anything worth drinking. California also boasted the largest small vineyard, a single vine planted in 1783 by a Mexican woman named Maria Marcelina Feliz, and known to have yielded upward of five tons of grapes. The European vine was introduced into California in 1770 by Franciscan missionaries, who brought over with them what were supposed to be Malaga cuttings and planted them around their missions from San Diego up the old Camino Real as far as Monterey and Sonoma. But the grapes they planted were not of any very good variety, and the wine they made was nothing to boast about.

We can safely say that when the Forty-niners arrived on the coast, they found no very good wine awaiting them. People of almost every nationality made a contribution of some sort to early California wine-making. A Hungarian nobleman and a Finn were leading pioneers; Chinese labor was used almost exclusively in the vineyards until 1890; a member of the Japanese royal house was, for several decades, the owner of one of the state's best vineyards; German emigrants became winemakers; a score of leading Frenchmen planted vines and gave their vineyards French names; and a large part of California's present wine production is in the hands of Italians. Thus a sort of viticultural League of Nations has existed in the state, with almost every race that played a part in the building of America contributing its penny's worth to the creation of California's vineyards and wines.

Among these strangers who appeared on the scene was a remark-able individual who came as Count Agoston Haraszthy, but presently had Americanized himself into plain Colonel Haraszthy. He intro-duced, it is said, the Zinfandel grape; and the cuttings of this variety, carried off and planted all over the state, undoubtedly changed the whole trend of California viticulture. It became an industry and began to grow like the prairie towns of the same period. California made up its collective mind to "go places," and the familiar American cycle of boom-and-bust was under way.

The "bust" was due to perfectly evident causes. The first boom lasted a little more than ten years. Most of the get-rich-quick planters knew very little about grape varieties, and still less about wine. Huge crops were harvested, but the wine was poorly made, and found no ready market. Then, to cap the evil days, the phylloxera arrived, that parasite which devours the roots of grapevines. The disastrous effects it had on the vineyards of California were hardly less than those it wrought a few years later on the vineyards of France. Whole vine-yards were wiped out and abandoned; all conceivable remedies, from those of science to those of witchcraft, were tried, with little or no success.

But the vine dies hard. By 1876 in California it was on its way back.

The resurrection was due largely to the efforts of two individuals, Professor George Husmann and Charles A. Wetmore. Professor Husmann was America's first wine technician of real consequence, and did more than any other person in this country to develop the phylloxera-resistant roots on which not only all California wine grapes, but virtually all European wine grapes as well, are now grafted.

Mr. Wetmore's contribution to the second boom now about to begin was that of a vast enthusiasm and a better knowledge of grape varieties which he had acquired on his pilgrimage through European vinelands: Returning from that tour, he labored to impart this enthusiasm and this knowledge to the wine producers of California. Those whose interest in vineyard culture was not altogether speculative soon began to plant good grape varieties. There were also people of independent means who began to produce fine wine as gentlemen wine growers; and thanks to the cheap Chinese labor which was then available, acre after acre along the steep slopes overlooking the Sonoma, Napa, and Santa Clara valleys was cleared of brush, plowed, and planted in vines. Storage cellars were dug back into the hills; and big, cool, thick-walled stone wineries began to spring up all over northern California. A good many of these carried simply the names of their owners; others were given classical or purely fanciful or foreign names.

There must have been a hundred such vineyards, within fifty or sixty miles of San Francisco Bay, that were relatively famous in 1890, and even more famous at the turn of the century. Some had changed hands, but most of them were going their sound and prosperous way in 1910. A decade later, the cultivation of a fine vineyard had become a millionaire's or a bankrupt's occupation; and all but a pitiful few of the great wine names of California had disappeared.

It is difficult, across the chasm of twenty-five years, to see national Prohibition as the better California vintners saw it. One of the principal arguments of the Prohibitionists was that essential foodstuffs were being diverted by the liquor industry; but wine grapes are not raisin or table grapes, and what could the growers do with wine grapes except make wine? Good wine grapes are grown on hillsides where little else, least of all cereals, will grow; then why were vines torn up which had taken a decade or more to come into full production? The wine growers of California had seen their fathers make wine, and their friends and their fathers' friends drink it without drunkenness, and with real enjoyment. It is not a pleasant thing to be told, when you have loyally and honestly pursued an occupation which has been honorably regarded since the beginnings of human literacy, an occupation which your father and grandfather pursued before you, that your occupation is criminal. But that was the law. So the upland vineyards were uprooted, and the equipment and the cellars were allowed to fall into disrepair.

It looked at first as though Prohibition meant the end of the wine-grape industry in California—but not for long. California farmers actually found it profitable between 1915 and 1934 to plant one hundred thousand acres of red-wine grapes.

Now a word about the grapes that were planted during this period. The public in the East wanted and demanded what were euphemistically described as "juice grapes," and was prepared to pay fancy prices for them. These home winemakers knew little about wine and less about grapes. As it happens, almost all of the fine-wine grapes of the world are small, thin-skinned, fragile, and not particularly prepossessing. They ship poorly. On the other hand, the thick-skinned, tough, common varieties—Alicante Bouschet, Mataro, Carignane—travel well; and it was these which the winemakers of New York, Philadelphia, and Boston wanted and secured. As a result, hundreds of acres of superior wine grapes in California were torn up and replanted in these varieties, which never could yield, even under the best conditions, anything but mediocre wine.

The damage Prohibition did to California is not likely to be repaired for another fifteen or twenty years. With a few notable exceptions, those who had created the traditions of wine producing in California, and had maintained its standards, did not survive Prohibition. The industry fell inevitably into less scrupulous hands. The decline in the quality of California table wine is partially due to this. Also, let it be remembered, the poor-quality grapes that were planted during the Prohibition era to satisfy the demand of the home winemakers are still there, still producing.

How long it will take for the wine industry of California to recover from Prohibition and its succeeding evils is difficult to estimate. This hoped-for recovery has been further delayed by the mistaken policy which many of the wine growers adopted after Repeal. Instead of frankly admitting at that time that there was almost no sound, well-aged wine on hand in this country, California's wine industry decided to brazen it out; no more dishonest and disastrous policy was ever adopted by a major industry. Wines that were poor, unsound, artificially "aged," artificially flavored, misrepresented, and mislabeled became the rule rather than the exception on the American market. It is to our everlasting credit that we recognized these for the frauds they were, and turned instead to cocktails and highballs. California wine producers have gone through difficult years since the end of Prohibition, but most of the difficulties were very largely of their own making.

Since 1936 and 1937 the situation has changed remarkably and for the better. The intelligent producers of California have begun to plant fine-wine grapes, to make their wine with vastly more attention and care, and to put out wines which are quite able to hold their own against all but the really great wines of Europe.

This country for just and valid reasons condemned the California wines that were being marketed in 1934 and 1935. For no less just and valid reasons, we should now welcome with open arms the excellent California wines which are being produced today; for the vine, at long last, is beginning to receive in the better California vineyards the respect and study and loving care which it deserves, and which it can so richly reward.

April 1941

American Names for American Wines

Frank Schoonmaker

When the New Year came in with a hurrah (and confetti) and a huzzah (with horns), the average American wine producer was not out celebrating. He probably heaved a sigh of relief as we shut the door on 1940—his seventh lean year was over and done with, and it looked as if a few fat years—perhaps seven, certainly two or three—were on their way. Wine consumption, at long last, is on its way up in the United States, and people as a whole are beginning to show a genuine interest in American wine.

Seven years ago, at the time of Repeal, American wine producers had a chance such as few ever get: this country had no drinking habits worthy of the name, people were favorably disposed toward wine, ready to try anything, and, after the Prohibition years, to accept anything good.

American vintners proceeded to muff the chance, miss the boat. This was largely their fault, but as we look back on December 1933 across the intervening years, we can see pretty clearly why the muff was made, why it was more or less inevitable, and why the United States did not become overnight (as a good many people rashly predicted it would) at least as much of a wine-drinking country as Argentina or Chile.

First, there were, in 1933, scarcely a dozen fine vineyards in North America. Plenty of raisin grapes, plenty of table grapes, but a pitifully few thousand acres of wine grapes. A good many California producers had torn up their superior vines during Prohibition and planted in their place the tough, common, heavy-bearing varieties then in demand as "juice grapes" for the home winemaker. A certain number of good vineyards had been simply abandoned.

Second, at the time of Repeal there was only an infinitesimal amount of good, properly aged American wine on hand. But most American producers, underfinanced if not in actual financial straits, had to sell what they had available, good or bad, mature or fresh from the fermenting vat. And they did.

Third, instead of explaining, to a public then definitely sympathetic, their problems and plans and hopes, American vintners, with a few notable exceptions, decided to brazen the thing out. They announced that their wines were quite as good as the better vintages of Germany and France and Spain—but any beginner with a couple of dollars in his pocket could buy two bottles and find out that this was not by any means true.

Fourth, American vintners insisted on selling their wines under European names to which these wines had no moral and precious little commercial right—St.-Julien, Château d'Yquem, Pommard, Chablis. The government finally stepped in and stopped the worst of these abuses; meanwhile American growers had, by inference, admitted that their wines were imitations and invited the public to compare the imitation with the original. The public did, and for the next two or three years almost all of the American wines sold were sold on a price basis.

Fifth, and this is not the fault of the vintners, there appeared, with Repeal, a collection of self-styled connoisseurs, most of them quite as ignorant as the public they pretended to instruct, who published, generally with the imprimatur of some wine merchant, enormously complicated vintage and service charts which baffled and embarrassed the average housewife—anyone was a barbarian to serve a '24 claret after a '29; an average Sunday dinner required three wines, none of which, in the majority of cases, the local liquor store carried; good wine should not be served to those who smoked, when all of one's friends smoked.

Faced with all this, after one or two unfortunate experiences with widely advertised domestic wines, the American housewife decided to concentrate on Martinis or Manhattans and highballs, and I can only praise her good sense.

American wine will never take the place which it deserves on America's dinner tables until it is honestly presented to the American public, and by "honestly" I mean under American names. California and New York and Ohio have now, after seven years, the vineyards to produce good wine, and considerable and fairly adequate stocks of good wine laid by. In justice to the wine and to ourselves, this ought to be sold for what it is. Let us look into this subject.

What is a French Chablis or a French Sauternes? And what is a California "Chablis" or a California "Sauternes"? Well, a French Chablis (unless shipped by a downright thief) is a wine made from Pinot Chardonnay grapes, incidentally one of the four or five best white-wine grapes in the world, either in the township of Chablis itself or in one of nineteen adjoining townships which enjoy the same climatic conditions and have pretty much the same type of soil. A French Sauternes is a wine produced in a delimited district about one-fourth as big as a California county, from Sauvignon, Sémillon, and Muscat grapes. Well, what is a California "Chablis"? Legally, it is any white California wine which the producer (who has probably never tasted a good French Chablis in his life) thinks tastes like Chablis. It can be made from Pinot Chardonnay grapes or from culls thrown out by raisin pickers, in the best viticultural district of California or the worst. A California "Sauternes" can be made anywhere in a state nearly as large as the wine-producing area of France, and it can be made of any kind of grape that the winemaker happens to have or cares to buy, including Tokays, Muscats, and Concords. Actually, I do not believe there are five thousand acres of true Sauternes grapes in California, and I am certain there are not three hundred acres of Pinot Chardonnays.

The trouble, therefore, with European names for California wines is not primarily that they are wrong or dishonest: It is simply that they mean absolutely nothing, that they give the consumer no idea what he is buying, no guarantee, and no information; that they give the producer of superior grapes and the owner of superior vineyards no advantage and no higher prices; that to the merchant they mean endless complaints and explanations. No two American "Sauternes" taste exactly alike.

Despite this lack of standards, these foreign type names, as Harold J. Grossman says, in his excellent *Guide to Wines, Spirits, and Beers,* "are more appropriate when applied to California wines than to American wines, as they do bear some resemblance to the originals, which is not true of the Eastern types."

Wine, it is important to remember, is not a manufactured article but a farm product, and its excellence or mediocrity is primarily the result of the soil on which the grapes were grown and of the grape variety which the producer chose to plant. Thus, in all of the great wine-producing countries of the world the local wines take their names from the factors which make them what they are—the place from which they come, the grapes from which they are made. We have our full share of pleasant and picturesque place-names in this country, and there is no reason why we should be unwilling or reluctant to use them. A few progressive wine growers have already started using them, and the public response has been overwhelmingly favorable.

Away, then, with California "Moselle," New York State "Burgundy," and the whole crew of hyphenated Americans. The fine vineyard districts of the United States are these: the Napa Valley, the Sonoma Valley, the Livermore Valley, and the foothills of the Santa Cruz Mountains in Santa Clara County, California; the Lake Erie Islands off Sandusky, Ohio; the Finger Lakes district of New York State, especially the shores of Lake Canandaigua and Lake Keuka. Other districts will, no doubt, soon come into production, and some of them may prove every bit as good as those already known.

The fine-wine grapes grown in this country are, in California, the Pinot (from Burgundy), the Cabernet (from Bordeaux), the Gamay (from the Beaujolais), the Riesling, Sylvaner, and Traminer (from the Rhine and Alsace), the Folle Blanche (from the Cognac country), the Sauvignon and Sémillon (from the Graves and Sauternes districts). In the East the grapes are native grapes, and the best of them, all of which yield white wine, are the Delaware, the Elvira, Moore's Diamond, the Catawba, the Diana, the Dutchess.

These, then, are the names one should look for on American wines, the names of the American districts in which the wines were made and the names of the grapes from which they came.

March 1941

RETURN TO THE NATIVE

Frank Schoonmaker

Nature seems to have planned the United States to be a nation of wine drinkers. Even apart from California, the wide expanse between the Atlantic Ocean and the Rocky Mountains, and from the Great Lakes in the north to the Gulf of Mexico in the south, is the greatest natural grape-growing area on the earth's surface. More species of grapevines grow here than grow in all other parts of the world combined.

"Vinland" the Norse explorers called this country nearly a thousand years ago, from the profusion of wild grapevines they saw along the seacoast; and no more appropriate name has ever been bestowed upon any of the continents.

Five hundred years after Leif the Lucky's voyage, the white settlers, clearing the land, remarked the same striking luxuriance of wild vines; yet, with the blind prejudices of the newcomer, they saw no value in this untamed growth. The presence of such strange abundance in the New World served only to remind them of the cultivated vines of the Old, so that, far from striving to adapt the native vines to cultivation and use, they uprooted them everywhere, making room for vineyards of imported European vines. The latter, however, sickened and died in their new environment, consumed by insect and fungus plagues (to which the native vines were resistant) or killed by extremes of temperature to which they were not accustomed. Nature was willing—but as usual, on her own terms.

Some there were who seem to have realized that the future lay in the development of native grapes, that this new land was not an experimental garden for all the imported plants of Europe, but an entirely new kind of "garden," wherein the gardener, if he were to succeed, must learn new rules and follow them. In 1616, we find Lord De La Warr writing to the London Company from Virginia:

"In every boske and hedge, and not far from our pallisade gates, we have thousands of goodly vines running along and leaving to every tree, which yealds a plentiful grape in their kind. Let me appeal, then, to knowledge if these naturall vines were planted, dressed and ordered by skilfull vinearoons, whether we might not make a perfect grape and fruitfull vintage in short time?"

His appeal was answered; a company of French vine dressers and winemakers appeared the following year, but unfortunately they brought with them their European prejudices and a large collection of European vines. These were promptly planted with confidence and expectation, while the "naturall" vines remained ignored. But the new arrivals, as usual, soon perished in their new home; and the "vinearoons," one may surmise, found other occupations.

Among the influential colonists of the period, the Dutch governors of New Amsterdam, the English governor Nicoll, successor to the Dutch on Manhattan, and William Penn, were all eager to promote viticulture and winemaking in their colonies. But almost without exception, the same mistakes were made; they strove to make the land conform to their own ideas, or to the ideas of overseas experts, instead of taking their cue from Nature and adapting themselves to conditions as they found them.

Thus, at this early date one can discern the beginnings of that unconscious depreciation on the part of American vineyardists of the products of their own vineyards, and that corresponding adulation of European methods and practice. It may fairly be called the curse of American viticulture, since it certainly delayed the development of native grapes for some two centuries; and it has its vestiges today in the use of European wine names to denote wines as different from the European as our American moose is from the European elk. Think of our native wines, therefore, as *American* wines, rather than as transplanted European types. To understand better the distinction between the two, one should have some knowledge of American wine sections.

The important wine-producing districts of the East, the South, and the Middle West can all be numbered on the fingers of two hands. Outstanding in point of quality is, perhaps, the Finger Lakes region of Western New York State, closely followed by the Lake Erie Islands district, north of Sandusky, Ohio. Lesser districts include a small section of the Hudson Valley; parts of Berrien and Van Buren counties in southern Michigan, along Lake Michigan; scattered spots in southern New Jersey; and areas around Charlottesville and Petersburg, Virginia; Aberdeen and Tryon, North Carolina; and Nauvoo, Illinois.

THE FINGER LAKES REGION

The long, narrow, and deep lakes which spread out on the map like the fingers of an outstretched hand in the west central part of New York State have given their collective name to the most important of Eastern wine districts. The region is one of rolling hills, stony, well-drained soil, and steep banks sloping down to the lakeshores. It is also a region of severe winters, but the accompanying heavy snowfall usually protects the vines from freezing.

From the standpoint of wine producing, the most important of the Finger Lakes are Keuka and Canandaigua, although some vineyards are also found along the shores of Lakes Seneca and Cayuga.

An Episcopalian minister, the Reverend William Bostwick, planted the first cultivated grapes in this district at Hammondsport in 1829, thus happily preserving in the North American wilderness the traditional affinity between church and vine. (The Gospel and the grape, it is interesting to note in passing, had already been jointly introduced into Spanish California some sixty years before by the Franciscan friars.)

About 1860 the champagne industry was started here by Hammondsport, and, except for the interval of Prohibition, has flourished here ever since, so that today American champagne is the leading wine of the region. The most important champagne houses and wineries are the Pleasant Valley Wine Company, the Taylor Wine Company, and the Urbana Wine Company, in the Hammondsport district, and Garrett & Company, in Penn Yan, at the northern, or outlet, end of the lake. The champagne process of fermentation within the bottle is, in most cases, carefully followed; the grapes, of course, are not the true Champagne grapes of France, and hence the wine can hardly be said to be an exact imitation of the French original; it is, on the other hand, an agreeable and well-made sparkling wine, with the pleasant, characteristic flavor of the American grapes from which it is made.

The grape varieties used in making American champagne include Delaware, Iona, Elvira, and Catawba, to which is generally added a considerable amount of neutral white wine from California.

The second important wine-growing district in the Finger Lakes area is that of Lake Canandaigua, westernmost of the larger lakes of the group. The industry here has its center in the small town of Naples, a few miles south of the southern end of the lake. The dry floor of the so-called Naples Valley is actually a continuation of the glacial cleft in which the lake lies, but it was raised above the water level centuries ago. The steep hillsides above the valley floor are mantled with flourishing vines, the finest vineyard plots being mainly those in the sheltered exposures of the southeast. Widmer's and Maxfield's Wine Cellars, Inc., are the leading wineries.

Here, without doubt, is one of the finest regions in the country for the production of dry white table wines. Such varieties as the Elvira, Diana, Dutchess, Diamond, Delaware, Vergennes, and Salem attain, in favorable years, a perfection rarely found elsewhere. The wines (we speak now of the dry whites) are full of zest and delicacy, and recall, in general character, those of prewar Alsace or Germany.

The outstanding winery in the district is that of Widmer Brothers, founded in 1888 by the father of the present proprietors. Most of its steep, rocky vineyards are entirely hand cultivated, it being impossible to run machinery or horses through the rows. At the vintage season, the grapes are packed in boxes which are loaded one atop the other, on massive wooden sleds. Horses then haul these heavily laden sleds down the slopes to the winery.

THE LAKE ERIE ISLANDS DISTRICTS

Toward the western end of Lake Erie and just north of Sandusky, Ohio, a number of low-lying, rather rocky islands make their appearance—the Lake Erie Islands, which, together with vineyard acreage on the nearby mainland, make up the second most important wine district in the East.

The most important vineyards are on Kelly's, North Bass, and Put-in Bay (South Bass) islands, and Middle Bass Island, as well as Catawba Island, which is actually a part of the mainland, and other nearby areas.

Catawbas and Delawares are the principal wine varieties planted, with smaller acreages of Norton, Ives, Bacchus, Elvira, Iona, and others. The white wines, as is the general rule throughout the East, are superior to the reds. Champagne making is an important branch of the industry here, Delawares and Catawbas being mainly used for this purpose, sometimes with an admixture of California wine.

Lovely and charming though the Sandusky–Lake Erie region is, the wines are decidedly disappointing. Too many—far too many—wines are falsified, are heavily "dosed" with sugar, or are blended with cheap California wines. They are usually too strong in alcohol—the result of too much sugar having been added to the mash before fermentation—and they are nearly always lacking in true regional character. There is too much emphasis placed upon age—particularly age in the wood; and consequently the freshness and fruity qualities of our Eastern wines, which are among their greatest attractions, are lost by the time the wine is bottled.

OTHER EASTERN WINE DISTRICTS

Although hardly a wine district, the Chautauqua grape belt deserves some mention, if only as a tremendous source of juice and table grapes, from some of which a little wine is occasionally made. The belt begins in Chautauqua County, New York, and continues westward, through the "neck" of Pennsylvania which reaches to the lake, and for some miles into Ohio. A high escarpment rises a few miles back of the lake and runs parallel to the shore for a hundred miles or more. The vines are planted between the escarpment and the water's edge—actually on the ancient lake beach.

Nearly all the vines are Concords, with Niagaras a poor second. Under the circumstances, it is, of course, useless to look for any really good wine from the Chautauqua district in the near future, although great wine-growing possibilities are undoubtedly there. The output of the Chautauqua belt is either shipped as table grapes or pressed for grape juice in any of the several neighborhood factories.

A small but flourishing grape-growing area extends along the west bank of the Hudson River, northward from Newburgh, for about twenty miles. Concord is the predominant grape and most of the production is packed in baskets and trucked to New York. One successful winery has, however, been operating since 1907: the Hudson Valley Wine Company, of the Bolognesi family at Highland, which owns considerable plantings of Catawba, Delaware, Iona, and Bacchus vines.

In New Jersey may be mentioned a few small, scattered vineyards, among them that of Herman Kluxen at Madison in Morris County, and the winery of H. T. Dewey and Sons, and that of Renault at Egg Harbor, where some plantings of Ives and Norton grapes provide fair red wines.

Vineyards around the village of Nauvoo, Illinois, on the Mississippi River, were first planted in 1851; and today wines are made there from Catawba, Ives, Norton, and Concord grapes, although table grapes and juice take most of the production.

Of the once numerous small vineyards and wineries which lined the banks of the Missouri River west of St. Louis, only a few remain.

Prohibition, of course, closed up many of them in 1919; and burdensome state regulations kept them from reopening after Repeal. It is to be regretted that Missouri, for years among the two or three top wine-producing states of the Union, sees fit to hamper agricultural enterprise insofar as it concerns the wine-growing activities of her citizens, to the extent that, far from being among the top three, the state is now well below the first ten or twelve in wine production.

June 1941

VIN ORDINAIRE IN AMERICA

Frank Schoonmaker

As far as its gastronomic resources are concerned, this country is already the envy of the civilized world. I suppose it will be doubly so when we somehow arrange to produce and distribute widely and market at a really low price a few sound and pleasant table wines. Please note that I am not talking about rare vintages and old bottles, but about the lowest common denominator of wine—something that we could all afford to drink every evening or as often as we chose, as a beverage and not as a ceremony.

How many of us can recall, before the war, after wine-drinking holidays in France or Italy or Spain or the Rhineland, our return to a bleak cocktails-then-ice-water regime in this country? A good many of us were goaded into action of some sort—we tried to make our own wine, and came to the reluctant conclusion that this was a job for professionals; occasionally we found an Italian grocer or gardener who would sell us gallons, but the wine proved uneven in quality and hard to keep; finally, after Repeal, we shopped around in our local liquor stores for a dependable and palatable American wine at a price we could afford, and generally, after a few disappointing months, we gave up.

Even American wine producers will now admit that most of the wines which they marketed between 1934 and about 1940 were a long way from what they should have been. And in the past five years we have hardly seen any real *vin ordinaire* (by which I mean a common, *inexpensive* table wine) sold in America. The humble gallon jug virtually disappeared in 1943 from our wine merchants' shelves; instead, the undistinguished reds and whites from the mass-production areas of California appeared in fancy dress at a fancy price, and elaborate advertising campaigns were launched to convince us that bottles which we used to buy reluctantly for 60 cents were suddenly worth $1.50 and were being sold us as a special favor.

The real purpose of this article is to say that today, at last, a potable American *vin ordinaire* is not altogether a mirage; it may be less distant than a good many of us have believed. Grape prices in California are back to reason this fall, the great wine boom is over, and from here it looks as though, for wine-thirsty Americans, 1948 would be the pleasantest year since 1917.

This may be as good a time as any to attempt to draw a clean line of demarcation between common table wine, of which the United States produces annually some thirty million gallons, and fine table wine, of which we produce about one fiftieth as much. The former, in terms of food, is what we eat 360 days a year; the latter is turkey at Thanksgiving and plum pudding on Christmas Day. Fine wines, whether produced in Burgundy or on the Rhine, in California or in the Finger Lakes region of New York State, will never be plentiful and will never be cheap; if *vin ordinaire* is not cheap, there is no excuse for its existence. When you pay $1.50 or $2 for a white Pinot from the Livermore Valley or a Cabernet from Napa, you have a right to the equivalent of a filet steak—a vintage wine from a top district, properly aged both before and after bottling, made with great care out of the unusual, shy-bearing grape varieties which yield outstanding wine not only in this country but in France. When you buy *vin ordinaire,* you are altogether in a different league, and you should judge what you buy as you judge coffee or milk or beer. The vintage (or lack of vintage) is of no consequence, for you want a young wine, and it may please you to remember that 90 percent of all French wine is drunk when it is less than two years old. As with coffee or beer, you have a right to something which is sound and palatable, with no off taste or off color; your wine will have little or no bouquet (for this comes with bottle age), but what aroma it has should be agreeable; you can serve it in tumblers or mugs or cocktail glasses, at the temperature you like and with any dish, including pickles. It is, as I have said, a beverage, not a ceremony.

The idea of converting America into a nation of wine drinkers through the pleasant evangelism of cheap native wine is not by any means new. It has been tried every couple of decades for the past hundred and fifty years, and by persons and organizations as diverse as Nicholas Longworth and Leland Stanford, Thomas Jefferson and the Wine Advisory Board. "The introduction of a very cheap wine into my neighborhood, within two years past," wrote Jefferson, "has quadrupled in that time the number of those who keep wines and will ere long increase them tenfold." (I wonder where the cheap wine came from, and what it was that finally killed off that promising little nucleus round Monticello.)

If you reread today the yellowed pages of the reports and chronicles published on behalf of wine in California, between 1850 and 1900, you find, over and over again, expressed with varying degrees of optimism, as the market went up or down, this same idea, as ineradicable, apparently, as the vine itself. Sooner or later the Golden West would bring the inexpensive fruit of its expanding vineyards to "the populous cities of the East." The case, in those days, was well argued. A quarter of a million immigrants a year were arriving in the United States from the wine-drinking countries alone; most of the restaurants in large cities were run by Frenchmen or Germans or Italians; the "upper classes, arbiters of fashion," already drank wine, and where the upper classes led, "the rest would follow."

Alas for the upper classes and alas for Bacchus! The best California wine, as late as 1910, sold for six dollars a case, but in those easy and pleasant days you could buy a case of bonded whisky for the same six dollars. Now it is a disillusioning and unpleasant truth that the popularity of various alcoholic beverages, the world over and throughout history, has always been in direct ratio to their alcoholic content and their price. The fiction that deep-seated racial preferences exist, that Frenchmen like wine, Germans like beer, Cubans like rum, and Americans like whisky, is nothing but fiction and has been disproved a hundred times over. Move a family from Munich to Rüdesheim or from London to Bordeaux or from Chicago to Paris, and you will have a family of wine drinkers within twenty years. Ninety percent of your rum-drinking Cubans come of wine-drinking Spanish stock. The Normans are French, but they drink cider like their neighbors in Devonshire across the Channel, and like the Spaniards in Asturias, for the excellent and sufficient reason that cider is cheap and wine comparatively expensive in the districts where they live.

To bring the comparison a little closer home, how can we explain, except on the basis of availability and price, the fact that the average citizen of California drinks four times as much wine as the average citizen of West Virginia or Michigan or Vermont or Texas? There is no longer, either in California, or elsewhere in America, any large body of foreign-born who still cling stubbornly to the eating and drinking habits which they formed before they came to this country. The overwhelming bulk of the wine which the American public will buy and drink during the next ten years will be bought, not on account of old taste habits, but because it seems, to the present generation, to go well with American food, and because it is fairly cheap. A gallon of wine for $2.50, or a bottle for 60 or 70 cents, is a better buy than $3 gin or $4 whisky by any criterion, even by the tough, unpleasant, but final criterion of alcoholic content.

The important part which price plays in this matter was long ago recognized in California. Competing with spirits at fifty cents a bottle, the table wines of pre-Prohibition days had to be cheap as well as good if they were to be sold at all, and a possible saving of three or four cents a gallon in transportation costs was a matter of major interest to the entire industry. As recently as 1910, most of the wine shipped east from California came by steamer or sailing vessel around the Horn, at some three cents a gallon plus the cost of the oak or redwood barrels in which it was customarily shipped and sold. Rail rates were considered almost prohibitive, and it was not until the first refrigerated tank car appeared in 1910 (a tank car designed for milk being used as a model) that the railroads began to play a really major role as carriers of cheap wine. At seven cents a gallon, coast to coast, these tank cars were rated at first as something pretty luxurious and expensive, and a good many of the old-school vintners continued to claim as well that a wine which had twice "crossed the line" in wood had received a sort of "aging" which time itself could not duplicate. It was more or less in support of this theory that a lady journalist, Mrs. Frona Eunice Wait, once wrote that even the Spaniards, in order to age their sherries, shipped them to "the Equator, in the Mediterranean Sea."

The opening of the Panama Canal in 1914 made wholly academic any further discussions of this sort; it also brought to light a good many novel possibilities in the field of shipping wine. By the end of 1915 plans had been completed for a double-hulled tanker which would carry wine from dockside San Francisco to dockside Brooklyn for one cent a gallon, and which would carry steel rails to California on its return voyage. Before the keel could be laid, there came the steel shortage and the war and Prohibition and, so far as the California wine industry was concerned, the deluge. It is interesting, however, to note that some twenty years later the French constructed a very similar steamer, which they quite properly named the *Bacchus,* and which carried on every trip across the Mediterranean, in its capacious belly, enough Algerian wine for an army on the march.

The unhappy story of the Prohibition years has no rightful place in an article such as this. Briefly, those who were unwilling to do without their claret or their *vino rosso* began to buy what were euphemistically called "juice grapes" in the large Eastern cities, in order to make wine at home. Now, the finer wine grapes are thin-skinned and fragile— they will not stand transcontinental shipment. The demand, therefore, was for the tough, thick-skinned, and common varieties which would travel; fine vineyard after fine vineyard was grafted over to such vines or replanted, and the superior varieties, little by little, tended to disappear. Today, fifteen years after Repeal, most of this debris is still there, and even today there are fewer acres planted to superior vines in the better California districts than there were when the Eighteenth Amendment became the law of the land.

Nearly a decade and a half after its great and apparently final de-

feat, the California wine industry was rather abruptly called on to reform its ranks and begin where it left off. Obviously, this was altogether impossible. Most of its conscientious and honorable leaders
had retired or died, many of the producers were bankrupt, the majority of its wineries were in ruins, the beautiful oak cooperage in most
cellars had dried out or gone moldy through sheer neglect, the better
vineyards had been regrafted or abandoned—there was less left than
most Californians care, even today, to admit.

The inevitable result was a five- or six-year period of poor wine,
wine so bad that much of it could not be sold at any price, even in a
country where wine was a new and glamorous toy; wine made from
raisin grapes or table grapes or culls, hastily and carelessly fermented;
wines labeled "Sauterne" and "Moselle" and "Chablis" and "Rhine
Wine," although all four were drawn from the same tank; wines that
would make a beer drinker out of anyone who tried them, and a good
many people did.

Most California producers were just a step ahead of the sheriff in
those days. In 1939, grapes sold for $20 or $25 a ton, well below the
cost of growing and picking them, and bankers estimated that California's wine inventory of 115,000,000 gallons was worth an average of
24 cents a gallon, which was perhaps an exaggeration.

If the war years did nothing else, they at least put the California
producers on somewhat firmer financial ground, and now that grape
prices are down again we have a right to expect from our friends on
the West Coast something a good deal better and a good deal cheaper
than anything they have sent us since Prohibition. Congress has seen
fit to tax spirits at a rate which makes them no longer competitive with
wine, and if California misses this chance, she may never get another
so good. I do not think, however, that she will miss this chance.

Having by now (I hope) awakened a moderate thirst and a certain
spirit of anticipation in my readers, I am compelled in all honesty to
admit that it will probably be more difficult than it sounds to find really satisfactory American *ordinaires,* at least for the next few months.
Such wines will certainly be produced and will certainly be for sale;
the problem will be to find them, to put one's finger unerringly on pre-

cisely the right jug or precisely the right bottle in the carnival of fancy names and gay labels. To do so, we shall probably have to abandon some of our carefully nurtured prejudices.

I, for example, very much dislike buying a wine called "Chablis" unless it tastes like Chablis, or a "claret" which resembles nothing so much as a lesser wine of the Rhône Valley. When I buy a superior American wine I insist on knowing not only where it came from, but also out of what grape it was made. When we are dealing with *vin ordinaire,* this is altogether out of the question. If we buy a jug labeled "Moselle" and the wine tastes likes Graves, we have no complaint so long as it tastes like good Graves. Actually, it is impossible to distinguish, either by chemical analysis or by tasting, between California Burgundy and California claret, and the one axiomatic statement that we can make about both of them is that neither is ever made from the same grape as its prototype in France. Apart from a few regional and varietal names (Sonoma and Santa Clara; Zinfandel, Cabernet, and Riesling, for example, the former referring to districts and the latter to grape varieties), California table wine names are utterly without meaning. A producer is at liberty to call his white wine Chablis or Rhine Wine or Hock or Dry Sauterne as he sees fit, and legally he can draw all four out of the same barrel. This, of course, has nothing to do with the intrinsic quality of the wine, which may be excellent, but it does render a good deal more difficult the selection of a bottle on a wine merchant's shelves.

Before Prohibition, California clarets were generally (but by no means always) lighter in color and body than Burgundies and contained a high proportion of wine made from Zinfandel grapes, whereas Burgundies were made from the Petit Syrah, the Carignane, and the Refosco. But the most celebrated "Chablis" of the 1890s was a Gray Riesling, "Moselles" were made largely from Folle Blanche (which is the cognac grape), and a half dozen more odd fish of the sort could be pulled up at will out of this wide ocean of confusion without limit or bottom.

Such nonsense need not concern us greatly when it comes to selecting a cheap wine for our daily dinner table—the producer can label it "Château Fujiyama" or "Napa Red," providing the wine is good.

Another widespread and legitimate prejudice is one against tank-car wine. Since a certain amount of bottle age is absolutely necessary to a fine wine, and since practically everything shipped out of California in bulk and bottled in the East goes to market as soon as it is bottled, and finally since the *raison d'être* of tank cars is cheap transportation, we are justified in complaining if a tank-car wine is anything but cheap. But if we are buying *ordinaire*, we can afford to look on the despised tank car with affectionate respect—it may save us as much as a dollar a case.

All this is rather negative—perhaps a few positive suggestions would prove helpful.

First, confine your searches for *vin ordinaire* to wine from California. Neither in New York State nor in Ohio nor in Michigan can grapes be grown cheaply enough to permit the sale of well-made wine at much under a dollar a bottle, and here we are talking of wine at 60 or 70 cents.

Second, try, if possible, to get a wine from one of the north coast counties—Sonoma, Napa, Santa Clara, San Benito, Alameda (which includes the Livermore Valley), and Santa Cruz. Far too much of the wine produced in the central valleys, around Lodi, Stockton, Manteca, Modesto, Madera, Fresno, and Delano, is made out of what are known as "three-way grapes." This innocent-sounding term means a raisin grape which can be sold as a table grape when raisin prices are low or, if worse comes to worst, can be used for wine. Such wine may be passable raw material for the manufacture of cheap domestic sherry, but it goes to market all too often as Chablis or Sauterne; it is flat, neutral, and about as appetizing as colored water.

Third, remember that the post office address of a winery on a label means precisely nothing at all. A "producer" in Napa can sell unblended Fresno wine if he sees fit, and a single winery near Livermore has actually bottled and sold, in the last five years, at least twice as much wine as the whole Livermore Valley produced. If you want to be sure of the origin of your wine, insist on some appellation like *Sonoma* Claret or *Santa Clara* Zinfandel.

Fourth, if you are experimenting in an effort to find something you like, tell your wine merchant what you are doing and give him your frank and outspoken opinion of the wines you try. Other people may be doing the same thing—they can benefit by your experience and you by theirs.

A great bottle of wine, in a well-ordered house, has its quiet and respected place in the cellar, and its last mile to the execution block on the dining-room table is as hedged round with etiquette and ceremony as a Spanish bullfight. A *vin ordinaire*, on the other hand, is a friendly and familiar little job, and the less etiquette the better. My own favorite way of serving it is in an earthenware carafe, or in a wooden *pichet* made out of beautifully coopered little oak staves, with a copper handle and copper lip—I bought it years ago in France. But a simple glass carafe will do as well and will give your guests and yourself the impression that you are drinking, not the fixed contents of a bottle, but as much or as little as you happen to want. Which, incidentally, is the way to drink *vin ordinaire*.

Belonging as it does in the kitchen, and not in the padlocked wine cellar, *vin ordinaire* should be consumed as one's thirst dictates, but it should never be wasted. To throw away half a bottle or half a gallon of wine is as poor housekeeping as to throw away half a chicken or half a leg of lamb. Wine, even common wine, it is true, has to be handled with a certain amount of care unless you want vinegar on your hands, but the rules for storing wine are simple and require no special equipment or special knowledge.

1. Wine is liable to spoil if kept for more than a day or so at a temperature of over 80 degrees Fahrenheit.

2. Wine will certainly spoil within a matter of hours if exposed to the air; I never, therefore, try to keep a half-empty bottle or half-empty jug, even in a refrigerator, and even if corked.

3. The best plan is to have on hand a collection of empty bottles of various sizes and a few corks (ordinary conical drugstore corks will do); as soon as you open your gallon or half-gallon jug, or your full bottle, pour off the wine that you do not expect to use immediately, into one or more of your empties, and cork them, leaving not more than a quarter of an inch of air space between the wine and the cork. So rebottled, the wine will be good for at least two or three months.

4. Bottled wines with corks should be stored lying down—this

keeps the corks moist and tight. But such precautions are unnecessary if you expect to use the wine within less than a week.

5. You can keep white *vin ordinaire* in the refrigerator indefinitely, but the ideal temperature is between 50 and 60 degrees. Repeated chillings, if the wine is allowed to warm up each time, will damage any wine.

6. The best storage temperature for red wine is 60 degrees, but 10 degrees higher or lower are of no importance to an *ordinaire*.

7. Most jugs, gallon or half-gallon, are hermetically sealed with a screwcap, and it makes little difference whether you store them standing upright or on their side. The latter is perhaps preferable if you propose to keep them for any length of time.

8. Sunlight is bad for wine, especially wine in clear white bottles or jugs.

9. The cheapest way to buy wine is in gallon jugs, which come four to the case, as compared with six half-gallon jugs (3 gallons) or twelve bottles (2.4 gallons).

10. Forty million Frenchmen, and an unknown number of Italians, Spaniards, and Americans, have demonstrated the fact that *vin ordinaire* is habit-forming. The author wishes to state in closing that you will have a hard time finding a more pleasant habit to form.

October 1947

San Francisco

Frank Schoonmaker

PART ONE

Sometimes, if there is a strong west wind blowing, your plane heads due west after the take-off, Mills Field drops away, and you can see the Pacific almost at once, restless and dark blue and as big as the sky.

Then, as the plane banks, you are flying south, high above the noiseless white surf of a rather desolate coast, with the shallow southern reaches of San Francisco Bay on your left. Between bay and ocean, seen from above, there is a widening triangle of wooded hills and wild broken country, green even during the parched summer months with redwoods and live oaks, with madrones and California holly and manzanita. Here and there, as the Peninsula hills increase in height and become the Santa Cruz Mountains, you can see scattered patches of vines.

There are vines, too, off east of the Bay on the low hills round Mission San José, and back of the hills in the shimmering saucer of the Livermore Valley. There are vineyards on the lower slopes of Mount Hamilton, and along the western rim of the Santa Clara Valley, from Saratoga and Los Gatos almost all the way to Gilroy. For this is "dry wine country," already famous for the excellence of its vintages in the 1850s; and if we are ever to have wines in America that can honestly be called "great," this is assuredly one of the districts from which they will come.

The fine-wine producing counties south of San Francisco are four—Alameda and Santa Clara, which bound San Francisco Bay on the east and south; wild, mountainous Santa Cruz, between Santa Clara and the Pacific; and hilly San Benito, of which only the extreme northwestern corner is of any interest or consequence. There is not a single good vineyard in any of the four which is over fifty miles from salt water, nor a vineyard which regularly requires irrigation if planted to superior vines, nor one which could not, with proper plantings and proper care, produce wine vastly better than what is commonly drunk in France. A good many of them are producing such wine today.

The basis of this regional superiority is neither complicated nor obscure. All fine wines owe their excellence to a combination of natural and human variables: proper climate; good, not overly productive soil; the appropriate grape varieties, correctly cultivated and correctly pruned; the knowledge and the unfailing care of the man who finally makes the wine.

In this small district south of San Francisco (as in Napa and Sonoma to the north, of which I shall have more to say another time), nature has been kind. The average temperatures during the growing season, as scientifically measured and recorded, range between those of the Moselle and those of the Rhône Valley. The grapes ripen about a month earlier than in France, and they are generally picked during warm weather rather than cool. The Burgundians often have to heat their fermenting rooms during fermentation, whereas it is standard practice in the fine, small California wineries (which are, alas, not very numerous) to cool the fresh must, or juice, as it comes from crusher or press. A great deal of wretched wine has been made in California by vintners of French or German origin who chose to ignore these facts and who, remembering rather hazily that the best wines of their native country were made from grapes picked late, blithely assumed that the same rule held good six thousand miles away. A wine made from overripe grapes can be, in certain areas and under certain extraordinary conditions, an extraordinary wine. As a whole such wines are flat, common, harsh, too dark in color, and lacking in freshness, if white; undistinguished, too high in alcohol, and without bouquet or softness, if red. These are the traditional but unnecessary faults of many California table wines, and in years of drought and exceptional heat such as 1921, 1945, and 1947, they are faults which French vintners, too, have to be at some pains to avoid.

This brings us rather deviously to the question of California vintage years. All of us have listened, with a certain amount of legitimate skepticism, to statements to the effect that "every year is a vintage year in California." Surprisingly, this is not too far from the truth, although one could certainly say, with equal justification, that "no year is a vintage year in California."

Such an apparent contradiction is really no contradiction at all. The weather in California is almost invariably fine during the critical weeks of the wine grower's year—the *floraison,* or flowering, on which the crop depends, and the vintage, when the grapes are harvested. As a result, the difference between a good year and a bad in California, *in terms of quantity,* rarely exceeds 20 or 25 percent (it is often twice and sometimes three times that in the fine districts of France and Germany). In terms of *quality,* California is even more strikingly consistent. Any amateur taster can tell the difference between a 1943 Burgundy or Moselle and a 1944 from the same vineyard. I do not think that any expert, no matter how competent, can distinguish between vintages in California, at least in any broad, general, and useful way which would permit setting up a valid vintage chart. This is not by any means to say that California can produce Château Lafite 1934 or Romanée-Conti 1929 or Piesporter Goldtropfchen 1937 five years out of five or even one year out of fifty. It may do so eventually; it never has.

What the growers in a few favored California counties can do, if properly encouraged, is to produce and sell, year after year and at a fair price, wines that are wonderfully sound and clean and good—not, with a few possible exceptions, crown jewels, but *wines certainly superior to the average European wine which has reached this country since Prohibition.*

The good California districts, however, are few, the really conscientious producers not very numerous, and most of them receive a good deal less in the way of public recognition and encouragement than they deserve.

Most of them are small. They produce annually somewhere between the average output of a little vineyard in Burgundy (1,500 or 2,000 cases) and the annual yield of a major Bordeaux château (10,000 to 20,000 cases). A few are larger, and instead of having just one specialty, as would be the case abroad, they produce a half dozen or a dozen different wines, red and white, still and sparkling, etc. Even so, the maximum, if we are talking of fine wine, seems to be around 50,000 cases annually.

This figure, curiously enough, is not just an American maximum, based on the fact that we are not as a whole a wine-drinking people— it is an international maximum. There does not exist and has never existed in France or Germany a vineyard producing a single famous wine, sold under the name of that vineyard, with an annual production of even 40,000 cases. Meanwhile, in the mass-production districts of California, there are a half dozen plants with a bottling capacity of between 5,000 and 10,000 cases *a day*.

It goes without saying that the small, fine producers, who are really farmers, with anywhere from ten to five hundred acres under vines, rarely make much of a splash in the way of publicity or advertising. They sell to their friends and their friends' friends, and to a few alert wine merchants who take the trouble to hunt them out. They label their wines, almost invariably, with the name of the county or district in which they live, or with the name of their special vineyard. Generally they add the name of the particular grape out of which the wine was made.

A few of them, in the past ten years, have become famous. A good many more of them deserve to be. They have added a new and fascinating chapter to the history of one of the oldest of all arts, that of winemaking; and they have inscribed a whole series of new, *American* names on the roster of the world's districts of fine wine.

The four fine-wine counties south of San Francisco chalked up an extraordinary series of victories last fall, at the California State Fair in Sacramento. The tasting, as always, was done by a jury of experts, and "blind." Now Santa Cruz, Santa Clara, San Benito, and Alameda produce between them less than 5 percent of California's 100,000,000 gallons of wine a year; they nevertheless accounted for fifteen first places and were judged to produce the best Cabernet, the best Pinot Chardonnay, the best champagne, sparkling Burgundy, pink champagne, Riesling, Sylvaner, Sauvignon Blanc, sweet Sémillon, sweet Sauterne, *vin rosé,* and Ugni Blanc of California; they even got first place in sweet vermouth.

SANTA CRUZ

Of the four counties, the most picturesque, although by a considerable margin the least important in total wine production, is Santa Cruz. Few native Californians, I dare say, are even aware that its vineyards exist. These are anything but numerous or large or famous; most of them are set well back from the magnificent modern highways that sweep through the valleys and over the lower passes of the Santa Cruz Mountains; they are in what might be called the "backwoods" of this little county of summer resorts. The Santa Cruz Chamber of Commerce, so proud of its five or six state parks, its cottage colonies at Boulder Creek and Ben Lomond, its impressive redwood trees, and its beaches, never sees fit to mention such odd corners as Vine Hill and Bonnie Doon. The most recent history of Santa Cruz devotes more space to the founding of the W.C.T.U. than to the fact that the county's vineyards once ranked, and certainly will one day rank again, among America's best. And a casual tourist who stopped for lunch in the dull roadside taverns of Boulder Creek or the mediocre seafood houses of Santa Cruz itself, would have a hard time believing that he was in a district of fine wine, a district which could and should be one of the most gastronomically interesting in the United States.

Back in the hills, however, there are a good many families, most of them Italian, that live largely off the country and live exceedingly well. Certainly I have never seen elsewhere in America land posted, not against hunters or trespassers, but against mushroom pickers—signs that read "NO FUNGHI" (which apparently requires no translation) are common enough along Santa Cruz Mountain roads, and if you care to poach you will find not only the commoner varieties but even *cèpes,* and *morilles* in the woods and upland meadows. There are trout and crayfish in the brooks, frogs are plentiful in the occasional ponds, the district is rich in game, and I have more than once eaten evidence that would lead me to believe that the game wardens are not so efficient as they might be. To those who own mountain vineyards anywhere in California, the deer and rabbits that feed on young grapevines and the birds that feed on grapes rank high on the list of public enemies. "And when the poor things are dead," as I was once told by an old woman near Ben Lomond, "it seems a pity to waste them." Instead of being "wasted" in the Santa Cruz Mountains, they are marinated in red wine, served with mushrooms from the woods in which they were born, and appreciated right up to the end of their corporeal existence.

Most of the celebrated old vineyards, for which Santa Cruz was famous in the years following the Civil War, are overgrown and forgotten today. The first of them was planted by "one Réné, a Frenchman" in 1852 or 1853. A decade or so later, a Mr. J. W. Jarvis, who had given the name "General Grant" to an enormous redwood tree on his property, was patriotically operating the Union Vineyard at Vine Hill; by the late 1880s he had founded the Santa Cruz Mountain Wine Company and had dug a whole series of tunnels or "cellars" into the sandstone along Branciforte Creek. Ninety acres had been planted to vines in the high limestone country west of Ben Lomond, and the white Ben Lomond wines were beginning to command a premium in the opulent hotels and better restaurants of San Francisco. There were vineyards, too, at Bonnie Doon, west of Felton, and Santa Cruz County was being described by members of the State Viticultural Commission as "pre-eminently the light dry wine district of California."

It is that today. It is the coolest major wine-producing county of the West Coast, certainly the most likely to give us an American equivalent of Rhine wine or Moselle, the one county where snow falls every winter in the vineyards, a county where not all the years are vintage years, and where, one day, we shall possibly make something comparable to the best of Germany and France.

Despite the fact that most of the existing Santa Cruz vineyards were grafted over to inferior varieties during Prohibition, there are a few encouraging beginnings. Near Felton, Mr. Chaffee Hall, a San Francisco attorney, has planted some dozen acres of Cabernet and Riesling, and is producing in his immaculate little winery called Hallcrest two wines which will be famous before long. Around Bonnie Doon and on the limestone hills near where the vanished Ben Lomond winery once harvested its grapes, there are new vineyards which are outposts of Almadén, itself over on the rim of the Santa Clara Valley to the east.

SANTA CLARA

The European vine was introduced into what was then known as Alta California about 1769, probably by Father Junipero Serra, and was first planted around the missions of San Diego and San Gabriel. As the chain of missions was extended northward, the vine went with them, and there is apparently no doubt that altar wine was being made in the Santa Clara Valley by about 1800. It cannot have been very good, since it was made by the most primitive methods imaginable from a mediocre wine grape (the Mission) and stored in skins, so it is hardly surprising that a couple of decades went by before any commercial winemaking was attempted. The Santa Clara Valley in the north and the Pueblo de Los Angeles in the south seem to have been the first centers of a modest little trade which, in the north at least, never achieved any importance until '49, when the gold rush created almost overnight a considerable market for wine in nearby San Francisco.

Thereafter, things went very rapidly indeed. By 1852 the first vines had been planted in what is now the Almadén Vineyard by Charles Lefranc (the name Almadén, after a famous old quicksilver mine in the nearby hills, came later). And by 1860 or thereabouts a half dozen producers—Pierre Sansevaine, Antoine Delmas, Louis Pellier, and a few others, mostly French—were shipping wine by wagon to the "port" (long since sanded in) of Alviso, and thence to San Francisco by boat. Throughout the early days Santa Clara shared with Sonoma the pre-eminent place as supplier of San Francisco's best wines.

Like Sonoma and Napa, Santa Clara has been from the beginning a district of small vineyards and small family wineries. Today, with eight thousand acres under vines and forty-six bonded wineries, it has the smallest average acreage per winery of any major wine-producing county in California. This, of course, means that there are comparatively few well-known "brands" of Santa Clara wine, and yet it is precisely under such conditions that the best wines are made, not only in California, but the world over.

Most of the enormously fertile, irrigated bottomland of the Santa Clara Valley is better adapted to prunes and apricots than to wine grapes, and the county's superior vineyards, without exception, are planted in the rolling foothills to the east and west. There is a little cluster of such vineyards around Monte Bello, which overlooks San Francisco Bay, and another little cluster farther south, between the village of Gilroy and picturesque Hecker Pass. There are some three or four good ones on the lower slopes of Mount Hamilton, east of San José, and others near Saratoga, near Los Gatos, near Morgan Hill and San Martin. Not all of these, of course, bottle their own wine or have their own label, and even of those that do, the majority deserve and have acquired only a local reputation. There are perhaps four or five that are nationally known and some four or five others that are working in the direction of quality and will bear watching.

Almadén, some five miles south of San José, is probably the oldest commercial winery now operating in California. Its owners have undertaken since 1940 an extremely ambitious program. Several hundred acres have been planted to Pinot Blanc, Pinot Noir, Pinot Chardonnay, Cabernet, and the like, which are the classic grape varieties of France. The cellars, already famous for their collection of old oak casks and puncheons, have been rebuilt and re-equipped, and on the whole it is hardly surprising that five Almadén wines, including its champagne, its Cabernet, and its *vin rosé,* were ranked first in their categories at the California State Fair in 1947.

A few miles west of Almadén is the Novitiate of Los Gatos, an important Jesuit seminary, which has been producing wine since the late 1880s. For sheer beauty, and for exposure as well, the Novitiate's magnificent hillside vineyards are unsurpassed in California, and from the point of view of the average wine drinker it seems rather too bad that the lay brothers in charge have so far chosen to concentrate on sacramental wines (over 80 percent of their present output) and on sweet wines, rather than on light dry table wines, especially in this "dry wine country."

The Paul Masson Champagne Company, founded by the son-in-law of Charles Lefranc (who planted Almadén), consists of a spectacular hilltop vineyard and small winery back of Saratoga, and a modern plant in the valley near Cupertino. The wines include one of the better California champagnes and a few excellent varietals—Pinot Noir, Pinot Blanc, etc.

Some other producers with at least a few wines well above the average are P. L. Mirassou & Sons of San José, San Martin Vineyards of San Martin, and California Wine Producers, Inc., of Evergreen.

SAN BENITO–MONTEREY

Except for a few vineyards in the high country directly north and south of Hollister, San Benito County could hardly be described as a district of fine wine. Two or three small growers have produced something pretty creditable near the Santa Clara county line, southeast of Gilroy, and what was once known as the Palmtag Vineyard, in the Cienega Valley, was purchased in 1942 by W. A. Taylor & Company. After extensive renovations and replantings, it now produces most of the white wines sold by that organization under the Valliant brand.

One small experimental vineyard in Monterey County, which has no winery as yet, is perhaps worthy of a line or two. It lies back of a village quite appropriately called Soledad (or Solitude), at an altitude of nearly two thousand feet, in a strange, desolate, almost rainless country of calcareous soil. Its owner, Bill Silvair, has planted it to Pinots, and on the basis of its present showings it may well prove one of the most interesting vineyards of California.

ALAMEDA

Per square mile, Alameda County is perhaps the most densely populated wine-producing district in the world; it includes the whole busy East Bay area—Berkeley and Oakland and Alameda, and towns such as San Leandro and Hayward which have grown to almost unrecognizable proportions since before the war. And yet, as happens so often in California, you can travel a dozen miles and come to an altogether different sort of country—an empty brown landscape of rolling hills, broken only occasionally by the green of vineyards, with hardly a house, sometimes, as far as you can see.

The vineyards, fifty years ago, were about twice as extensive as they are today, and on a good many slopes there are still traces of abandoned vines—gnarled trunks exactly eight feet apart and a few green leaves generally withered by late August. Fifty years ago, as now, there were two entirely separate vineyard districts in Alameda County; the older consisted of the hills that sloped down to San Francisco Bay round Mission San José; the larger and more important was the Livermore Valley.

The great name in Mission San José in those days was Gallegos, a family which dated back to the original period of Spanish "grants." The best vineyard today is Los Amigos, which owes its renaissance since the repeal of Prohibition to the late Bob Mayock, ex-newspaperman, great wine lover, and extraordinary host. Other producers include Weibel, specializing in champagne, Riehr, and Darrow.

Directly back of Mission San José there is a break in the hills through which, dependable as the sun, the cool bay wind blows eastward every afternoon in summer. Thanks to this wind, the dry, stony, almost treeless Livermore Valley has become one of the most celebrated vineyard districts in the West. Without this wind it would be as hot as the raisin-grape country around Lodi, unfit for agriculture unless irrigated, a virtual desert.

Most of the good California vineyards are on hillsides; in Livermore, however, they are not—the vines are planted on a gently undulating, incredibly rocky plain, and their roots in many cases have been found to go down thirty feet in search of moisture and sustenance. Their yield per acre, on this barren soil, is low, hardly ever exceeding two tons and, in the case of finer varieties, even less.

Ever since the first vineyards were planted in the 1880s, Livermore has been considered white wine country, and most of the leading producers today specialize in what Californians call "Sauterne" (without the final *s* of its French prototype)—a full-bodied white wine, either dry or slightly sweet, which should be made, and in this district usually is, from the Sémillon and Sauvignon Blanc grapes. A few progressive growers, however, have proven that Livermore's possibilities are by no means so limited—the Pinot Chardonnay, the Pinot Blanc, the Sylvaner, and the Grey Riesling of Wente Brothers, for example, all rank among the best white wines produced in the United States.

Apart from Wente, who is the undisputed leader in this field, the major producers are Concannon, Cresta Blanca, Garatti, and Ruby Hill.

PART TWO

In general, as you go north, almost anywhere in Europe or the United States, the climate becomes consistently and perceptibly colder, practically county by county, sometimes mile by mile. There are a few exceptions—climatic eddies and backwaters, so to speak—districts such as the great wine-producing area north of San Francisco Bay, where, on a weatherman's map, the isothermic lines and the lines of latitude form a patternless tangle of hot northern valleys and cool southern plains, where the hilltops are often warmer than the lowlands and where, traveling due north, you can move from the climate of northern France to that of central Italy within thirty miles.

This whole extraordinary country, approximately sixty miles long and half as wide, consists principally of Napa and Sonoma counties, plus perhaps a corner of Contra Costa. It is actually farther south than Washington, D.C., or Rome, and it is indebted for its long, fairly cool, dry summers and adequate winter rainfall to its proximity to the ocean and to the fog and damp winds that blow in over San Francisco Bay and up the Russian River Valley every evening nearly twelve months out of the year. The farther you get from the bay or the ocean, going north or east, the warmer it is, and whereas the village of Sonoma and the town of Napa, which are both practically on tidewater, have summer temperatures much like those of Burgundy, in France, Calistoga and Cloverdale, farther north in the same county, are as warm as southern Italy or Spain.

All of the really distinguished table wines of California come from about five or, at most, seven counties which, in the order of their annual overall production, are as follows: Sonoma, Napa, Santa Clara, Alameda, Contra Costa, San Benito, Santa Cruz. Here we shall attempt to deal only with two, but with the two most important—Sonoma and Napa.

It may be just as well, however, to give in passing a few further words of explanation as to why seven little counties, which produce no more than 10 percent of California's total annual gallonage, are responsible for over 90 percent of the fine table wine made in this country. Climate, of course, plays a major role, as does the fact that most of the northern coastal vineyards are planted on hills, or at least on fairly unfertile, rolling ground which does not require irrigation. But the question of grape varieties is even more important. No fine wine, anywhere in the world, has ever been made from anything except wine grapes, and all the best of it comes from a dozen or so varieties, useless for making raisins and poor or, at best, passable as table grapes.

As I write these lines, in December, California wineries have reported a total crush, for the 1948 vintage, of 1,281,495 tons of grapes (a ton of grapes yields from 150 to 160 gallons of table wine, or from 90 to 100 gallons of fortified wine). Now out of this total of 1,281,495 tons, 319,397 tons, *according to the reporting wineries themselves,* were table grapes, 523,333 tons were raisin grapes, and only 438,765 tons (under 35 percent) wine grapes. In other words, only about a third of the 1948 California wine that Americans will drink has been made from wine grapes to begin with, and only a fraction of this third from wine grapes of superior quality.

On the other hand, about 85 percent of the wine produced in the north coast counties is made from wine grapes (as against 35 percent for California as a whole), and these counties include almost every commercial planting of superior varieties on the West Coast. At the 1948 State Fair in Sacramento, all the gold and silver medals for table wines, without exception, were awarded to wineries in the north coast counties, and no really outstanding table wine has, to my knowledge, ever been produced in California outside of these counties. It is therefore hardly surprising that most of the best American wines carry on their label not only the name of a specific wine grape, but also the name of a north coast county. And now back to our subject.

Sonoma and Napa counties form, in general, the northern shore of that rather considerable inland sea known as San Francisco Bay. They are not, by any means, exclusively wine-producing districts: the great naval base of Mare Island is in Napa County, and there are as many pear orchards and duck blinds as vineyards. Sonoma is hardly more famous for its wines than for its chicken farms (the town of Petaluma calls itself "the egg basket of the West") and its cheeses and its summer resorts. In neither county, as you travel through, do you get the impression that wine is the livelihood and lifeblood of the countryside. You can get good Napa wine, if you insist, in a few restaurants and lunchrooms in Napa and St. Helena and Calistoga, and good Sonoma wine, rather less easily, in Sonoma and Santa Rosa and Healdsburg. In both counties the waiters and waitresses are astonished when an outsider orders one of their local wines by brand name and seem surprised even when you ask for a wine from Napa or Sonoma. Yet the economy of both counties is to a considerable extent based on wine, and nowhere in the United States will you find so high a proportion of laborers who prefer a glass of red wine to a glass of beer or whisky.

Let us hope that before long some of the better wine producers come to realize what a remarkable asset they possess in the way of an extraordinarily lovely district. If they gave a little guidance and help and advertising to a few enterprising restaurateurs, they could make of Napa and Sonoma a second Côte d'Or and second Rhône Valley, loved and praised and remembered by thousands of tourists every year.

Except in the fall, when the leaves are gone from the vines and the parched lowlands not yet green, Napa and Sonoma are both spectacularly beautiful. To one who knows Europe they recall southern Tuscany, or the hilly country behind Gibraltar, or the Valley of the Durance, east of Avignon. In every sheltered corner of the hills there are orange and lemon trees; the venerable live oaks and madrona trees stand alone in their fields like trees in a Poussin landscape, and the whole district has a sort of half-classical, almost Roman air.

As far as the vineyards are concerned, Napa consists of the Napa Valley. Sonoma, farther west, includes not only the shallow little valley of Sonoma Creek, but the much more extensive and more important Russian River country, around Guerneville and Healdsburg and Asti, to the north.

The two valleys, Napa and Sonoma, some fifteen miles apart, run northwestward like parallel fingers from the marshy lowlands along the bay shore. Neither one, at its southern end, looks much like a valley—rather like a little depression in a district of irregular and rolling hills. But the hills, as you go north, become higher and more impressive, their upper slopes heavily wooded and covered with an almost impassable tangle of manzanita and laurel and California holly. The vineyards, few at first and scattered, become larger and more numerous, covering the whole narrowing floor of the valley, running back into the hills, forming a patchwork of lighter green among the firs and cedars of the uplands.

Together the two valleys, with the range of hills—known as the Mayacamas Mountains—which separates them, form one of the great viticultural districts of the world, capable of yielding with time and patience wines as fine as any that France and Germany have produced. Three quarters of a century ago, it seemed that this promise was well on its way to fulfillment, and Robert Louis Stevenson, who spent some months near St. Helena, in the Napa Valley, could write:

Wine in California is still in the experimental stage. . . . The beginning of vine-planting is like the beginning of mining for precious metals: the wine-grower also "prospects." One corner of land after another is tried with one kind of grape after another. . . . So, bit by bit, they grope about for their Clos Vougeot and Lafite. These lodes and pockets of earth, more precious than the precious ores, that yield inimitable fragrance and soft fire; these virtuous Bonanzas, where the soil has sublimated under the sun and stars to something finer, and the wine is bottled poetry: these still lie undiscovered; chaparral conceals, thicket embowers them; the miner chips the rock and wanders farther, and the grizzly muses undisturbed. But there they bide their hour, awaiting their Columbus; and nature nurses and prepares them. The smack of California earth shall linger on the palate of your grandson.

By 1900 there were at least sixty or seventy prosperous wineries in the Napa Valley; scores of little corners in the Mayacamas uplands had been cleared, in search of those "Bonanzas" of which Stevenson wrote; Napa wines had become famous, not only in San Francisco, but in New York; and they had even won medals and acclaim in expositions abroad. Over eighteen thousand acres in Napa County were planted to vines, a high proportion of the vines were of good varieties, and a high proportion of the vineyards were on the upland slopes, rather than on the flat, alluvial, too-fertile valley floor.

All of this peaceful, picturesque, and industrious little world, which had been so laboriously created, mostly by French and German settlers and Chinese labor, over a period of six decades, was destroyed by national Prohibition in a matter of months. The hill vineyards were abandoned to the tangled brushwood that surrounded them; the lower vineyards were replanted in tough, productive grapes that would stand transcontinental shipment to home winemakers in the East; the wineries, one by one, fell into disuse and ruin. Only a few survived the holocaust and by making sacramental wine eked out a precarious existence until Repeal. Out of more than threescore Napa producers in 1917, Inglenook, Beaulieu, and Beringer alone are still operating on a major scale and still in the hands of the families that owned them prior to Prohibition.

The past fifteen years have undone a good deal, but by no means all, of the mischief worked by the Eighteenth Amendment. The wineries are busy and most of them prosperous again, even if some of the old buildings proved beyond repair. The rolling foothills are once more covered with the orderly regiments of newly staked young vines, and a few courageous pioneers are even trying to bring back into production the mountain vineyards that once were responsible for Napa's finest wines.

The shady and sleepy little town of Napa, at the valley's southern end, has never been much of a center of the wine trade—its major vineyard before Prohibition was Judge Stanly's La Loma, which,

southwest of the town, slopes gently down behind its enormous eucalyptus trees to tidewater. Napa Creek is really an estuary rather than
a river, and a mile south of the town, as often as not, you can see the
funnels and superstructure of an ocean-going ship rising out of what
appears to be pastureland, with no water in sight.

Two parallel roads and an unimpressive little single-track railway
line run northwest from Napa into the vineyard country. One of these
roads (the poorer, incidentally) is the picturesque, winding Silverado
Trail, of which Stevenson wrote, in his *Silverado Squatters,* over sixty
years ago; the other, less romantically named Route 29, skirts most of
the major vineyards and passes within a few hundred yards of the important wineries. In Yountville, a dozen miles from Napa, is the old
brick Groezinger winery, once the valley's largest and at last active
again under the name Mountain View. A little farther north, near
Oakville, is To Kalon, where, fifty years ago, Hiram W. Crabb used to
make what was regarded as the best Burgundy of California. It is now
owned by Mr. Martin Stelling and undergoing a major renaissance.

Another mile or two and you are in Rutherford, with Inglenook's
venerable, ivy-covered stone buildings set back under live oak trees
on your left, and Beaulieu's winery like a windowless fortress on your
right. The former was founded in 1879 by a Finnish sea captain, Gustav Niebaum, who had made an early fortune out of Alaskan furs. The
châtelaine of Beaulieu is Madame Georges de Latour, whose husband
for nearly forty years was one of the leading viticulturists of northern
California.

From Rutherford north, through St. Helena and Calistoga, there
are almost as many wineries as houses. A great many of these producers, of course, sell their wine in bulk; of the fifty bonded wineries
listed by the Wine Institute, eight or ten, at the outside, put out bottled wine that can be purchased in Chicago or New Orleans or New
York—the others, to the average consumer, can have little more than
an academic interest.

In the Napa Valley, as almost everywhere else in California, there is
a direct and generally predictable relation between the quality of any
producer's wine and the varieties of grapes that he grows in his vineyard. In this respect, Napa still has the unhappy legacy of the dry

years to contend with—acres of Alicante Bouschet and Carignane and even Mission on the bottomland, all too few Pinots, all too few Cabernets, all too few Rieslings, and, as a whole, too few vineyards on the hillsides, too many on the flat. But, especially in the new plantings, the proportion of better grapes is extraordinarily high, and it seems probable that the name of Napa will fully regain its old luster, especially if it is safeguarded and restricted and advertised (as it deserves to be but at present is not) by a strong association of local growers.

The fifteen years since Repeal have been less kind to the Sonoma Valley than to Napa. For this little district, birthplace or at least cradle of the fine-wine industry in California, where, over ninety years ago, General Vallejo made twenty thousand gold dollars in a single season out of his vineyard of five thousand vines, seems to have fallen on evil days. There are still a few good vineyards, but there is not a single bottler of superior wine in the Sonoma Valley. Most of the fine grapes go elsewhere—those from the Goldstein Ranch, now known as Monterosso, over to Louis Martini's winery in St. Helena; the Rieslings and Traminers from the old Bundschu place, south to Almadén in Santa Clara County; the Cabernets from the Kunde hillsides, in most years, to Fountain Grove. And yet, all the way from Vineburg to Glen Ellen and from the bay north to Los Guilicos, this can and should be, has been and will be again, almost another Côte d'Or or another Rheingau.

The Sonoma Mission, California's northernmost and last to be established, was founded in 1823 and christened San Francisco Solano. A year later, the mission vineyard consisted of over a thousand vines, and it seems reasonable to suppose that by 1825 or 1826, wine of a sort was being made in Sonoma by the Franciscan padres.

Sonoma's Golden Age, however, began in the 1850s, and it owed its development in large part to the activities of one extraordinary individual, Count or (as he later chose to call himself) Colonel Agoston Haraszthy. Forced to leave his native Hungary on account of his liberal leanings, he made his way, after a remarkable series of adventures, by way of Sauk City, Wisconsin, and San Diego, to San Francisco; in 1858 he purchased a farm, or ranch, known as Buena Vista, on the low hills southeast of Sonoma. In the following decade, making and losing a couple of fortunes en route, he completely transformed and modernized the wine industry of California and traveled through Europe as the governor's special agricultural delegate, bringing back with him over one hundred thousand cuttings of "1,400 varieties," a good many of which, on the basis of present evidence, would seem to have been mislabeled. He found time, meanwhile, to construct a series of "champagne tunnels" at Buena Vista, to write an outstandingly interesting book, to build a villa in the Renaissance style, to make what was called California's best brandy, and a "Tokay worth eight dollars a gallon."

A ridiculous political dispute in the state legislature made it impossible for the good Colonel to distribute his imported cuttings in an orderly manner, as he had planned. Financial troubles ensued, and although the Colonel's sons, who had been sent to spend an apprenticeship in the vineyards abroad, unquestionably were the most competent wine men in California, Haraszthy eventually lost control of his cellars and vineyard. Indefatigable and undiscouraged, he set up a sugar plantation in Nicaragua in 1868 and a year later disappeared into a river "infested with crocodiles."

Haraszthy, however, had provided the momentum for the take-off; the rest was comparatively easy. Two itinerant German musicians, Kohler and Frohling, parlayed a little vineyard near Los Angeles, which they purchased in 1854, into a wine empire which included vines in Sonoma, ten great "wine vaults" in San Francisco, a resident agent in New York, and an export trade, around the Horn, to Denmark, England, and northern Germany. Arpad Haraszthy, who remained in charge of the Buena Vista Cellars after his father's departure, produced California's first successful champagne, Eclipse, which became famous. Emil Dresel and the Gundlach-Bundschu Wine Company planted, along the lower foothills of the Mayacamas Mountains near Vineburg, the Riesling, Traminer, and Sylvaner grapes which even today, in their old age, yield some of the best Rhine type of wines of California. The whole fertile little valley was rimmed with vines by 1900.

Most of these, alas, are overgrown today and gone. It is a disheartening sight, as you drive northward from Sonoma to Santa Rosa, to see, on acre after acre of what could and should be some of America's best wine-producing country, the faint patchwork squares of abandoned vineyard. A few hardy farmers continue to grow grapes—they sell them, for a good deal less than they are worth, either outside the valley or to one of five or six bulk-wine producers in Sonoma or Kenwood or Glen Ellen.

Back in the wooded hills west of Glen Ellen are the fire-scarred ruins of Jack London's once celebrated home. And near Glen Ellen is the one winery that offers anything of interest to a thirsty lover of picturesque and ancient buildings. Most of us who are not Californians or who are of more recent vintage are inclined to forget that the great earthquake in 1906 did not stop at the city limits of San Francisco but devastated a whole countryside. Charlie Pagani's Glen Ellen Winery, being as durable as they come, suffered a minor casualty—it was bent, not broken, by the tremors and survives today, incredibly and magnificently sway-backed but as solid as ever.

The little chain of hills that forms the western slope of the Sonoma Valley peters out after a few miles, and once you cross the low saddle at the head of the valley, you still have the Mayacamas Mountains on your right, but a wide plain on your left. With one exception, in this fertile country of orchards and hops round Santa Rosa, there are no vineyards of consequence. The exception is Fountain Grove.

It is true, of course, that in a country where Germans and Italians and Frenchmen, Finns and Chinese and Russians and New Englanders, counts and trappers, musicians and colonels were all numbered among the original settlers, the extraordinary becomes commonplace. But even in such company, the history of Fountain Grove is unusual. For a number of years it was one of those curious "cooperative commonwealths" that sprouted up like mushrooms, under the guidance of self-appointed "prophets," all over America during the latter half of the nineteenth century. The "prophet" of Fountain Grove was one Thomas Lake Harris, whose disciples included members of some of the most distinguished families of England and whose principal acolyte was a prince of the Royal House of Japan, Kanaye Nagasawa. It was Nagasawa who created Fountain Grove as it now exists; toward the end of his life, proud of the rolling vineyards that he had planted to Cabernet, Zinfandel, Riesling, and Pinot Noir, he became known as one of the best judges of wine of the West Coast. The vineyard is owned today by Errol MacBoyle and is one of the few in Sonoma which, in grape varieties and cellar equipment and general all-round quality, deserves to rank with the elite of Napa.

This northern half of Sonoma County, from Santa Rosa to Asti and Cloverdale, is, incidentally, the only important part of California's fine-wine country which lies outside the basin of San Francisco Bay. It is drained instead by the Russian River, a picturesque, meandering little stream which rises in the north near Ukiah, flows south parallel to the coast, and then, at Healdsburg, cuts abruptly west through the magnificent redwoods of the Coast Range to the Pacific. Its valley, between Healdsburg and the ocean, is thick with summer cottages and picnic grounds, and there is only one winery of consequence—the old stone champagne plant of the Korbel family, at Guerneville. The Korbels, originally from Bohemia, made a fortune in the lumber business, and some of the gigantic stumps of their original redwoods are still to be seen among the vines.

A high proportion of the early vineyardists in the Sonoma Valley were Germans, and French settlers were largely responsible for the development of Santa Clara, but the Russian River Valley, from Healdsburg north, is a sort of little Italy. Even the countryside, with its rolling, irregular, reddish hills, looks surprisingly Italian and recalls nothing so much as the Monferrato, the classic district of fine wine southeast of Turin. The wines, too, are much more like those of Italy than of France—sturdy, full-bodied, heavy in tannin and rich in color—though it would be hard to say whether this is due to a combination of soil and climate, or to the grape varieties used, or to traditional Italian methods of vinification. In any case, northern Sonoma has always specialized in red wines and concentrated on the production of something sound and honorable and inexpensive, rather than of something rare. Most of the small growers sell their wine in bulk, and almost all those who bottle, like the Italian Swiss Colony, for example, do so on a very large scale.

Of Sonoma County's 20,000 acres under vines, about 9,000 are planted to Zinfandels, 3,000 to Petite Sirahs, and 2,000 to Carignanes. These, of course, are not varieties likely to produce a Chambertin or a Château Latour. What they can and do produce, in gratifying abundance, is something that we can all afford to drink, and drink with enjoyment, at our daily dinner table.

April 1948 / February 1949

WINE AND WAR

New Wines of France

Frank Schoonmaker

This spring, after six long weary years, we shall have them back—the old, well-remembered bottles, the familiar, famous names. Lordly Chambertin . . . Romanée-Conti; the magisterial clarets of the Bordeaux country, Latour and Mouton-Rothschild at their head; gay, crackling Vouvray, with a single strand of wire holding down its impatient cork . . . venerable Hermitage . . . pale Chablis with its color of ripening wheat and its aroma of gunflint; the Alsatian white wines in their tall, slender green bottles.

A good deal of water and a fair lot of wine have gone under the bridge since these cheerful ambassadors of France were last with us. We shall have to cope with a whole generation of new vintages: 1940—the vintage of Dunkirk; 1941—the wine of Pearl Harbor; 1942—*cuvée* of the North African landings . . . and so on through 1945, vintage of Victory and, appropriately enough, probably the best year since 1900.

During the German occupation, a few odd scraps of "information" reached us regarding French vineyards and wines. Almost all of the news was bad.

The Germans have seized all the cognac in France and are using it for motor fuel . . . they have broken up the cognac stills for copper scrap . . . requisitioned all the champagne in Reims and Epernay ... there is no sulphur, and the French vineyards have been riddled with mildew ... all of the Burgundian vineyards have been torn up and potatoes planted on the Côte d'Or ... as a result of the manpower shortage, the vines have been abandoned over most of France ...

Luckily, all this proved to be nonsense. The French, as was altogether to be expected, took great care of their vines; the damage in general was substantially less than during the war of 1914–18 and was extensive only in Alsace, around Colmar. The town of Chablis was badly hit in 1940, but the vines escaped injury; a few *chais* (winemaking plants) and cellars in Bordeaux were wrecked by Allied bombings; the village of Comblanchien on the Côte d'Or was burned to the ground by the Germans in 1944. That is about the total, and a remarkably small total it is.

Furthermore, France was exceedingly fortunate in the matter of weather. Never, certainly, in the last half century have the French vineyard districts known a comparable succession of dry summers (which means a minimum of mildew) or a higher average of good or creditable vintage years.

Lastly, of course, the French did an extraordinary job of hiding and protecting their stocks, walling up portions of their cellars, burying their more precious bottles, bilking, cheating, duping, and deceiving the Germans on every possible occasion and in every possible way.

As a result, there is probably about as much fine wine in France as there ever has been in our lifetime.

This is not at all to say that fine wine (let alone *vin ordinaire*) is easy to come by in France, or cheap, for it is neither. The stocks, for once, are not in the hands of the wine merchants, but hidden away in the cellars of small producers. The thousands upon thousands of little reserves of this sort make up together a not inconsiderable portion of the hidden wealth of France; they are the fruits of frugality and they have been assembled with peasant shrewdness and great care. The bad bottles, most of the doubtful bottles, and in general those incapable of long life, were sold to the Germans or the rich collaborationists or the black market. What is left is the precious cream of seven bitter years. Despite any and all devaluations of the franc, and come what may in the way of export subsidies or bonuses, it will be sold slowly, in small lots, for high prices, and at what the grower feels is the propitious moment. This propitious moment will come when the grower finds it possible to buy what he needs—agricultural machinery, clothes for his family, coffee, sugar, tobacco—at prices he thinks are bearable.

It may, therefore, be considered certain that there will be no great abundance of good, cheap French wine on the American market in the near future. Our California friends have nothing to fear—any French wines which are plentiful here will be either overpriced or poor. But a certain number of small lots discovered, bargained for, and imported by our more knowing merchants, are likely to be of very high quality indeed.

Champagne, of course, is a case apart. Most of the large houses have adequate stocks. Some of them will send their best—and some will not—to the American market, which, I think, is not generally regarded with sufficient respect in Reims and Epernay. One thing is sure: there will be no imported champagnes at $2.50 or $3 a bottle, as there were before the war.

There are a great many pitfalls which await the unwary in all this business. French wines have been, in the past, among the most consistent in the world. M. Dupont's 1929 Pommard was like a fixed star—if it was good it was always good, and if it was bad it would never surprise you by being better than you expected. Lafite 1928 was Lafite 1928 the world round; Lafite 1934 was another matter and superior to the 1928 not three times out of four but one hundred times out of one hundred. Well, it is useless to expect any consistency of this sort from the wines of the wartime vintages; granted the best will in the world, the growers were shorthanded, lacked material, lacked everything, including the most elementary necessities.

Just for example: red wines are customarily "candled" as they are bottled, and again before they are packed for shipment. This process, which sounds mysterious and complicated, is not. It involves holding the bottle between a candle and one's eye to make sure that the wine is clear. In occupied France there were no candles to be had, and most of the time no electricity to light the cellars.

In the old days, fine red wines were generally clarified with white of egg, a matter of a half dozen egg whites being stirred into a barrel; settling, they carried with them any floating particles which remained. But in the hungry France of 1940–46, an egg was a meal.

Dry white wines, especially the good ones, decline rapidly in quality if not bottled after eighteen months or two years in wood, and red wines a little less rapidly after two years or three. There was a general and disastrous bottle shortage in France throughout the war, and some wines have been or will be bottled long after the termination of their normal stage in barrel.

There was no sugar *shortage* in France during the German occupation; there simply was no sugar. Period. Now, sugar is absolutely necessary to the manufacture of champagne and is widely used in the production of Burgundies of poor vineyards or of mediocre years. Those who were not fortunate enough to have stocks of sugar on hand had ... well, no sugar. This means that a good many champagnes, especially those of unknown brands, were held longer in barrel before their secondary fermentation in bottle than would normally have been the case, and some of them may well have suffered by it. On the other hand, many of the commercial Burgundies, which are often *chaptalisé* (given more body and alcohol with the addition of sugar during fermentation), had to be made as God and nature intended that they should, and you will find many of them somewhat lighter and less powerful, though no less *bouqueté,* than you remember them.

Incidentally, this same sugar shortage is responsible for the continued absence of French liqueurs, as well as for a slight but significant change in the character of French cognac.

Most commercial cognac, before the war, was sweetened or "softened" with caramel or burnt sugar. There was nothing at all reprehensible about this practice, any more than there is about the "dosing" of a semisweet champagne. But with sugar unprocurable, many of the cognacs we are receiving today are drier than they used to be. A number of them, by the way, are also older and better than they were. And now that the franc has been devalued, they can be counted on to come down, at least a little, in price.

Whatever happens, however, it will be a long time before we wine drinkers find ourselves back in the easy atmosphere of the 1930s, with sound clarets at $12 a case and '29 Burgundies at $2 a bottle. Our old friends are coming back at last. They will be scarce at the beginning, and expensive, and not altogether as dependable as we might wish. But, God bless them, they are coming back—a sign, if you wish, that France, like the vine, will once again be green.

May 1946

RETURN TO BORDEAUX

Frank Schoonmaker

When, on your way south from Paris, you take the ferry at Saint-André-de-Cubzac, with the warped and rusted skeleton of the once-celebrated road bridge down in the Dordogne River on your left (by courtesy of the Germans), and the spidery outline of Monsieur Eiffel's great viaduct oceanwards on your right (by courtesy of a German mine which failed to explode), you are already in the Bordeaux country. If it happens to be a late September afternoon, hazy and calm, with a gray sky with a few patches of pale sunshine, you will see the Bordeaux country at its best, wistful and graceful and old-fashioned, like an eighteenth-century print.

With its cobbled quays and its formal gardens, its long, low, windowless buildings (the *chais* of its great wine merchants), and its old, elaborate houses, spacious, high-ceilinged, and cool behind their gray façades, the city of Bordeaux has something of this same remote eighteenth-century charm. It is slow and easy-going, as befits an inland seaport with a wide, slow-moving river at its doorstep.

Bordeaux's river, the Garonne, joins the Dordogne a few miles north of the city, to form the broad tidal estuary of the Gironde. These navigable rivers and the proximity of the ocean have made Bordeaux's history and molded its whole character.

A hundred and fifty years ago the great Bordeaux clarets were still almost unknown in Paris; but they had already been famous for centuries in England and in Scandinavia and in the cities of the Hanseatic League, and they were even being shipped in considerable quantities to the United States. In the names of a score of châteaux—Talbot, Brown-Cantenac, Boyd-Cantenac, Lynch-Bages, Léoville-Barton, Smith-Haut-Lafite—there are reminders of the fact that Guyenne was once a British province, that the "wine-fleet," plying between Bordeaux and London, consisted of over a hundred and forty vessels as long ago as 1350, of the fact that a British monarch—Edward II—once ordered a thousand barrels of "good Gascon wine" for his coronation.

In its quiet way, Bordeaux, before the war, was one of the most international of French cities. The sons of its mercantile families (most of which had intermarried) spoke English, and often German and Spanish and one of the Scandinavian languages as well. They had their wine-producing châteaux up in the Médoc, their summer villas at the nearby beach of Arcachon, their town houses in Bordeaux. They knew how to live, and the cuisine in their favorite Bordeaux restaurants was one of the best in France.

Like most regional cuisines, that of Bordeaux is based on the gastronomic resources of its own countryside. Traditionally, this is the province of *cèpes,* those magnificent and delicate mushrooms, thick as a steak, which we in America rarely see except *en conserve*. It is the home of steak *marchand de vin,* which anyone can make who has shallots and parsley and butter and a little sound claret; the home of *rougets,* those little delectable red mullets, caught in the Gironde off Royan—but for these you will have to go to Bordeaux, to La Mère Catherine, or Dubern, or the Chapon Fin, or the Château Trompette. There are oysters from Arcachon and Marennes, *moules* from Chatelaillon, fresh sole from the Atlantic, and the famous incomparable mutton from the salt meadows of the Pointe de Grave. For those whose tastes run to rarer dishes there is lamprey, one of the strangest of fishes, traditionally served with red wine, not white; in September there are even ortolans, those tiny succulent birds no larger than a man's thumb, which have been famous among gourmets for two thousand years.

Particularly, and especially, there is wine. Fresh young Graves *en carafe*, fruity young Médocs and Saint-Emilions from the lesser vineyards, and the whole impressive, interminable assortment of *Grands Crus* and great years. The Bordelais never seem to forget that their principal industry is wine; toward the end of September, particularly if the weather continues fine, the forthcoming vintage becomes almost the only topic of conversation. And the vocabulary of these conversations is a very special one indeed.

Will the wine be a *vin de primeur*, maturing early, like the 1936s and the 1944s, or a *vin de garde*, slow to come around, like the 1928s and the 1937s? Will it be *maigre*, like the 1939s, or *gras*, like the 1943s? Will it be *dur* and *tannique*, like the 1926s, or *souple* like most of the 1942s? Will it be *petit* or *costaud*, *ordinaire* or *racé*, *délicat* or *puissant*? Will the year rank as a *grande année* or a *mauvais millésime*, or will it be one of those *années jalouses*, in which the wines are of uneven and uncertain quality?

The determining factor, of course, is the weather, and by the first of September most of the cards, so to speak, are dealt. But a single rainy week can turn the most promising year into disaster, and occasionally, as in 1924 and again in 1946, a month of miraculously warm and sunny days just before the vintage will transform what looks like a bad year into a *grande année*.

During the whole month of September, everywhere in the Bordeaux country, a fall housecleaning is under way—a prodigious brushing and scrubbing, sweeping and scouring—as the fermenting rooms and presses are made ready for the grape harvest. The owners, many of whom have been away for the summer, move back to their châteaux to keep an eye on things, and if the prospects are good, a kind of gay excitement seems to pervade the whole countryside.

There is a good deal of friendly rivalry between the producers as vintage time comes on; in general, "he who picks last, picks best," but there is the constant and increasing hazard of autumn rains, and it takes a good deal of nerve to risk one's entire crop for the thin margin of added quality which a few days of September sunshine can give. It was with a definite note of triumph that the owner of a small Médoc château announced to me last fall that "Lafite is already picking, but I have not picked a grape and the weather is still fine."

The Médoc at vintage time, in a good year, is a sight worth seeing. The villages are deserted, and everyone from seven to seventy is in the vines—the women picking into flat wicker baskets and generally singing as they work, the young men emptying the baskets into the *hottes* on their backs and carrying them to the nearby roads, where the old men are waiting with two-wheeled carts and the slow, shuffling oxen that draw them. Around every château there is a sort of invisible aromatic halo, made up of the scent of fresh-crushed grapes and the sweet unmistakable odor of fermenting wine.

Really to understand the Médoc, or the Bordeaux country as a whole, you have to know something of the strict, almost feudal system which has made, out of a generally unfertile province, the most celebrated wine-producing district of the world.

The Bordeaux country, which is about one twentieth the size of New York State, and about one seventieth the size of California, produces more than twice as much table wine as the whole United States. About four fifths of this total is red, and the majority of it is nothing more than sound, pleasant table wine, which always has been and always will be consumed in France. Made from the Cabernet grape, plus a certain admixture of Merlot, Malbec, Petit Verdot, and Carmenère, it is blended, intended to be drunk young, and sold generally as "Bordeaux Rouge," for this name is the lowest common denominator of all red Bordeaux wines. Literally it means a red wine, *any* red wine, from the Bordeaux country, and clarets from the better districts are never so labeled—they are entitled to other, more specific and more honorable names. The less famous and less important such names include Côtes, Côtes de Blaye, Côtes de Bourg, Néac, and Fronsac; the more famous are the Médoc, Graves, Saint-Emilion, and Pomerol.

All of the great red wines of Bordeaux—those responsible for claret's international and enduring fame—come from these last four districts and, with a few exceptions, from certain especially favored townships, perhaps a dozen in all. The regional characteristics of each one of the four major districts are fairly pronounced, and the wines of each can generally be recognized without too much difficulty. Superficially and quickly, they can be defined as follows:

Médoc—north and west of Bordeaux. The classic fatherland of great claret and a whole wine country in itself. See farther on.

Graves—west and south of Bordeaux. Produces more red wine than white, although better known for its white. Its best reds (which include Haut-Brion) are excellent, a little softer and less definite in character than the Médocs. Someone once said that the Médocs are like gloss prints of a photograph, the Graves like prints on soft paper.

Saint-Emilion—east of Bordeaux, on the north bank of the Dordogne River. Its wines have been called "the Burgundies of Bordeaux." To an uninitiated taste they will seem "sweeter" than the Médocs or Graves (actually, no red Bordeaux wine is in the slightest sweet); they are ready sooner, somewhat shorter-lived, a bit higher in alcohol; they generally have less tannin, are softer, more obvious, less distinguished.

Pomerol—adjoins Saint-Emilion, and there are wines on both sides of the arbitrary border that *no one* could tell apart. The average quality of Pomerol is perhaps a little higher, since the officially delimited district is smaller, but there are a few Saint-Emilions (Ausone and Cheval Blanc, for example) better than the best Pomerols.

The Médoc, which produces not far from half of the world's supply of really distinguished red wine, is a little triangle of gently rolling country, bounded on the west by the dunes and pine woods that fringe the Atlantic beaches, and on the east by the estuary of the Gironde. There are a few sleepy, gray villages (most of them world-famous) set down among the vines, and, scattered over the landscape, each with its little *parc* or formal garden, its clump of trees, and its extensive vineyard, there are several hundred large country houses, which the French call *châteaux*.

Wines from the less celebrated of these châteaux are usually purchased by Bordeaux wine merchants, blended, and sold either as

Médoc, or under the name of the village from which they come, such as Margaux, St.-Julien, or St.-Estèphe. The better châteaux, on the other hand, usually practice what is known as "château-bottling"—the wine, unblended, is bottled at the château under the owner's supervision. A few particularly careful growers refuse to château-bottle their wines in poor years, but unfortunately such scrupulousness is the exception rather than the rule, and the *mise du château*, although a guarantee of authenticity, is not the assurance of quality that it could and should be.

September 1947

Red Wines of the Côte d'Or

Frank Schoonmaker

So, four or five hundred years ago, they celebrated the excellence of Burgundy in the taverns and cabarets of Paris: "If I had a gullet five hundred ells wide, and the Seine ran this good wine of Beaune, I would go down under the bridge, stretch myself out, and I would let the Seine run down into my belly."

Heart-warming and *joyeux,* heady, big of body, magnificent and Rabelaisian, this is Burgundy. Surely not, as Maurice des Ombiaux has said, a wine for a man with a cold and lazy stomach, since those who make good Burgundy are about the most industrious vintners of France, and Burgundy in turn, as Francis Bacon might have said, maketh a warm man.

I am always astonished when people compare Burgundy with Bordeaux, as if the two were similar, for they are as different as noon and twilight. In Gevrey-Chambertin or Beaune, when there is an honored guest or a great occasion, the linen *nappe* and the great crystal glasses are on the table by noon, and one is well into the *coq au vin* and the best wines by one-thirty. In Bordeaux, such meals are served by the light of chandeliers, and the greatest of the *vieilles bouteilles* only make their appearance in their gleaming decanters two or three hours after sundown. In Bordeaux you eat *sole frite* with a little white wine at lunch, thinking of dinner, and in Burgundy you take an omelette, or the simplest *grillades*, with mineral water at dinner, remembering lunch. The most celebrated poet of Bordeaux, Biarnez, wrote of the châteaux and the wines so dear to his heart in cool and measured Alexandrians reminiscent of Racine. Burgundy is celebrated in bawdy tavern songs.

The immemorial and indestructible and universal fame of red Burgundy is based on the russet-brown soil of one narrow, not particularly fertile hillside, and on the incomparable quality of one extraordinary grape. The hill, of course, is the Côte d'Or, or "Golden Slope," of which I shall have more to say later. The grape is the Pinot Noir.

The origin of the Pinot is unknown; it is probably as old as France. In the first century A.D. a vine, "one of several grown in Gaul . . . the smallest and the best," was identified and described by the Roman agronomist Columella in terms that make it reasonably certain that he knew what we call the Pinot, and had tasted its wine.

By about 1400, in any case, these "best and most precious wines of the Kingdom of France," as Philip the Bold called them, had become celebrated throughout the civilized world. The Dukes of Burgundy were as proud of the title "Lords of the Best Wines of Christendom" as they were of their dukedom, and in 1366 the Italian poet Petrarch could even charge that the Papal Court, then installed in Avignon, refused to return to Rome because of its fondness for the wines of Beaune.

It was about this time, too (if not, indeed, before), that there appeared in Burgundy a lowborn rival of the Pinot, the prolific and inferior Gamay. Planted in the fertile lowlands at the foot of the Côte, this "most evil and disloyal vine" yielded *"très grande abondance de vin,"* but a wine so bad, in the words of a fourteenth-century chronicler, that it was "full of very great and horrible bitterness, and becomes all stinking."

The battle between Pinot and Gamay lasted five hundred years. Essentially, it was a battle between quality and quantity, between the authentic and noble wines produced on hillside vineyards from the shy-bearing Pinot, and cheap, common wines made from the productive Gamay on the plain. Thanks to the French wine laws of 1937, the Pinot is now definitely in the ascendant, and no wine containing

Gamay can legally be sold as Burgundy, except as "Bourgogne Passe-tout-grains" or "Bourgogne Ordinaire." But fraud, they say, is as old as the devil, and much of what is shipped to America as Burgundy, even today, is certainly not worthy of that venerable and honored name.

The essential problem, from the Gamays that were used to *"tromper les étrangers"* before Columbus was born, to some of the magnificently labeled "Pommards" that many of us have found disappointing since the war, is a simple problem. It would have delighted Adam Smith. It is a problem of supply and demand. Everyone wants Chambertin—there are seventy acres of true Chambertin in the world; one year out of three, at best, ranks as a great vintage; in the most favorable of years, an overall production of ten thousand cases is a magnificent crop, and there are autumns like 1945 when a September hailstorm will destroy in fifteen minutes all that a peasant *vigneron* has laboriously created in twelve months. Great Burgundy, as long ago as 1400, was considered a wine for *"notre Saint Père le Pape, Mons. le Roy et plusieurs autres seigneurs."* The population of the world may double and its wealth increase a hundred times over—Chambertin will remain Chambertin, a closely planted little hillside of tiny, not very productive vines. And, if you please, Pinots.

Good Burgundy, therefore, is never cheap, and no one has ever made much money, let alone a fortune, out of the *good* Burgundy he has produced or bottled or sold. We in America perhaps got a false impression during the 1930s when you could buy a case of Clos Vougeot for the price of a ringside seat at a prize-fight, and drink Romanée-Conti at $4 or $5 a bottle. This is no longer the situation and may never be again—it was based on a rate of exchange—and the great wines of Burgundy will always be for the few, not necessarily for *notre Saint Père le Pape,* or *Mons. le Roy,* but for those who take the trouble to find them, and realize that they are bargains at whatever price is asked for them in the wine marts.

The Côte d'Or, from the standpoint of wine, is a hill, or chain of hills, running from north to south along the western edge of the Saône valley, from Dijon to Santenay, some thirty miles in all. You can see the vineyards from the windows of a Paris–Riviera train—a narrow green ribbon of vines, hardly ever a mile wide, sloping up from the valley to the oaks or pines or outcroppings of yellow rock along the crest of the Côte. Every two or three miles, nestling among its vine-yards, is a sleepy little village with a world-famous name.

Some fifteen miles south of Dijon a break in the slope divides the Côte d'Or into two more or less equal halves, and each half takes its names from the most important of its little towns—the northern Côte de Nuits from the village of Nuits, the southern Côte de Beaune from the town of Beaune. With one or two minor exceptions, the Côte de Nuits produces red wines only, and these, on the whole, are bigger and more robust, greater and longer-lived, than their charming sisters of the "Slope of Beaune."

November 1947

R.N. 7: Wines of the Rhône

Frank Schoonmaker

The River Rhône leaves Lake Geneva like a child getting out of school. It runs precipitously west out of the foothills of the Alps toward Lyon, forgetting the tranquillity and calm of Montreux and Lausanne and Thonon; forgetting even its *omble chevalier,* that incomparable creature of deep Alpine lakes which is the noblest, and which Prosper Montagné has called the best, of all the freshwater fishes of the terrestrial globe.

Impatient, swift, sometimes surprisingly deep, but on the whole not very formidable except during the spring freshets, the Rhône scampers down to Lyon. Its banks are the Elysian Fields of the gastronome—Bresse on the right, homeland of Brillat-Savarin, of the capon and pike, of quenelles and frogs' legs and good butter; Savoie on the left, with trout and crayfish and Gruyère cheese and a hundred kinds of *gratins.* There is even one little wine which, however, I have never drunk outside the country of its birth—a cool, pale, dry little wine, occasionally a bit *pétillant,* or sparkling—Seyssel.

By the time it reaches Lyon, the Rhône has acquired a touch of the grand manner; it runs smoothly and evenly, as if it knew very well where it was going, under its twelve bridges, past the stone quays and the tall gray houses, within a stone's throw of La Mère Brazier and a two minutes' walk of La Mère Fillioux, past Garcin and Morateur and Sorret (the splendid and memorable restaurants of the gastronomic capital of France) it runs through Lyon, not like a gourmet, but like a young man in a hurry.

Then, at the southern tip of Lyon, back of the vast iron-and-glass half-sausage of the railway station of Lyon-Perrache, the young Rhône joins the young Saône, and the two take off on their bridal flight toward the Mediterranean, like a couple pursued by an angry father.

I find, when I mention Lyon-Perrache, that I remember with extraordinary vividness three or four or a half dozen frosty mornings when the southbound *rapide* stopped for its scheduled ten minutes in the still, dark station and I climbed down out of an overheated compartment to drink hot coffee and eat warm *croissants* on the icy platform.

When I speak of Lyon itself, I remember not the wartime city of broken bridges, but early departures southward by car after a night in the Terminus or the Carlton, with half the city still asleep in the gray winter dawn, and a luncheon in Châteauneuf-du-Pape in the offing.

R.N. 7, the *Route Nationale* that runs south from Lyon to the Mediterranean, is by all odds the most exciting road of France, especially in December or January, for it runs broad and inviting and easy toward the sun, like the Rhône, which it parallels all the way to Avignon. On a clear winter morning you can begin to notice, as you go south, the signs of the south—a Roman monument in Vienne, a great hill of vines facing due south at Ampuis (Côte Rôtie), more vines and an errant cypress or two at Tain l'Hermitage, the first olive trees near Montélimar, squares with plane trees, old Romanesque churches, towns that are increasingly low, tile-roofed, biscuit-colored. Finally, far off to the left, smoky and blue against the eastern horizon, you see the great six-thousand-foot summit of Le Mont-Ventoux—you are in Petrarch's and Mistral's country, you are in Provence.

A hundred and fifty years ago the trip southward from Lyon must have been vastly more exciting, even if it could not be made in a morning or a day. There were no railways; one "fell" down the Rhône by barge; you got off, if you were timid, while your barge passed under the narrow, dangerous stone arches of the "Bridge of the Holy Ghost," or Pont-St.-Esprit; you tied up at night and ate the food and drank the wine of the country. It was an adventure.

It was probably less of an adventure fifteen hundred years before, when R.N. 7 was the great Roman road of trans-Alpine Gaul, the line of communications to Paris and Germany and Britain, when senators drank what we call Châteauneuf-du-Pape in what we call Avignon, and proconsuls asked for Côte Rôtie in what we call Vienne.

R.N. 7, then as now, was doubtless a highway celebrated for its food. The gastronomic resources of the Rhône Valley are infinitely varied, if not quantitywise very large, and the cuisine is generally in the great Lyonnaise tradition, with just a trace of the flavor and fire of Provence. At La Mère Germaine, in Châteauneuf-du-Pape, in ante-bellum days, you were served *pâtés* of lark and quail, of woodcock and partridge and wild duck, of hare fed on rosemary and thyme, and wild rabbit which had fed on God knows what, as daily hors d'oeuvres. At Condrieu you ate freshly caught perch, as sweet as the almonds with which they were cooked; at Orange and Avignon you could get truffled *brandade de morue* and *aïoli*, Mediterranean dishes, full of oil and garlic and Provençal sunshine. Chez Pic, in Valence, you were served those wonderful little goat's-milk cheeses of St.-Marcellin, which look like old, corroded silver watches when you buy them, but are snowy white when skinned, and go perfectly with the end of a bottle of red Hermitage at dinner.

But the greatest restaurant of the Rhône, and incomparably the best of France, is and has been for a decade the Restaurant de la Pyramide in Vienne, otherwise known after its fabulous proprietor and chef as "Point." I have heard Point called *le roi* even by the director of the Tour d'Argent in Paris, which is praise indeed, and I doubt whether there is any chef or restaurant owner in western Europe who would have the pretension to call himself Point's equal today. During the war he was twice closed by the Germans, but within a week after the liberation of Vienne by the Seventh Army, his lovely bubble-thin baccarat glasses were back on his linen tablecloths, and his food was as good as any I have ever eaten.

Fernand Point is six feet three inches tall and weighs somewhere in the neighborhood of three hundred pounds. He has worked and lived in the kitchen since before he was ten; he has a prodigious memory, a great deal of imagination, an absolutely unfailing taste; when he is in a good mood, which is most of the time, he is as shy and simple and sensitive as a child. Like most great chefs he is capable of towering rages and black despair, and when you have seen him thus, it is easy to believe the story of Condé's chef, Vatel, who committed suicide when the fish for the king's dinner failed to arrive on time.

The dining room and cellar of the Restaurant de la Pyramide is the best possible starting point for any visit to the Rhône vineyards. The wines are all there, chosen with loving care by *"le gros Fernand"* himself—white Condrieu, pale and fragrant; rare Château Grillet, golden, heady, with a trace of muscat in its bouquet; sparkling St. Péray; white Hermitage, honey-colored, long-lived; the sturdy, authoritative white wine of Châteauneuf-du-Pape; pink Tavel, the most famous *vin rosé* of France. And then, *grande bouteille* after *grande bouteille*, the orderly regiment of the reds—Côte Rôtie, Crozes, Hermitage, Cornas, Châteauneuf-du-Pape.

Like the wines of many another district, the Rhônes have had their periods of favor and glory, their declines and resuscitations. Côte Rôtie was a vineyard before the Romans came to Gaul, and was celebrated by Plutarch and Pliny and Martial and Columella. Hermitage, too, in all probability, was a vineyard under Rome, although there are those who say that its grape, the Syrah (having originated in Shiraz, whence the name), was brought back from Asia Minor by a returning Crusader. Châteauneuf-du-Pape was already famous in the days of the Great Schism, when the Papal Court was installed in Avignon, and Provence was the center of culture in the West.

The Rhône wines were popular, too, in nineteenth-century England. Mr. Saintsbury speaks of Château Grillet as "a favorite here in the days of the Regency"; today it is almost unknown, even in France. Saintsbury mentions, too, an Hermitage 1846, "the *manliest* French wine I ever drank," though he drank it when it was forty years old; there are perhaps some of our modern Hermitages, but not many, which will last as long.

The most recent eclipse which Rhône wines have suffered was

brought about by two factors: first, inadequate laws and controls, which permitted all sorts of inferior wines to be sold fraudulently under the famous old names (Châteauneuf-du-Pape, during the early 1920s, was almost in the class of "grocer's claret") and thus brought down the price; second, the understandable reluctance of peasant growers to cultivate their steep and terraced vineyards by hand when, with wine prices down, they could hope for no more than a miserable living in return for the most backbreaking kind of work.

Thanks largely to the efforts of one man, Baron Le Roy de Boiseau-marié, President of the Wine Growers' Association of the Rhône, the necessary legislation has been passed. Rhône wines are now produced under the most stringent controls, and they are well on their way back to the high place which they deserve and once occupied in the hierarchy of the *Grands Vins de France.* They are still not so expensive, comparatively, as they will be, and an American wine buyer will probably get better value in red Rhônes than in any other wines shipped out of France since the war. There are a few points worth remembering:

First, vintage years are less important in the Rhône Valley than in any other district of France; the faithful sun of Châteauneuf-du-Pape is not the pale sun of Chablis, and the Rhône growers, like those of California, can say with some trace of justification that "every year is a vintage year." To be sure, there are variations, large crops and small, but a really bad season comes four or five times a century, not four or five times a decade, as on the Côte d'Or.

Second, the more general the name that a wine carries, the less good the wine. A Côtes-du-Rhone is a wine, almost any wine, from the Rhône Valley; Châteauneuf-du-Pape is a wine made from certain specific grapes in one of the best districts of the Rhone; Châteauneuf-du-Pape–Château Fortia is a wine from one of the few choice plots of that district. No Château Fortia is likely to be sold simply as Châteauneuf-du-Pape and no Châteauneuf-du-Pape as Côtes-du-Rhône.

Third, although Rhône wines, especially the red and white Hermitages of exceptional years and outstanding vineyards, are long-lived, there is no reason to make a fetish of old age and to keep something for twenty years which is as well drunk after five. Tavel, like most *vins rosés,* is better before its third birthday than it will ever be again; the white wines, after their third or fourth summer, tend to lose in freshness what they gain in bouquet; to the producers of Côte Rôtie and Châteauneuf-du-Pape a good 1937 is already an old bottle. The trend toward younger wines is general the world over in this impatient age, and there is nothing much we can do about it except lay away a particularly good Hermitage when we find one, in the hope that the world will be less impatient twenty years from now.

December 1947

Champagne

André L. Simon

Champagne is the best of all wines—at times. There is no wine that is the best all the time; so much depends not only upon one's taste but upon one's mood, upon conditions, circumstances, and the company. Let us imagine, for instance, that we are having lunch at Ascot or Goodwood: The choice is lobster salad or cold Scotch salmon. You have the one and I have the other, but we both will call for champagne. Claret or Burgundy would be entirely out of place, and vintage port quite unthinkable. Now as the afternoon wears on, imagine that you back losers consistently for the first three races: It is just a hypothetical situation, but it has happened to me and it may one day happen to you. And go on supposing a little further—that you, in sheer desperation, put your shirt on the outsider with the longest odds in the 3:30, and it romps home. That calls for a celebration; you must have the best. Are you going to call for a bottle of Château Latour 1929, or Les Grands Echézeaux 1923, or Cockburn 1908? They are all great wines, and you and I could write whole books about them, describing their bouquet, body, and breed, but at the moment you would not have any of them even as a gift. What you want is champagne, and no other wine would be acceptable.

Champagne is not only sparkling wine, but it is the best of

sparkling wines because it is made of better grapes and with greater care than the others. It is said that from the man who picks the grapes which are to be pressed to make champagne to the one who will wrap the bottles for dispatch, each bottle of champagne passes through one hundred different pairs of hands. This indicates the infinite care necessary to bring a bottle of champagne to the remarkable degree of perfection which justifies its high price.

Costly as the intricate processing and infinite care of champagne may be, these things are responsible for the fact that champagne is better able than any other wine to stand the trials and shocks of life. Just think of it. A bottle of champagne has spent some years, never less than three and often as many as ten, in the cool peace of its Reims, Ay, or Epernay cellar, many feet down in the quarried chalk. Then the "call" comes; it is hauled up to the light of day, washed, dressed up with label and foil, wrapped in colored tissue paper, cased and sent by rail to Antwerp, Havre, or any other port. It may be the depth of winter, but that makes no difference. The wine will be left overnight on the quayside, then it will be flung down the hold of a steamer which will carry it, shaking, throbbing, pulsating, and rocking all the time, through the hell of the Red Sea to the still hotter hell of the concrete quays of Mombasa, before it undergoes another thorough shaking on its way by train to Nairobi. There it may have a rest under the stifling tin roof of some wine store until at last somebody with a thirst and a purse gets hold of it, sticks it into a bucket of crushed ice, and leaves it for an hour or so. And after all this, when the cork is set free and the wine is poured out, it bubbles forth clear as crystal, crisp, fresh, delicious, all smiles, as if it had received nothing but kind and considerate treatment all along. Is it not wonderful? Of course it is, and there is no other wine that can endure what champagne can endure.

If by now you believe, as I do myself, that champagne is really an unusual wine, you might like to know why it is so remarkable.

Le vin de Champagne, or *le champagne,* for short, is the wine that is made from the grapes that are grown in the vineyards of La Champagne, one of the ancient French provinces that were split up into smaller *départements* at the time of the French Revolution of 1789. La Champagne lies due east of Paris, southwest and west of the Ardennes and Vosges Mountains, its far from effective natural defenses against the Hunnish hordes of Tartary of long ago and the mechanized hordes of Germany in more modern times. La Champagne is mostly flat and drab: Its great plains and its few hunched-up sets of hills are in turn swept by icy winds from the east during winter, and scorched by merciless heat during summer. It has one fair river, the historic river Marne. The soil of La Champagne is light and poor, without any depth of humus upon a subsoil of white chalk. In that part of the Valley of the Marne, west of Châlons-sur-Marne, where a range of hills rises between Reims and Epernay, the soil is no richer, but it has proved highly suitable for growing winemaking grapes during the past fifteen hundred years, or the past two thousand years if we agree that the Romans were the first to plant grapes where dense forests had formerly flourished.

Today the vineyards of La Champagne grace the slopes of two opposite ranges of hills of the Valley of the Marne, above and below Epernay. The more important of the two, on the right bank of the Marne, between Epernay and Reims, is called La Montagne de Reims: Some of its best vineyards, from west to east, are those of Rilly-la-Montagne, Ludes, Mailly, Verzenay, Sillery, and Verzy, all facing Reims. Then passing south, at the bend as it were of a huge horseshoe, we come to Trépail, Ambonnay, and Bouzy; and with our back to Châlons-sur-Marne, away to the east, and proceeding due west, the vineyards of Avenay, Mareuil-sur-Ay, Ay, Dizy, and Hautvillers higher up, all face the right bank of the river Marne and Epernay. There is another range of hills opposite, at some distance away from the left bank of the Marne, known as La Montagne d'Avize; its best-known vineyards are those of Pierry and Chouilly, nearest to Epernay, and then, going east toward Châlons-sur-Marne—Cramant, Avize, Le Mesnil, Oger, and Vertus.

In La Montagne de Reims vineyards, some 80 percent of the grapes grown are black grapes, black Pinot grapes, and 20 percent are white Pinot grapes. In La Montagne d'Avize, white Pinot grapes are grown almost exclusively. The Pinot grape, whether black or white, is one of the great aristocrats among winemaking grapes: It ranks with the Cabernet of the Médoc, the Sémillon of Sauternes, and the Riesling of the Rhine. These are all grapes which possess that most elusive and attractive of all wine virtues which is called, for lack of a better word, breed. Pinot grapes are also grown in the vineyards of La Bourgogne, yielding wines which possess this same quality, though differing from those of La Champagne because the nature of the soil is entirely different. It is because the soil of the vineyards of La Champagne is so very poor that the noble Pinot grape can be made to produce an exceptionally light and delicate wine which makes a far better sparkling wine than would grapes with a greater volume of bouquet and body. But one must not forget that it is entirely due to hard work, the only hard currency that Nature accepts, that the poor chalky soil of the *champenois* vineyards has been made to yield, in the course of centuries, a wine of such unique excellence and appeal that it has been the source of undreamed-of wealth.

Champagne was not always a sparkling wine: For hundreds of years it was a still table wine, red if made of black grapes, white if made of white grapes. Sparkling champagne was first heard of at the end of the seventeenth century, but, until about one hundred years ago, sparkling champagne was the exception and still red champagne was the rule. Dom Pérignon—he was born in 1639 and died in 1715—has been hailed as the discoverer, inventor, or creator of sparkling champagne, but he made no claims to any accomplishment of the sort, nor did any of his contemporaries claim any such honor for him. All who knew him praised his kindly disposition and his professional ability: "He loved the poor and he made excellent wine." Dom Pérignon, cellarer of the Abbey of Hautvillers, never wished for a better epitaph; he would certainly have resented being hailed as the first man to have "put bubbles into champagne," when neither he nor anybody else was ever responsible for these bubbles. The bubbles in sparkling champagne are the same as the bubbles in bottled beer: They are tiny drops of liquid disturbed, whipped, and chased by escaping carbon dioxide or carbonic acid gas.

If we want wine to be sparkling, all we do is prevent the carbonic acid gas from escaping into the air. We must bottle it up, cork it up, and make sure that the cork is tightly and safely wired or tied so that the gas inside the bottle cannot push it out. That is where Dom Pérignon comes in. He was the first to use stoppers made of cork bark in place of the stoppers of wadded hemp or the drop of olive oil previously used to keep dust and dirt out of the wine. Sparkling wine and also still wine matured in the bottle did not and could not exist in France before corks made of cork bark were imported from Spain.

All that was quite a long time ago. Let us see now how champagne, sparkling champagne, the favorite type of this wine, is made today.

As soon as the grapes grown in the vineyards of La Champagne are ripe, they are picked by hand, of course, as many of the bunches are hidden under the foliage of the vines. They are brought in small baskets to the nearest roadside, spread upon large osier trays, and looked over, bunch by bunch, by a number of sharp-eyed expert old women, armed with long, pointed scissors, who remove unsound, unripe, or otherwise defective berries from all bunches. The bunches are now piled in great baskets, which, when full, are loaded on cart or van and delivered with the least possible delay to the nearest *vendangeoir.* There they are weighed and tipped into the *pressoir,* a square oak press holding four tons of grapes when filled to the top. This press has a heavy lid made of thick oak boards which can be raised or lowered by means of an electrically driven screw. When the lid is brought down upon the heaped mass of grapes in the press, the grapes are crushed and their sweet juice runs down a wide groove into a large vat on the floor below. This vat is pegged on the inside, and as the rising flow of grape juice reaches the 450 gallons peg, the connection between the press and the vat is switched over to another vat. The lid of the press is then raised, and the wet mass of disfigured squashed grapes is heaped up in the center of the press; down comes the lid again, and greater pressure than before is applied in order to extract every drop of juice that remains in the grapes. It is obvious that the wine made from this last turn of the screw will not be so good as that made from the first.

Let us watch those first 450 gallons of white grape juice which were pressed out of four tons of ripe grapes and are now in the pegged vat below the press. It will not be long before we notice that there is something happening; bubbles are beginning to appear on the surface and very soon now the grape juice ceases to be dull and dormant. It frets, it gets hot, it throws up a froth, discarding the dust and dirt that came in with the grapes; it is "fermenting." As a matter of fact, it has now ceased to be grape juice at all. Some of its grape sugar has already escaped as carbon dioxide and some has become alcohol, which means that we now have wine instead of grape juice in the vat. So we promptly draw our very new wine into ten casks, each holding 44 gallons, as the original 450 gallons have lost 10 gallons in the course of fermentation.

The casks of new wine are usually sent by motor lorries to the cellars of their owner, be he an individual *vigneron* or one of the great shipping houses, and they are left more or less alone for the next six months or so. This gives the wine a chance to continue fermenting very slowly and to settle down sufficiently for the *chef de cave* to taste it critically and to make up his mind how best to "assemble," or blend, his various *cuvées*.

In any champagne house of repute there are in the early spring of the year many hundreds of casks of new wine—that is, of wine made from grapes vintaged during the October of the preceding year from a score or more different vineyards. The *chef de cave* has a most difficult duty in deciding how best to blend these different wines to achieve the highest possible standard of quality and a sufficient degree of distinctiveness to ensure that his *cuvée*, his choice, will have a greater appeal among champagne connoisseurs the world over than the *cuvées* of his competitors, the other champagne shippers. All the great houses have large reserves of wines made in the best vintage years, wines which are kept in casks to be blended with the new wine of later and less-favored years in order to raise their standard of quality. When the *chef de cave*, after many careful tastings and trials, is satisfied that his *cuvée*, the wine of the year, is worthy of the reputation of the house whose name it will bear on its label in years to come, his next problem is to make sure that when the time comes to offer this *cuvée* for sale, the wine will be sparkling, with neither too much nor too little carbonic gas in it. This means that the wine must be bottled; that it must be securely corked so that no gas from within can push the cork out; and that there is in the wine, at the time of its bottling, just the right amount of sugar to produce, after fermentation, the proper amount of gas. Too little sugar would result in flat champagne, which is dull; too much would burst the bottles, which is worse.

Scientific instruments enable the *chef de cave* to test the wine which is about to be bottled with such accuracy that he may add to it just the right quantity of sugar to produce the desired quantity of gas. Time is the next headache, for time is money, capital locked up and interest running up. But there is nothing to be done about it. The new wine, that is, the newly blended *cuvée* with its right "dope" of sugar, has been bottled and safely corked up, and now must be left alone, stacked in great piles of many thousands of bottles in deep, cold cellars cut out of the chalk rock, and given a chance to do its appointed work in perfect peace. Its work is to transform through fermentation every bit of the sugar in it into alcohol and carbon dioxide, and the new wine will do it perfectly, provided always that you are in no hurry and can afford to wait, eighteen months to two years. By then there will be no sugar left in the wine, but there will be something else besides the carbonic acid gas to make the wine sparkling: There will be a crust, or sediment, the inevitable "discard" of all fermenting wines. You cannot decant champagne as you decant old claret or vintage port, leaving the sediment in the bottle, so something must be done to get it out of the champagne bottle before it leaves its home cellar. This is a tricky job, one that demands time and skill.

When the bottles are lifted from their stacks, where they have had a long rest in a perfectly horizontal position, they are stuck into specially made grids, or racks, head or cork first, the punt slightly tilted up, and every other day an expert *remueur,* or "shaker," a man with strong hands and a light touch, seizes each bottle in turn by the punt, gives it a few rotating tremors, pushes the bottle slightly forward to leave the punt tilted a little higher than when he first came to it. After quite a long time of this gentle assistance, the sediment inside the bottle has been made to slide down a little nearer the cork, until, in the end, the bottle is almost in a vertical position, the punt uppermost, the bottle standing practically on its head, or rather on its cork. Now comes the turn of the *dégorgeur,* also quite an expert at his job, which is to release the clamp that holds the cork firmly in the bottle, letting the gas inside the bottle blow out the cork and all the sediment that has been so laboriously packed upon its inside face. That is easy enough if you do not mind how much wine and bubbles rush out of the bottle; but, of course, that must not happen and the skill of a trained *dégorgeur* is such that hardly any wine and bubbles are allowed to escape. Nowadays the work of the *dégorgeur* has been made much easier by a refrigerating machine which has been devised to freeze just that one inch of dirty champagne with all the sediment which has arrived upon the inside face of the cork in the bottle. It is safer and quicker to remove the cork with the small lump of frozen wine and dirt stuck to it, leaving the rest of the wine in the bottle absolutely starbright. The wine is also dry, since every bit of sugar that was in it at the time of bottling has by now been completely fermented.

Now is the time to settle a very important question: Is the wine in the bottle too dry? The answer is, ninety-nine times out of a hundred, in the affirmative. The next question is: How much or how little sugar ought we to put in each bottle of wine before corking it for the second and last time? The answer depends entirely upon the taste of the people who will eventually be drinking the champagne: sweeter for the French, who drink champagne at the end of the meal with *gâteaux* and *dessert*, and drier for the great majority of the English champagne connoisseurs, who enjoy it before a meal or with fish and white meat. To make sure that he will have some champagne to please all and sundry, the *chef de cave* adds 5, 3, 2, 1, ½, or ¼ percent of liqueur to different bottles of wines, after the sediment has been removed and before the second and last cork is forced in and securely wired on. This liqueur is made of sugar candy melted in champagne, with sufficient pure spirit of wine or brandy to ensure that the added sugar cannot possibly start fermenting at a later stage.

All that remains to do now is to give the wine which has been liqueured a long rest so that it has time to assimilate the added sugar—which it does in a few weeks' time—and then it may be sent for and sold. But there is no hurry; on the contrary, there is much to be gained by leaving the wine alone for another year, maybe two or even three, before it is sold. It will gain in quality by losing some of its original acidity.

Champagne bottles are more smartly dressed than most other wine bottles. This tendency began when the cork was held in place not, as at present, by a neat wire guard, but by a long piece of twine which was wound many times round the neck of the bottle. To protect the twine from damp as well as from rats, it was covered with a tight-fitting cap made of pewter or tin. Gradually this cap was made more attractive by making it longer and of various colors, becoming eventually the "foil" as we know it today. Besides the foil, which gives the champagne bottle a festive appearance, the bottle bears never less than one and often quite a number of different labels or notices, each containing some items of information, such as the name of the shipper, the house responsible for the wine inside the bottle, his or their home address—usually either Reims, Epernay, or Ay, but occasionally also Châlons-sur-Marne, Mareuil-sur-Ay, Avize, and other place-names—usually also the badge, crest, or trademark of the shipper, the date of the vintage—that is, if all, or at least if most, of the wine inside the bottle was made from grapes picked and pressed in the year the date of which appears on the label—some indication of how dry or sweet the wine may be, either *Brut* or *Nature,* which should mean a wholly unsweetened wine, *Extra Sec* or Extra Dry, which means a drier wine, *Sec,* sweet, *Demi Sec,* sweeter; and, for the Commonwealth, the Royal Arms, which means that the shipper holds the Royal Warrant and that his champagne supplies the royal cellars. Sometimes the *cuvée* is described on the label as *Spéciale* or *Reservée.*

Champagne should always be served cold, but not overiced. Too cold, too sweet, or too much champagne means an unholy thirst the morning after, but no headache.

When the wire which holds the champagne cork in place is removed, the bottle should be held in a slanting position so that the wine and gas do not rush out madly as soon as the cork is released, which they will do if the bottle is held in a vertical position. As soon as the cork is out, pour a little wine into a glass and bring it to the tribunal of your nose; smell it with care to be sure that the wine is free from the taint of a moldy cork or any other possible blemish. It is also important to make sure that champagne is served in dry, well-polished glasses: When glasses are at all damp, the champagne bubbles will rise in a sluggish instead of a lively manner. To beat the bubbles out with a "mosser" or a fork is sheer waste of money and good wine. Anybody with a diaphragm allergic to bubbles had better order a still wine or still champagne, which is entirely different from flat champagne.

The color of champagne is straw color, golden. But there is also some champagne which is made pink: It is neither better nor worse than golden champagne.

Vintage champagne is, by definition, the wine of one and the same year or vintage, a year when the grapes were perfectly ripe and sound. In practice, however, when the demand for a very popular brand is greater than the supply, or for other economic considerations, a vintage champagne can be a blend of wines, a large proportion of the blend coming from grapes gathered in the year the date of which appears on the cork and label, while a smaller proportion is made up of usually less expensive wines of former vintages. Any champagne which is sold without the date of a particular vintage may safely be considered to be a blend of the wines of different years; such a wine is always cheaper than the dated wines, and sometimes it is very good indeed and undoubtedly a better value than many dated vintage champagnes.

There was no lack of sunshine during the war summers of 1941, 1942, and 1943, and all three years were shipped as vintage years by various champagne shippers. If one remembers that when the wines of those three vintages were bottled, France was occupied by the Germans, in 1942, 1943, and 1944, it is quite remarkable that they were so good when shipped to us after the war. It is fairly obvious that the lack of skilled labor and the shortage of new champagne bottles and first-quality Spanish corks must have made it particularly difficult for the champagne shippers to keep up the high standard of quality of their various brands. The 1945 and 1947 vintage champagnes have rightly been hailed as the best that we have had since the war.

Champagne is the best wine, as a matter of fact the only wine, one can enjoy the last thing at night and the first thing in the morning, at a ball in the early hours, and at eleven o'clock the next morning, when a gentle pick-me-up is so welcome. At mealtime dry champagne is excellent with *hors-d'oeuvre,* fish, entrées, and all white meats, but it is also most acceptable throughout the whole of a meal: This is not mere hearsay, I can assure you, but personal experience of many years.

In a less topsy-turvy world than the one in which we happen to be living at present, the money which is now being spent on deadly armaments could be far better used on free champagne at eleven A.M. for everybody every morning; then we could claim to be a civilized people.

June 1953

VINTAGE TOUR

James Beard

PART ONE

It was early in 1949 when the French commercial counselor in San Francisco bethought himself a most pregnant idea which later in 1949 became a successful reality. It was his conviction that a group of American wine-lovers, all of whom were members of the various branches of the Wine and Food Society in these United States, should set out on a voyage of discovery in the various wine districts of France. His plan immediately interested not only the French Bureau of Tourisme but also the various viticultural organizations in France and the division of the French government which has to do with the wine industry.

So it was that ten avidly interested wine and food lovers, whose creed it is that "an intelligent approach to the pleasures and problems of the table procures a greater recompense than the simple satisfaction of the appetite," set out on probably the most comprehensive trip through France's vineyards ever planned for laymen.

During the twenty-two days, this group tasted over three hundred bottled wines, well over one hundred wines yet to be bottled; were entertained at more than thirty official luncheons and dinners and numerous *vins d'honneur;* and visited a surprising number of the world's greatest vineyards. That we all returned happy and with our digestive apparatuses working admirably is a great brief for the continuous use of wine and for French cuisine. I might add, however, that girths were noticeably expanded during the course of so much vinous and gustatorial indulgence.

It is obviously impossible to give a complete, day-by-day report of this trip, so we have chosen to treat some of the districts rather briefly and to include our comments on those menus and wines of the greatest popular interest.

TOURAINE-VOUVRAY-ANJOU

Our first four days were spent in this particularly historic and beautiful section of France, whence come some of its most delicate wines.

The first day we absorbed much of the matchless scenery as we rolled along in our chartered bus with frequent stops. In Chartres we visited the magnificent cathedral, to me one of the masterpieces of the world's architecture. We prowled the magnificent châteaux of Blois and Amboise, and finally, late in the afternoon, we arrived at Tours for our first major engagement. This was a dinner offered by the Chamber of Commerce of Tours, our initiation into serious tasting. The menu included some nine wines of the district, both still and sparkling. We discovered again the charm of young wines, especially the delicate whites, which charm made it a thoroughgoing pleasure to taste a Saché 1947 and a Vouvray 1948. It was interesting, too, to compare the Vouvray of 1948 with a rather lordly and distinguished wine of 1919 that was served with our dessert. It was the first of many times we were to be served *brochet,* one of the great white fish of France, and also the first of many times we were to be served partridge. Speeches, too, and the formalities of official entertaining prepared us for the days to follow.

Our second day was filled with adventure, specifically, our introduction to the *caves.* In the Vouvray district the *caves* as well as some of the houses are built right into the solid rock. We visited one home which had been built into the rock with only a façade of stone. Our luncheon was preceded by a tasting offered by the vintners of the district, and we had a choice of some eighteen different Vouvrays. Here we discovered another of the few women who are the heads of great wine companies. This was the Comtesse de Casteja, who, like Madame Bollinger of Ay-Champagne and Mrs. de Latour of Beaulieu in California, is thoroughly at home in the vineyard and in directing the business end of production.

During the afternoon we visited Azay-le-Rideau, Chinon, and Fontevrault, and arrived in Saumur just in time to attend another *vin d'honneur,* offered by the Chamber of Commerce, and an official dinner. The outstanding wine of this district, to my mind, was a 1947 Vin Rosé de Saumur. This little-known *vin rosé,* which contains a great deal of the Cabernet grape, has great charm, a pleasant texture, and a most delightful bouquet.

Our third morning was devoted almost entirely to a tour under the supervision of the Baron de Luze, of the Ackerman-Laurance plant and cellars. The delicious and delicate wine which is known in this country as the Ackerman-Laurance Dry Royal is produced by the champagne process in a plant entirely hewn out of the side of a hill. Our final afternoon and evening were spent in the Anjou district where we visited the famous vineyards of Coteaux du Layon and Coteaux de la Loire. The physical beauty of this particular region is magnificent, and the wines which Anjou produces reflect this magnificence.

Deviating a bit from wine, we spent a most agreeable hour in the Cointreau plant, one of the most modern and efficient in France. The pungent aroma of orange peel still returns to haunt us.

Robert Cointreau and some of his associates had planned a diverting dinner party for us in the historic Château de Brissac. This château, which was rebuilt within the original thirteenth-century walls, has many memorable legends woven into its history. Here some sixty of us dined and wined by candlelight. The dinner had been planned to cater to American tastes. Robert Cointreau had stated that Americans liked lobster, beef, and ice cream—and these were the mainstays of the menu!

COGNAC

Our sojourn in Cognac was notable for several things. Firstly, at a small inn en route—the Grand Hôtel de la Breche, in Niort—we ate what proved to be one of the outstanding meals of our trip. This was proof that one need not visit the great restaurants exclusively to discover fine food. Secondly, it was interesting to find out what an impregnable kingdom is this district of Cognac. It is dominated by two great firms, whose families have for generations controlled the major part of the world's Cognac drinking. Thirdly, we were obliged to stay overnight in what is universally known as the worst hotel in the world: Le Grand Hôtel de Londres. It was particularly fascinating to visit the great plants of Hennessy and Martell; to watch the fine art of blending Cognacs; to see the almost endless warehouses where it ages; and to taste many different Cognacs of varying ages.

At a dinner given us by the Chamber of Commerce, Maurice Hennessy startled us with the information that the tiny country of Venezuela drinks more Cognac than is consumed in the entire United States. He feels that those of us who appreciate wines and good food should give more attention to fine brandies as a *digestif* and particularly to their use in cooking.

BORDEAUX

The night of our arrival and before starting our three-day tour of the Bordeaux district, several of us decided to do a little extracurricular tasting of our own. We repaired to the famous restaurant Le Chapon Fin, known to have one of the greatest cellars in existence. We chose wines which we guessed we might not have many more chances to enjoy. Among them were a Château Haut Simard of 1934 and two wines from Château Ausone, both of which are known to be great— those of 1928 and 1929, the latter, for my money, one of the greatest clarets I have ever tasted. We followed this with a 1920 Château Cheval Blanc, one of the noblest of the wines from that château. A fitting climax was an 1878 Armagnac, itself reason enough for a visit to the Chapon Fin.

Saturday morning's degustation began at an early hour at Château Haut-Brion in Pessac, where both red and dry white wines are produced. We tasted the Haut-Brion Blanc 1948, which everyone declared a delightful and promising wine. As one member of the tour described it, "Young and tender. Jail bait." The 1947 red, though still in its very early youth, gave hints of its future excellence.

A long and interesting stop was made at Château Carbonnieux Villanave d'Ornon, which is known almost exclusively in this country for its white wines, but whose red wines we sampled as well. M. Paillet had decided before our arrival, and wisely so, that it is sometimes much better to taste wines with food. As a result we tasted the white wines with oysters and the red wines with tiny strips of bread well buttered and sprinkled with peeled green walnuts. Naturally, each of these helped to accent the wines we were tasting. This was our last stop before lunch, over which the first major disagreement on wines occurred. It was a friendly debate, however, and brought forth no fisticuffs.

The remainder of that afternoon—after a three-hour luncheon period—was spent in tasting wines in the Barsac and Sauternes districts. It goes without saying that the medal of honor went to Château d'Yquem. Baron de Lur-Saluces offered us some of his greatest vintages and escorted us around the estate, which is so situated that it, like its wines, dominates the entire district. The view of the surrounding country from Château Yquem is breathtaking in its beauty. After visiting Château Ricaud and Château Loubens, where we tasted more dessert wines, a tired but exhilarated group of wine amateurs returned to the hotel.

After a bit of freshening, the sturdy three who had spent the evening before at the Chapon Fin made a return pilgrimage. This time we compared the great Cheval Blanc 1920, which we had tasted the night before, with another great wine of the same year, Château Latour.

Early Sunday morning two of us were invited by Monsieur Sicart of Le Chapon Fin to visit his remarkable cellars, where I am confident you will find the greatest treasury of Bordeaux wines in the world. It has been his life's work and pleasure to maintain this cellar and to

offer only the greatest of wines to his guests. Sicart has a long background in the business, and the son has been trained by the father to
succeed him. Here were all the great names and the great years—the
1920s, the 1921s; the 1900s and the 1906s. M. Sicart proudly displayed
his favorite bottle—a magnum of Château Lafite 1864, which he is
keeping for a souvenir of its greatness. The collection of Bordeaux
was fabulous, but there was a noticeable lack of the great Burgundies.
Sicart explained that he felt no especial warmth toward them and that
they were too heavy and too strong. He hastened to assure us that this
was not true of the white Burgundies.

The list of old Cognacs and Armagnacs is as distinguished as the
list of famous persons who have made visits to this great cellar. The
guests include almost every crowned head of the last century and all
the great notables of our age.

Though it was only ten in the morning, we were bidden to taste two
of the rarest of his Cognacs—an 1810 and an 1830. As we were sampling these liquid treasures, M. Sicart gave us a dissertation on brandy
drinking in general. He feels that a straight-sided glass of large proportions is preferable to the balloon or tulip glass, and he eschews the
custom of nursing the brandy to sniff the bouquet. Not at all, says he.
"Drink your brandy. Tip the glass upside down and hold your hands
around the bowl until it is completely dry on the inside. Then and
only then can you get the true perfume of the brandy." We tried this
and found that our olfactory senses were pleased.

Sunday was Médoc day. It had for its initial event one of the most
distinguished meals we enjoyed during the entire trip, luncheon at the
Château du Taillan, where we were entertained by Monsieur and
Madame Jean Cruse. The château itself and its fabulous collection of
porcelain and pottery and antiques are worthy of an entire article.
The luncheon consisted of *filet de sole à la Joinville* accompanied by a
Cruse Monopole Blanc, followed by *canetons à la Neva*, which brought
forth a Château Pontet Canet of that very great year 1945. The ducks
were boned, stuffed, rolled, and roasted to a perfect state of doneness.
A Château Rausan Ségla of 1929 vintage, and served from magnums,
proved a great and distinguished wine. This was served with *cèpes à la*

bordelaise. The *cèpes*, those remarkably flavored and textured mushrooms which grow in such profusion throughout this particular section, had been picked on the estate that morning. M. Cruse brought forth a rare 1865 Château Pontet Canet to serve with the cheese. This venerable wine showed remarkable signs of its past greatness and was not too old to have a lively interest for present-day drinkers. A magnificent 1929 Château d'Yquem accompanied the dessert of *crème Beau Rivage.*

As I said before, the Rausan Ségla 1929 was a liquid treasure. Relative to this, M. Cruse said to us after luncheon: "The 1929 vintage was something that has never happened before and will probably never happen again. Even Bordeaux wines ceased to be Bordeaux wines and became a special thing which no one here had ever experienced. It is my opinion that 1929 is the greatest year we have ever had."

There are many people, however, who claim that 1945 and 1947 will both outdistance the 1929s. There has not yet been time to tell that, but having tasted a number of the 1929s, it is my opinion that there is a long way to go to outdistance them.

This was to be one of our greatest tasting days, for after our Cruse luncheon we proceeded through a trail of other vineyards. These included some of the great names in Médoc such as Château Pontet Canet, Château Margaux, and Château Lafite. Here we tasted the young wines not yet bottled, as well as some rare ones, and there was much note-taking for future reference.

This was the first day that a long and elaborate luncheon preceded a long and more elaborate dinner. We were the guests of the Baron Philippe de Rothschild at Château Mouton-Rothschild for a tour of the vineyards and the *cave* and then for a formal dinner in the great banqueting hall, which opens into the vast storeroom and which is separate from the château. This is a unique spot where excellent showmanship is combined with tradition. The storage and pressing rooms are spotless, and the lighting is startlingly modern and theatrical to a degree. There are walls decorated with fascinating bits of equipment and curios of other days, all arranged for dramatic effect. Here we tasted a wine which will no doubt be of the greatest of the

1947 vintage—the Château Mouton-Rothschild. Naturally, it has not yet been bottled, but it will be available soon and should be laid down to mature.

Whereas our luncheon at Château du Taillan had been informal and unusual in table appointments, the dinner at Mouton-Rothschild was sheer elegance from beginning to end. Madame Cruse at Château du Taillan had arranged her table simply, with a duck, a rabbit, and a huge goose of faïence and had surrounded them with autumn leaves and colorful vegetables from the garden. It was one of the most charming tables I have ever seen. The table at Mouton-Rothschild, on the other hand, was laden with candelabra in silver and in gold; the table service was also a combination of both metals. Notable arrangements of flowers were artistically arranged, and the entire atmosphere was one of Old World luxury and beauty.

The menu: delicious French oysters—to my taste the finest anywhere—accompanied by a really pleasant Graves, an Agneau Blanc 1945. A *crème Doria. Soles menière.* A remarkable *contre filet de boeuf bouquetière,* followed by a simple salad and cheese. Finally, a *glace pagode* which was perfection—thin layers of crisp meringue with ice cream between and a *sauce chocolat* over all.

In addition to the Graves, we tasted a Château Mouton d'Armailacq 1940, a Mouton Cadet 1943, and two Château Mouton-Rothschild—jeroboams of 1923, which we found in every way distinguished, and for the record book, *impériales* of the 1881 vintage from the private stock of the owners. While it was a remarkable wine, it lacked the distinction of the 1865 Ponte Canet which we had tasted at lunch. An Agneau Blanc Sauternes 1945 rounded out the wines, but with our coffee we tasted some of the *marc* which had been made at the château. Different from the great *marcs de Bourgogne* and those of Champagne, it was a most interesting and earthy brandy nevertheless. It is strange that Americans have never developed much feeling for *marc.* There is such demand for it in France. However, we did find on the trip that there was great interest among a few of our party in this natural and somewhat rugged *digestif.*

You may well believe that it was a weary but well-victualed group that trudged to its rooms to make notes of the day's doings. All the wines tasted and drunk during the day added up to a staggering total.

Off early next morning to visit, first of all, the formidable cellars and offices of the great firm of *négociants*—A. de Luze and Co. These people, who are probably the greatest wine shippers in the world, have acres of space on the waterfront where wines are stored, bottled, labeled, packed, and shipped to every corner of the globe. I was completely engrossed by the shipping room and pondered over the stencils cut for firms in practically any city in any country you might care to name. Madagascar, Reunion Island, Papeete, Boston, San Francisco, Oslo, Beirut—all these names made you realize the magnitude of the wine business and its far-reaching influence. This was our first view of the mass-production side of the industry and gave us material for comparison and contemplation.

Then out of Bordeaux into the Saint-Emilion district where we made an early-morning stop at Château Beauregard, a brief stop at one of my favorites, Château Cheval Blanc, and from there on to the town of Saint-Emilion. There the monolith temple, which had originally been a pagan temple, after that a Catholic church, and now a museum, started up some provocative discussion.

Through the town of Saint-Emilion we rode, past several bakeries where they make nothing but macaroons, for this town is one of the macaroon centers of France. We drove on to the really beautifully situated Château Ausone, where we marveled at the perfection of the surrounding landscape and the tidy vineyards with their ripe juicy grapes almost ready for the pickers. Then back to the Château Clos Fourtet, which boasts a tunnel actually over a mile in length.

Luncheon that day at the Hostellerie de Plaisance was made doubly interesting by the presence of Professor Portmann, one of the most active members of the well-known "Medical Friends of Wine." Also, I had as my vis-à-vis, Monsieur Challon of Château Ausone, who was slightly wary of this group of pilgrims. When he found that two or three of us were violent protagonists in his favor, he warmed up a bit. The final capitulation occurred when cooking was mentioned. For the balance of the meal he offered to me in detail some of his favorite recipes. He is an avid cook and goes to no end of trouble to perfect a dish he happens to fancy. Luncheon was a most satisfactory finale to the full and absorbing experience in Bordeaux.

PART TWO

From Saint-Emilion, where we bade *au revoir* to the Bordeaux district, we made a brief sally into Gascony, stopping in Bergerac for the night. Here antiques enthusiasts and beret collectors reveled for several hours, and most of the crew collected tins of *pâté* and truffles to be sent home.

Dinner that night, notable for good bourgeois cookery, was also notable for some unusual wines. We were all delighted with the charm and dryness of the Château Panisseau. This rather little-known white wine is one you might choose with pleasure when you find it on a wine list. The *gigot de mouton* which was served us that night should have been preserved as a lesson in how to cook lamb or mutton to the point of perfection. Each slice was hot and juicy and pink; it was one of the dishes so perfect in its simplicity that everyone starred it even after the trip was over. Just another proof that the simplest dish may be gourmet food if it is lovingly and knowingly prepared. With the lamb we drank another wine of the district, a red Pécharmant 1943 of charm and grace, though in no way great. The famous sweet white wine of the region, Monbazillac, came with our dessert, and for a fancier of the really sweet wines this is a most delicious example.

A winding trip through the narrow streets of Bergerac preceded a pleasant evening spent on the banks of the Dordogne discussing—of course, wines and food.

Off early the next day through some particularly wonderful country with a stop for sightseeing at the historic town of Montpezier, a tiny walled village which the English built as a fort during the Hundred Years' War. There is a charm and flavor about the place far more English than French. Then on to Millau, a zooming manufacturing town and very close to Roquefort. We paused for two days as far as wine was concerned and concentrated our tasting powers on cheese, specifically on Roquefort—the king of cheeses.

ROQUEFORT

It amazed me to learn that the town of Roquefort is responsible not only for the great cheese that bears its name, but also for fine gloves, glue made from the bones, gelatin used in clearing wines, a good deal of the lamb and mutton eaten in the district, and woolen cloth. The cheese industry requires a great deal of ewe's milk, for which large herds of sheep are raised on the rocky crags; most of the young are killed when one month old to guarantee the milk for the cheese. The other industries are the outgrowth of this cheese manufacture.

We were taken through one of the finest glove factories in France and saw the hides prepared from the raw wool-covered article to the most expertly cut and finished gloves imaginable.

Then on to Roquefort where one of our finest meals awaited us. We had been told that we should find good food there, but few of us were prepared for the really excellent luncheon. I think this is one of the menus worth repeating in full:

Les Perles du Charentais au Vin de Liqueurs
(Balls of perfect melon which had been marinated in
fine port and were served well chilled.)

Le Feuilleté Roquefortaise
(The most exquisite puff paste, light and delicate and
filled with a paste of butter, Roquefort, pepper, and salt.
The puff paste slices were at least three inches high.)

Le Gratin de Queues d'Ecrevisses à Notre Façon
(This was the first of many times we were to taste this
dish of crayfish tails in its several versions. This one had a
very rich brown sauce and was gratinéed under the
broiler before serving. It was smooth and flavorful.)

Le Coq des Causses au Vin de Clairette
(An admirable version of *coq an vin,* but covered with a
tasty crust and baked in the oven.)

> *Les Petits Pois à la Saveur du Jambon du Pays*
> (Tiny French peas cooked with bits of smoked ham
> which gave distinctive contrast to the chicken.)

> *Gigot de Mouton du Larzac Rôtis à la Broche*
> (Leg of lamb cooked *à point*—meaning that it had its
> juice and its pinkness and worlds of flavor.)

> *Le Roquefort, Roi des Fromages*
> *Bombe Belle Hélène*
> *Petits Fours*
> *Fruits*
> *Moka*

After such a luncheon, we needed the strenuous exercise of climbing the rugged cliffs and trekking up and down through the fabulous natural cellars which have been divided into a many-storied building underground. These caves have been used for untold generations for the storage and seasoning of cheese, and no other place where such cheese is prepared can achieve quite the same flavor. Perhaps the most interesting angle of our trip to Roquefort and the caves was to discover the different flavors and stages of curing which are used in various cities and districts. Monsieur Mittaine had a table arranged with nine different cheeses, each marked with the name of a city. We sampled and found tremendous difference in each one. Paris and New York, for instance, have almost the same taste in the length of time the cheese should be aged. Marseille wants a riper cheese, a city in South America prefers one less well aged, and so on. I found that my taste coincided with that of the people of Roquefort, who prefer their cheese really well aged and filled with the blue mold which gives Roquefort its great and unique character.

On we rolled, down through as rocky and picturesque a country as one can find in France, to Montpellier, and then over to Arles for a day of shopping en route to Avignon and a trip through the Rhône Valley.

We made a brief stop at Les Baux-en-Provence for a trip to the incredible ruins atop the hill and a viewing of the Provençal Festival which had been arranged for us. There has since the war been a greatly revived interest in the traditional songs and dances of regional France. Young people have joined together to study the charming customs of other times and give occasional performances in traditional style. We had a delightful evening of Arlesian songs and dances.

RHÔNE VALLEY

Our trip up the Rhône Valley had a most distinguished beginning. It has always been my contention that the wines of the valley of the Rhône were not well enough known and far too little appreciated. They have a rare quality about them which is always pleasant, usually satisfying, and sometimes great. I treasure the knowledge I have of them and am grateful to the person who first introduced them to me.

Our first day in the district began with luncheon at what is to my mind one of the fine restaurants of the south of France—La Mule du Pape at Châteauneuf-du-Pape. Our luncheon was built around the wines we were to taste. There were among the other guests the mayor of Avignon, my luncheon partner, and the Baron Le Roy, who is so well versed regarding this section of France.

We tasted a Tavel Rosé 1947 with our *hors-d'oeuvre*. This is always a most refreshing wine and certainly the most versatile member of the entire wine family, for it is at home with practically any dish from *hors-d'oeuvre* to dessert.

Two different vintages of Côtes-du-Rhône Blanc, those of 1942 and 1945, came with our entree, a *moussaka provençale*. They showed to great advantage, although the 1945 proved the greater. The 1933 Châteauneuf-du-Pape was an ideal partner for the partridge. However, it was with dessert that we had the pleasantest surprise: a Châteauneuf-du-Pape Blanc—a rarity of a wine, dry and pleasant. I must admit its interest was mainly a matter of curiosity, for it is not so great as other white wines of the Côtes-du-Rhône.

This was a day of unusual experiences, for after we had toured some of the vineyards of the district around Châteauneuf-du-Pape, we drove along to Valence to spend the night. Much to our bewilderment we found not only a press conference awaiting us but also one of the most perfectly appointed cocktail parties—in the true New York manner—that you could imagine. Young Roger Latry, whose father was for many years chef of the Savoy Hotel in London and who has been honored in this country several times, is the manager of the small hotel in Valence, and a most progressive and thoughtful one he is. Our dry Martinis were perfectly made and well chilled—an accomplishment of major proportions in France—and the *canapés* were varied and wonderful. Roger Latry had also planned dinner for us. We ate some excellent foie gras, a velvety cream of chicken soup, and a *poularde de Bresse demi-deuil,* and those delicate mushrooms, *morilles à la crème.* We sat long with the Latrys discussing the hotel business in America and Europe.

The next day was to be the high point, gastronomically speaking, of the entire trip. We started early in the morning for Tain l'Hermitage where we were to tour the vineyards and lunch with a group of the vintners. Tain l'Hermitage is most picturesque, for the vineyards which cover practically every inch of the great hill are really fabulous. We visited with M. Chapoutier the vineyard of the Chante Alouette, which yields one of the great white wines of the Rhône Valley, and also the Hermitage vineyards; then back to Tain for a bountiful luncheon. The *pain d'écrevisses du Cabaret* was a triumph, and many gave it the highest score of all. It was a *gratin* of crayfish tails topped with what could be described best as soufflé pancakes cooked separately and then rolled. With that, we drank an Hermitage Blanc La Chapelle of 1942 vintage, a brisk, full-bodied white wine with wonderful bouquet. The Hermitage Rouge Cuvée de la Sizeranne 1929 was also a memorable wine. I sat next to M. Chapoutier, who was justifiably proud of his wine. This we had with our cheese, and a better combination of flavors is hard to imagine.

More vineyards after luncheon, those of Côte Rôtie and the tiny vineyard of Chateau Grillet, which produces an infinitesimal quantity each year, making it perhaps one of the most prized of all white wines. We were to learn its delightful qualities that evening at dinner.

The crowning tragedy was that after this Gargantuan luncheon, so masterfully prepared, we were to be introduced to the great temple of gastronomy—the Restaurant de la Pyramide in Vienne. M. Point had advised us two days before that they were already preparing things for us. We beseeched heaven for the power and space to consume two superb meals in one day.

CHEZ POINT

It certainly became evident upon our arrival *chez Point* that he had made a special event of our visit. Monsieur himself in all his colossal grandeur made us welcome. Perhaps a short description of Fernand Point is in order. He towers more than six feet and is broad to a degree. His chest descends, ever-widening, to well below his waistline. There is a rotundity about the man which is mindful of perpetual good living. As is usual with people who live exceedingly well, there is a benign and comfortable expression on his face and a general aura of well-being. You are at once aware that here is a man who knows living and all its embellishments, master of his particular art, and certainly one of the world's most knowing persons on the subject of food and wine.

Our reception was warm; we sat on the terrace overlooking the garden and drank a *pétillant* wine of the district, well chilled and served in capacious pitchers. The wine was mixed in our glasses with *crème de cassis*. Madame Point joined us, and we found her to be the very soul of charm and as efficient as an IBM device. At just the proper moment, as if there were wires and lights to signal the Points from the kitchen, we were ushered into the large dining room and seated at a beautifully appointed table. Just as we were all comfortably settled, two waiters entered carrying a tremendous silver platter with a stunning piece of food artistry on it. This was our first course—*volailles de Bresse en chaudfroid* with *salade de truffes*. The slices of breast were arranged in elegant design around the three large chickens which were the center of interest. Naturally, the decoration was of truffles on the slices and on the chickens, which were filled with *pâté de foie*. Beautiful silver *attelets* (which were old ones, and I know how difficult it is to find them) pierced the chickens. These skewers were decorated with oversized whole truffles and carved vegetables and whole tomatoes, in the manner of Carême. With this bit of gastronomical artistry, we had a salad of fresh truffles, subtly and deftly seasoned so that the glorious perfume of the fungus was predominant. Felix Point chose to offer us from the treasures in his wine cellar a Château Grillet 1947. Point and one other restaurateur capture the bulk of the wine of this vineyard, and there are those who will journey far for a taste of it. A delightful and rewarding wine it is, dry and well bodied.

Our second *hors-d'oeuvre, oreiller à la Belle Aurore,* was another optical- and palate-pleasing treasure. This great pillow of pastry was stuffed with a *pâté* of venison baked to a glorious golden-brown. With this we drank an excellent Beaujolais of 1945 vintage, properly chilled as is my taste with Beaujolais. Monsieur Point's famous *gratin de queues d'écrevisses* came next. The velvety smoothness of the sauce and the delicate flavor of the crayfish tails blended into a happy amalgam.

The *pièce de résistance*—as if all of them weren't—was *feuiletés de per- dreaux Pyramide.* Each partridge was browned very quickly in butter and then wrapped in puff paste with the head protruding through a hole in the pastry. They were cooked to a toothsome and visual glory. Then the eyes were painted with a tiny white ring and the whole served on a beautifully arranged tray. Some mousseline potatoes— pureed, seasoned, and whipped to foamy froth—were the only em- bellishment. With this, one of the most perfect Rhône wines I have ever tasted, an Hermitage 1937. This aristocrat of the vine was mel- low, round, and luscious.

We continued with the same vinous triumph for the Saint Mar- cellin cheese, a specialty of the house. Our dessert, *ananas en surprise,* was another *pièce montée* breathtaking in the delicacy of its arrange- ment. The silver platter was arranged with three tremendous pineap- ples at the back, and slices of the fruit were in balanced groups in front. Then mounds of fresh raspberries accentuated the golden color of the pineapple, and a thin cloud of spun sugar covered the entire platter. With this, a tray with the famous Pyramide done in nougat as the center decoration and a sumptuous selection of *petits fours.*

Liqueurs, coffee, and cigars followed on the terrace, and after re- laxing chatter and compliments and pictures, the final mark of hospi- tality was offered us—a drink for the road, as it were: Veuve Clicquot Rosé Champagne.

It was a tired group that arrived in Lyon at two o'clock in the morning. And, I may say, gourmets as replete with marvelous food and drink as it is possible for gourmets to be. Paeans of praise rose in every throat, for the next day was a day of rest. I lunched with several others off Bollinger champagne and we dined very lightly, for there wasn't a hunger pang among us. In fact, even the following day, as we wandered through the Beaujolais district, the thoughts of eating were not too appealing. As a matter of record, I skipped out on what proved to be a very poor luncheon and then drove off, with another member of the party, to the delightful Hôtel Relais des Compagnons de Jéhu to sip a bottle of bubbly in the garden and relax. This is a country hotel you should all remember. It is situated near Pontanevaux and has just about as much charm and beauty as is possible for a country hotel. Monsieur Faure will show you every courtesy there, and you may be assured of good food and excellent wines, especially the *vins du pays*.

BURGUNDY

Our stay in Burgundy was all too short, but when one is on a schedule as full as ours, it is difficult to apportion the time. We did get to see most of the historic vineyards and to learn a great deal about the methods of this particular part of France's wine production. As one drives through this district, one is so aware of the small vineyards and of the demand for the fine wines from that section. The beauty of the district and the craftsmanship in planting and caring for the wines are outstanding. We were fortunate in sampling a goodly number of wines and meeting key people in every part of the industry. One notable extracurricular experience fell into our laps—at least into the laps of four or five of us. We were invited to one of the old firms to taste some rare wines.

As we visited the cellars of Champy, Père & Cie, we were suddenly introduced to what might almost be described as a bit of Hollywood. A button was pushed, and one of the great *cuves*, which usually holds many gallons of wine, opened to disclose a completely equipped tasting room. It was in this novel spot, surrounded by a wealth of wine curiosa, that we sat and tasted. We were given our choice of anything in the working cellars or from the private collections of the owners. One of us asked to taste a rare white wine and another to taste a rare red. The white was one of the most joyous tasting sensations I have ever had, and my feelings were shared by the rest. This was a 1904 Grand Montrachet. I know that many of you will say that is much too old for a white wine and that it must have passed its prime. Not at all. From the moment that the golden liquid was poured into the mammoth tulip-shaped glasses, we knew we were experiencing one of the great vinous thrills of our lives. The bouquet confirmed it and the tasting emphasized the fact. It was a sensuous pleasure we would have been sorry to miss.

We were next introduced to an 1898 Clos Vougeot which, though noble in stature and a rarely delicious wine, had begun to show definite signs of its age. It was not quite so distinguished as the Montrachet, but of great interest to taste.

We topped these with a Marc de Bourgogne 1915—a great example if that earthy drink is your pleasure, and it is one of mine.

We were fortunate in having Monsieur Drouhin to guide us through the historic Hospice de Beaune. At the end of the tour we visited the historic cellars and saw the 1949 vintage being brought in. It has been a sensational time in Burgundy, these last few years, for there have been so many consistently good years. Of these the excitement seems most pronounced over the 1947s. They are, in the opinion of a great many experts, wines which are absolutely unbelievable in greatness. The white wines of that year, many of which seem to be ready for drinking now, are really unprecedented, wines which one wants for great occasions. The reds of 1947, too, are maturing quickly and in some cases are being drunk already. Monsieur Drouhin said that word of the greatness got around before the annual auction at the Hospice de Beaune. As a result, the wines brought the biggest prices ever paid at the sale, which provides the money for the perpetuation of the hospital.

Our parade of memorable meals was added to in Burgundy by one really remarkable dinner and an excellent luncheon. For dinner we were guests of the Syndicat des Négociants en Vins Fins de Bourgogne in their headquarters. There were some notable wines, among them a Meursault Genevrières 1946, which was delicate and flowery, and a 1929 Demoiselle-Montrachet, which was sheer molten gold and so delicious it should have been crowned with some special type of honor. The Nuits-Saint-Georges, Château de Gris 1929, which we drank with our pheasant, and the Clos Vougeot 1923, which accompanied the cheese, were both aristocratic examples of the grandeur of red Burgundy.

The food, too, offered us specialties of the district: *brochet en croûte,* which added another style to our repertoire of dishes featuring pike; *jambon à la crème,* one of the noblest dishes from that particular region; and a savory pheasant. It may interest you to know that a woman prepared this dinner for twenty-five of us in a very small kitchen. It was a major accomplishment!

Luncheon the following day offered by the Chamber of Commerce of Beaune was another journey into gastronomic excitement. A wonderful *tarte au foie gras,* an excellent *poulet demi-deuil,* and a perfectly cooked *gigot* were the outstanding dishes, with some amusing *frivolités bourguignonnes* to begin with. The outstanding wine was the Chambertin 1928, which had great distinction and roundness.

We visited many of the vineyards and cellars in the district. A few of the great cellars in Beaune extend under the streets and under several other buildings as well as the one entered. It is an intriguing network of cellar space which houses fortunes in wines. I noticed casks of wine from the previous year's sale at the Hospice de Beaune, which were marked for purchasers in all quarters of the globe, including several for Señor Peron in Argentina.

ALSACE

The outstanding incident of our trip from the Burgundy district to Alsace was, in addition to the magnificent scenery through the Vosges mountains, a perfect wine served to us en route. We stopped at the Feuillée Dorothée high in the Vosges near Plombières. The setting is breathtakingly beautiful, for one lunches on a terrace that literally hangs from the side of the mountain. The wine we had, which was served with that famous hot *hors-d'oeuvre* of that part of the world—*quiche Lorraine*—was a Traminer, Reserve Exceptionelle. It was one of the most flowery, light, and enchanting wines of that district, where the lush quality of grape flavor is so prominent in all the wines. Alsatians are delightful, unpretentious wines which should be drunk when they are young and gay.

The following day we drove through the lovely country from Colmar to Riquewihr, which should be catalogued in your next French itinerary as a must. Riquewihr, a relic of seventeenth-century France, is built on a rather steep hill. The houses, the streets, the market, and the surrounding walls are sheer enchantment, and the general feeling one has in the town is one of utter and complete detachment from the world. Here we trekked through the streets and peered into dooryards and were given a tasting of some of the choicest of Alsatian wines. With it we had as palate cleaner a towering *Kougelhof,* a coffeecake perfectly flavored and beautifully baked in its mold.

The wines we tasted were young, mostly 1947s and a few 1945s. Such charm and light poetry they have, these young Alsatians. The Traminer, the Riesling, and the Pinot Gris grapes produce them. It was an assortment of the finest wines from all the great houses in Alsace, including Willm, Dopff, Hugel, and several others.

At luncheon we tasted more wines of the district, after touring through their picturesque vineyards. There was an especially notable Grand Riesling Reserve 1945.

CHAMPAGNE

A brief overnight stop in Strasbourg gave us a slight respite, and then on to the Champagne country. Our stay there was all too brief, but we covered some notable ground. On the Sunday of our final week we were the guests of the Comité Interprofessionel du Vin de Champagne at a delightful luncheon in the beautiful home of Comte Bertrand de Vogüé. In this charming atmosphere and with a group of distinguished neighbors in the district, as well as André Simon from London and a minister from the French cabinet, it was a gay and interesting luncheon. We drank some delightful Champagnes: a 1943 Roederer and a 1923 Veuve Clicquot, which was a most distinguished wine and one of which the Comte de Vogüé may well be proud. The day was enhanced by a birthday visit to the gracious Madame Bollinger at Ay. She had told me that the Sunday of our visit would be her birthday, and, as far as we were concerned, it was one of the happiest celebrations in a long line of gaiety. We trouped through the winery, where the *vendange* was just being completed, to watch the press and note the care which this remarkable woman takes with her wines. Then we tasted the fresh press and the grapes. We continued across the road to Madame's home, where we toasted her in what is probably the greatest Champagne still in existence—the 1929 Bollinger. It is truly a sensation to drink this superb wine, and we felt honored that she had offered it to us for our mutual celebration.

After this we toured the long lanes of cellars, which during the war years sometimes served as a place to sleep as well as a storehouse for the thousands of bottles of Champagne. It would be an eerie place to sleep at any time, but with disturbances of war going on above, it must have been terrifying.

We motored back to Rheims and dined with André Simon, who had joined us the day before. It is always a joy to talk to André, for his enthusiasm knows few bounds, certainly not those of age, and his knowledge is tremendous.

Our last day on tour was spent in visiting the vintners of Pommery and of Moët and Chandon, through all the miles of cellars and the various stages in the preparation of Champagne. Then finally, we bussed back to Paris, much the wiser in mind on food and wine and much the rounder in girth. Is that surprising?

The following night was the climax, and a most glamorous one at that. Monsieur Vaudable of Maxim's had invited us to a farewell party and he had planned it to a fare-thee-well. He had invited a number of Parisians who have made the greater appreciation of good living one of their prime delights in life. Our dinner was beautifully planned and was served in the traditional grand manner that has come to be expected of Maxim's. We started with a Château Rayne Vigneau 1921, which was chilled to a very low temperature. With this came smoked salmon, caviar, and other *bouchées.* Then to table. Great plates of *marennes,* the best oysters in France, to my taste, and with them a beautiful 1934 Montrachet. The wine went on through the next course of *rouget en papillote.* The red fish made a most dramatic appearance as they were rushed in encased in their voluminous paper coverings, and the aroma was overpowering as they were torn from their sheaths before eating. Pheasant Souvaroff, with *its* wonderful aroma dough-sealed into the casseroles, proved to be sheer joy to eat as well as to whiff. An excellent Château Haut-Brion 1919 in magnums accompanied the pheasant, and we toasted Mr. Weller of that vineyard who was one of Monsieur Vaudable's guests. Mr. Weller is one of the few Americans actively engaged in the production of French wines.

Our dessert was a refreshing pineapple sherbet served in great bowls of carved ice, which were lighted from the inside and covered with a film of spun sugar. With this magnificent presentation there was the 1929 Moët & Chandon, Cuvée Dom Pérignon. Then came coffee and a venerable brandy, Rémy Martin's Les Barbotins—truly an experience in brandy drinking.

We were to be permitted one more gastronomic episode *à la française* before our feet again touched American soil, sailing home, through the waves, or as I did, through the clouds, in ships that carried France across the ocean with us. The excellence of the cuisine aboard the airliners that bear the crest of Air France is proverbial. Food, service, and wines were, as always, reminiscent of the best to be found in France, with the added charm of being specially adapted to meet the particular requirements of dining aloft. There was a split of Moët and Chandon champagne on the attractive tray which held our subtly seasoned, exquisitely prepared luncheon on board the Air France ship which carried us home, and with this we drank a last sentimental toast.

"To France, her great wines, her matchless food, her overwhelming hospitality!"

January/February 1950

LA VENDANGE

Frederick S. Wildman, Jr.

Every year two events stir the imaginations of the French. The first is an international bicycle race, complete with heroes and villains, pathos and skulduggery, that tempts France to an orgy of speculation and gambling. The bicyclists, their entourages, and the cheering throngs form a vast snake which crawls across the countryside, blocking traffic and bringing business to a halt. This affair is euphemistically known as the "Tour de France."

The other event is the *vendange,* or grape harvest. To understand why such a basic agricultural activity should assume such importance in France, one must for a moment examine the tastes of the country. The ultimate purpose of the *vendange* is the making of wine, and wine to the Frenchman is far more than a national beverage. A German will drink his beer—and an American his Martinis—with pleasure, but unthinkingly. In France a good wine is examined; it is peered into and through; it is fondled in the glass; it is sniffed, tasted on the tongue, rolled against the palate; it is savored and discussed. Wine is a source of nutrition, merriment, conversation, and aesthetic enjoyment. To its growers and devotees it is even more; it is—in that cliché of clichés— a way of life.

Consequently the *vendange* and the weather leading up to it are objects of a collective concern that other countries reserve for such events as beauty contests. In France last summer, the sun rose day after day in a cloudless sky. Gardens wilted, grass burned, and public parks were seared to a barren yellow. Milk became scarce, the price of vegetables spiraled upward. Most nations would have considered this an unmitigated disaster, but in France it was greeted with rejoicing. Why? Because the vine, showing an egotistical lack of compassion for its neighboring vegetation, blossomed with grapes. The vintage of 1959 was on its way toward joining the immortal 1929 and 1911.

By the middle of August all reports pointed toward a great vintage year, so, without further ado, I decided to join in the *vendange*. Labor is in short supply at the vineyards, and volunteers are more than welcome. By the first week in September I was en route to Europe.

Stopping in England, I purchased a high, black 1949 London taxi-cab (an excellent year in taxis as well as in wine). After being ferried across the Channel, I headed for Beaujolais, the vineyard area in southern Burgundy which produces the fruity and amiable wines of the same name. The taxi performed effortlessly as it rumbled down the *routes nationales* of France. Better yet, its somber and unfamiliar shape struck terror into the hearts of the usually fearless French drivers, guaranteeing me a clear road ahead. Past Beauvais and Paris, Auxerre and Chalon, the gallant machine swept down the tree-lined roads. Sleepy white Charolais cattle shook their heads in bovine disbelief; dogs of every conceivable and inconceivable breed contributed choruses of canine surprise; in the villages small children clustered around, vainly attempting to pronounce the "For Hire" above the driver's seat.

Finally, on the eighth of September, the taxi and I arrived at Saint-Léger, a rustic hamlet thirty-five miles north of Lyon in the heart of Beaujolais. My destination was Corval, a charming sixteenth-century house, seat of the Pasquier-Desvignes family. There I was greeted by M. Claude Pasquier-Desvignes, patriarch of a spirited ménage consisting of seven children, countless grandchildren, a benign and wondrously calm wife, and numerous itinerant foreigners. M. Claude, a speculative philosopher whose every conversation is modeled on a small essay of Montaigne, combines this role with that of a shipper of wines. It was he who warned me to get to bed early. The *vendange* had already begun; on the morrow I would be called on to help.

Sure enough, my head had barely touched the pillow when I felt a hand on my shoulder and heard a voice telling me it was five o'clock, time to get up. Fighting off the urge to go back to sleep, I climbed out of bed, fumbled my way into my clothes, and descended to the kitchen. There I was greeted by Bruno, a son of Monsieur Claude. Bruno thrust a bowl of steaming coffee into my hands and added several ounces of a clear colorless liquid. The fluid turned out to be the highly alcoholic French elixir known as *marc*—unaged white brandy made from grape residue after it has been pressed for wine. Within seconds a warm glow suffused brain and body. Bruno, seeing signs of revival, began to outline the day's endeavor.

First, we were to proceed to the house of M. Champagnon, chief of the *troupe* of local *vendangeurs,* or grape pickers. There the members of the *troupe,* fifteen in all, would gather at six o'clock for an enormous breakfast, after which we were to march off to the vineyards.

By now the first traces of dawn began to illuminate the eastern horizon. As we approached the Champagnon farm we saw workers, who had arrived the evening before from Lyon to help in the picking, emerging from a neighboring barn, combing hay out of their hair. From the opposite direction another band approached, a small cluster of swarthy men whom Bruno identified as gypsies.

The gypsies and their colorful caravans had descended on Beaujolais en masse for the *vendange*. Every few kilometers there was a cluster of gaily painted trailers and wagons, dark women in full-skirted dresses, dozens of small children, and the lean dogs the gypsies train to be some of the finest hunting (or poaching) dogs in the world. The aid of the gypsies in grape harvesting was something of a mixed blessing. With so many additional workers the grapes could be picked on time, but the concomitant decimation of the neighboring rabbit and chicken population was *"épouvantable"* to the local farmers. Being French, they did not suffer in silence.

The different groups met in front of the kitchen door of the farmhouse. Hands were shaken, and we entered the kitchen, in the center of which was a long, low table. An unshaded lightbulb, suspended from the ceiling by a strand of wire, bathed the room in its hard electrical glare. The table in the center was laden with bowls and plates, tableware and glasses, an enormous coffeepot with a faint curl of aromatic steam sighing from its spout, and a huge tureen filled with thick hot soup. On one side of the room Madame Champagnon presided at the stove over mountainous quantities of vegetables and a large roast of beef. M. Champagnon entered, welcomed us briefly, and asked us to sit down; we were a little late getting started.

Bruno explained that a breakfast of this size was a necessity to the *vendangeur.* There would be six hours of very hard work before lunch. Anyone would be exhausted by ten o'clock without a hearty breakfast.

By six-thirty all of us were stuffed, and, patting our stomachs amiably, we were shepherded out the door by the *chef de troupe.* Fourteen of us were promptly equipped with pruning knives, named rather prosaically *couteaux de vendange,* and *seaux,* small metal buckets to put the grapes in after we had cut them. The fifteenth member of the group, a heavyset boy named Marius, carried a large wooden container called a *jarlot.*

It was Marius's job to walk up and down the rows of vines dumping grapes from our *seaux* into his *jarlot,* which he emptied from time to time into one of the still larger wooden containers called *bennes,* placed at intervals along the edge of the vineyard. When these *bennes* were filled, a horse and wagon took them to the shed where the press was. There the contents of the *bennes* were emptied into a *cuve,* a wooden barrel ten feet high. The grapes were to rest in the *cuve* a few days, so that the juice could absorb the tannin, color, and flavor of the skins before pressing.

As we set off down the road toward the vineyard, the green countryside of Beaujolais with the Montagne de Brouilly in the background was etched in the clear light of morning. The grapevines in the Champagnon vineyards, a ten-acre plot, were tied to individual stakes, not to long rows of wire. The grapes, like most wine grapes, were far smaller than table grapes. The variety used in Beaujolais is the Gamay, a grape that produces an enormous amount of juice in proportion to the number of vines planted, and consequently is looked upon with some disfavor by the growers of the more exclusive

Pinot Noir grapes of northern Burgundy. Nevertheless, the Gamay grown in the unique soil of the area produces a charming and quickly maturing red wine with a characteristically fruity taste.

The first hour and a half of picking was a delight. Cool zephyrs eddied between the rows of vines. From time to time wine or water was passed up and down the rows. But the atmosphere steadily warmed with the rising of the sun, and as I continually bent, stooped, squatted, and rose, long-unused muscles began to protest. After three and a half hours of these calisthenics, we stopped picking and sat down to enjoy refreshments of cheese, sausages, and wine. Never was a respite more welcomed. Then back to work. The grapes piled higher and higher in the *bennes* at the edge of the vineyard. Suddenly M. Champagnon called another halt. I wearily wiped the sweat from my brow, peered over the vines, and asked Bruno what had happened. He told me that we were through for the day. Usually it takes a full day to fill a *cuve*, but in 1959 the grapes were so plentiful and easy to pick that we had picked our daily quota by noon.

That evening, revived by a hot bath and an apéritif, I accepted with alacrity M. Claude Pasquier-Desvignes's invitation to work next day on the press. The old press was a curiously archaic piece of wrought iron and woodwork dating from the late nineteenth century and called, for some unknown reason, a *"presse américaine."* Beside it were four enormous *cuves*, one filled with the grapes we had picked that morning, others filled with grapes picked on the previous two days, and the fourth partially filled with freshly pressed and still fermenting wine. Though the wine this year in Beaujolais was taking only three days to absorb enough color and tannin from its skins, and thus could be run through the press with great speed, the grapes were coming in even more rapidly, and there was no place to store them. That was why our work had been cut short earlier in the day.

The next morning I was awakened at the comparatively civilized hour of seven, and Bruno, his brother Marc, and I had our bread and coffee without the need of any more invigorating stimulants. My muscles were stiff from the previous day's unusual exercise, but this made everything seem more worthwhile. A little suffering adds to one's sense of contribution.

At the press we three were joined by three others. The first step was to open the spigot at the base of the *cuve* filled with three-day-old grapes; from it drained a steady stream of partially fermented red wine which had been pressed by the weight of the grapes. Since not all the natural sugar in the wine had yet had enough time to convert into alcohol, the red juices now pouring forth were *vin doux*, sweet wine.

My task was now assigned. I was told to man an ancient centrifugal pump which transferred the *vin doux* from the wooden containers at the base of the *cuve* into an enormous wine barrel. Bruno and Marc stripped down to their shorts, washed off their legs and feet, and leapt into the draining *cuve* to trample the grapes, thus releasing still more of the residual juice. The crew stood guard nearby. Trampling grapes is a dangerous job. Fermenting grapes throws off a toxic gas which every year asphyxiates several workers throughout France.

In due course the stream pouring from the tap dwindled to a thin red trickle. Bruno and Marc climbed out to join us for sausages and wine and a few minutes of relaxation. A wooden chute was put into position, running from the *cuve* down into the *presse américaine*. Marc and Bruno climbed back into the *cuve* and shoveled the remains of the grapes onto the chute. These slithered down into the press and were spread around evenly by two men with shovels.

The *presse américaine* looks something like a guillotine surmounting a large, fat barrel. There are two major differences, however. At the place where the blade hangs in the guillotine, the press has a flat lid affixed to an enormous screw. When this screw is turned, the lid lowers down into the open barrel, pressing the grapes. The walls of a barrel are ordinarily solid, but this one was constructed like a picket fence with a half-inch space between slats. The juice seeped out from between the slats, trickling over the base into a small trench carved in the wood at the barrel's base, and was finally led into a large wooden tub at the press's feet. When the grapes were pressed as much as possible, the lid was raised and the *gâteau*, or cake, of grape residue was broken up with mattocks and pressed again. Finally the cake, pressed completely dry, was removed, watered down and allowed to ferment, and distilled into *marc*.

Our day at the press was a spectacular success: The quality of wine pressed from the grapes was excellent; the chemical analyses showed that the wine had perfect equilibrium: Its constituent elements of tannin, alcohol, acid, sugar, and water were perfect in quantity and balance.

As the late afternoon sun insinuated itself into the cool shadows of the shed, I rushed into the house, grabbed three cameras, picked up extra lenses, light meters, strobe lamp, and film, and hurried back to take photographs. I placed a ladder against the newly emptied *cuve*, climbed it, and began shooting.

I decided that one more high shot would make the day perfect photographically as well as viniculturally. I advanced the film, checked my light reading, set the camera, and climbed one rung higher up the ladder. I leaned back a little to bring the press and my co-workers into the camera's field. Suddenly I found myself flying. The last little movement up and back had converted the ladder into a top-heavy seesaw. With a thunderous crash the ladder and I landed on the bottom of the *cuve*, ten feet below. A hailstorm of lenses, light meters, and sundry camera equipment followed. What ignominy for a wine lover to end his career by falling into an empty cask! Even the Duke of Clarence had the good fortune to be drowned in a *full* butt of Malmsey!

In a few moments I got my wind back. By now assistance was pouring over the top of the *cuve*; I was quickly plied with sturdy draughts of Beaujolais and even more invigorating doses of *marc*. I crawled out of the *cuve* under my own steam and was immediately whisked away to be X-rayed. I discovered that three of my vertebrae had been chipped. This was hardly monumental damage, but it was enough to allow me to retire in good conscience into the role I liked best. No more five-o'clock risings, no more sweating in the heat of the noonday sun. I could now sit back in peace and sip the lovely wines of Beaujolais, observe the buzz of activity, and smugly reflect that I had given my all to the vintage of '59.

September 1960

GREAT WHITES

THE LAST *KELLERMEISTER*

Everett Wood

Heinrich Allinger, *Kellermeister* of Schloss Johannisberg, one of the fabled castles on the Rhine, is more in harmony with his work and his environment than anyone else I know. This does not mean that he feels an affinity for his century—or for its technical achievements, some of which have invaded even the world-famous wine cellar over which he presides. But within the circumscribed limits of his domain, where he tends single-handed hundreds of barrels and thousands of bottles, Herr Allinger is uniquely happy and at home.

Like Thoreau, who had traveled widely in Concord, Allinger has voyaged for fifty-seven years through the tiny village of Johannisberg. The other three years of his life were spent fighting for his country in France, which, though only a few hours by train from the Rhineland, must have seemed like the other side of the moon to him. Since his return in 1919, he has spent the greater part of every day underground, in the enormous cellar of the Schloss, as the men of his family have done for more than a hundred years.

Such extraordinary devotion to a cellar and the juice of the grape has made Heinrich Allinger something of an oddity, even along the Rhine. This same devotion caused the only known instance of friction between Prince Metternich, the owner of Schloss Johannisberg, and his faithful wine keeper. In the spring of 1950, when Allinger had put in thirty-one years of service without a day away from the cellar, Prince Metternich decided to take action. Having failed repeatedly to persuade his *Kellermeister* to take a vacation, he decided to surprise Allinger into doing so by a subterfuge. Secretly, he booked the unsuspecting man on a three-week bus tour through the wine regions of France and Spain. All expenses of the trip were paid and application was made for a passport and the necessary visas. The trap was ready when word reached Allinger from the government that his application for a passport had been approved and the document was awaiting his disposition. Thunderstruck, the near victim of a three-week vacation made frenzied inquiries and discovered the plot just in time.

When the whole ruse and its intent were clear, Allinger made a characteristic decision. As much as it grieved him to disappoint the Prince he had served so well, he respectfully refused to leave Schloss Johannisberg for as much as one day. "Out of the question," was the way he described it to me later. "Who would have cared for the cellar while I was gone?" His round plump face wrinkled with conviction. "And besides, Herr Wood, you know I'd never ride anywhere in a bus."

It was on this point that Prince Metternich's well-meant plan had ended in failure. Because Allinger, although he lives in the age of the motor vehicle triumphant, is no patron of rapid transportation. He has yet to step inside an automobile of any kind, much less ride in one. Where he wants to go, speed is of no importance.

Thinking back on it now, I can see how fortunate it was that my first visit to the historic Schloss Johannisberg was made on foot and, moreover, that on that particular day it was raining. I had taken the train from Frankfurt to Geisenheim and had walked the last two miles through the vineyards—getting soaked and picking up a considerable deposit of January mud on the way. As I approached the castle, I lost confidence momentarily. Would an itinerant enthusiast be allowed to buy a few bottles of Schloss Johannisberger, I wondered? Or wasn't it more likely that these famous wines were sold only in wholesale quantities to the buyers who came here from around the world?

I needn't have worried. A secretary in the office of the administrator of the Schloss assured me that they did occasionally sell wines in small quantities, and that if I could find a certain Herr Allinger, who was undoubtedly around the cellar somewhere, he would find the wines I wanted and perhaps tell me a little about them as he did so. How monumental an understatement that was I couldn't guess at the time.

Fortunately, the man who might tell me a little about the wines was just about to enter the cellar when we met. My first impression was of a heavy-set, monkish man whose ruddy face belied his years and the time he had spent underground. The traditional leather apron of his trade hung loosely about his waist, and in his left hand he carried a candle. I introduced myself and asked if he was Herr Allinger. He nodded.

"And you," he ventured, eyeing my drenched clothing, "are a wine lover, or perhaps even a *Kenner* (connoisseur) who has walked here through the vineyards in the rain. In the summer, when the weather is fine, hundreds of people visit the Schloss—mostly by car these days. But in the winter our visitors are few."

I assured him that it was my love for wine that had brought me here.

"It's the love that counts," he said, in his Rhenish dialect, and beckoned me below, where the barrels and bottles were stored.

Twenty-two steps lead down to the cellar of Schloss Johannisberg, stone steps worn down through the centuries. Before descending them, my guide paused to light his candle. Though the Schloss has been lighted by electricity since 1905, Prince Metternich's *Kellermeister* usually visits his mossy domain by candlelight. At the bottom of the stairs we were in a world of cool temperature and slow time. In the huge vaulted chamber that runs under the west wing of the castle, I could see what appeared to be two endless rows of barrels.

I began to sense the extraordinary intimacy that existed not only between Allinger and this, his dedicated place of work, but between him and each separate barrel. Every wine maturing in the three-hundred-odd barrels that lined the cellar had its own story of success, hope, or disappointment, which was carefully recorded by Allinger and known to him as the condition of a patient is known to a physician. This intimacy was so real that on two occasions that day he interrupted his torrent of information to address a barrel directly.

"Don't worry." He was speaking to a '48 Spätlese. "Fifteen months in the barrel and already you're smooth and harmonious. A year more in the bottle and you'll have bouquet, too. Keep it up. You're going to make it."

To another barrel he was less complimentary. "*Ach*, you! Is that all you could do? We had such hopes in you, too!"

More than an hour later we had reached the far side of the second great chamber, and I noticed six smaller barrels that held three hundred liters apiece. In these, Allinger explained to me, were mellowing some of the noble Auslesen, wines made from specially selected late-picked grapes of the previous year. *Spitzenweine* of the '49 vintage, he called them; later they would take their places among the century's great Rhine wines. Reminded of the original purpose of my visit, I asked if I might have a couple of bottles of *Spitzenwein*.

"Gladly, if you promise to show them every respect—every honor," he answered. "Such wines are wonders that can't be brought about each year."

Just how great were the wines he selected for me only one versed in the noblest products of the Rheingau or Pfalz, Germany's outstanding wine-producing areas, could ever know. Entering another huge chamber, where thousands of bottles were arrayed in separate bins, he withdrew one and placed it gently in a metal carrying tray.

"A 1945 Auslese from barrel number forty-five," he said. "A dark year in most respects—but the sun shone late into October, and what few grapes we did harvest were mostly *Edelfäule*." He referred to the so-called noble mold.

He picked another bottle, deep gold in color, from the next bin, and laid it in the tray as carefully as if it were fragile Dresden.

"A 1945 Auslese from barrel number fifty-four—our finest barrel of the year." Even after wines have been bottled, Allinger, like most cellar masters, still refers to them by the number of the barrel in which they matured. "An Auslese," he added, "which in color and body and bouquet truly resembles a Beerenauslese."

He stopped speaking for a moment and seemed to make a decision. Whether it was the thanks I managed to express for the wines he had just chosen, or whether he was moved by the mud on my trousers that told him I had come to Schloss Johannisberg more as a pilgrim of the grape than as a buyer, I do not know. Whatever the reason, he disappeared abruptly behind the farthest row of bins and returned with a dust-covered bottle that he held up for me to see. It was a Beerenauslese that he had nursed personally from the wine press to the glass. Lovingly, he recalled the three barrels in which it was made, calling them his "three sisters of 1943." He told me the total hours of sunshine the vines had been blessed with that year; on what day in early November the overripe grapes had been selected from all the bunches to make this wine (cherished memories to him); how long the juice from these grapes had fermented in the barrel; how, on a February night in 1945, the wine had been hurriedly bottled by candlelight, to the sound of approaching gunfire from across the Rhine, and hidden in a secret cave of the cellar; and, finally, how the wine had been retrieved four years later and discovered to be one of those noble rarities—a truly great *Spitzenwein,* which cannot be described but which, once tasted, is remembered forever. Herr Allinger said of this one simply, "Exquisite."

Ah, yes, Heinrich Allinger, old friend and companion of so many hours talked away underground! That wine was indeed exquisite and I shall never forget it—any more than I can forget that when I left that day it was you who thanked me for the visit and asked me to come back again.

In time I became a frequent visitor to Schloss Johannisberg, though I avoided weekends and the summer months; there were too many information-seekers about then even for Herr Allinger. In one respect I did fail consistently in my wish not to impose on him; no visit was ever as short as I'd promised myself it would be. Allinger's reminiscences carried both me and my intention away every time.

Each trip through his cellar was at once a lecture on viniculture and an insight into happenings long ago. It seemed unbelievable to me that anyone could know so intimately wines and people who had flourished centuries before he was born. But Allinger does. All of Schloss Johannisberg's yesterdays are part of his today. He seems, in some inexplicable way, to have lived it all. And from his devotion he has developed his own frame of reference.

Once, when I asked him about the winter activities of a *Kellermeister,* I mentioned casually that winter was my favorite season. I was born in February, I said, and added almost automatically the year—1916. Allinger's reaction to this unhistoric fact was as prompt as it was startling.

"No! Not 1916!" he exclaimed. "How sad. Now, that was a *Mistjahr* if ever there was one."

Mist in German connotes no good, so I thought he must be referring to the fighting that year on the front where he was in action. I was wrong.

"That 1916," he continued, "was one of those years that a *Kellermeister* must suffer through. From early June on, the vineyards fell victim to every insect imaginable. By midsummer there was hardly a healthy grape on the vines, and no sunshine! Instead of the usual three hundred barrels, we managed to fill exactly three and a half. A mere two thousand one hundred and seventy-five liters for the whole year. Think of it!" And then, perhaps to comfort me for having appeared in the world at such a woeful hour, he added, "I was born in a *Mistjahr* myself—1896."

That was really a dark year in the history of Schloss Johannisberg. It rained so steadily during the whole summer that the sour results of the vintage were dubbed privately "Moses Wine"—a name befitting anything that had survived so much water. What little was made of the stuff was sold later by local tavernkeepers for fifteen pfennig a liter—with a piece of cheese to take the taste away thrown in.

"No," concluded Allinger philosophically, "not all of us can share the fame of a great vintage. But it's periods like ours that provide contrast for the truly noble ones." His memory moved back over the years and he mentioned '49, '37, '21, '11, '93, '68, and '57.

I discovered in time that Allinger—although unmistakably the *Kellermeister,* historian, and incomparable champion of Schloss Johannisberg—was by no means a narrow-visioned *Lokalpatriot* incapable of appreciating things outside his own realm. The Riesling grape, wherever it grew, was his province. And with an enthusiasm for his competitors and an impartiality found too seldom among his compatriots, he directed me to the greatest vineyards of the Rheingau and Pfalz. Sometimes, after these trips to other cellars, I would bring a bottle back to Schloss Johannisberg. This procedure was reminiscent of bearing coals to Newcastle, but necessary if I wanted to get my mentor's evaluation of my purchase. As may be imagined, such evaluations were always full of overtones.

Allinger's approach to any wine I brought him was unvaried. First he would open the bottle and eye the brand marks on the cork and then, with piercing intensity, the wine itself. Next he would pour his glass a quarter full and subject its contents to a searching nose test, the step in his examination that revealed the most. Finally, and almost as an afterthought, he would sip a few drops. With that done, he was ready to analyze the wine's whole history of triumph or failure, while I listened—and finished the rest of the bottle myself.

I was unable to get down to the Rhineland during most of 1955 and consequently was out of touch with my friend. When, after eight months, we did meet again, he welcomed me with his usual "*Grüss Gott,* Herr Wood," and inquired, without pausing, what I'd been doing during the eight months, five days, and nine hours since I'd been away from the Schloss. It didn't surprise me that he knew the exact date and hour of our last meeting. By now I knew he was incapable of forgetting anything. But what did astonish me, a moment later, was the telephone I saw on Allinger's desk. For one who had never stepped into an automobile or seen a motion picture or given his blessing to electric lights, such a modern device seemed a painful compromise with his convictions. I asked him for an explanation.

"Herr Labonte, the administrator, had it installed," he said. "But don't worry, I haven't answered the thing yet. And since I wouldn't dream of calling anyone myself—I don't think it will be of much use around here." He shook his head. "Wine is a matter of time, of years," he insisted. "If anyone is really interested, he'll come here, as you have, and see what we have in the cellar."

Old friend, I thought, forgive me for my moment of disbelief. I should have known that you, of all people, wouldn't submit to the tyranny of such a gadget. Not you, for whom vintages are the measure of time!

Yet I couldn't help wondering what attitude Herr Labonte or Prince Metternich might have on the matter. Would they be pleased or displeased that their *Kellermeister* had so little use for the telephone installed in his office? I asked Allinger.

"You know, I've thought about that myself," he conceded, "but I think it will be all right. After all, Herr Wood, they've known for some time that I'm a *Sonderling*—and I'm still here."

A *Sonderling*, he had said—an odd stick, a character. Certainly I knew by now how well that description fit him, at least in the subtler sense. But there was something in the way he had used the word, suggesting the distance between his world and that of his contemporaries, that made me a little sad and reflective. Perhaps it was the very frankness of his remark and the silence that followed it that encouraged me to speak of a matter I had never dared to mention before. "Herr Allinger," I asked, "how does it happen that you never married? Don't you think that's too bad? Even worse, perhaps, than being born in a *Mistjahr*? If you don't make a move pretty soon, a tradition is going to die at Schloss Johannisberg. For four generations your family—"

"Herr Wood," he interrupted, laughing, "there just hasn't been the time, that's all, time enough to take care of both a wife and a cellar."

His answer was far from convincing and I told him so. After all, his father and grandfather and great-grandfather had married and been cellar masters of Schloss Johannisberg. Somehow they'd managed both responsibilities. How could he, a lover of tradition, treat his own family's tradition so lightly?

"*Ja, ja,* I know. But it wouldn't make much difference now, anyway," he sighed. "In a generation or less there won't be any *Kellermeister* as we know them today. It's not just the family—it's the profession itself that's dying."

I asked him to explain.

"Wine is becoming more of a science every day," he said. "A profession like mine won't last much longer. In the future a cellar will be run by two people: a chemist and an engineer."

It saddened me to hear him say it, for I knew what he meant. Already I had seen the first six-thousand-liter tanks installed at Schloss Johannisberg. In these huge pressurized vats, the intricate process of wine fermentation can be more accurately controlled than in the smaller temperamental space of a wooden barrel. Skillfully operated, these tanks can achieve a greater similarity of product each year. The resulting standardization of quality, though regrettable in certain ways, is particularly important to these vineyard owners along the Rhine whose wines vary so enormously, not only from year to year, but from barrel to barrel in any given year.

I shook my head. I could not believe that the Rhine wines of the future would be solely the product of pressurized tanks presided over by chemists and engineers—at least not the great wines, those that Allinger called "exquisite." Such *Spitzenweine* must always be the glorious result of ingredients beyond control: the amount of sunshine on the vines each year, the chance of *Edelfäule* in the vineyards before harvest, the affinity of the *Kellermeister* himself for the juice of the grape, breathing, maturing, coming to life in a wooden barrel. "I can't imagine a wine cellar without a *Kellermeister*," I protested. "Or, at any rate, I don't want to."

We stood together on the terrace of Schloss Johannisberg. From our vantage point above the Rhine, we watched the night come on and the lights appear in the villages whose names are known to all who know fine wine. And we could see other lights: the stream of trucks and automobiles on the highway below, aircraft cruising overhead (the Schloss lies directly on the air route from Frankfurt to all points west), the new factory in Geisenheim, which was doing its best to illuminate the whole December sky. I mentioned these intrusions of the century to Allinger, thinking they must surely distress him. But they didn't. Since they weren't of his world, he seemed hardly to notice them. What he saw were the timeless things, the great river flowing west through the vineyards, the village of his birth, and above them, Schloss Johannisberg. This was his world, and in it he was at one with the scene, and happy.

As I drove away I saw candlelight shining through his window. I knew that before the light went out he would note in his diary all his observations and impressions of the day. This diary fills over two dozen volumes by now and makes memorable reading for any wine student who can decipher the script. It would be a shame if his notes on wine lore and local history were ever destroyed. But I doubt that the loss would trouble their author much. Everything that has happened at Schloss Johannisberg he knows, and will remember always.

December 1957

Thirteen Rows of Baiken

Everett Wood

In my cellar, awaiting the right moment to be opened, is a bottle of noble wine. I look at it now and then, salute it in spirit, and read the label, the letters of which are beginning to fade:

1953er

RAUENTHALER BAIKEN

Riesling   Beerenauslese

Original-Abfüllung   Chr. Sturm & Sohn

Anyone with a knowledge of German wine would know why I cherish that bottle. He would know from the label, at a glance. The label is a wine's pedigree; it reveals vintage, village, vineyard, grape, condition of grape when picked, where bottled, and by whom. But sometimes a label can symbolize more: It can be a page in an album recalling vine-covered hills and wines tasted in dark cellars by the Rhine. . . .

Looking back, it seems strange how long it took me to find my way to Rauenthal. During the first years I lived abroad, I haunted all the little villages whose wines are the fame of the Rheingau—all of them, that is, except Rauenthal. And I might not have gone there at all had I not read in the *Rheinischer Merkur* one day (on the financial page, of all places!) that Baiken, a tiny vineyard of six acres in the village of Rauenthal, had been assessed as the most valuable property per acre under vine cultivation in Germany. That report changed the direction of my travels. As soon as I could, I left Frankfurt by train to learn more about those six acres.

Rauenthal is only ten minutes by bus from the nearest station. But I arrived at that station on a morning in late May and there were paths through the vineyards. I decided to walk there instead. In less than a mile, I approached the hill, the Rauenthalerberg, which hides all of Rauenthal save its steeple, and has made the village a name in the world of wine. Two hundred eighty acres of impeccably groomed vineyard rose before me, but looking up its terraced slope, it seemed more like a green sea rising in waves above the Rhine. Here, if anywhere, the vines planted so many centuries ago have conquered the landscape. The Rauenthalerberg is a monument to the triumph of the Riesling grape.

On the path that wanders to the crest of the hill, I saw vineyard workers in blue attire trimming the new shoots on the vines. I asked one if he could locate Baiken for me, and perhaps tell me something about that remarkable vineyard. His answer was small help. "It's over there," he informed me, pointing to the west shoulder of the slope, and then he lapsed into silence. Thinking that he had no more information to offer, I was about to move on when he added: "If you're interested in Baiken, why don't you look up Herr Sturm? He owns part of the vineyard." I thanked him for the suggestion and made a mental note of the name.

No one who knows Rauenthal would call it a showplace on the Rhine. Unlike its neighboring communities, it has no castle or romantic ruins. It is a *Weindorf* with three streets and a cluster of red-roofed houses—a village dedicated to wine. But when I think of Rauenthal it means more to me than its famous product; it recalls horses drawing carts over cobblestones worn smooth, and Father Scheuermann, the abundantly bewhiskered curate, blessing the vines in his frock; it means the endless work on the slope by the river, the dread of frost, the fear of hail, the tension when the vineyards are closed, even to their owners; it means the harvest bells ringing in October when the grapes are ready to pick; it means the sound (eerie beyond belief when you first hear it) of barrels mumbling aloud as the juice ferments into wine, the coolness of dark cellars, women in long shawls walking children down the street, and—above all—the kindness of Herr Sturm and his son Otto, who gave me that bottle I cherish.

But, of course, that's what Rauenthal means to me now when I look at the label on my wine bottle. On that morning in May I was still a stranger there and did what most strangers do after a climb in the vineyards; I went to the nearest *Weinstube,* ordered a glass of wine, and asked the whereabouts of Herr Sturm. "Herr Sturm, *der Ortslandwirt?*" the waitress asked. (I wasn't too sure of the word she had used but guessed that it meant the local overseer for agriculture.)

"I believe so," I said. "I'm told he owns part of Baiken."

"Then you haven't far to go. He lives in the house across the street, the house with the big wall around it."

No name was posted on the gate that I knocked on, and, as there was no answer either, I turned the knob and stepped inside. In the courtyard I saw a man in vineyard worker's clothing leading a horse. As I came closer I could see he was a somewhat elderly gentleman of slender build, almost bald, with a fine white mustache. His face, round and kind, had the color that comes from working long in the sun. When I was close enough to him, I excused myself for the intrusion and asked if he was Herr Sturm. "Christian Sturm," he answered, with a slight bow. "And how may I be of service?"

I told him I was a pilot who spent his free time in the vineyard country and of my interest in learning something of Baiken. "Oh, Baiken," he said, pleased at my mention of the name, and then, referring to my profession, made a little joke that put me at ease immediately. "In that case, sir, you've landed at the right place and on schedule. My son is sampling our '53s in the cellar. If you would care to join him . . ."

I descended the stairs in the left wing of the barn into the moist coolness and scent of grapes that always go with a wine cellar. The cellar was small by Rheingau standards, but wonderfully neat. The first chamber held rows of bottles stacked in bins. The second contained about twenty barrels; here Herr Sturm's son was siphoning wine from one of them with a rubber tube. Even in the dim light I could see he wore clothes like his father's, and had his father's friendly face, but was of a more robust build. Again I was conscious of imposing, but Otto Sturm welcomed me with heart-warming courtesy.

He was sampling various wines of the '53 vintage, he explained, to determine their development and when they would be ready to bottle. Successively he sampled wines from Langenstück, Siebenmorgen, Wülfen, and Kesselring—all vineyards owned in part by his father. Although barely seven months in the barrel, they were already perfectly clear and smooth, and showed traces of the harmony and delicious fruity taste I learned later to associate with wines from the Rauenthalerberg. Promising as these young wines were, I was not prepared for the last wine we sampled on that occasion. It came from a smaller barrel, of the three-hundred-liter size, identified merely with the number 1 in chalk.

"We have great hopes for this barrel," Otto Sturm told me. "In good years we leave our grapes longest in Kesselring and Baiken. This is a Baiken from grapes harvested last November."

It wasn't necessary to taste the wine he offered me in a small *Probeglas* to recognize its greatness. Dark golden in color, the wine clung to the side of the glass as I turned it in my hand, and it had that infinitely delicate, yet almost overwhelming bouquet that comes only from the Riesling grape that has turned *edelfäule*, or "nobly overripe," when allowed to hang late on the vine in years of extraordinary weather.

"Magnificent," I agreed. "But how can a wine become like that after only seven months in the barrel?"

Otto's father, who had entered the cellar as I spoke, answered my question. "It's a Baiken Beerenauslese," he said simply, but in his voice I sensed the pride I would recognize so often when Herr Sturm mentioned the word Baiken.

How amply that pride was justified I learned shortly afterward from the awards that decorate Herr Sturm's living-room walls and give testimony to why Baiken, as well as Christian Sturm, are held in such esteem. Among them I saw the German Republic's Medal of Merit awarded "in recognition of services rendered in the cause of viniculture" (the citation was dated April 10, 1954, and signed by President Theodor Heuss); the State of Hessen's Victor Prize for the greatest wine of the '46 vintage, a Baiken Auslese; and a facsimile of the Gold Medal Certificate from the World's Fair in Paris, awarded to a Baiken Beerenauslese '93 produced by Peter Josef Sturm, Herr Sturm's grandfather.

Impressed as I was by these and the other awards I saw, what struck me most was my host's attitude toward them. To say he did not feel personally honored by such achievements would be false. He did. But as he spoke of them, they seemed to honor even more the six acres known as Baiken.

On the pretext of watching that marvelous wine I had tasted grow "nobler in the wood" (it was finally bottled in March 1955, after seventeen months in the barrel), I returned often to the cellar where I had met Otto, walked through all the vineyards that constitute the Rauenthalerberg, and had the pleasure of numerous talks with Herr Sturm. Although Baiken is his heart's joy, and provided the subject of much of our conversation, his whole life has been devoted to the welfare of his village. Not only as twice-elected *Ortslandwirt*, but as Chairman of the Harvest Committee (like his father before him), his work is reflected in the integrity and quality of every wine produced and bottled in Rauenthal. It is the Harvest Committee that determines when to close the vineyards in September; on what days during the harvest the grapes may or may not be picked; and last, but of enormous importance, it sets the date for the *Spätlese*, or "late harvest," a crucial factor in the production of German Rieslings and one that explains a large part of their greatness. German vineyards, wine cellars, and labels are controlled vigorously by law. But the members of the local Harvest Committees act as the first defenders of their village's proud reputation.

On only one occasion was Herr Sturm unable to answer one of the countless questions I posed to him about Rauenthal. Strangely enough, it had to do with Baiken. I asked him how the vineyard got its name.

"The name is very old," he said. "It appears in our earlier records. But where it came from or what it means, I don't know. When it *became* a name, however, I do know." And then, as though it had all happened only yesterday, Herr Sturm (whose family also goes back to the earliest records of his village) told me of the tribulations and first triumph of Rauenthal. Every name he gave in full, every date without pause, every detail with the pain or joy it bore. Yet he spoke of events witnessed by his grandfather a century ago.

"Such a series of bad wine years," he began, "no one could remember. The year 1850 was a *Nassjahr* with no sun on the vines. What few grapes survived the rain were watery and bitter, and made miserable wine. And then, who could believe it, the next six years were the same. Mercifully, 1857 was somewhat better. Not a good year, but one to live on and give hope again. Finally, and as reward perhaps for our seven lean years, came the date unique in our history, 1858—the greatest vintage we had ever known and the first wine to make Rauenthal a name beyond the Rhine."

Warming to his subject, Herr Sturm described the honor bestowed on his village when sixteen barrels of their incomparable '58 vintage were purchased for the Congress of German Princes, which opened in Frankfurt on August 16, 1863. The wines produced by Georg Wilhelm Siegfried were Riesling Auslesen from Baiken and Wieshell. It took eight horse-drawn wagons to haul the barrels from the cellars of Herr Siegfried to those of the Central Hotel in Frankfurt. Their departure was an event in the annals of Rauenthal.

"Of our eight hundred inhabitants," Herr Sturm continued, "all who could walk were on hand to cheer the procession off. As the gaily decorated wagons moved down the hill toward Neudorf, the church bells rang. From the top of the Rauenthalerberg our whole artillery, three cannons, fired volleys across the Rhine. Everyone waved. Everyone sang. Believe me, our hopes rode the long way to Frankfurt that day with those barrels of Baiken Wieshell. In time, the wine was delivered to Herr Wilhelm Sarg, director of the Central Hotel, where it was served in the ballroom and caused a sensation among the princes. One royal guest—William III of Holland—was so . . ." Herr Sturm closed his eyes to find the word, "so *begeistert* that he paid the unheard-of sum of eighteen thousand gulden for a single barrel to bring back to his court. That barrel was the first Rauenthaler to bear our name to the world outside."

If Herr Sturm seemed more to relive than retell this moment of local history, it was because he had himself so often known the same cycle of misfortune, hope, and occasional reward. Since 1884, when he was born in Rauenthal, numerous *Nassjahre* have drowned the grapes on the vines; a dozen (but no more) superb vintages have increased his village's fame and brought prices that were indeed unheard-of (at auction, the top Rauenthaler wines bring bids that amaze the uninitiated); while the other years have provided, at best, "something to live on and give hope again." As might be expected, Herr Sturm has accepted the years of disappointment with composure and a vineyard man's philosophy. *"Der liebe Herrgott wird uns nicht im Stich lassen,"* I have heard him say—"The good Lord will not fail us."

Quite by accident one day I discovered the one thing he cannot accept philosophically, and never will: the steady acquisition of local vineyards by the *Staatsweingut,* the State Domain, which now controls almost 40 percent of the Rauenthalerberg. I hadn't meant to touch so sensitive a point. I had merely asked him who were the present owners of Baiken.

"Count Eltz from Eltville is one of them," he said, "and from here Johan Wagner, Heinrich Schuth, and myself. We are the last private owners of Baiken. The rest, a good half of the vineyard, belongs to the State. They bought it from a broken man—my neighbor, Heinrich Kimmel, in 1924."

In the conversation that followed I sensed that Herr Sturm's opposition to the *Staatsweingut* was deep-rooted, irrevocable, and based on principles that have guided his life. As a devout Catholic, he does not approve of the secularization of church properties in the nineteenth century which gave the State Domain its first vineyards. ("Secularization means stealing," is the way he put it to me.) As a native Rauenthaler, he believes his village's treasure, the Rauenthalerberg, should remain in native hands. And as a lifelong producer of wine, he feels that the relationship between a private owner and a vineyard is one of the secrets of great wine.

"A vineyard is more than a possession," he told me. "It is an obligation—an obligation to cultivate, to sacrifice, and to care. If one cares deeply enough, it's a reason for being alive."

After such an expression of conviction, I wondered how he would react to any attempt by the State to buy him out, as they had Herr Kimmel.

"Did the *Staatsweingut* ever approach you about Baiken, Herr Sturm?"

He turned the stem of the glass in his hand several times before answering. "No, they haven't," he said. And then in words that sounded strange from so gentle a person, he concluded with finality: "On that subject they know that I'm a man of iron."

In December of 1956 I was notified of my transfer to New York, and I paid a last call on the Sturms to thank them for the many hours I had spent in their company. They were out when I arrived, but I found Otto soon afterward, inspecting posts in Kesselring. Together we walked to the west shoulder of the hill, to the six acres that had brought me to Rauenthal. There, between the holdings of Count Eltz and the *Staatsweingut*, were the rows of Baiken that belong to Herr Sturm. For the first time I counted them. There were thirteen. From this tiny patch of vineyard (barely the size of five tennis courts) had come the wines that had won the Victor's Prize for the greatest Auslese produced in Hessen in 1946, had brought back the Gold Medal from the World's Fair, in Paris, and had helped make the bells ring on that day so long ago when eight wagons left Rauenthal for their rendezvous with the German princes in Frankfurt.

As we stood on the steep slope, Otto picked up some soil in his hand. *Schieferboden,* he called it, an almost claylike texture that holds the moisture for the vines in dry years. As I looked at the soil, and then at Otto, I realized that he resembled his father not only in facial features. Someday those rows will belong to him. Like his father he will tend them with his hands and his heart. And, should anyone try to buy his thirteen rows of Baiken, he, too, will be a man of iron.

Later that afternoon the Sturms gave me the bottle that I'm keeping for a special occasion. But what occasion now, I wonder, can equal the memories that the label evokes.

February 1959

VIENNESE MEMOIR

Lillian Langseth-Christensen

The ever-illogical and beloved Viennese may house only the most precious vintages in their own cellars and their palates may be educated to appreciate only the noblest wines, but when the first green bush appears from under the eaves of a vintner's house in the little suburb of Grinzing, they are off—as one man—to the *Heurige* to drink Grinzinger 1957.

In German the word *heurig* means "this year's" or just "this." It is most often used in describing *heurige Kartoffeln,* new potatoes, words without romance or music. But Vienna speaks an enchanted language of her own. There, *Heurige* means the fragrant, fresh, new wine of Grinzing and all that surrounds the lighthearted, carefree drinking of it. It means the place, the wine, and the age-old customs. The Viennese go to the *Heurige* and they drink *Heurige* and they call it all by the single word. It means *Schrammelmusik* and zither playing; it means the indescribable atmosphere, the *Stimmung,* the charm, the green wine hills, and the first taste of the cold, pale golden wine. It means the effect of the wine, different from that of any other, and the feeling of gaiety and happiness, of romance and enchantment. It means the traditional vendors who carry their heavy wooden trays of sweets and confections through the village from *Heurige* to *Heurige.* It means good food—*Wiener Backhendel, Grinzinger Salat,* and *kalter Aufschnitt*—it means Vienna and it means spring.

The green bush that signals that a vintner is pouring new wine is a small bunch of evergreen boughs tied to the end of a staff and hung out from his low white house. The moment it is in view, word travels fast and far that Poldi's or Franzl's wine is ready, and every heart in Vienna begins to sing. From Jani the shoemaker's assistant right up to Herr Graf and Frau Gräfin there is no one in Vienna who is going to miss the *Heurige.* It is said that a passing stranger once observed, "There must be a hole in heaven—over Grinzing."

Heurige cannot be bottled or transported; it must come straight from the casks in the vintner's cellars to the tables set out in his garden. Since the *Heurige* cannot go to the Viennese, the Viennese, with Mohammed's wisdom, go to the *Heurige.* They go right out to the grape arbor at the back of the vintner's little house and, while they happily drink Grinzinger '57, Grinzinger '58 grows green on the wine hills behind them.

Ever since the first vintners poured out their new wine to avoid taxes and discovered that the young golden wine was, in fact, a gold mine, there have been established procedures which are still followed. Originally, all the vintners drew lots, and each hung out his green bush only after the casks of the *Heurige* next in line before him had been drained dry. But as the taste for the new wine grew, it was possible for several vintners to hang out their bushes at the same time. Thus Jani and his Resl could find a primitive *Heurige* to suit their simple tastes, while Herr Graf and Frau Gräfin went to the *Heurige* that their fathers and grandfathers had patronized before them. Fortunately the vintner always provided a son and heir to the vineyard, while the Graf and Gräfin produced an heir to the title, so the noble family could go on for generations with a *Heurige* that they considered practically their own.

Austria is the only country in the world that grows most of its best wines within the city limits of its capital. Jani and Resl, who couldn't possibly afford more than a few tumblers of wine, packed their sausage, bread, and cheese in a rucksack and walked out to Grinzing. They chose a *Heurige* that provided only the wine and the rough wooden tables and benches in the garden; itinerant musicians might stop to play *heurigen Lieder* and pass the hat for coppers before they moved on. Jani and Resl sat arm in arm in a garden that overlooked Vienna. They watched the sun setting and they ate their heavy slabs of black bread and sausage. They drank the delicious new wine from thick tumblers as casually as they would have drunk water, and they saved their last coppers for the sugar-men whose tempting trays were piled high with traditional confections. There were always little sticks strung with sugared dates and figs, which were sold by the stickful. For those who could afford such sweets, there were wedges of *Pischinger-torte* or little chocolate confections wrapped in foil. The wine was cheap and the Viennese were born musicians. Many brought their own guitars, and all linked arms and sang as the magic of the evening drew them together.

Herr and Frau Müller went out to Grinzing on the tramway, from which they alighted at the last stop on the Grinzinger Platz. They walked up one of the steep cobbled streets that wind through the wine hills of Vienna's suburbs and chose a slightly more pretentious *Heurige,* one with a large garden, with lanterns and checkered tablecloths, a *Heurige* with four musicians. They selected a *Heurige* that served just enough food to counteract the effect of the wine and to enable the guests to stay from late afternoon through the long evening without bringing their own supper. The Müllers could request their favorite songs from the musicians, who went from table to table, and they could order any of the numerous *kalte Aufschnitte,* large tempting platters of cold meats. These became increasingly elaborate when Herr Müller ordered a *feiner* (or even a *sehr feiner*) *kalter Aufschnitt. Feiner* meant the addition of butter rosettes and salads, *sehr feiner* always meant a little goose liver pâté. When the vintner's wife was enterprising, the Müllers could order *Cobenzl* eggs, named for the hill behind Grinzing, and *Sulze.* They invariably missed the last streetcar back to the inner city at midnight so that they could walk home with the musicians.

Herr Graf, on the other hand, approached the whole thing quite differently. He was, after all, a connoisseur of wines and pleasure. Having kept a careful eye out for the days of sunshine and the days of cloud or rain during the previous spring and summer, he knew just about what to expect of his *Heurige*. He had also gone out during the winter to spend a few quiet, pleasant evenings with Pepi and Mina Huber, his family vintners, to determine how the young wine was coming along. He had sat in the small low-ceilinged room with its warm tile stove and lovely old guitar. He had enjoyed a pipe and tasted the new, as well as some very good old wine.

When the wine was ready and the day was set, Herr Graf and Frau Gräfin invited their guests. Pepi Huber was not only a good vintner, he had the added advantage of a strong baritone voice and a repertoire that included all the beloved old songs, and he could accompany himself on the guitar. Herr Graf engaged a zither player to entertain while Pepi was drawing the wine, for he considered the ensemble required for *Schrammelmusik* too pretentious. Pepi Huber's Mina knew what was wanted from her. She fattened her pullets and slowly dried golden rolls for perfect bread crumbs. She churned butter, and when the day finally came, she prepared crisp, juicy *Wiener Backhendel* and served it with an enormous *Gurkensalat* and *heurige Kartoffeln*. Her dessert was invariably the same. Ever since Oskar Pischinger, Vienna's famous nineteenth-century confectioner, had contrived his *Pischingertorte*, it had been the accepted *heurigen* sweet. Mina made the richly filled *Torte* herself.

The Graf and his guests enjoyed their *Heurige* as sincerely and simply as Jani and Resl enjoyed theirs. They loved the primitive garden with its benches and long table, the scent of lilac and linden in bloom mingled with the delicious fragrance of *Backhendel*, the soft twang of the zither and Pepi Huber's *Lieder*, and they looked forward to the *Heurige* all year. For all of them it was a part of Vienna that could not be imitated anywhere—to drink new wine in the landscape that has produced it, in Grinzing, an ageless, unchanged Grinzing.

April 1958

THE WINES OF
HUNGARY AND AUSTRIA

Hugh Johnson

Without ever really thinking about it I find that I have subconsciously formed associations between various flavors in my mind. There is a country kind of taste, associated with rather coarse, garlic-scented terrines, that makes me relax at once, knowing I will be more than satisfied. And then there is the very opposite—the taste of oysters. Nothing relaxing about them; they have a challenging sort of appeal. Oysters make me stop and think about their strange complex of flavors—each one is another little dish by itself—keeping me on my toes until they are all gone.

There are also faint and luxurious tastes such as grilled sole or capon. Then there are seasonal tastes, such as tangerines and almonds, whose Christmas overtones are so strong as to constitute their whole character.

I would not say that the dishes that form such groups taste alike. Only that in some almost metaphysical way they belong together. And precisely the same thing happens with groups of wines: They detach themselves from the others and dwell together in the same part of the mind.

The particular group—a sort of ethnic group, it seems to me—that fascinates me by its almost human character is that of the old Austro-

Hungarian Empire. With my shaky historical knowledge I have no trouble in detaching a large lump of Middle-to-Eastern Europe—east of Switzerland, south of Poland, north of Serbia—and labeling it The Old Empire. We are dealing with Vienna and Budapest, above all—but also with the towns and countries that were touched by their influence in the Empire's eighteenth- and nineteenth-century heyday. This group includes Northern Italy—the more so the farther east one goes—Northern Yugoslavia, and Romania in parts. I will leave boundaries out of this piece; but the palate traces its own frontiers.

How would one characterize this land? Baroque, horses, waltzes, woods, monocles, opera houses, game, paprika, chocolate cake? Marvelous, rather ironic manners? Short bursts of passionate energy? Mist and mud, and a slow river brimming through a desolate plain?

Almost as vivid as any of these images in my mind is the picture of yellow wine, with a sort of reticent sweetness, an edge of fire, a feeling that the grapes were almost too ripe—that the juice dripped out of them like molten candy to ferment like bubbling-hot oil. The apple-like freshness of Germany, which Switzerland has been known to catch, is far away. The imperial taste is warm and strong; sometimes even fierce. These wines are not for delicate sipping; one does not catch one's breath at their elusive freshness. They are a stirrup cup before battle.

One great wine sums up the qualities of this region; indeed, almost caricatures them. Tokay is the only Middle-European wine to belong in the same class as port and sherry—certainly the only one that most wine amateurs all over the world have heard of. Its name is really much more familiar than its taste. I have tried—with only partial success—to express what that taste is. The nearest I have come is the phrase "celestial butterscotch." It is dark golden wine, very sweet (in its best qualities), and almost buttery rich. There is a shade of toffee in the taste, too, these days, which represents a change of style and technique ... but I'm running ahead of the story.

———

Tokay belongs in history as the favorite dessert wine of a world that thought dessert wine the *summum bonum* of gastronomy. Tokay was loved by the Hapsburg Court of the Holy Roman Empire, the Russian

Imperial Court, and the nobility of Russia and Poland. The town of Tokay (Tokaj) is only a few minutes from the Russo-Hungarian border—it's interesting that its location is still the Hungarian side, and that the czars, after the emperors, were the big customers. Also the wine merchants of Warsaw, who had stocks going back three hundred years, which they lovingly opened, sniffed (I imagine), and recorked every twenty years or so.

There was Tokay of various qualities and ages and degrees of sweetness—and there was, in a class apart, Tokay Eszencia, something that even czars allowed themselves a go at only on very special occasions. The secret of Tokay lies in this quasi-mystical fluid, which, when old half-liter bottles of it from the early years of this century come up for auction at Christie's, regularly fetches several hundred dollars a bottle. Eszencia, or quintessence of Tokay, is the self-expressed juice of extremely ripe grapes; the tears, so to speak, of grapes that are leaking their concentrated sweetness and flavor.

They leak because of the same curious rot that makes Château d'Yquem and the great Sauternes and shrivels the grapes for the Trockenbeerenauslesen of the Rhine and Moselle. Botrytis is a sinister-looking form of mold with purely beneficent results. This mold appears only during long, warm, misty autumns. The presence of a river not far off is a help in providing ground-hugging moisture at morning and dusk as the days shorten. Sauternes has the Garonne River; Tokay has the Bodrog. Grapes with river-induced botrytis look as though they will taste moldy; instead, they taste more honey-sweet than ever. Somehow the mold softens the grape skin and makes it porous. And it is the water content that finds its way out. What is left inside the grape is the sugar and the unanalyzable essences that constitute its flavor. Both are concentrated by the absence of water to an intensity they could achieve in no other way.

Just crushed and made into wine in the ordinary way, these grapes create something very luscious and satisfying. But the Hungarians have a characteristically theatrical way of going further than anyone else. They simply pile the grapes on a grating or sieve, and what is squeezed out, without any mechanical aid, is the true Eszencia.

And strangely there is a scientific foundation for this ancient practice. The first and most gentle pressing of any grape makes the best wine, for the first juice to run comes from a zone midway between the pips and the skin, from flesh that has been in contact with neither.

Tokay Eszencia contains so much sugar that it is very reluctant to ferment at all. It is analogous to jam; the sugar keeps the equilibrium. I have two half liters of it in my cellar (I had to go to Tokay and be very polite to the boss to get them) and neither of the wines has started to ferment noticeably, although one is six years old. In fact, my cellar is probably too cold; the State cellars of Tokay are dank but not chilly.

Eventually, the theory goes, this most remarkable grape juice does become wine of a sort: very low in alcohol, sweet and concentrated in flavor. It is this wine that has always been held to have the power of bringing men back from the dead, or at least death's door. There are innumerable tales of Magyar or Polish nobles or bishops on the point of giving up the ghost when somebody hastens to the hushed bedside with a flask of Eszencia. Hardly has the elixir moistened the graying lips than we find his lordship up and playing golf. (I mentioned my little hoard to the life insurance company, thinking that they might reduce my premiums on the strength of it. Their answer, I may say, just shows how far the commercial motive has clouded men's view of what is great and noble.)

Whether any Eszencia finds its way to the Kremlin these days I could not discover. But clearly such a superaristocrat of wines has no place in a Communist state. What the wine growers of Tokay do with it now, sensibly enough, is use it for blending with and improving their standard sweet wines.

Tokay today is often a mixture of a strong white wine and a very sweet one—the sweet made from botrytis-infected grapes and added in certain set proportions to produce different grades of the final product. The most luxurious Tokay sold is all *aszu* (the word for sweet wine); the plain everyday one has none. *Szamorodni*, as the latter is called, is a good aperitif rather than a dessert wine.

The intermediate degrees of sweetness are indicated by the number of measures of *aszu* added to the base wine. The measure is a seven-gallon tub called a *puttonyo;* the barrel, a *gönci,* holds thirty-five gallons. Five-*puttonyos* Tokay is therefore all *aszu* (since five sevens are thirty-five); four *puttonyos* (or *putts*) has seven gallons of *szamorodni,* and so on. All Tokay, except plain *szamorodni,* has a little neck label showing the number of *puttonyos,* so that its sweetness is readily known. The bottles, incidentally, hold only half a liter (or two thirds the contents of an ordinary wine bottle). At about five dollars a half liter they are not inexpensive.

———

Tokay itself is probably the least visited of all the world's famous wine towns. Its position about forty miles from the Soviet border may have something to do with this. Tokay's atmosphere is remote—enough with the sort of memorable stillness of a small provincial town in a Chekhov play. The center of its social life is the incongruously grand *halasczarda* (or fish restaurant), opposite the broad poplar-fringed Bodrog River. From the window tables, above the gables opposite, the wavy crest of a hill of vines can be seen. In the gloom inside one eats hot, substantial, peppery dishes: soup with *pontj,* the rich freshwater fish of Hungary; bulky noodles with smoky bacon and sour cream cheese; flaky pastries resembling those in an Eastern bazaar; and coffee as good as in Budapest.

The ordinary house wine is not Tokay, or not strictly the type of Tokay one came to taste. It is the Furmint of the district; the table wine made of just one of the Tokay grapes—but the one that epitomizes Hungarian originality; a grape of pungent fruitiness and searching astringency. Furmint is, it could be said, the starting point of Tokay. Into the vat with it go smaller quantities of two other grapes, the Hárslevelü (or lime-leaf grape) and a Hungarian form of the muscat.

The winemaker's problem with any sweet wine is always how to keep it stable so that any refermentation does not cause it to arrive at its destination fizzing. In ancient times in Tokay the stabilization was done with brandy, as it still is in the making of sherry. The modern method, though, is to pasteurize the wine by raising it to a high temperature for a short time to kill any remaining yeasts. I have no positive proof, but I suspect that the trace of toffee in the taste of modern Tokay may come from the pasteurization; that, in fact, the classical wine of Hapsburg and Romanov was a shade different.

The notes I made while tasting a wide range of Tokays in the State cellars bring the whole experience back to me vividly. The cellars are what one might call small-bore tunnels; men of any stature keep brushing their heads on the mildewed roof. Candles are the only light: Each visitor takes a long-handled candlestick and plunges into the Stygian labyrinth, up and down ramps and little stony ladders, past endless files of diminutive barrels—the *gönci* are only a little over knee-high. Here and there at the far end of a gallery one will see a conspiratorial group, heads and shoulders crouching in the flickering light, as cellarmen taste or maneuver a barrel. There are no cellars in the world like these for the feeling of being in the bowels of the earth. The analogy with a gold mine is irresistible, particularly when one comes to the little circular cave of a tasting room and samples the golden wine.

—

But Hungary is not all Tokay, and it is a mistake to associate Hungarian wine too much with great age and imperial banquets. The bulk of Hungarian wine (which is a big bulk; most of the country grows wine in one form or another) is white, pale, and ready to drink within a year of its making. Isolated regions of hills—most of the country is flat—provide the better wines. The best natural vineyard situation of all is the north shore of Lake Balaton, Central Europe's biggest lake, which gives the Hungarians their only seaside. A number of old volcanic stumps rise almost from the side of the lake. The sort of outstanding soil-and-climate situation that occurs all too rarely—in Burgundy's Côte d'Or, for example, or the middle Moselle—is found on the slopes of Mount Badacsony.

Badacsony white wines are probably Hungary's best. There is no getting away from the fact, however, that they could be, and clearly have been in the past, better than they are today. With the State control system there is no opportunity for the great individual winemaker. The best winemakers are probably in charge of the largest wineries, where the widest range of grape qualities go into the brew. It is rather as though, let us say, all the wine of Meursault, Chassagne-Montrachet, and Puligny-Montrachet in Burgundy were made in a fine modern cooperative together. One would expect the wine to be very good. But it could never have the quality of that of great vineyards on their own. Exports are all State-controlled by the excellent Monimpex organization. One will not be disappointed by the standard wine they ship.

On the other hand there are private vineyards and wine cellars in very good situations. A visitor, if he can make himself understood in Magyar, or has an interpreter, can discover enchanting little cellars where both the machinery and philosophy of winemaking are purely nineteenth century. In one, an octogenarian dame mimed the whole winemaking process for me perfectly. Then she tottered up a ladder in her laced-up boots with a pipette on her shoulder to fetch me a sample from the top of a vat. After one year the wine was still fermenting. Hungarians like to drink it that way; as cloudy as milk and marvelously sharp and fizzy. But her older wines, above all those made of the unpronounceable Szurkebarat and Kéknyelü grapes, were as full and penetrating in their flavor as very good white Burgundy. I like the word "stiff," which they use for these dry and pungent wines. They are very well worth looking out for and drinking with thoroughly rich and well seasoned food.

The district name and the grape name are all one will find on a Hungarian wine label. Badacsony is the best of Balaton; if the wine is labeled Balaton it will probably be slightly less impressive—though still quite good. The grapes of this district, which are named on the label after the district, are Olaszrizling (the Italian Riesling—here at its excellent best); Szurkebarat (Pinot Gris—also at its best here); Furmint, as in Tokay; and the splendid Kéknyelü. I would hesitate to try to distinguish one wine from another in words: All have Hungarian boldness and yet considerable subtlety.

Mór and Somló are two much smaller hill areas that make wine of long tradition and great quality. Móri (the final "i" is adjectival, as is the "er" of Bernkasteler) wine is probably the driest and most delicate of Hungarian white wines. The grape is the Ezerjó. Somlói wine is more like that of Balaton with the same volcanic soil and the same grapes. Many of the best Somlói wines, however, are on the sweet side—rather in the manner of the great hocks of the German Palatinate.

———

These wines are the most distinguished white wines of Hungary. Red wines are in the minority. But two regions are known primarily for their reds: The one in the north, outside the splendid Baroque market town of Eger, is very well known even abroad. Egri Bikavér, or Bull's Blood of Eger, is analogous to red Bordeaux in some ways. One of the grapes in its blend is the Merlot, as in Bordeaux. There is a hint of a claret scent in the young wine. This is as far as most bottles get, however: Few people think it is worth laying down wine that costs so little in the first place.

The only mature bottle of Bikavér I have ever had was one I kept in my cellar for eight years. It was of the 1959 vintage. I can best liken it, in its mature state, to an excellent old Chianti. It had a similar warmth and sweetness. Again, here is a wine one should buy to keep—not, as almost everyone does with relatively inexpensive wines, to drink up and forget.

The State cellars of Eger are so celebrated for their Bull's Blood that few people know their white wines at all. Yet I was as impressed by the white wine as by the red when I visited the cellars. Leanyka is the chief local white grape and white wine. It is pale and delicate for Hungary—although from the age of some of it still in the mighty red hooped casks of the State cellars it is no weakling. I tasted a seven-year-old Leanyka that was rather soft but still quite flavorful and not at all tired.

The other red-wine district is only just becoming known as it begins to concentrate on its best red-wine grape variety. The Pinot Noir of Burgundy has proved so successful in southern Hungary, in the Mecsek district around Villány and Siklos, that I expect we shall soon get a chance to buy it here. Villány is the name most often seen on the label, usually followed by the word "Burgundi." Again, this is a wine brimming with color and flavor, which wants keeping several years.

This survey is necessarily a rapid tour of a country whose wines are all worth looking at. There are other historically famous names, notably Sopron near the Austrian border, whose wines I am only on nodding terms with. And there are other developing districts growing Italian Riesling and the Kadarka (a Balkan red grape, which plays a large part in Bull's Blood and has real quality). I would not be a bit surprised to taste a very good wine from any of them. It is always encouraging to hear of more good things being made in more places. Hungary is certainly to be watched—and so, in just the same way, is Austria.

—

If Hungary is slightly handicapped by the overcentralization that comes with State control, Austria in the past has had exactly the opposite disadvantage. It has traditionally been a land fragmented by thousands upon thousands of small growers, none big enough to enter the market with consistent fine wine.

To this extent the customary picture of Austrian wine as a tavern drink is accurate. Still, most of the best vineyards supply light, fruity, hurriedly made wine of almost miraculous characteristics straight from the barrel. But once in bottle (if anyone is so rash) they become a dreadful disappointment.

I believe it is only really in the last few years that the export potential of the wine they make has hit the Austrians. I said that no bottle of fine wine out of Hungary would surprise me. Until a couple of years ago any bottle of fine wine out of Austria would have been astonishing—whereas today it is already accepted as the normal thing.

For a city as sophisticated as Vienna, Austrian wine does seem a bit rough-and-ready; yet in its context, from the cask in a *Heuriger*, it has a captivating heady freshness. There is no exact translation for the word *Heuriger*. It means both the new wine and the grower's hospitable cellar or terrace where he offers it for sale from the barrel.

Vineyards still occupy what must be some of the most valuable suburban land in Vienna: as central as, for example, Montmartre in Paris, Morningside Heights in New York City, or Hampstead Heath in London. The vineyards infiltrate the beginnings of the Vienna Woods to the north, commanding a superb view of the city and the Danube. And scattered among them, in residential districts and out in country lanes, *Heurigen* attract the Viennese of all classes. In most, one can eat;

in some, dance under the trees; in all, drink new wine until one has one's fill.

Grinzing is probably the most famous of these wine districts in Vienna. But between Grinzing and Nussdorf and Kahlenberg and Sievering, and their respective Grüner Veltliner (the most Austrian of grapes and my personal favorite), Traminer, Sylvaner, and Riesling there are a thousand debates and, no doubt, duels fought every night.

Viennese wine, however, is a perfect example of what is meant by saying that a wine does not "travel." To take it out of context by exporting it would be absurd. To this extent it is typical of the Austrian wine-growing tradition—and long may that tradition continue.

In all Austria only two districts have a real tradition of exporting wine, and even they have rarely exported their best. The Wachau is the more distinguished of the two, but there is something about the name Gumpoldskirchen, the other, that makes it easy to remember (or perhaps hard to forget).

The Wachau vineyards occupy one of those sites that God clearly intended for vines. At a point about fifty miles above Vienna where the Danube River flows in broad curves eastward, the north bank rises in broken hills to a thousand feet above the water. The pivot of this region is the little town of Dürnstein, under which the road burrows in a tunnel. Dürnstein has Austria's largest and best *Winzergenossenschaft*, or cooperative winery—a union of nearly all the growers on these difficult and fragmented slopes. Their bottlings are some of Austria's finer and more reliable wines.

Dürnstein also has one of those truly memorable hotels at the water's edge where setting, food, and wine are all, in the words of one guidebook I treasure, a lyrical outburst of "typism." Richard I, King of England and crusader, surnamed Coeur de Lion—the Lionheart—was a captive in Dürnstein castle while, the story goes, his faithful minstrel, Blondel, was looking for him all over Austria. Can you bear to be told that Blondel stood below the castle walls, wistfully plucking the notes of his royal master's favorite song, when his heart leaped to hear the well-remembered voice answering with the words from within?

The hotel, in any case, is called the Löwenherz, and it makes the logical base for a visit to the Wachau. One is directed by the manager to a simple *Heuriger* in a lane by the river. This particular grower, a lusty old chap in a stocking cap, produces a Grüner Veltliner with true panache.

The bulk of Wachau wine is made of the common Sylvaner grape for rapid consumption. Under the name Schluck, this wine has created a reputation for being adequately fresh and fruity at a very low price.

But the *pièces de résistance* of the Wachau are the Grüner Veltliner and the Rhine Riesling—the latter being a more complex and distinguished wine, the former, the characteristically full and forthright kind. Fritz Salomon and Petermichl both bottle good ones. The place-names to look for are Weissenkirchen—sold by the cooperative as Achleiten—Dürnstein, Stein, and Krems.

Just downstream of the town of Krems, the hills move away from the north bank of the river and wander off northeastward. The small town of Röhrendorf, just around the corner, has a particularly important place in viticulture. It is the headquarters of the firm of Lenz Moser, one of the most original and skillful winegrowers in Europe.

Lenz Moser has given his name to a revolutionary way of growing vines widely spaced and relatively high above the ground, producing more and better wine from fewer plants with less work and less chance of disease. He has also demonstrated that it is not only the traditional vineyards of Austria that can make its best wine. At a tasting in his cellar I met wines from districts I had never heard of, which were among the best Austrian wines I have had.

One was a Grüner Veltliner from Mailberg in the north of Austria, in the district known as the Weinviertel—which, although the name means wine quarter, has always been more famous for quantity than quality. Another was a Riesling from a strange and rather depressing district down near the Hungarian border—the sandy shores of the shallow, reed-fringed Neusiedler See. The west shore of this distinctly odd lake, which is said to be wadable right to the middle, boasts one historic wine town, Rust. Ruster Ausbruch—*Ausbruch* is Austrian for what the Hungarians call *aszu*—was once famous as a near-Tokay. But this wine came from the east side of the lake, from the little-known village of Apetlon.

I look on my Apetloner Rheinriesling Auslese, now that I have some at home, as the perfect wine for startling and baffling friends who think they know German wine backward. It has the quality of a very fine German wine but it also has the Austro-Hungarian attack, the stirrup-cup-before-battle feeling. What greater pleasure is there than finding a new source of really marvelous wine?

I may have been less lucky with my Gumpoldskirchners. It is easy to get the wrong idea when every *Heuriger* offers a different quality— and when even the bottled wine seems to vary enormously in character and style. Sweetness was the one thing they all had in common: Some had the acidity and fruit to back it up; others did not.

Gumpoldskirchen lies along the Sudbahn, the railway south from Vienna, which has given its name to the vineyards stretching due south from the city. These slopes are the last gasp of the Alps in the face of the central European plain. Their name of *Thermenalpen* comes from the hot springs that break the surface at Baden and Bad Vöslau and furnish the wooded slopes with hundreds of little stucco villas suitable for convalescents who take the waters. Alsace, the Côte d'Or, and the Middle Haardt are all famous wine districts with almost identical sites: foothills facing east over a flat landscape.

Gumpoldskirchen is the white-wine center of the Sudbahn; Baden and Bad Vöslau specialize in red wine. Neither, in my opinion, is a world-beater, probably due to the local grape varieties, which are very much in the majority. There is as much pleasure in these charming places as in any of Austria's *gemütlich* wine towns; but essentially these are wines to drink in *Heurigen*.

Trying to view Austrian wine as a whole is difficult at the moment. Export strategy is just developing. We may see estate-bottled wines quite soon from remote districts. Klöch in Styria is one. The latest arrival, however, is a good representative of the modern trend in everyday wines toward lightness, good balance, and basic anonymity. The Hirondelle range, which has just been announced, is a blend without a district name. It aims at being fresh and attractive, slightly sweet and very inexpensive.

Time will tell whether the old imperial style can survive in the modern world, or whether Hungary, too, will adapt its wine, making it paler and lighter and less gloriously characteristic. I was drinking a bottle of Furmint last night and holding the glass against a white napkin to admire the lovely color, like beech leaves in autumn. I could just hear a modern winemaker dismissing it contemptuously as oxidized, which indeed it was.

This tale has a moral—or I would not be ending with it. The moral is to keep an open mind. There are more great tastes in heaven and on earth (thank heaven) than come from the "great growths," whose names we all know. And one of the greatest tastes of all lives in the heart of the old Holy Roman Empire.

April 1972

THE
AMERICAN REVOLUTION

THE WINES OF CALIFORNIA

Hugh Johnson

It may seem curious that I, a visitor from Europe, should be telling Americans about the unrecognized glories of some of their country's produce. The tendency to regard imported things as in some way superior is not an American peculiarity; in Britain it is *très snob* to drive a Lancia or a Mercedes—the same price and speed as many British cars but somehow much more stylish. In America it is still *très snob* to drink Beaujolais and Moselle, even Chianti and Verdicchio. No one, I believe, really asks himself the obvious question: Are they better than wines grown in my own country? He just assumes that they are, or that his guests will feel better entertained if they are served the imported variety.

With the thirsty curiosity of a visitor, with an open mind and an iconoclastic nature, with no bones to pick and no axes to grind—you can already guess what I am going to say. California is making wine as good as the wine of France—at the peaks not quite so good, but on the average maybe better.

Why should we be surprised? Because everyone knows that France is the world's greatest wine country, and the nearer her neighbors cluster around her, the better the wine they make. Because she has been making wine for two thousand years, and California, in effect, for thirty-six. And because we have had the greatest meals of our lives in France, the food and the wine combining to produce something we could never find elsewhere.

———

I am in a dismal little restaurant in the Napa Valley. Since it is the only eating place for miles, the policy is to charge the famine price for hamburgers. You order them rare; they come charred. I've brought a half gallon of Mountain Red from a nearby winery. I fill a glass and commiserate with myself about the menu (I haven't yet seen what an overstatement it is). I swirl the wine about and look at it. I sip it and chew at it a bit. Suddenly I'm interested. I realize that what I have in my glass is exceptional, even beautiful. What I'd bought as basic comfort—can you remember what *"onze degré"* comfort tastes like in France?—sings to me. Down into the portmanteau for words. Yes, it's gentle, yet it's gutsy. It's firm and dry and yet the taste it leaves is distinctly sweet. It has individuality, no doubt about that. I'd know it again.

Or, I am on a terrace overlooking the sparkling bay at Sausalito. San Francisco hovers in the smog above the yachts. The Sunday brunch crowd is warming up over glasses of milky, frothy, icy gin fizz. I ask for a glass of white wine from the jug. Marvelous. The slight grapy beginning on the tongue, just a kiss of fruit, and then the clean, dry, expanding flavor of well-made wine all the way down.

———

The first, extraordinary lesson of California for the visitor is that the state is sitting on an artesian well of sensationally good, plain, everyday wine. Due, more than anything, to the managerial qualities of people like the Gallo brothers, very good wine at very low prices can be taken for granted, and not just in California but in every enlightened part of the United States. I can't remember when I have been as impressed by anything as by the Gallo enterprise. Three hundred million bottles of wine last year. A glass factory in the winery. There's nothing else like it in the world. Cynically, I would have thought it possible only for childish fizzy drinks, or at best for the sort of sweetened wine, designed for an unsophisticated market, that some European countries ship across the Atlantic. But no, it is real wine, dry, made naturally with only the aids that technology can offer to prevent it from going wrong.

The emphasis today tends to be on the varietal wines of California, at the top end of the market. There is certainly much to say about them; to wine lovers they are where the interest of the subject lies. Yet the quality of Gallo's Chablis, Vin Rosé, and Hearty Burgundy was the opening revelation of my California journey.

I arranged a little tasting in New York for a feature writer from the *New York Post* to show her why I praised these wines so highly. She thought I was some kind of eccentric, but I amazed even myself with the outcome. We compared a glass of Gallo Chablis from a half-gallon jug with the best French-bottled Chablis *premier cru* on the Sheraton-Russell Hotel's list. The Gallo was—Gallo. Clean, fresh, in perfect condition, and very pleasant. The Chablis Vaudésir (at three or four times the price) was quite out of condition; the sulphur that had been used to keep it safe for the long journey had only added to its problems. It was flat, stale, and oxidized. And yet I have had so many bottles of European white wine in America that have been, if not as bad as this, at least tired, that I hesitated to send it back. "That's the way it comes," would have been the answer. Too true.

I risk sounding partisan if I insist too much on these questions of value and the condition of the wine. Yet it bothers me to think of potential wine lovers' being put off by paying a premium for wine that can only disappoint them. Far better, it seems to me, to buy something really reliable and not pay a premium. And then one can explore the heady realms of estate bottlings in one's own time.

To go on about value for money, however, is not why I asked *Gourmet* to let me report from California. It was 1966 when I last did a winery tour there. Exactly four years later I was back, to find so many eggs hatched, so many chicks become full-grown layers, so much bustle and excitement about the place, and so many new ideas being pushed through with so much enthusiasm that I was reminded of (though I never saw it) Hollywood in the 1900s, when tailors and lawyers and dentists with names like DeMille and Mayer brought their energy and vision to a bit of unknown countryside and started building dreams.

The hardest-headed businessmen in San Francisco can talk about doubling the United States' consumption of table wine (that will be from one gallon to two gallons a year for every man, woman, and child) in the next five or six years. Already Americans drink more wine than the English. The thought of growing and selling another 150 or 200 million gallons has brought companies that used to put all their faith in hard liquor onto the scene. They have noticed, too, that the campus parties that used to be based on liquor have changed to wine. Publishers can suddenly sell books on wine by the tens of thousands. Without a blow struck, a benign revolution seems to be taking place in America. It is not just a question of fortunes being made in what was once a backwater of agriculture; it is a change for the better (at least so I think) in the whole life style of the nation. There are several streams all tending to the same object. The great volume producers I have been talking about are by far the biggest and, for the moment, the most important. They can lead their smaller, poorer rivals in many techniques. But there are areas where it pays to produce on a modest scale and not to be committed to national distribution. Vital experiments are often made by the devoted individual—a figure more common on the California terraces than you would believe.

Take Bob Mondavi. His family has owned Charles Krug for many years. Krug wine was already excellent, but Bob believed he could make it even better. He shifted down the road a few miles, built a new winery with financial backing from members of a Washington brewery family (finance is not one of the problems today; if you doubt it, try to find a winery that will accept your investment), and even before the roof was on had started using revolutionary new equipment to make immensely attractive wines the way he felt they should be made.

The slight remaining tinge of inferiority complex that American winemakers still tend to have was an added spur. Without it would Bob Mondavi have traveled to France to pin down the very oak that gives that special mealy taste to Meursault? Would he have had his barrels made in the same Limousin cooperage? And would he pride himself so much on the admittedly uncanny resemblance of his wine to white Burgundy aged in the same oak?

But then who, even in France, had ever really pinned down the part oak plays in the final taste of a wine? It was a revelation to me, at the Mondavi and also the Mirassou wineries (the young Mirassous are eager disciples of Mondavi) to be able to isolate the Limousin flavor for the first time, and even to compare it with the flavor of oak from other woods.

As Brother Justin, winemaker at The Christian Brothers, says, in California all the winemakers watch each other's experiments with skepticism, have a good laugh, and then try the same experiments themselves. In his mountain monastery he has one of the most advanced wineries of all—the last laugh?

As technique expands, so does territory. For years the problem of housing subdivision supplanting vineyards on the best Bay Area land has been one of the wine industry's headaches. The snag was that the cooling influence of the Bay is vital to premium table wines; farther inland or farther south the days and nights are warmer, and quality is lost.

But a climate survey by the brilliant wine department of the University of California at Davis showed that ideal conditions for grapes exist in new areas that had been more or less desert before—above all in the long valley that runs northwest up to Monterey Bay, which apparently acts as a cool-air corridor.

The pioneering Almadén and Paul Masson (both of whom are feeling the southward pressure of San Francisco on their home vineyards), Wente Brothers from the Livermore Valley to the east, and Mirassou from San José have among them planted about thirteen thousand acres of completely new premium table-wine vineyards. The whole Burgundian Côte d'Or is only twenty-two thousand acres.

At the same time the possibilities of the hills around the Napa Valley are being exploited. It has always been known that the extra cost of hill plantings is rewarded with higher quality. Small wineries such as Stony Hill and Souverain, with the highest quality as their one object, naturally started in the hills. Louis Martini has long had the famous Monte Rosso vineyard. Now the southern foothills of the Mayacamas Mountains between the Napa and Soma valleys, known as Los Carneros, are coming into the picture as high-quality vineyards in an ideal situation.

Perhaps most exciting of all to me was my first contact with a mechanical grape picker. If labor problems were the mother of this invention, they will be quite forgotten when its virtues are fully realized. For here, in one machine (cumbersome though it looks at the moment, like a Heath Robinson device that removes your hat, polishes your shoes, and fixes you a Martini), are the answers to half a dozen of the most puzzling problems in California winemaking.

Its speed is perhaps its greatest asset. It gives the grower the best possible chance of choosing the ideal moment for the vintage, and gathering the grapes exactly when he wants. Better still, it can work at night, when the grapes are comparatively cool. It leaves unripe berries on the vine; it damages fewer grapes than human hands do; it cleans the grapes and dumps them in a truck alongside as it trundles down the rows. True, its use is limited to comparatively flat vineyards, but these are precisely the ones where the quality is most in the balance, and the extra freshness of the fruit picked at night, avoiding over- and underripeness, can make the difference between a dullish wine and a truly enjoyable one.

Men, machines, new acreages to make a Frenchman turn green with envy, if not white with fright—but I am a romantic at heart. Most memorable to me are those places where the wine grows as it grew in Eden—some private vineyards in the hills, such as the one Robert Louis Stevenson described, where all human happiness seems to be summed up in a scene of calm fertility.

Schramsberg—the winery that Stevenson so delighted in—after a long period of neglect once again embodies everything that is most seductive about California. Jacob Schram's cool and lofty old frame house, as ornate and dignified as a Nob Hill mansion, is now the home of Jack and Jamie Davies. Their labor (and labor is the word) of love has been to restore everything—to replant the breathtaking vineyards in the woods with the best vines of Champagne, to restock the long vaults cut into the mountain with racks of the best wine that their talent and dedication can produce. To walk around the steep, forest-fringed vineyards with Jack, to visit the spring and the little theater Schram made in a grove of redwoods for his friends, and then to sit in the shade and drink the delicate uplifting Schramsberg wine seems to me as much as any man of goodwill can ask from life.

And yet there is a more uplifting and exciting experience still in store: a new winery that demonstrates that this idyll is not just a nostalgic one, but something we can look forward to in the future. High on Pritchard Mountain, hundreds of feet above the floor of the Napa Valley, looking downward and out to the northwest over lake, forest, and the Mayacamas Mountains, looking Mount St. Helena right in the eye, stands the most remarkable wine cathedral (there is no other word) of the modern world. A vast natural amphitheater, cleared of forest, has been planted in the great grape varieties—Cabernet, Chardonnay, Riesling, and Chenin Blanc. Right in the natural stage of the amphitheater is a huge, red-gold, three-sided pyramid—a building of the space age, pure and deliberate in line and function. There is no avoiding the comparison with a cathedral—the scale and a sense of aspiration suggest it immediately. Still more inside, where the single vast cool space is aisled with pillars and the floor is completely uncluttered. A file of gleaming tanks and the rhythmic bulk of barrels are monuments and congregation.

The name of the new winery is Chappellet. Donn Chappellet, tall, bearded, and soft-spoken, and Phillip Togni, his winemaker, are like men with a secret. Pride and modesty combined keep them reserved. To taste the brilliant wine they are making and to watch their faces, inquiring and yet confident, is to see the antithesis of the salesman—the craftsman of genius who knows that the world will beat a path to his door.

October 1970

FINE WINES OF CALIFORNIA

Frederick S. Wildman, Jr.

PART ONE

"California, here I come" may seem a strange utterance from someone who has spent half a lifetime tasting the wines of Europe. But during the summer of 1965 there I went, wandering through what is now known as one of the world's great vineyard regions—the necklace of counties that surrounds San Francisco Bay. I came, I saw, and I savored, and the hospitality and goodwill of the winemakers was overwhelming, the landscape was lovely, and many of the wines were excellent. All conspired to make my tour memorable.

It is agreeable to observe how the fine table wines of California have come of age these past few years. No longer suffering from the inferiority complex that made them ape European place-names, the best California table wines are appearing more and more under their own appellations—with the place where they are grown and the grape varietal from which they are made clearly stated. This deserves applause, as there is something inherently sad in seeing a good, honorable wine masquerading under the name of some other great vineyard region.

California wines have had a long, hard climb over three decades, and the fact that they have done so well in what by European standards is a preposterously short space of time is due in large part to the dedication and experimentation on the part of a few vintners, and the guidance given them by the research team of the University of California at Davis.

Thirty years ago California wines were at their nadir. Prohibition may have been an amusing time for the Stutz Bearcat set, but for those who loved the wines of California it was an unmitigated disaster. For seventy years before the enactment of the "noble experiment" in 1919, viticultural pioneers such as Colonel Agoston Haraszthy, the Hungarian nobleman, political philosopher, and agronomist who, before dying in the jaws of a Nicaraguan crocodile, systematically introduced and experimented with the best European grape varietals in California; and the Finnish adventurer, entrepreneur, and sea captain Gustav Niebaum, who founded Inglenook vineyards, produced wines that Americans had good reason to be proud of.

Then came Prohibition. America plunged into an epoch of bathtub gin and other potables too dubious to mention. The result was a jading of a generation of palates, and the uprooting of hard-to-acquire, hard-to-plant, and hard-to-protect vines. Even worse, when Prohibition was finally pushed into oblivion in 1933, few people could afford fine palates even if they had managed to keep them. The Depression was on. Banks were failing. Breadlines were forming in the streets. Consequently, the bulk of California's revived wineries concentrated on making fortified wines of which the only boast possible was that they were highly alcoholic and cheap.

During this gloomy period a few idealists such as John Daniel of Inglenook, Louis M. Martini, Georges de Latour of Beaulieu, and the Wente and Concannon families of Livermore waged what appeared to be a quixotic battle. Against the overwhelming tide, they kept their standards high. And, as the general reputation of California wines sank, it seemed inevitable that these few holdouts would not survive for long. But an unforeseen event was to bring them recognition.

From that sad day in June 1940 when the Germans occupied France, the fortunes of California's wines of quality began to turn. American oenophiles, who formerly had spurned California wines, now found themselves cut off from their beloved Chambertin and Château Haut-Brion. But where were they to turn? California was the only answer. Firms that had hitherto only imported European wines canvassed the northern counties and soon discovered those few wineries that had maintained high standards. They began distributing their wines, and by so doing introduced American wine lovers to the good wines of their own country.

By the late 1940s the established vineyards attempting to produce wines of superior quality were more or less those that exist today. Among them were Almadén, Beaulieu, Beringer, Buena Vista, Christian Brothers, Concannon, Cresta Blanca, Inglenook, Korbel, Krug, Louis M. Martini, Paul Masson, Mayacamas, Martin Ray, Sebastiani, Souverain, Weibel, and Wente.

These, in conjunction with such skilled counselors as Frank Schoonmaker and the research team at the University of California headed by M. A. Amerine and A. J. Winkler, began codifying areas in terms of their average temperature during the growing season, and then experimenting with grape varietals to see which ones went best where.

California vineyard areas were divided into five regions. Region I is the coolest, corresponding to Germany and the northern regions of France, namely Champagne and Chablis. Region II parallels such areas of middle temperature in France as Bordeaux and the Côte d'Or. Region III is much like the warmer regions of France, such as the lower Rhône Valley, and the northern sections of Italy, Spain, and Portugal. Region IV is similar to most of Italy, Spain, and southern Portugal, and Region V is akin to Andalusia, Sicily, Algeria, and Morocco. It was theorized that the best areas for fine European table-wine varietals were in regions I, II, and, to some extent, III. Nearly all of these, to no one's surprise, turned out to be in eight counties around San Francisco Bay—San Benito, Santa Cruz, and Santa Clara to the south; Alameda and Contra Costa to the east; and Napa, Sonoma, and Mendocino to the north.

At this the visiting gourmet can rub his hands in Panglossian glee. Gastronomically speaking, it is "the best of all possible worlds." For, as the late Lucius Beebe so exuberantly informed us, San Francisco is an epicurean watering spot of the first order, with Oriental, Middle Eastern, Latin American, Italian, French, and American restaurants scattered among its hills and wharves. And, as most of the best vineyards and their attendant tasting rooms are within an easy two hours' drive, one may easily spend a Lucullan week here—the days tasting the products of the vine, the evenings sampling the works of the town's master chefs. It is an experience guaranteed to expand both the spirit and the waistline.

—

Upon arriving in San Francisco, I needed someplace to begin my vineyard explorations, and, since an alphabetic approach seemed as reasonable a one as any, I started by visiting the San Francisco offices of Almadén. I was greeted hospitably by their vice president and general manager, H. Peter Jurgens, who invited me to lunch on Fisherman's Wharf. We dined on abalone, lightly cooked in vermouth and gracefully complemented with an Almadén Johannisberger Riesling. After lunch he generously made arrangements for me to visit those vineyards I could in my short stay on the coast.

The first, needless to say, was Almadén itself. The next morning I found myself traveling southward to its enormous new vineyard at Paicines in San Benito County, where over three thousand acres have been planted in the very best varietal grapes—about a third of the total production of fine-wine grapes in America. These European vines, moreover, are grown from their own original rootstocks, a great rarity in the northern hemisphere. To understand the significance of this, a little viticultural history is in order.

In the second half of the nineteenth century a deadly blight struck both the vineyards of Europe and those of California where European grapes were being raised. This disease, the phylloxera, was caused by an aphis which attacked the vine roots, wounding them and ultimately causing the vine itself to die. For a frantic twenty years every device known to science was used to kill these mites, but to almost no avail. European wine production fell catastrophically. Only the best vineyards managed, by dint of constant work and great expense, to keep these minuscule marauders at bay.

The phylloxera aphis, it transpired, was a native of the Eastern seaboard of the United States, and it had arrived accidentally on experimental vines sent to the continent and California. In the densely planted wine vineyards, the disease spread like wildfire.

Finally, after two decades, it was reasoned that because the eastern American vine roots had survived, evidently they had developed some sort of natural immunity to the phylloxera. The best solution then would be either to graft European vines onto American roots, or to develop hybrids that combined European quality with American immunity. As the former of these solutions took less time, it was the one generally chosen, and as a result the aphis was brought under control. Most of the vineyards of Europe and California were replanted with American vines, and the European shoots were grafted onto them. What few pure European vines managed to survive succumbed during the Second World War, when proper pesticides all but disappeared.

The wines made from these new graftings were to most extents and purposes the same as the old ones. The graft, as anyone knows who has seen three or four kinds of apples growing from the same tree, carries the characteristic of the fruit, not the root. Nevertheless, many an elderly wine purist maintained that although the new wines were very good, they were not quite up to the famous vintages of his youth. Whether or not this was a case of looking back through rose-colored glasses will probably never be decided to everyone's satisfaction. However, Almadén, when planting its enormous vineyard at Paicines, took advantage of the fact that no vines, and hence no phylloxera, had ever been in the region before. Modern techniques can now keep the aphis at bay, and so it was decided to grow all the fine European grape varietals directly from their own rootstocks. The vines are now coming into production in larger and larger quantities. From the care taken in growing them and in making the subsequent wine, they should prove an interesting addition to the gourmet's table.

———

Supper that evening was beside the pool at the Paicines ranch, a lovely, sprawling single-story house on a hilltop. As far as the eye could see the rolling countryside was covered with vines, the dark outline of the Gabilan Mountains cradling the sun as it set. The host and hostess were Louis Benoist and his charming wife, Katey. Louis is an ebullient San Franciscan with a look of jovial innocence that belies his astuteness as a financier, businessman, developer, and sometime inventor. As the president of Almadén he has dedicated his sprightly mind and manifold resources to making it as fine and as large a vineyard as he can.

The meal that night was a splendidly aged filet of beef with, aptly, *sauce marchand de vin.* Accompanying it was one of Almadén's very good Cabernet Sauvignons. We ended with a lovely Brie, ripe but not runny, and a few glasses of one of Almadén's most recent additions— a California Blanc de Blancs made, as are some of the finest champagnes, entirely from the Pinot Chardonnay grape. It was dry and light, with a delicate bouquet, certainly one of America's best sparkling wines and the perfect way to end an evening.

Early the next morning I was taken on a tour of the vineyards and shown the extraordinary built-in sprinkler system, a field of a thousand whirling spiders spinning rainbows into the noonday sun, which guarantees a perfect annual rainfall. The tour continued through the enormous cooperage warehouses, all kept at perfect cellar temperature. We visited a brandy still and a private plastic pipe-making plant to fabricate tubing for the mammoth irrigation net. We then set forth northward in the direction of San Francisco to Los Gatos in Santa Clara County. Here the original Almadén vineyards were planted in 1852 by the Bordeaux vine grower Etienne Thée. Santa Clara County is rapidly becoming urbanized as the San Francisco–Oakland complex sprawls farther and farther afield. Nevertheless, it is still the home of some of California's finest and best-known vineyards—Paul Masson and Martin Ray among them.

The Paul Masson Company, incidentally, lays claim to 1852 as its founding year, basing this on the date Etienne Thée planted the vineyard Almadén now owns. The reason for this demands a little knowledge of Etienne Thée's family tree. Thée left his vineyards and his company to his daughter and son-in-law, Charles Lefranc. Lefranc in turn left the company and vineyard to his ebullient son-in-law, Paul

Masson. The company Masson founded has since sold Thée's vineyard, which is now owned by Almadén. So both companies claim 1852 as the year their vineyards were founded.

The present Paul Masson Company not only owns a few small vineyards at Saratoga in Santa Clara County, but some years back purchased the San Ysidro ranch near Gilroy in San Benito County. Here it is planting fine grape varietals to make its own wine. The head of the firm, Otto Meyer, is a music lover of note, and every Sunday afternoon in the summer has public concerts of excellent classical music in an outdoor bowl near his Saratoga vineyards. The firm of Paul Masson has an equally distinguished reputation as a vintner. It produces a number of good sparkling wines; a Cabernet Sauvignon, Gamay Beaujolais, and Pinot Noir among its red wines; and a Pinot Chardonnay, Sémillon, and Chateau Masson, a dessert wine, among its whites.

Almadén has also kept its original vineyard going, but that has been overwhelmed in scope by the huge new vineyard at Paicines. However, the old buildings are still utilized for the making and storing of wine, and the delightful old farmhouse of Thée and Lefranc is used to entertain guests.

It was here, before lunch, that we had a comparative tasting of varietal wines from Almadén and several other California wineries, a regular occurrence so that the Almadén winemakers will know how their own wines stand in comparison to others. It was extremely interesting and very objective. It is perhaps a pity, though, that at no California tasting I attended was there a good European regional wine of the varietals compared. It would have provided an outside referent to avoid any natural tendency to parochialism there might be among California winegrowers. In view of the effort that is going into the raising of standards of quality, however, this is a most minor criticism.

There followed a lunch of a perfectly splendid *poulet à la créme* accompanied by a cool bottle of Pinot Chardonnay that did it grace. So fattened, I retreated to San Francisco for a well-deserved steam bath at the Pacific-Union Club and a pleasant siesta.

———

The next day I was up early and on my way southeastward across the Bay to Livermore, home of the Cresta Blanca, Concannon, and Wente wineries. Here I was met by Karl L. Wente, grandson of one of California's viticultural pioneers, Carl H. Wente. The original Wente was an enterprising German who emigrated in 1880 and by 1883 had done well enough to purchase land in Livermore and start making wine. In general the Wentes have concentrated on making fine white wines, though lately some Pinot Noir and Gamay have been planted to make reds and rosés.

Karl showed me around his family winery and then invited me into his ranch for an agreeable cold lunch *"en famille."* One of the problems that had lately sprung up in Livermore, he told me, was that the great burst of nearby Oakland's population had tapped the subsoil reservoir of water, dropping the water table precipitously. Artesian wells were the only answer, and these had to be driven deeper and deeper. Ultimately a limit would be reached, and unless some method of conservation or irrigation was devised, the problem could be fatal for wine growing.

After lunch we tasted a cross section of Wente wines—the Pinot Chardonnay, which was very good, quite dry, full in bouquet and flavor; the Dry Sémillon, again a full bouquet, flowery, and semisweet; a Sauvignon Blanc called Chateau Wente, quite sweet and full, something like a Monbazillac with less of a taste of glycerine; the Pinot Blanc, which was pleasant, but a little young when I tasted it; and the Gray Riesling, at present a great success among American wine drinkers. Made from a grape named the Chauché Gris, it is not considered especially noteworthy in France. However, its light body and taste seem to agree with the current American palate. *De gustibus non est disputandum.*

The word *Riesling,* incidentally, is used widely among American vintners to cover a multitude of grapes. There is the aforementioned Gray Riesling, or Chauché Gris; the Franken Riesling, which in Alsace is usually called the Sylvaner; an Emerald Riesling that is an American hybrid; a Mainriesling; a Wälschriesling; and even a Missouri Riesling, which is probably another name for the native American Elvira. One of the reasons for this *"embarrass de Rieslings"* is that the wine-drinking public knows it to be one of the world's finest white-wine grapes, and so the name is being cashed in on by grapes that have no relation to it. The true German Riesling in California is nearly always called the Johannisberger Riesling, and here it produces a fine, light wine, not too similar to its German counterpart, but still with a dry elegance that marks it as a wine of considerable merit.

PART TWO

After making visits to some of the vineyards to the south of San Francisco, I next traveled northward across the Golden Gate and on into the lovely Napa Valley. The entrance, south of the town of Napa, is flat and broad, but the valley gradually narrows and deepens as one travels north. The flanks of the low mountains bordering it are covered with grapes and trees. At the northern end is Mount St. Helena, named after the patron saint of Princess Helena Gagarin, the wife of the Russian governor in the days when Russia's Pacific empire stretched in a vast semicircle from the Amur River in Siberia to northern California. Grapes are everywhere, and scattered among them are odd pylons surmounted by what appear to be airplane propellers. Whenever there is a frost, the propellers are used to stir up the cold air which otherwise would sink to the valley floor and wither the vines. Every few miles there are signs bearing the name of some famous vineyard: Beaulieu, Beringer, Christian Brothers, Inglenook, Krug, and Louis M. Martini among them.

My first stop was with John Daniel, Jr., at Inglenook. The winery itself is a massive stone building constructed by his great-uncle, the almost legendary Gustav Nybom or, as he "Americanized" it, Niebaum. Niebaum was a Finn when Finland was a duchy attached to the Czar's empire. He took to the sea, and at an early age he was sailing off the coast of Alaska, then a Russian colony, when Seward purchased the area for the extravagant figure of $7.2 million. America not only gained an enormous and extraordinarily rich chunk of real estate; it also got the enterprising Captain Niebaum. After making a fortune in the seal trade, he moved to California, studied viticulture there and in Europe, and dedicated himself to producing the finest wines possible. Since then, under his nephew John Daniel, Sr., and great-nephew John

Daniel, Jr., Inglenook has continued as a leader of fine-wine making in California.

Consequently, the wine world was astonished to learn in the summer of 1964 that Inglenook had been sold to United Vintners, better known as Petri, an enormous California firm specializing in bulk wines. There were, of course, dark murmurs that this was the end of Inglenook. But, so far at least, quite the contrary. Recognizing the great increase in the demand for wines of quality, Petri has left Inglenook autonomous, and these vineyards may well provide the framework for Petri's own entrance into the fine-wine market.

John Daniel, Jr., met me in his office and, when questioned about the sale, he explained that although he had sold the name of the winery and half the vineyards, the other half of the vineyards and all the winemaking remained in his hands and those of his cellar master. There had been no change in the growing of fine grape varietals, none in the making of the wine—only in its marketing and distribution. John is a quiet, soft-spoken man who pauses before he speaks and then pinpoints the most nebulous idea in five or six words. To me, a born chatterbox, this trait is downright miraculous.

After exploring the Inglenook cellars, we went off for a pleasant lunch in a local restaurant, accompanying it with a lovely bottle of Inglenook Cabernet Sauvignon. Unlike most other California winemakers, Inglenook allows the grape juice to stay a good length of time "on the skins," as is done with fine Bordeaux. This practice gives the wine a full, deep color, and a flavor that is rather tart and harsh when young, but it compensates by causing the wine to develop slowly to far greater heights. Mayacamas, another small vineyard on the mountainside above the Napa Valley, follows the same procedure, as does Martin Ray. Commercially, a wine of this sort may cause trouble, as it often throws a deposit, and the bulk of the wine-drinking public does not yet seem to know that sediment is normal. So storekeepers are loath to handle wines that have it.

As I wanted to take some pictures of the vineyards, John suggested that I come back the next morning and accompany him in his light plane for a tour of the valley.

The rest of the afternoon was spent with Brother Timothy in the Greystone Winery of the Christian Brothers at St. Helena. The Christian Brothers are a Roman Catholic order of teaching friars founded in France in the eighteenth century by Saint Jean Baptiste de la Salle. Funds are necessary to keep their schools going; they raise them partly by producing wines in the Napa Valley. The winery is an impressive building filled with the most modern winemaking appurtenances. The afternoon ended with a tasting of the Christian Brothers' various vintages. Although most were wines for popular taste, the Cabernet Sauvignon was particularly noteworthy.

At ten the next morning I met John Daniel at a tiny airstrip near Rutherford, and we took off in his sleek little Cessna for an aerial sweep of the valley. It was a grand day, with bright sun and fleecy clouds. As we climbed over the mountains that separate Napa from Sonoma County, a number of unexpected small vineyards appeared, perched high on the slopes. Mayacamas was one of them, its contoured terraces, like long tendrils, grasping into the bends of the hills. Deer, which are great aficionados of the tasty vine leaf, are a constant menace to California vineyard owners, and some had obviously been nibbling on Mayacamas's vines. We flew over Louis M. Martini's Monte Rosso vineyard on another hillcrest, a mass of red rock surrounded by vines. John told me of an additional hazard—rattlesnakes that like to sun themselves on the warm mountain stones between the vines. This tends to make the California vigneron rather more cautious as to where he puts his feet than his French cousin.

When we landed, John took me to a luncheon meeting of the Napa Valley Association, and here I met Louis P. Martini, the son of Louis M. Martini, and representatives of other fine vineyards such as Beringer and Beaulieu. We discussed the University of California's system, mentioned earlier, of grading areas by their average growing season temperature, matching these to their European temperature counterparts, and then choosing the grape varietals accordingly. I brought up the point that some north European grapes seem to lack acidity when transplanted to areas I or II. In Europe it is well known that a year of great sunlight is apt to produce wines high in sugar, and hence alcohol, but low in acidity. Consequently, it seemed to me that although the University of California had done considerable research with temperature, they might with profit also examine the effect of sunlight—perhaps "solar radiation" is a more descriptive expression. The process of photosynthesis, after all, depends more on light than on temperature. And the vineyards around San Francisco Bay, though cooled by breezes from the Pacific, still lie between the thirty-sixth and fortieth parallels, level with southern Spain, Sicily, and the northern coasts of Algeria and Tunisia. The San Francisco area may be as cool as the Rhine, but the angle of the sun there, and hence its intensity in terms of radiation, is Mediterranean. Bordeaux, by contrast, lies just south of the forty-fifth parallel, Burgundy around the forty-seventh, and the Rheingau on the fiftieth. It seemed to me no quirk that, whatever the temperature charts say, by far the best California red wine is made from the Cabernet Sauvignon, a grape from Bordeaux in *southern* France. From Bordeaux also come two of the finest white-wine grapes, the Sauvignon and the Sémillon. The other outstanding white-wine grapes grown in California—Riesling, Traminer, Pinot Chardonnay, and Pinot Blanc—all do well around the forty-fifth parallel in northern Italy, and the Italian versions of them are in many ways similar to the Californian. Moreover, the finest rosé of California is made from the Grenache grape. In Europe the best example of this comes from Tavel, forty-four degrees north latitude near the mouth of the Rhône River.

Now, the temperatures in the University of California's temperature area I correspond to vineyards that lie at about fifty degrees north latitude in Europe. If one were to strike an average between this fifty degrees and their actual positions—approximately thirty-seven to thirty-nine degrees north—it would come out at about forty-four degrees north—almost exactly the same parallel as Bordeaux, the Rhône at Tavel, and great vineyards of northern Italy; in other words, just where the grapes that are most successful in California flourish in Europe.

Is this a coincidence? If not, this mean between the solar and the temperature latitude might provide a simple rule of thumb for choosing good, susceptible European varietals for California's vineyards. For instance, it might be interesting to try some of the other good grapes from around the forty-fifth parallel in Europe, in temperature regions I and II. The real Syrah (not the Petit Syrah, which is already grown in California) from the Rhône Valley might do well, or the excellent Nebbiolo from the Barolo and Barbaresco regions of northern Italy. The wines made from these grapes are slow-maturing and thus might not be popular as a broad-scale commercial venture, but they still could provide some additional welcome material to California's winy arsenal.

Almost underlining my thoughts, a charming bottle of Beringer Grignolino, fruity and full, was uncorked and put on the table. The Grignolino grape is grown in the region adjacent to Barolo and Barbaresco, and if the Beringer wine is an example of what a good Italian grape will do in regions I and II, then other such varietals should certainly be tried.

The discussion proceeded to the idea of forming some sort of local classification system to protect and develop the reputation of the Napa Valley. The possibility of a registered mark, a Napa Valley *"supérieur,"* perhaps, to be affixed after the name of the vineyard and the grape varietal, certifying that the wine in the bottle had come from certain grapes grown only in the Napa Valley and had passed stringent controls, was bruited about. But winegrowers are pretty independent by nature, and they don't want to tie their reputations or freedom of action too closely to their neighbors, so the idea soon bogged down in disagreement. This is a pity. Château Mouton-Rothschild doesn't suffer because Château Lafite or Château Margaux are equally well known. Far from it. They have all developed their reputations together. Because of the high qualitative standards they have jointly set, the whole area, in this case the Haut-Médoc, became known, and everyone prospered. If the Napa Valley Association could arrive at some classification for its superior wine, there is little reason that its fame shouldn't spread and soon rival some of the best vineyard areas abroad. A joint effort could achieve this. As the late John Kennedy once observed, "a rising tide lifts all the ships."

After lunch I thanked everyone for a cordial meal and an interesting exchange of views, and then headed westward over the mountains that separate the Napa Valley from Sonoma County. My destination was the Buena Vista vineyard in the town of Sonoma. The vineyard was founded by Count—or Colonel, as he later called himself—Agoston Haraszthy, who may properly be considered the founding father of fine wines in California. He was a dynamo of a man: Despite his belonging to the nobility, his liberal opinions forced him to flee his native Hungary in the 1840s. He founded a town in Wisconsin; then, when California began to open up, moved on to San Diego and became its first sheriff and representative to the new California State Assembly. Shortly before the Civil War he moved to Sonoma, opened the Buena Vista vineyard, and turned with characteristic energy and intelligence to making wine. He dug caves out of the hillsides with Chinese coolies, built himself a charming winery, and was commissioned by the governor of California to go to Europe and bring back the best grape varietals he could find. This he did, bringing back hundreds of types for experimentation. Although the phylloxera wiped out most of these vines—and his fortune as well—it may be safely said that the systematic growing of fine wines in California is based on Colonel Haraszthy's early work.

In 1943, Frank Bartholomew, the present head of UPI, bought the rundown vineyard and winery and revived it. The wine now produced there is pleasant, with several good varietals represented. The spot itself is idyllic—verdure, high trees, and gray stone—a historically interesting place to visit and a splendid site for a picnic.

The next day I continued up to Guerneville on the Russian River to visit the Korbel winery. The countryside is very agreeable, with a road winding down the riverbank through piny woods. After a few miles I arrived at the large Korbel building. Korbel has the reputation of being one of the oldest and best sparkling-wine producers in America. Started in 1881 by the Korbel brothers from what is now Czechoslovakia, the winery was purchased in 1954 by another group of brothers, Adolf, Paul, and Ben Heck. Descended from a family of Alsatian winegrowers, the brothers Heck have been involved with wine all their lives. The winery is a spirited, gregarious family affair; the Hecks obviously love their work and do it well. Their champagne, especially their *nature* and their *brut,* is excellent—certainly far better than most European sparkling wines. They are now embarking on a policy of broader wine production, and if their new varietal table wines come up to the standards set by their sparkling wines, the thirsty gourmet may look forward to additional bounty for his table.

My tour of the vineyards was over. As I headed back to San Francisco, I couldn't help musing over a theory that crops up from time to time in nearly all oenophiles' conversation—that civilization and wine seem inextricably intertwined. As Edward Hyams recently expressed it in his interesting book, *Dionysus: A Social History of the Wine Vine,* "The central and most sophisticated territory of the wine vine seems always to correspond to the central and most sophisticated territory of Western civilization at any given time." When Greek philosophy, language, and art were paramount in the Mediterranean, so, too, were its vintages. When Caesar bestrode "the narrow world like a Colossus," Falernian wine was recognized as the *ne plus ultra* of civilized drinks. As the vineyards of France burgeoned through the late Middle Ages into modern times, so, too, has French culture achieved a dominance far out of proportion to its population. The age of Goethe, Schiller, Heine, Bach, and Beethoven also marked the beginning of the great epoch of Rhine and Moselle wines.

If there is any truth in this thesis, it is indeed a pleasure, both as a wine lover and an American, to observe how good many California wines have become. They may have a way to go before they can challenge the finest growths of Burgundy, Bordeaux, and the Rheingau, but they are improving at a rate that should cause European winegrowers to start casting nervous looks over their shoulders. Who knows? Perhaps the wandering folksingers, the busy laboratories, the artists on the Big Sur, and the student effervescence are all harbingers of a switch of the Western cultural center from the shores of the Atlantic to those of the Pacific. If so, the wines of California's northern counties will certainly have their role to play.

May/June 1966

THE JUDGMENT OF PARIS

Gerald Asher

In the early 1970s Steven Spurrier, an English wine merchant, and Patricia Gallagher, his American partner, had a small wineshop in Paris in a cul-de-sac near the Place de la Concorde, where, in an adjacent building, they also gave courses in wine to their enthusiastic customers. Almost inevitably, Spurrier and Gallagher developed a considerable clientele among expatriate Americans. The U.S. Embassy was a block or two away, the substantial offices of IBM were almost next door, and American law firms were scattered all around them. Through word of mouth, their Caves de la Madeleine became a regular stop for California wine producers and others making the rounds of the French wine scene. Often these visitors brought a bottle or two with them, and Spurrier was able to taste what he has described as "some exceptional [California] wines."

At their shop Spurrier and Gallagher dealt in French wines (except for a few of the most ordinary commercial blends, there were no California wines available in Paris at that time), but they decided to use the excuse of the United States' bicentenary to show a selection of California wines to French journalists and others connected with the wine world. They were sure that they would make a good impression on the French and thought they might even surprise them. They hoped, too, that any stories generated in the press might bring in a new client or two.

With their bicentenary plan in mind, Gallagher visited California in the fall of 1975 and Spurrier followed in the spring of 1976, during which time he picked out six Chardonnays and six Cabernet Sauvignons, all of recent vintages, that he thought would give a fair picture of what was going on in California. He needed two bottles of each, and, knowing he might have difficulty bringing two cases of wine through French customs, he arranged for a group of twelve tennis enthusiasts on the point of leaving for a wine and tennis tour of France to carry two bottles each in their hand baggage.

To give the wines a context and ensure they would be judged without prejudice, he decided to offer them for tasting in unidentified, wrapped bottles and to mix in among them a few white Burgundies and red Bordeaux. He knew he would have to choose among the very best of these or risk the suspicion that he and Gallagher had set up the California wines to score off the French. He knew, too, that because he would be showing the wines blind—that is, unmarked—and asking the tasters to rank their preferences, the credentials of those participating would have to be impeccable; otherwise any approving nods toward California might be dismissed as stemming from a lack of familiarity with the niceties of French wines.

The tasting took place at the Inter-Continental Hotel. The panel members—experienced and of high repute—were all French: Pierre Brejoux, then chief inspector of the National Institute of Appellations of Origin; Aubert de Villaine, part owner of Domaine de la Romanée-Conti; Michel Dovaz, a wine writer and enologist; Claude Dubois-Millot, from *Le Nouveau Guide;* Odette Kahn, editor of the influential *Revue du Vin de France;* Raymond Oliver, the celebrated chef and owner of Le Grand Véfour; Pierre Tan, owner of Château Giscours, a *cru classé* of the Médoc, and secretary-general of the Syndicat des Grands Crus Classés; Christian Vannèque, head sommelier of Tour d'Argent; and Jean-Claude Vrinat, owner of Taillevent.

The Chardonnays brought by Spurrier's tennis players from California bore the labels of Spring Mountain '73, Freemark Abbey '72, Chalone '74, Veedercrest '72, Chateau Montelena '73, and David

Bruce '73. He added to them four white Burgundies: Meursault-Charmes, Domaine Roulot '73; Beaune Clos des Mouches '73, from Drouhin; Bâtard-Montrachet '73, of Ramonet-Prudhon; and Puligny-Montrachet, Premier Cru Les Pucelles '72, from Domaine Leflaive.

Spurrier's Cabernet Sauvignons were Clos du Val's '72; the '71s of Mayacamas and of Ridge Vineyards' Mountain Range; Freemark Abbey's '69; Stags' Leap Wine Cellars' '73; and Heitz Cellar's Martha's Vineyard '70. I wondered why he had not included wines such as Robert Mondavi's '69 Cabernet Sauvignon or the Georges de Latour Private Reserve '70—both of these wines yardsticks by which other California Cabernet Sauvignons were being measured at the time.

"I simply didn't get to taste them," he told me recently, whereas he had already tasted a number of the wines he did select, and the rest had been chosen based on visits to wineries made on the advice of friends.

Nothing was left to chance in his choice of Bordeaux to put alongside the California reds. They were Château Mouton-Rothschild '70, Château Haut-Brion '70, Château Montrose '70, and Château Léoville-Las-Cases '71. A formidable group of wines.

Members of the jury knew only that some of the wines were French and some from California. Once they had graded the ten white wines—poured from their wrapped bottles—on a scale of twenty points, they did the same with the reds, and a group order of preference was determined. Among the journalists present as spectators was the Paris bureau chief of *Time,* and in the magazine's international edition of June 7 he announced the group's decisions to the world.

Among the white wines, California's Chateau Montelena headed the list, followed by the Meursault-Charmes, Chalone, Spring Mountain, Beaune Clos des Mouches, Freemark Abbey, Bâtard-Montrachet, Puligny-Montrachet, Veedercrest, and David Bruce. A California wine, the Stags' Leap Wine Cellars '73, was first among the reds, too. It was followed, respectively, by the Château Mouton-Rothschild, Château Haut-Brion, Château Montrose, Ridge Mountain Range, Château Léoville-Las-Cases, Mayacamas, Clos du Val, Heitz Cellar Martha's Vineyard, and Freemark Abbey.

—

In California, growers took the news calmly—"Not bad for kids from the sticks" was the reported response of Chateau Montelena's owner, Jim Barrett. But in France, and particularly in Bordeaux, there was consternation and, one might say without exaggeration, a degree of shock. It was not that California's success diminished in any way the real quality or value of the French wines—they had been used, after all, as the measure by which the others were judged—but the published results challenged the French in a field where they had assumed their superiority to be unassailable.

The French experts who had participated in the tasting, greatly embarrassed, felt a need to excuse themselves: Sophisticated arguments were put forward to explain away their choices. But, even allowing for every extenuating circumstance and accepting—as Spurrier has since said repeatedly—that another jury, or even the same jury on another day, might have placed the wines in a different order, it was clear that California had arrived. Regardless of the statistical reliability of the point system Spurrier had used to establish the group preferences, serious California wines, tasted seriously by serious judges, had at the very least stood shoulder to shoulder with French wines produced from similar grape varieties.

The tasting gave California a shot of confidence and earned it a respect that was long overdue. But it also gave the French a valuable incentive to review traditions that were sometimes mere accumulations of habit and expediency, and to reexamine convictions that were little more than myths taken on trust.

The French were soon all over California—a place they had until then largely ignored—to see what was going on. In no time at all the first of many of their sons and daughters had enrolled in courses at Davis or begun working a crush in California, just as many young Americans had always done in France. And within the year, Baron Philippe de Rothschild, of Château Mouton-Rothschild, was in deep negotiation with Robert Mondavi to form the joint venture we know today as Opus One.

In a recent article in the British publication *Decanter*, commemorating the twentieth anniversary of the tasting, Steven Spurrier said that the recognition given California twenty years ago was recompense for the state's investment in research and equipment. To some extent he is right. As a consequence of Prohibition, California vineyards had been replanted with coarse shipping varieties; winemaking standards had been seriously compromised; and most wineries had fallen into disrepair. The University of California had had to send its professors on the road to show vintners who had missed traditional father-son instruction how to make clean, flawless wines again. They never claimed to be teaching the art of making fine wine; their task—much more basic—was simply to reestablish the essentials of the craft, to reconnect post-Prohibition wine producers to a heritage that had been lost.

Certain vineyard sites that today are recognized for the quality of the wines they yield may well owe their survival to the professors' tour—but in fact many were first cultivated a century ago. Robert Mondavi's Reserve Cabernet Sauvignon is essentially the product of a vineyard, To Kalon, originally planted by Hamilton Crabb in the 1880s. Spring Mountain now occupies the winery built by Tiburcio Parrott in 1884. (Parrott's house is familiar to viewers of *Falcon Crest*; in the 1890s he produced there an exceptional Cabernet Sauvignon.) And, as our subject is recognition, the Liparita winery on Howell Mountain, now active again, took a gold medal for its Cabernet Sauvignon at the Paris Exposition of 1900—then, too, in competition with French wines.

———

A few weeks ago I saw the actual scores awarded each wine by individual members of the 1976 Paris jury—as opposed to the final rankings published at the time. I was struck first by the fact that all nine judges had given their highest scores for white wine to California—either to Chateau Montelena or to Chalone. That, it seemed to me, was indeed an endorsement—at least for young wines—of California grape maturity, technique, and hygiene.

And yet something about Spurrier's attribution of California's success to equipment—to technology—bothered me. I thought, for example, of Richard Graff's Chalone Vineyard as I had known it in 1974. Graff had always been a maverick among California wine producers. His vineyard, waterless and difficult to reach, was planted with an old clone of Chardonnay that he had cultivated vine by vine. Neither his methods of cultivation nor his winemaking had much to do with modern California technology. Chalone had little equipment to speak of; in 1974 it was still generating its own limited supply of electricity. And most important of all, at a time when California was only beginning to flirt with oak barrels, Graff had spent a year in France researching a treatise on oak and, probably alone in the California of that period, was fermenting his Chardonnay in the barrel and aging it on the lees. Now, more than twenty years later, that practice is commonplace.

Mike Grgich, then winemaker at Chateau Montelena, was born into a wine-growing family in Croatia and had perfected his craft first with Lee Stewart at the old Souverain winery on Howell Mountain (now the home of Burgess Cellars). A legend in California in the 1950s and 1960s, Stewart, self-taught, was obsessed by the details of winemaking. For him, it was the small things that counted. "I learned from Lee to watch over a wine as I would a baby," Grgich told Richard Paul Hinkle in a recent, anniversary interview for the trade publication *Wines & Vines*. From Stewart, Grgich moved on to André Tchelistcheff, the man behind the success of Beaulieu Vineyards' Georges de Latour Private Reserve, "who taught me to look at wine from the vineyard," and then to Robert Mondavi, "who made me aware of temperature control and French oak." When Grgich went to Chateau Montelena, he applied what he'd learned. "By then I knew how to handle a wine gently," he told me. "To disturb it as little as possible." The grapes for his winning 1973 had, like Graff's, also come from an old Chardonnay clone.

The Stags' Leap Wine Cellars Cabernet Sauvignon was the only California red to place among the first four. Surely it is more than coincidence that Warren Winiarski, the man who made it, should also have been an alumnus first of Lee Stewart, "a fastidious man who applied himself to every aspect of his wine," then of André Tchelistcheff, and finally of Robert Mondavi. "André gave us the soaring, the poetic vision. He had the gift of articulating what wine was to be, raising our horizons," Winiarski told Hinkle. "Robert provided the push, the thrust to get things done. Details and vision are nothing without the will to execute them."

It took a while longer for California's new crop of younger winemakers to learn these same lessons: to free themselves from technology; to abandon their expensive high-speed pumps and centrifuges; to reassess what "cellar hygiene" means (it doesn't mean keeping nature at bay with laboratory-prepared yeasts, preventing contact between a wine and its lees, and avoiding malolactic fermentation, the bacterial change that softens a wine and draws its disparate elements together); and to understand that fine wine is indeed made in the vineyard. In fact, it was a traditional, low-tech California that was honored that day in Paris in 1976. What the French recognized in wines they'd never tasted before was not equipment and rampant technology. It was the quality inherent in mature California vines; the skill and artistry of men like Richard Graff, Mike Grgich, and Warren Winiarski; and the vision of those who had gone before them.

January 1997

SALUT!

ADVICE

Hilaire Belloc

Throughout his crowded life Hilaire Belloc was peculiarly dependent on a small circle of friends (depleted with the years) to whom he could always constantly resort for hospitality, affection, and appreciation. Some of the most intimate of these was the family of Aubrey and Mary Herbert. Readers will remember his lines, "On the Ladies of Pixton": Three Graces; and the mother wore a grace, But for profounder meaning in her face. *Bridget Herbert was the second of these Graces and the first to marry. When she did so, Belloc was sixty-five years old and approaching the long silence in which his literary life ended. He gave her as a wedding present the manuscript book of advice from which these pages are printed. His surviving friends will recognize the precepts which were often, in one form or another, on his lips. His interest in food, wine, and domestic economy was strong and idiosyncratic to the verge of perversity. He believed that in those matters the rich were ready dupes; that excellence was rare and found in obscure and humble places. Some of the information given . . . is already obsolete; some of it expresses crotchets; but the bulk is a garnering of wisdom and in every turn of phrase may be heard the unmistakable authentic tones of the great man.*

EVELYN WAUGH

ABOUT WINE

WARMING IT

Never warm red wine. This deleterious practice is called by the vulgar "taking the chill off." Wine—red wine—can be just as good with the chill on: especially in early Autumn when the weather is fine. Rabelais, who knew more about wine than Dionysos and Noah put together, thought that, nay, affirmed it that, in Summer wine should come cool out of the cellar, and he was right. He spoke of *Chinon* wine, known also as the *Fausse Maigre*, for it has more body than the first and superficial acquaintance allows to it.

But if you *must* warm red wine do this: Take it out some six hours before drinking it; put it on a sideboard far from any fire—but in a room with a fire, or other heat. Take the cork out a little before drinking it—say half an hour before—to give it air after this slow warming. Then drink it.

To put red wine into warm water (I mean, to put the bottle into warm water) or to put it near the fire turns it into vinegar. This is not so true of Port, which is not a wine: but it is God's truth of Claret and Burgundy, Touraine, the Rhône, the Etruscan, the Spanish, and indeed the Algerian. The Rhine. All red wines.

COOLING IT

Do not cool white wine too much. All white wine is the better for cooling, but beyond a certain point, it kills the taste.

An excellent way of cooling white wine is this: Get a Bath oliver biscuit tin—2 or 3 is better than one, for you may want to have several bottles cooled, and to wait for cooling when one has begun drinking is damnable. These biscuit tins are just the height of a bottle or a little more, and, *what is their special point*, a *little* wider. Put the bottle into the tins and pour water in till it reaches about one inch or less below the top. There is then, a jacket of water all round the bottle. Put broken ice—not much—into the water at the top: not so much as to choke it, but only so much as can float in the water. This ice gradually melts, the cold melted ice sinks, and therefore very soon the whole water jacket is at 32° Fahrenheit, and, being a thin layer, doesn't freeze the wine.

A good permanent instrument to have about the place is a leaden roll of this shape and size well fastened, and with handles fixed on. See that it is wide enough for champagne.

BAPTIZING IT

All—or nearly all—red wine is the better for having just one or two drops of water poured into the *first* glass only. Why this should be so I know not, but so it is. It introduces it. This admirable and little known custom is called "baptizing" wine.

Some also, on seeing a little wine left in a glass throw it on the ground or ashes of the fire, crying "Cottabus," KOTT and BUS; this is a superstition, but not to be despised. It is said to placate the gods.

UNCORKING IT

It is strange that the clear and necessary doctrine on the uncorking of wine should be so little known. Get it firmly in early wine-drinking and it will make all your life the easier.

It is this. Always uncork wine with a *Lazy-Tongs.* Like this

You screw in the screw with the Lazy-Tongs, flat like this

Then you pull at the handle and as it extends like this

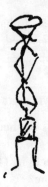

the corks come out, however stiff, with perfect ease, as though pulled by a giant.

If I can remember I will give you one to serve as a model.

Never be without one.

All other forms of cork pulling are exasperating, and many of them dangerous.

The butler-way of putting a bottle between one's knees, holding it with the left hand and fighting the reluctant cork with the right is a perilous waste of effort; and often doesn't even come off after a long sweat. It can rupture the puller and, if he has a weak heart, kill him stone dead.

All fancy cork screws other than the *Lazy-Tongs* are a fraud. There are dozens of them: with auxiliary screws: with a grip: with a little catch to rest on the bottle neck: they are *all* unsatisfactory.

Many waste their lives in dealing with the corks of fizzy wine—including ciders. These are corked with a sort of mushroom shaped excrescence like this

and baffle men.

The rule is to take a sharp knife and cut off the excrescence, leaving the rest of the cork flush with the top of the bottle. Then pull it out as you would an ordinary cork.

UNCORKING ROTTEN CORKS

When a cork has rotted in part it does not follow that the wine has been affected: but it does follow that your cork screw does not pull out the cork at first go. Before you get it out enough to pour there is sure to be a lot of little bits of cork and cork-dust on the top of the wine.

Therefore, on first discovering that the cork screw pulls though without lifting the cork right out, get a piece of clean linen (*not* muslin—which is not fine enough) put it over a jug (not a bottle, for that is too narrow) make a sort of cup of it over the top of the jug and strain the wine through that.

Then you can put it into an empty bottle or decanter with a funnel.

ON DECANTING WINE

This is the only occasion on which it is wise to decant wine. In all ordinary cases decanting wine is a folly. It looks genteel and makes the wine less good. That does not apply so much to the heavy wines like Madeira, or Muscatel, but it is most true of Claret and even of Burgundy.

However, if you have to—or choose to—decant wine, at least use the right kind of silver funnel such as was used by our fathers.

It is shaped like this

At the bottom of the cup is a strainer and the end of the spout turns sideways. The strainer prevents any big bit of cork or lees getting through and the turn at the end of the spout makes the wine flow softly down the glass sides instead of churning up the wine with bubbles.

If you *must* decant wine, at least see to it that decanters are (a) Washed with nothing but plain water—and that best cold. (b) Thoroughly dry before the wine goes in. It's impossible to dry the inside of a decanter except by letting it drain and then trusting to time, which does all things.

ABOUT BUYING WINE

Divide your buying of wine into two clear departments
(1) Buying ordinary wine.
(2) Buying special wine.
They are bought successfully in two quite separate ways.
(1) For ordinary wine—that is, for wine costing, at present prices with the pound still worth 12s. (God knows how long that will last) from 2s. or even 1s. 10d. up to 3s. a bottle (*never* pay more—2s. 6d. is quite enough). The rule is to find a place where three things are combined.
(a) A large stock and lets you taste.
(b) A man who knows you or your friends.
(c) A man who gives you what he says he will and doesn't substitute something else.
To these three characters you *may* add, if you like
(d) A man who will advise honestly but not push.
I have for some years found all this with Mr. Heath who runs the wine department of the Army and Navy stores. He shows you samples to any amount to taste before you buy, and he is just as pleased to sell you 1 dozen as 20 dozen. He will also, if you have little room, reserve a wine for you to draw on in detail as you need it.
But however much room you have don't lay in more than two years' supply of ordinary or gulping wine: better, six months, unless you strike a good cheap lot—like the 24 Tassegne I got for Bruton Street some time ago.
(2) Special wine: that is, wine the point of which is its excellence, should be bought by your own taste. No known recommendation can take the place of that—never let yourself be talked into buying a wine which you don't like.

And the rule in tasting is this: (1) Always taste in the morning, and better late in the morning: anyhow, long after having eaten food. (2) Take the merest sip of each sample. (3) Begin with the youngest. (4) Eat (a touch) of dry biscuit when you feel your taste getting doubtful. (5) Allow a minute or two between each taste.

Now very often you can't taste. They don't give you the chance. You have to buy the stuff in its bottles or leave it. In such circumstances *never* buy anything you have not tasted, apart from the bottles awaiting your purchase. If you have had a wine at a meal, and like it, then trust the wine man that he will sell you the same in glass. But don't buy wine by the name, or the year, or anyone's recommendation. Buy it by your own liking of it.

Some of the people who make a business of buying up bankrupt stock, and derelict stuff, and cellars at the end of a lease, etc., are not to be despised. People like Godfree Felton for instance. They always let you taste and are honest in delivering up to sample.

It is a good plan to go to the auctions also, but there you cannot always taste. The Cecil, for instance, was a great opportunity—and others will come.

BUYING IN WOOD

Don't buy wine in the cask in England: except Burgundy sometimes—on which, see below. Buy it rather from the wholesale man in France, and the best one for common table wine is *Théophile Guillon*, the big man at Nantes. But don't buy from him without *testing* first, go there and do it. Sleep at the Hotel des Voyageurs which has good comfortable rooms, large and clean—notably room 90—or the one that used to be 90. This hotel gives you coffee in the morning but no other meals and in big towns that is the rule in choosing an hotel—as I shall repeat later on. Eat other meals out. There is a very good restaurant just over the way in the Place du Théâtre.

Make Guillon blend your wine with Algerian. They hate doing it because they think it vulgar: but it is a most sound rule: *especially for our climate.*

It adds body and makes the wine last. African wine by itself is too rough. It is the wine on which are suckled young lions and the Foreign Legion. But though too rough all alone (and it has often hit me hard in the Lesser Atlas, while in the desert it kills), it is excellent added to the thinner French wine—e.g. wine of St.-Gilles, or anywhere in the Herault—in the proportion of 25 to 30 percent: but no *more* than 30 percent. The mixture of Algerian wine and water (often sold in England as St.-Emilion) is to be deplored.

Buy Burgundy (for drinking in England) *in the wood.* If you buy it in bottle it is always more—I mean, if it has been imported in bottle. Burgundy bottled *over here,* i.e. imported in the wood, is always better and smoother than Burgundy coming in in glass. Why this should be so none know, or knows. I found it out by accident like Columbus discovering America. I have tested it over and over again, and it never fails. If there is a wine merchant you really can trust, and whom you know, personally, to overlook the bottling himself, then taste his Burgundy from the wood, ask him the cost of bottling and order from him.

The '23 Burgundies, though still kicking, are magnificent wines: some I have already drunk with joy in spite of their youth. Notably a Nuits which I have at home. But of that later.

KINDS OF WINE

Of *champagnes* I know nothing. Besides which, champagne is not a wine but a drug. Invaluable when one is tired—I pant for it when I am tired, but it is not a wine. However, though I know nothing of its ages and makers, I do know that *Pommery and Greno* are always to be trusted, for I have known them all my life and they buy grapes from men of my connection. They are standard people. Never letting one down.

If you don't like dry champagne say so. A moderately sweet (or moderately dry) champagne is a human kind. A Brut is not. It is an acquired taste. It goes with meat and one can drink more of it, but it's rough stuff. However, that's all taste, and it's not for me to say as I only drink champagne to raise me from the dead—a thing I constantly need.

Vouvray, and Saumur, now, [are] another matter. These, though they sparkle, are wines. Real wines. I think, personally, that the wine of

Beaulieu (near Angers) whether still or bubbly is straight from heaven. But it often offends people used to dry champagne. I remember during the war when I had a drink of it, some of my acquaintances being starved for bubbly tried my Beaulieu—but they didn't like it. Those who *do* like it, like it enormously. I am one. *It must be drunk cold.*

You will get some good still Beaulieu at the Petit Riche, 21 rue le Pelletier, just out of the Boulevards, about half a mile east of the opera. They cook fairly well there too.

Of *Rhône* wines, I say, drink them on the Rhône. I never knew any that travelled properly. An exact Hermitage at Tournon or even at Nîmes is a thing to remember. But rarely in Paris and never in London.

Burgundies, as I say, have bottled over here. Remember that the best in Europe are in Belgium. Belgium always buys them up. When you see a parcel of 1911 *Nuits* or *Beaune,* buy it if it is reasonable. Remember what I said of the '23s. The '28s are the master wine of this world, but no one except God knows when they will be drinkable. They are as full of body as Homer, but they certainly won't be good to drink as a matter of course till, I should say, 1940. Of these very gigantic wines the *Richebourg* and the *Clos Vougeots* will be the leaders.

Richebourg '28 has all been bought up but one can get parcels of it. I bought a bottle of it in Salisbury at a grocers, and I am keeping it for my grandson. It was in his window. He did not know its value, and I gave him 8s., which was only fair. Also I once struck a dozen of remarkable *Nuits* in an inn at Llandovery. These things come by chance. E.g., in another inn at Instowe in Devon, I found a whole *cache,* or store, of admirable claret which I was told came there through a butler, as I can well believe.

If you like strong wine, remember *Vosne.* It is little known. It is full of iron. It is a good drink for the young, but too violent for the middle aged.

As for *Corton:* if it is soft, then it is good; but if it is not, it is not.

Chambertin is royal by nature, but variable: you must know it first.

To be certain of drinking good Burgundy as you travel, go to the Three Pheasants at Dijon. But don't order it right away: talk to them about it first and give them at least one hour.

Of the wines of the *Garonne,* called Clarets, I have no expert knowledge though God knows I am fond of them.

I warn you against the '23s: notably Haut-Brion '23 has gone off. The '24s are still good solid human wines. You can depend on the *Pichon-Longuevilles* with their Arch-label—at least, I find it always up to a certain standard wherever I go. I think they take a lot of trouble over making it—but I'm no use at the list. I go by taste and get what I like.

As with Burgundies, so with Clarets, you do not know them till you have eaten meat, or at the very least clear soup, before you drink them.

Of the *white wines,* a standby is Barsac, only take care not to get it too sweet. It can be like syrup, and cloying, but a normal cheap Barsac such as I have got for years from Gennaro in Old Compton Street is good with fish.

The wine of *Faye* in the extreme N.E. of Anjou is a good wine: rather dry (goes well with shellfish); (Beaulieu I have already told you of); in your travels get it at the Chapon Fin at Angers.

As for the white Burgundies, they are for those who like them. I never did. Not even Chablis and Hock. I neither know nor like. Those who do cannot seek it out too carefully and will sell their souls for it.

But I maintained and shall maintain till I die that of all white wines the one immediately from Paradise is that of *Orvieto.* Only remember this: it won't travel a mile, go and drink it at Orvieto, on a summer's day.

It being May and the day not too warm, sleep in the new inn at Bolsena—about the last house on the left at the top of the hill on the Orvieto Road. Then walk all morning from dawn to Orvieto, and when you get to that noble hill town which is as old as the gods, at once sit down and drink *cold* Orvieto wine. It is very, very good and two glasses make you immortal for a short time.

If I go on about wine I shall have no space for anything else. But before I leave Etruria I beg you to see the tombs of Tarquinia—called also Carneto—which are a linking of life and death and filled with majesty as is no other sculpture I know.

Do not sleep at Carneto, for you will not sleep.

January 1962

America's Madeira Tradition

Roy Brady

A list of devotees of Madeira from late Colonial days through the Civil War reads like a directory of American history. First in place, of course, was George Washington, who took a pint with his dinner every day; his portraitist Gilbert Stuart tossed off tumblers of Madeira "like cider in haying time." Jefferson and James Madison were Madeira admirers, and so was Ben Franklin. Chief Justice Marshall's parties for his lawyer friends were famous and the delight of the wine merchants. Up and down the Atlantic seaboard great families were known for their Madeiras as for their exploits in commerce, law, learning, war, and politics. In New York, names like Griswold, Lenox, and Goelet are linked with Madeira history. In Philadelphia, there were Cadwaladers and Butlers; in Virginia, Carters and Fitzhughs; in Charleston, Pinckneys, Rutledges, and Gadsdens. Above all, there was Habersham in Savannah.

Madeira, in a way the most American of wines, is produced on a Portuguese island in the Atlantic off the coast of North Africa. Adam Smith, writing in the year of the Declaration of Independence, explained how it came to this country. About one hundred years earlier Charles II had forbidden the American colonists to import European goods in their own vessels. Wine, in particular, had to go to England, pay English duties, and continue on in English ships. Somehow Charles's act made an exception of the wine of Madeira, and the colonists promptly took advantage of it to avoid the high cost of European wines shipped through England. Madeira was soon on the way to becoming American through adoption. (A taste for it was carried to England by British officers stationed there during the Revolutionary War.) During the eighteenth century it was drunk freely with and after meals. The tradition of drinking it ceremonially after dinner with emphasis on pedigrees of individual wines, thoughtful comparisons, and careful attention to minute details of the Madeira party flowered early in the nineteenth century (and faded in the twentieth). It was slow in developing, because in the early days Madeira was not at all the warm, amber wine as we know it today.

Winemaking began on the island soon after its discovery in 1419 by an expedition sent out by Prince Henry the Navigator, but for a long time grapevines were less important than sugarcane. The wine was mostly dry and red and, beyond doubt, not very good. Little is known about its early history, although by lucky accident the letter books of William Bolton, an English merchant, have survived from the years 1695 through 1714. Bolton came to Madeira from Shakespeare country to conduct his business out of the principal town of Funchal. His letters are full of information about his problems with rival merchants, Portuguese authorities, and his London firm. They tell of the risks of trade, of slave running, and of a visit to the island by Mr. Halley whose name was later given to the comet. Most important for us, his letters also show that he was shipping wine to Boston, New York, the Carolinas, and other ports in North America. He mentions Malmsey, later to be famous, which was already highly prized but scarce.

But the discoveries that were to make Madeira great lay in the future. The first was fortification—the addition of a little brandy to the wine. A Portuguese handbook of 1720 suggested the idea for Port, and sometime between then and the middle of the century the notion reached Madeira. As with much in the history of Madeira, the exact facts are obscure. At any rate, it was soon recognized that a little brandy suits the genius of the wine, allowing it to develop into something new and splendid, especially if made from white grapes rather than red.

The other essential discovery was that gentle heat is effective in maturing the wine. It was found in the eighteenth century that a sea voyage, especially through the tropics, did wonders for Madeira. By 1800, someone had learned that much the same results could be obtained at lower cost by storing the wine in heated buildings on land, being careful to maintain very mild heat for the finer wines. These buildings, *estufas,* quickly became a part of the Madeira scene and have remained so to this day, though for some wines the more romantic sea voyages continued to be used until recently.

Typical of the traveled wines were those sold at auction by a Mr. John Vaughan of Philadelphia on November 18, 1841. The Library of Congress has preserved a crumbling copy of the sale catalog with its characteristic descriptions. One wine was " 'Phelps, Phelps & Laurie's' Splendid Old East India Madeira, of two voyages in the wood, bottled in London Docks, under inspection. Stored at Natchez, Miss. from Nov. 1837, to April, 1839." There were 120 bottles of "Splendid *'Sercial.' Vintage of* 1806, of the Private Stock of Count Calvalhall. Exclusive growth of 1806. Confiscated by Don Miguel, and carried from Madeira to Lisbon, in 1829. Returned to the Calvalhall family on the restoration of the Queen of Portugal. Purchased of the family in 1834 by Wm. Phelps, Esq. Importers signature on the labels." Also noted was the ship that brought the wine, the *Powhattan,* in May 1835. These early descriptions of Madeiras are often explicit about where the wine had traveled, but just as often vague about other essentials. The mention of a grape name such as "Sercial" is decidedly unusual.

More than a century after John Vaughan another remarkable cellar was auctioned off in New York, and the Madeiras were described in the same detailed way. The auction was at the Ritz-Carlton Hotel in November 1943, and the wines were from the estate of Henry Walters, a Baltimore merchant. Baltimore was one of the old Madeira towns with many famous collections, and several of these had contributed to the Walters cellar at earlier sales. The label of an 1874 India Extra Madeira noted that it had been shipped "From Madeira to

London 1877. Thence Shipped June 1887 by Messrs Blandy Bros. & Co. per ship 'Star of Greece' via Cape of Good Hope to Calcutta and back to London 1888. Returned to Madeira 1888 from whence Imported Direct to Baltimore."

In my cellar there is a bottle whose label reads "SOLERA No. 1868 shipped by Cossart Gordon & Co. This wine was shipped March 1940 per SS 'Lima' to Lisbon, Portugal; thence by SS 'Vulcania' to New York. Transhipped per SS 'Mormacwren' to Buenos Aires, Argentina and thence returned to New York having twice 'crossed the equator.' Bottled Sept. 1940."

One milestone in the Madeira history of America was reached in 1895 with the publication of a curious little story, *A Madeira Party*. Written by S. Weir Mitchell, a Victorian physician, novelist, snakebite expert, and Madeira connoisseur, the story was apparently a popular one. The little book to which it gave its name went through repeated printings, and copies are by no means rare today. The plot of the story was simplicity itself:

Just after dusk one chilly evening "sometime early in the second quarter" of the nineteenth century, four gentlemen, all old friends, gathered in a Philadelphia dining room. The flickering light of a generous fire of hickory logs illuminated the warm colors of a fox-hunting scene on the wallpaper. On the table, china, glass, and plate glistened under the silver candlesticks while the elderly butler fussed over final arrangements until he was satisfied that everything was just right. It was a serious occasion. Presently the gentlemen sat down and soon finished a light supper of terrapin and canvasback. Then they turned their attention to the real purpose of their gathering. They were to taste and discuss a series of fine Madeira wines in a way that had become traditional during the preceding century of American history.

The half dozen highly polished decanters the butler placed on the table were all quarts. Anything smaller was regarded as bad for the wine; the old experts felt strongly about not confining Madeira too much. They imported their wines in casks and, after some time, transferred them to demijohns, large wicker-covered glass vessels holding at least five gallons. Here they remained for many years or generations. On the question of bottling there was a sharp difference of opinion. The Philadelphia experts were dead against it. One of the guests at the party said heatedly that it was almost impossible to get good Madeira in Boston or Charleston. "They bottle their wine. Incredible as it may seem, sir, they bottle their wine." He continued, "Madeira was never meant to be retailed. It improves in its own society, as greatness is apt to do." The statement reveals the patrician and sometimes snobbish quality of the Madeira tradition. The wine was not bought in bottles for current use, but by the cask to be drunk a generation or two hence. Hamilton, the host, remarked, "I have noticed that the acquisition of a taste for Madeira in middle life is quite fatal to common people." One guest thought it "rather remarkable" that a man he had known, "not a gentleman, either," had developed a good Madeira palate at the age of forty. The man died soon after—no more, Hamilton apparently thought, than he deserved.

Hamilton busied himself arranging the decanters in the proper order for tasting as he explained that the wines had been siphoned from their demijohns several days before and left in a warm room to mellow. Pouring was taboo because it might bruise the wine, and the decanters were passed "with the sun," for to send them around the other way would sour the wine. A peculiar-looking bowl of water stood in the center of the table to permit the guests to rinse their glasses between wines. Notches around the edge of the bowl held the glasses and prevented them from slipping all the way into the water.

The gentlemen discussed the wines one by one, sometimes with disagreements. One wine, for example, was called Madeira by some and Sherry by others. Although Madeira is a highly individual wine it does occasionally, in extreme age, approach the character of a Sherry of equal age. The party concluded with Cuban cigars which Hamilton was shocked to learn had recently gone to eighteen dollars a thousand.

The sudden and almost total disappearance of the American Madeira tradition is attributable to no one set of factors. The afflictions of the Madeira vine in the last century were certainly responsible in part. In the 1850s a fungus disease wiped out the vineyards so completely that for eight years hardly any wine was made. Recovery was far from full when, in the seventies, an insect, ironically from America, attacked the roots and spread destruction once more. At that point many growers and shippers gave up for good, and most of those who remained took to making standard blended wines rather than the fine vintages of former days. The system of landholding on Madeira added to the difficulties, as there were no great and wealthy wine estates and grapes were grown by small peasant proprietors who could not afford to ride out these two disasters. They turned to raising fresh vegetables for the London market and other cash crops less risky than the vine. But these problems did not stop the supply of Madeira; they only lessened it. Greater factors in the eclipse of the Madeira tradition were the changing social and economic conditions. Above all, the tradition was expensive and troublesome to maintain, demanding large houses and constant attention. Madeira was not laid away and forgotten in a quiet dark cellar, but often kept in glass-topped attics and periodically moved in and out of the sun. Even after a wine had been through the *estufa* or twice around the Horn to India, the old connoisseurs felt that it should be repeatedly moved, warmed, and sunned. Stuart Oliver, a Baltimore wine lover who collected many old Madeiras early in this century, complained that his wines kept him on the run, for he brought them up from the cellar for sunning and turning and then back down again to rest. Most men were not willing to expend the necessary time and energy.

The universal failure of the experts to leave any record of their knowledge and experience was another cause of the tradition's decline—one easily understood in view of the patrician nature of the Madeira mystique. The experts knew one another personally, moved in the same circles, and felt no need to write for the instruction of others, or to advertise their own knowledge. Men like Hamilton clearly had no interest in instructing "common people." Even Dr. Mitchell's book tells oddly little about the wines themselves. J. P. Morgan had a wonderful collection of old Madeiras when he published his cellar book in 1906. But as he had only about a dozen copies printed for distribution to friends, it is now probably the rarest of all American wine books and cannot have had any influence. Since the old cellars were large and the wines fabulously long-lived, they often outlived their owners, and were then usually sold privately, if at all, and did not come on the market to stimulate interest. The Walters sale was an exception.

Another view on the fading of the Madeira tradition comes from the late Julian Street, one of the most charming of American wine writers. He had the good fortune to experience many fine old Madeiras at the table of Dr. Mitchell's son, who had inherited many of his father's demijohns and used them for Madeira parties at his New York home into the 1930s. Street thought that Madeira lore vanished so quickly and completely because of the unique, casual, and at times downright frivolous way in which the old wines received their names. They were named after the ships that brought them, the merchants who imported them, the families who bought them, the places they had been, or after incidents or famous people who were in some way associated with them. All these names—Skylight, Painted Pipe, Forget-me-not, Wedding Wine 1795, W.T.W. Meda, Jenny Lind 1849, Old Baltimore (Oliver's own), Nabob, Mary Elizabeth, Jr., Gov. Kirby's original bottles, Constitution 1802, Thompson's Auction, to name a few—are colorful enough, but don't convey the slightest scrap of information about the type, quality, or character of the wines. Attention was often paid to dates—of vintage, importation, demijohning, bottling, and any other incident in the history of a wine—but other facts are scarce.

The system of naming adopted on the island in the eighteenth century did not find much favor in the United States until recent times. Madeira grapes gave their names to the wines made from them—the principal ones being Sercial, Verdelho, Bual (or Boal), and Malmsey, in order of increasing sweetness. (Sercial is fairly dry, but no Madeira is completely dry unless it has become so through great age.) In commoner Madeiras it is useless to look for differences of flavor among the various grapes, for here the names are likely to indicate no more than degree of sweetness. With the finer wines differences appear, though there is still similarity. Madeira is often compared to Sherry, and it is true they have a distant resemblance, but Madeira, like every great wine, is unique—thoroughly and completely itself.

Another name seen rather often is Rainwater, a type of Madeira that is, or was, exceptionally pale and dry. There are more conflicting stories about this wine and its origins than about almost anything else in Madeira history. How did it get so pale and dry? Is there some lost process for making it, or is it just a freakish wine that occurred naturally at times? If the latter, why does it not occur anymore—for the Rainwaters of commerce today are neither paler nor drier than Sercials.

Always associated with Rainwater is the name of William Neyle Habersham, and men have looked to him for answers to some of these questions. Born into a leading Savannah family in 1817, he enjoyed a long and successful career in the family shipping business. He was prominent in society and an accomplished amateur musician, trout fisherman, and horseman. His reputation as a Madeira expert was formidable, and probably led to all sorts of prodigies being ascribed to him. He was one of those rare men who could actually identify wines tasted blind. Once, after correctly identifying a wine, he added that it had been away from Savannah for some time and only recently returned. His judgment was confirmed. Another time a friend tried to confuse him by mixing two Madeiras. Habersham gently rebuked him saying that if he could believe his host capable of mixing wines he would say it was "half Catherine Banks and half Rapid." Right again.

Habersham had over his ballroom a great, glass-roofed Madeira room which only he and his cellarman were ever allowed to enter. Some writers believe that there he conducted secret rites that transformed normal Madeira into Rainwater, but, in fact, nothing is known of what actually went on in that room. A few years ago Mrs. Habersham's diary came to light, and there was a short-lived hope that she might drop a hint, but she did not even mention Madeira. The last Habersham cellarman was "Mediculous" Johnson, an ex-slave who outlived his employer but remained silent to the end about the Madeira room. (He got his name from a Habersham daughter, aged four, who watched him going about his duties one day and finally exclaimed, "George, you sure are a mediculous man.")

At any rate, the fame of Rainwater spread across the world, and to many it was the finest Madeira of all. Today it is a common enough name on labels, but the only true Rainwaters are the rare survivors from the last century.

If the Madeira tradition were only a memory it would still be a fascinating bit of Americana, but it is more than that. Madeira shows clear signs of reviving. There is a quickening of interest in it, and some wonderful old wines that have been forgotten for many years are finding their way to the market. The very eclipse of Madeira is to our advantage because it allowed grand old wines to escape earlier drinking. They are rare and expensive, of course, but it is possible to taste them and know to what heights Madeira can rise. Their scarcity is not so serious as it might seem, because a genuine old Madeira is a wine of such power, concentration, and intensity that it has to be drunk sparingly. A small glass will supply an hour's thoughtful drinking. Wine left in the open bottle actually improves for days and lasts, without injury, for weeks and months, where an old claret or Burgundy would be ruined by the air in a few hours.

But of more practical importance is the increase in good, sound Madeira for everyday use. So far its popularity has been growing in England faster than in the United States, but the increasing interest is encouraging the producers to make better wines that will be available to all. With the aid of the Portuguese government, inferior grape varieties that invaded the Madeira vineyards during the bad years are being uprooted in favor of the classical varieties. Even the delicate Terrantez grape, once almost extinct, has been planted again, and its wine will be known again for the first time in a century. Vintage wines are also coming back. Instead of blending everything together, as was done for so long, the producers are setting aside some especially good vintages to age by themselves. With continued encouragement of this sort, the great age of Madeira, it is hoped, will return.

December 1965

OUR CHRISTMAS MADEIRA

Nardi Reeder Campion

Most families cherish Christmas rituals. Our family's—my father's really—centered on a crystal decanter that glowed with ruby Madeira wine. It was a form of ancestor worship. I was only nine when my sister's beau, Raymond, derailed Father's ceremony, but my memory of that day is as crisp as a sunlit winter morning.

Debonair was the word for Father. In summer he wore saddle shoes with his white flannels; in winter he donned a velvet-collared chester-field and an initialed silk scarf. His shirts were monogrammed and so was the door of his Pierce Arrow. He prized good food, good wine, and good manners. He thought Prohibition was an evil, a kind of blas-phemy to be ignored, and enjoyed his evening Scotch and soda with-out ice. "Glenlivet," he was fond of saying, "helps a mon breast the brae." (Scotch always roiled up his Scottish blood.) Although Father was a courtly man, we all knew his gentle manner cloaked a red-hot temper. Once, after hitting four golf balls into the water, he hurled in his driver and stalked off the course.

On Christmas day Father dressed in his kilt, ruffled shirt, and Prince Charlie coatee. Then he stuck a *sgian dubh* (black knife) into his diced hose (argyle kneesocks)—the correct words were important. His father had presented him with the kilt when he graduated from the University of Michigan. It was a miracle of deep pleats of the Ancient Sutherland tartan, which is like the Black Watch but has an overlay of three red lines crossed by two white ones. Through years of good living, his girth had expanded, but so had the kilt because a clever tailor kept moving the leather fastenings.

My two brothers sported Sutherland neckties on Christmas day, and Mother and my sister, Julia, wore ankle-length Sutherland kilts. I did not own a kilt. I had to wear the black velveteen dress with lace bertha and pink sash that had been my sister's. A Scottish family does not waste money on something new if something old will do. My closet was hand-me-down headquarters.

Our Christmas ritual began after Mother served the dark plum pudding, swathed in blue flames and anointed with brandied hard sauce concocted by Grandma's "rule." Then Father brought forth a round silver tray bearing the crystal decanter of Madeira and seven tiny silver cups. We all trooped into the living room to stand before the portrait of the man responsible for our ceremony. When this ancestor had emigrated to America in the nineteenth century, he had joined the United States Navy, and he had been painted in uniform.

Father set the tray down on the marble-topped table as gently as he would a baby. When he was a boy there had been two decanters of Madeira, but the supply had dwindled to one, partially filled, which he husbanded with care.

"Our Madeira," Father would intone, "is almost a hundred years old and it hasn't faded. I don't think it will ever go off." He would drone on and on, boring us with details of how in the early eighteenth century sailors stopped at the island of Madeira for wine and then added brandy to the barrels as a preservative; and how the ship's roll heated the mixture, improving the flavor; and how the Portuguese winemakers copied the sailors, adding brandy and heating their own wine, thereby creating this exquisite dessert drink called Madeira. He always wound up by declaring: "And the best Madeira shines after dark as if the sunlight were still in it."

With a ceremonial flourish Father would pour a thimbleful of the precious wine for each of us. He then raised his little silver cup high, holding it delicately between thumb and forefinger. We raised ours in the same way. Father said, "To the clan." We echoed, "The clan!" And *very slowly* we sipped the tart, pungent liquid, inhaling its delicate aroma.

Every Christmas his blue eyes misted as he said, "In 1844 a case of this Madeira was brought to America by my great-grandfather, Commander Sutherland, who rebottled it thirty years later to ensure its longevity. Let us drink to the man who provided so wisely for his progeny. To Nathaniel Sutherland, Commander of the Ocean Seas. *In vino veritas!*"

We would turn and face the portrait in the ornate gold frame, lifting our silver thimbles to the young officer with gold epaulets on his jacket and black hair curling over his high, gold-encrusted collar. I half expected his snapping black eyes to wink at me. "To Commander Sutherland!" There was a burning in the throat and a warm glow as the treasured Madeira vaporized. It was like drinking history. We would have to wait a whole year for another nip of that nectar.

———

The December when I was nine, our house hummed with Julia's beaux. She was thirteen years older than I and had everything I yearned for—a soft gray squirrel coat, Grandma's gold cairngorm brooch, lace-trimmed teddies, My Sin perfume, blue satin mules edged with downy marabou. Although (as Mother kept telling me) Julia didn't drink or smoke, she was a flapper who danced a wicked Charleston and Black Bottom. Bobbed hair was the cat's meow, but she liked to be different. Her auburn hair was so long she could sit on it. She poufed it out over her ears with "rats" and pinned it into a glistening doughnut on the nape of her neck like the vamp Pola Negri. Everybody was crazy about Julia. Everybody except me.

Father called Julia's swains "goofers." He was not enchanted with any of them, but the current favorite, Raymond, had irredeemable faults. He went to Yale, he wrestled, he wore size fourteen shoes, he had a plate-rattling laugh, and he never knew when to go home. Raymond padded around after my sister with such devotion that Father referred to him as Julia's Saint Bernard.

"Your Yale goofer is always underfoot," he growled. "Doesn't he have a home?" Father and I saw eye to eye on everything.

After the Madeira ritual that Christmas afternoon, Father and Mother departed for an eggnog party. Their friends didn't think much of Prohibition either. Soon Raymond arrived, carrying a gift for Julia wrapped in silver paper.

I was nestled by the fire reading my Christmas book, *The Little Colonel's House Party.* I looked up to watch Julia, who, I had to admit, glowed in the flickering light. She untied the red velvet ribbon and, cooing like a dove, drew from the tissues a string of carved ivory beads. Raymond fastened their clasp beneath her chignon and gave her a kiss. Sickening. I went back to my book.

Some time later I heard Julia say, "Would you care for a drink, Raymond?" and Raymond answer, "Righto." I looked up again to see Raymond dropping chunks of ice into a tall glass. Then, before we realized what he was doing, he picked up the crystal decanter and poured all of the remaining 1844 Madeira over the ice. Julia gasped. She looked stunned but did not say one word. The room was very still.

A shiver ran over me. *Holy Ghost!* What will Father say? I stared wide-eyed at Julia. She wouldn't look at me. She was gazing at Raymond with a Pollyanna smile that said he was a wonderful man. But her cheeks were pale, and she was twisting her handkerchief into knots. Still she said nothing. I couldn't believe it.

Raymond, holding the tumbler in one hand, wrapped his free arm around Julia's waist and said, "Come on, girl, let's go into the kitchen." He heavy-footed through the door, pulling her along. I knew he wanted more smooching, and I was glad they were out of sight.

Nothing could be done. You can't unring a bell. I looked sadly at the empty bottle displayed on the shelf. After he filled the decanter for the last time, Father had mounted that bottle on a stand. On the brown glass a plain white label, bordered in black, read:

RARE OLD MADEIRA

IMPORTED BY

COMMANDER SUTHERLAND U.S.N.

1844

REBOTTLED 1874

What will Father say? All I could think of was his return, and in a way I longed for it. Father was at his eloquent best when he was angry, and Julia had it coming. After a while she and the Saint Bernard came back, but I pretended I was reading and didn't even look up. I bided my time.

———

It was growing dark when Mother and Father blew in out of the cold, eyes shining and snow glistening on their hair. Father took their coats to the hall and returned, kilt swinging as he whistled "Jingle Bells." I saw Raymond reach out for Julia's waist, but this time she frowned and pulled away. When Father neared the marble-topped table, he froze.

"What . . . happened . . . to . . . the . . . Madeira?" he asked. *Very, very* slowly.

Julia tried to speak casually. "I just offered Raymond a little Christmas drink." Her smile made me think of the crazy duchess in *Alice in Wonderland*. At that moment she looked as though she had never heard of the Sutherland clan motto that Father had drilled into us: *"Sans Peur."*

"A little Christmas drink?" Father's blue eyes were flashing electric sparks. There was a long silence, the quiet at the center of a cyclone when nothing moves. I held my breath.

Father stared, openmouthed, at the glass in Raymond's hand. "What is that you're drinking, young man?" he said evenly. "It's too dark for Madeira."

"Yes sir," Raymond agreed cheerfully. "It sure is. I don't like my booze straight. I always cut it with Coca-Cola." He held the drink aloft and smiled at Father. "Here's how!" he said and gulped the last of our Madeira. It won't be long now, I thought.

Father sank into a chair. He must have looked that way when he heard the Spanish-American War had quit on him before he could join Teddy Roosevelt's Rough Riders. He closed his eyes and massaged his forehead. When he exhaled a long, slow breath I imagined smoke coming out of his ears. We were all watching him, all except Raymond, who was happily crunching ice with his big teeth.

Father sat staring at the floor, quietly smoothing his Sutherland kilt with one hand and fingering his black knife with the other. I dug my fingernails into my palm, waiting for Julia to catch it.

But there was no explosion. After what seemed like forever, Father looked around with absent eyes. Then he got up in slow motion and stalked out of the room. That was all. He never said a word about the demise of his precious Madeira, then or ever. Some things are beyond speech.

Raymond came to our house only once after that. He was still mooning after Julia with those hangdog eyes, but as far as I know she never kissed him again. We may have lost the Madeira, but we got rid of Raymond.

December 1987

Let's Ration Water

Iles Brody

Monsieur le Comte de Soleillas, a gentleman living in France around 1600, had a beautiful mistress who was given to playing the prude. Today you'd call her a sourpuss. She evinced her heavy disapproval at court when she heard little jokes with cute double meanings, for harmless little sophisticated anecdotes were just as much the *bon ton* then as they are now. Well, it took a king to break down the fair lady's hypocrisy.

"This woman needs wine!" shouted King Henry IV at a state dinner when he found the count's mistress particularly strait-laced.

They brought her a gobletful of liquid ruby; she drank it all, and presently the little lady was pulling vigorously at the velvet sleeve of the monarch! "Tell me some more!" she chirped.

An ancient poet expressed even better what I have in mind: "Put a cup of wine into my hand that I may cast off from me the cloak of hypocrisy."

But I'll stop illustrating what I have in mind. I'll say it—wine is the secret ally of every host and hostess. It enlivens tedious dinner parties. It untangles one's thoughts, unties one's tongue, it stands for conviviality. It tends to strengthen and excite the spirits, cheer and comfort the languid, refresh the exhausted. It turns the dullest dinner companion into a charming and close associate. She may even seem pretty, all of a sudden.

I am waxing lyrical—but so did the poets of Greece and Rome when they wrote about wine. They attributed the invention of wine to the gods, to Osiris, Saturn, and Bacchus. Anacreon calls the juice of the grape ambrosial, and Homer deems it divine. Plato, the cautious, the sober, said that nothing more excellent than wine was ever granted by God to man.

Wine was indeed a great boon to mankind, but it wasn't altogether heaven-sent. In fact, the Egyptians were the first to know the rules for the culture and the preparation of grapes and wine. The science was inherited by the Greeks, and from them it descended to the Romans. The French came next as the true champions of wine; and now, finally, it is almost an American monopoly. This is the country that carries on today the great wine tradition.

It is no use denying that most of the things we know in gastronomy we learned from Latin countries, especially from France and Italy. The people of those two nations, whether rich or poor, always drank wine with their meals. For the first time in the history of America we can live in the same proper gastronomic fashion and be happy. The reason is that American wines today are better than ever and more abundant. We have plenty of the fine medicine. (According to Hippocrates, wine is nothing less than that; he himself prescribed it for many diseases, and advocated different types of wines for different constitutions. "Drink wine when you eat, and you'll be healthy," he said.)

This is not necessarily a treatise against water with your meals. Water is all right as a thirst quencher—but who wants to drink water to wash down oysters? Or a divine *coulibiac* of salmon? Or *boeuf bourguignonne*? Or even the lowliest stew? The habit of drinking wine with meals has lately increased tremendously, but the trouble with many Americans is that they think wine drinking during meals is a complicated affair and that it is the province and the privilege of the opulent. Drinking wine with meals is the most natural and most simple thing in the world, and much less expensive than myriads of other, inferior pleasures.

I couldn't imagine eating lunch or dinner without wine, even merely a sip of it, even a cheap *pinard*. I don't wish to lecture you on how to maintain your health while eating, for I am neither a medical man nor a nutritionist. But I am persuaded—and it sounds logical—that drinking ice water with hot meals cannot be healthy. I don't want to describe, either, what I think is going on when cold substance meets warm in your tummy; I don't like to paint unsavory pictures. (In the case of chilled wines, however, the innate fire of the wine balances the coldness.) But I want to tell you that the foremost thought in the mind of a gourmet, besides enjoying his meal (and how could he without wine, beer, or ale, as best suits his palate?), is to get up from the table light in girth. How can he accomplish that if he bloats himself with water until he fairly bursts? Water just dilutes your food—it doesn't blend with it, like wine. With all due respect to cattle, given so much to water drinking, H_2O just increases the appetite in an artificial way, and a gourmet abhors artificial stimulation.

You may remember watching children eat, children who were born cursed with reluctance in eating, unhappy youngsters who each time they swallowed a morsel, however tasty and flavorful it might be, had to wash it down with big gulps of water. When I was a youngster back in Europe, I wasn't a reluctant feeder, and I was properly educated at least in eating and drinking. I even took yeast—in the form of beer. For with the first course at luncheon, beer was always served. True, I didn't get the healthful and thirst-quenching beverage in as tall a glass as the grown-ups; but if I left as little as a half inch of it, there came the admonition: "Finish it, young man. It's good for you . . ."

A white wine, properly chilled, came next on the liquid menu. Until I was fourteen, mine was diluted with either plain or soda water. Finally I was poured a glass of red wine; and after I drank it with relish, I was still able to romp with my pony, Juliette, and my dogs, Moving Picture, a dachshund, and Foxie and Fixie, the terriers. It is an erroneous American conception that one gets drunk on wine, even when it is used in moderation. Wine, used in small quantities the way I have described from my own experience, strengthens the stomach.

To go back for historical testimony, this is exactly what Saint Paul said to Emperor Titus as he handed him a jar of light and delicate Setine.

There are very few real wine connoisseurs in this world, and so ordinary mortals should trust to their own palates to select their wines. There is a great deal of fashion and caprice in the rise and fall of wines; to rise above the ordinary it is not enough for a wine, it seems, to be possessed of real merit. Often, favorable circumstances and happy chances are needed to launch it, just as in the case of a singer or a dancer. Frequently I drink a ridiculously cheap wine and wonder why it isn't better known, when it certainly merits fame. On the other hand, an inferior wine may be popular, just because it once reached the right people and came recommended by someone who claimed to be a wine connoisseur.

I have only a few principles about wine. The first one is that I seldom drink an imported wine, no matter where I am. In France I used French wines; in Switzerland, Neuchâtel; in Austria, Vosslauer; in Italy, Montefiascone or Asti; in Hungary, Bull's Blood, and, if it came from a reputable cellar, Tokay; in England I drank Scotch, and rum in Haiti. In America I drink American wines, for more than one reason.

You see, I never believed that wines could cross the sea. As a matter of fact, I knew that there were only one or two types in France that could stand a long ocean voyage without being at least a little bit injured. (And a little injury to wine means a great deal.)

Furthermore—this statement is wholeheartedly sincere— American wines agree with me much better than any others. Here in this country, and elsewhere, I drank great wines, like a Romanée-Conti, or a Château d'Yquem, more out of curiosity than anything else, a kind of snobbishness, and because we, all of us, are collectors of rare items. But to my personal palate these great wines, no matter how expensive they were, didn't exhibit such a great deal of difference. They were made of grapes just like the cheaper ones. And the lighter, younger wines always charmed me more, to be utterly truthful. They seem to become a part of one quicker than the old and heavy wines, and they combine with food much better. The so-called fine French wines of old seemed to cause a bit of internal unpleasantness, in me at least. And when, on a few occasions, I became rebellious and said in a still, small voice that I favored an American wine to a French wine, there came admonitions from those self-appointed connoisseurs, and I kept my tongue again under control.

Today I don't have to remain silent any longer. American wines have come into their own, and I shout out loud that I love them! The other evening I played a little joke on an acquaintance of mine, a lover of *chichi*, French wine, and vintages. I poured a bottle of excellent American Burgundy into an empty bottle of Nuits-Saint-Georges, and served it with due ceremony. The gentleman, who thinks he can really judge wine better than anyone I know, held the glass against the light, contemplated the color, took a delicate whiff, and rinsed his mouth with a tiny portion. Then he stole a glance at the bottle, which I had placed so that he could see the label. He finally took a swallow, and his face, which had remained undecided during the operation, suddenly lit up. "What a wine, my boy, what a wine! Nuits-Saint-Georges! My favorite!"

My acquaintance is in love with a chimera; I can't really admire such a person. I have much more admiration for the great writer, H. G. Wells, who fairly saturated himself with native wines during his last visit to this country, saying that the best wines in the world are American, and that he simply can't understand why the lucky natives don't drink more of this liquid sunshine. That was when we still could import French wines. A war had to occur before the Americans really discovered what treasure they have in their own country.

There is a thought in that expression "liquid sunshine" that should captivate the imaginations of those who care about their health—and who doesn't? Despite its slightly "dry" taste, wine, like citrus fruit, has an alkaline ash. There are practically no carbohydrates in dry red or white table wine, but there are plenty of vitamins of the B complex group, riboflavin, thiamin, and B_1. And there is also pantothenic acid in it, which is an anti-grey-hair vitamin. Or haven't you seen the old Frenchmen or Italians of the wine regions? As a rule, they haven't a grey hair on their heads and have been drinking wine all their lives. And don't you remember the constant, gentle little smiles on their faces?

When I was a boy, I lived in a small vineyard, owned by my grandmother, during the months of September and October. In the evenings I sat with the peasants around a campfire and listened with rapt attention as the foremen told stories—the only pastime people had in those days. I can still close my eyes and see the faces of the peasants illuminated by the firelight as perfectly as though they were right before me. Those faces were kind, and simple, smiling and relaxed, free from every human pettiness and evil. They were the faces of wine-drinking people. One of the foremen often told stories concerning kings and wine. The kings' feats were always extraordinary. "Saint Stephen, coming home from battle one day, ate a whole barbecued calf and drank a barrel of Bull's Blood . . . " I believed every word of the foreman. I think I still do.

Talking of royalty, one should know that Henry VIII definitely didn't change his wine as often as he changed his wives. But of course, there is pride in proprietorship; Henry owned a few acres of vineyard in France, and was much more concerned about this small estate than about his mighty England. And I suspect that the famous regal bogyman was nothing else but a vintner at heart, in love with pretty bunches of grapes, their divine juice and excellent vintages.

There were many other royal vineyard owners, outstanding among them Charles V, François I, and Louis XIV. The latter, *le roi soleil,* was visited by a deputation from a famous wine district in 1666. "Sire," said the leader of the deputation, "we offer you our wine, our pears, our gingerbread, our biscuits, our hearts, and . . ." Louis XIV cut him short: "Well, where is the wine?"

Like kings, poets, too, hit on the truth sometimes. And I insert here the words of a forgotten one, who wished to prove that wine is even more precious than love. I almost agree with him.

> *On fait l'amour dans tous les temps,*
> *On ne fait du vin qu'en automne . . .*

October 1942

A MODEST CELLAR

Roy Brady

A wine cellar is a state of mind. I drifted into it nearly twenty years ago. At first, I simply bought an occasional bottle for a certain dinner. Then I started picking up interesting bottles here and there with no particular dinner in mind. They were stuck away in any convenient corner to await the right time. One idle Sunday afternoon I thought it would be a good idea to collect all the bottles together and see what there was. That did it. I cleared out a cabinet under the kitchen counter and gathered up the bottles, about two dozen, which half filled the cabinet. In the corner of a basement apartment near the University of Chicago the cabinet proved to be a good cellar, quiet, dark, and reasonably cool the year round. Some people would regard it as laughable to call such a cubbyhole a cellar, but it suited my purse and needs at the time. Since then, wherever we have lived in Chicago, New York, and Los Angeles, some nook has been found to house the growing collection. Now it is in an underground cellar and of a size that would have seemed preposterous twenty years ago.

After a certain point a cellar seems to take on a life of its own. For years I struggled to build up the reserve. It seemed impossible to have a real cellar on a modest income. Then I began to realize with growing astonishment that it was actually possible to accumulate more wine of one kind or another than was likely to be used before it got too old. With the collecting habit firmly entrenched, the problem could be, sometimes at any rate, having enough strength of character to reject all the good buys.

My early purchases ranged wildly, as they still do. I think the risk of a few indifferent or even bad bottles is worth taking. Sometimes a poor bottle is more instructive than a good one, and it certainly makes the next good one all the more enjoyable. There is no use in living on a mountaintop above the clouds if you never go down to see the plains. I did decide very soon to specialize to a degree, thinking it better to know a few wines well rather than many but slightly.

I had started with California wines, partly because the book that had aroused my interest in wine was about them, partly because they were easier to understand, and partly because good European wines were still scarce soon after the war. Meanwhile I became acquainted, by reading, with many European wines I had never seen. When importing began to revive, it 'was exciting to search out wines that had been only names in books. One could exclaim with Shelley: "The world's great age begins anew, / The golden years return."

The first specialization was red table wine, and Bordeaux was the obvious candidate for a reason that seems almost quaint today—it was rather inexpensive. The two great red wines are Bordeaux and Burgundy and, in the late forties, the former was distinctly cheaper and available in greater variety. I was able to try all the great first growths of Bordeaux, the châteaux Lafite, Latour, Margaux, Mouton-Rothschild, Haut-Brion, Ausone, and Cheval Blanc of the 1934 and 1937 vintages at never so much as four dollars a bottle. Only a few '24s and '29s went to five dollars, for a long time my top price. The very pleasing light vintages of 1938 and 1940 were then at their peak and much cheaper. I bought a good many bottles of Château Haut-Brion '40 at $1.96, and it seemed the very ideal of a sweet, light, fragrant claret.

It was a wonderful time to begin exploring the world of wine. Despite the enormous losses of World War II an abundance of wine had survived to maturity, and much of it came to this country at prices that seem absurdly low today. Château Cos d'Estournel '34 at $2.59, the '40 at $1.39. Château Bouscaut '40 was 95 cents. The '42s ranged from 98 cents for Château Léoville-Las-Cases all the way up to $1.89 for the great Château Latour. The greatest bargain of all was probably a beautiful Château Brane-Cantenac '24 at $1.95. Yes, it was a wonderful time. A profusion of wines that had been unavailable for years appeared on the market in all sorts of places.

To supplement red Bordeaux I chose its California counterpart, Cabernet Sauvignon. The first wine I ever bought by the case was a Beaulieu Vineyard Napa Cabernet Sauvignon '43. Until then the desire to experiment had limited purchases to one or two or three bottles of each wine. I still buy many odd bottles to experiment.

As a secondary specialty I chose Sherry, a very different wine. It is highly versatile and has the advantage of keeping in the open bottle much better than table wines. A dry one lasts for days in the refrigerator and a sweet one for weeks outside.

In 1948 I started keeping a cellar book listing purchases, dates of purchase and use, place of purchase, and price. In another book I have kept notes on wines as drunk, and both books are still going. One of the pleasures of a cellar book is in reading through it years later. Looking back to the beginning of the book I am surprised at a number of things. The first entry, a bottle of Wente Bros. Livermore Pinot Blanc '43, was on the fifth of September, 1948, and a year later the total stood at 399 bottles, rather more than I would have thought. Of course, some were for the reserve and quite a few were half bottles for sampling. It is not surprising to find that one bottle in six was a red Bordeaux, but to find almost one in four a Sherry is unexpected. On a restricted budget Sherry is attractive because it goes further than table wine. Also, in those days, merchants were still disposing of many excellent Sherries they had been forced to take on tie-in deals with liquor during the war. Good buys in Sherry were common, and I have always believed in adapting my taste to the state of the market.

After a few years we moved to a much larger, aboveground apartment, better for us but not so good for the wine. A large hall closet was convenient but a bit warm. Nevertheless, the cellar prospered and, apart from one disaster, the wine survived. The loss was a Romanée-

Conti '34 for which I had paid ten dollars after a long struggle with my conscience. By the time I noticed the leaking cork it was too late.

In its new quarters the cellar continued to grow slowly, and with a hundred bottles it seemed that an important milestone had been reached. Red Bordeaux, California Cabernet Sauvignon, and Sherry continued to predominate, but the cellar book shows that just about everything on the market was represented at some time: California reds and whites of all kinds, California Sherry, Port, Champagne, rosé, Madeira, and vermouth. There were red and white Burgundy, Sauternes, Chablis, Anjou, Rhône, Jura, Champagne, Moselle, Graves, Monbazillac, Tokay, Port, Madeira, and Beaujolais, as well as wines from Italy, Spain, Luxembourg, Greece, Sicily, Portugal, New York, Ohio, Maryland, Missouri, the Rheingau, Switzerland, Austria, Chile, and Argentina. Some became favorites and some, after one or two appearances, have not been seen again. I last bought a bottle of muscatel in 1953, and it is still in the cellar.

In 1951 we moved to California and, for a couple of years, I had nothing that could be called a cellar. Some wine was stored with a friend, but at home I lived a hand-to-mouth existence with a dozen or two bottles at a time. The next move was to a house in West Los Angeles, where an insulated closet in an unheated part of the house made a very satisfactory cellar. The mild climate near the California coast makes it easy to maintain a reasonable temperature. With a bigger and better cellar and some brightening of the financial situation I began to plan further into the future. It mostly took the form of laying down red Bordeaux and California Cabernets by the case. The mid-fifties were not so favorable as the late forties, but still halcyon days compared with the mid-sixties. The great 1945 Bordeaux reds were getting scarce. I got a case of Calon-Ségur at twenty-one dollars, half a dozen bottles of Château Mouton-Rothschild at a staggering eight dollars each, and an assorted dozen of other things. At the suggestion of a well-known New York merchant I made a case of Château Gruaud-Larose and two of Château Talbot the basis of my '47s. They were and are lovely but, like most '47s, relatively short-lived and now past their best. Still, a good wine drunk regularly over a long period becomes a valued friend, always welcome though getting feeble. The search after older vintages led to some neglect of the then easily found and excellent '49s. A couple of cases of Château Pichon-Longueville were a good start, and one of Château Lynch-Bages, lately become fashionable and costly, was a fine buy at nineteen dollars. Various half dozens and odd bottles of the first growths and others rounded out a nice little collection of '49s which I have used sparingly so that many remain.

The 1950 vintage did not enjoy much of a reputation in its youth; there were better years before and after it, so prices held to attractive levels. I bought most of the first growths and others by the case, as little as twenty dollars for Château Margaux, and used them freely. The next year had a very poor reputation, and I explored cautiously. On the basis of the 1940 and 1944 vintages I had got the idea that Château Haut-Brion was especially successful in "off" years and I invested in the '51. After a promising start each bottle seemed harder and more bitter than its predecessor, and I was glad to see the end. I missed out on Château Latour, which has proved to be the star of the year.

Then came the famous pair, 1952 and 1953. By the time they were on the market I had decided to buy a case of each first growth in good years and of châteaux Latour and Mouton-Rothschild in every year. That plan did not last long. The destructive freeze in February 1956, the small vintage of hard wines in 1957, the short-lived little wines of 1958, and the highly touted 1959 vintage successively drove prices upward until I gave up. After buying widely among the '52s, '53s, and '55s, I dropped back to only half a case of Château Mouton-Rothschild in 1959 and a third of a case in 1961. The other big names are down to a bottle or two each. I don't suppose that I will ever buy these wines by the case again, nor the lesser growths very often. Between the vintages of 1945 and 1961 prices have tripled.

At the same time, I was laying down California Cabernets of every vintage, especially from Beaulieu, Inglenook, Krug, and Hallcrest, in amounts up to five cases of the remarkable 1951 Private Reserve from Beaulieu. Now, on these too, I have somewhat backed off though not so much for price. Growing demand and lagging grape supplies have been forcing these wines on the market younger and younger. Cabernets made to be attractive when young cannot always be depended upon to improve greatly with age. Pleasing to begin with, they may not repay keeping. The producers, knowing that most people drink their wines soon after buying them, feel they must adapt.

After six years the West Los Angeles house was too small for the family, and the cellar was too small for the five hundred bottles. I was beginning to store wine with the merchants from whom it was bought. In the new house there was simply no place for a cellar. The bulk of the wine was stored in a friend's Bel Air cellar for more than two years while I looked for a permanent place to keep it. I did finally find a new cellar, much the best yet, underground and ample in size.

The years without a cellar were a period of rapid growth. When they were over, wine was stored from Boston to Beverly Hills. I had added eight dozen vintage Ports, including many of the excellent 1945 vintage from Sandeman, Silva & Cosens (Dow's), and Warre. There were several dozen very old Madeiras and a half dozen bottles of the splendid Imperial Pemartin Sherry from Sandeman. Red and white Burgundies had begun to appear in greater quantities, and there was a modest collection of Sauternes such as Château Coutet '52. It was frustrating to be unable to get at most of the wine, especially the old stock stored with the friend, but at least I was secure in the knowledge that it was safely stored under nearly ideal conditions.

I did finally find a new cellar, much the best yet, underground and ample in size. In the fall of 1961 I was looking forward to moving all the wine into the new cellar as soon as bins could be built to receive it. On the clear windy morning of November seventh I left the house full of pleasant thoughts about the neat arrangement of bins with everything accessible. I had an errand to do before crossing the Santa Monica Mountains for the office. I noticed a thin column of smoke rising from the mountains—a minor brush fire probably. An hour later when I started toward the hills smoke was billowing up in the wind—it might be something of a fire at that. At the foot of the hills the police had closed the road, the very road where the wine was stored. With mild concern I doubled back to a telephone and called my friend. Was the fire anywhere near? "Next door . . . can't talk . . . leaving now," he gasped, and the line went dead. It was the great twenty-million-dollar Bel Air fire that destroyed 450 houses that day.

I was too busy to get any further news until I saw my friend late in the afternoon, but the vast cloud of smoke stretching the length of Los Angeles was there for all to see. The firemen had warned my friends to get out. When they threw a few things into the car and started off the house next door was blazing wildly, and in a few moments they lost sight of their own house in the swirling smoke and ash. News reports showed that their house was near the center of the disaster. It could not have survived. The old vintage Ports, the ancient Madeiras, the clarets of 1949, 1947, and 1945, the . . . I didn't want to think about it. They were just puffs of steam in that sooty cloud above.

When we were able to get in next day we found nothing of the house next door but the chimney. A dozen more down the street were like it—but my friend's house had a slightly scorched railing along the patio, no other damage. The wines slumbered peacefully down below. Since then I am less reluctant about opening a rare bottle. Once it has done its duty at table and become a happy memory it is safe.

As quickly as possible I moved into the new cellar. The fifteen hundred bottles of today only half fill it, and I do not anticipate further growth. Reactions to it vary from "Good heavens, you'll never be able to drink all that!" (from a person who never bought two bottles of wine at the same time) to "Yes, it's a nice little working cellar" (from a wine merchant).

Once I had the new cellar, I began to do a little more drinking than buying. I had found that having too much old wine on hand not only risks spoilage, but it inhibits trying new things. Too much time spent attending to the senile and the moribund leaves too little for new acquaintances, and a good part of the delight of wine is in the new—new vintages, wines from new places, and wines heard of but not seen before. I enjoy having plenty of old friends in the cellar, but I like to have empty bins for the unexpected guests, too.

For similar reasons, wine adds to the interest of travel. Instead of drinking familiar wines I look for new ones. Last fall I started one afternoon to drive from Paris to Antwerp. Traffic was very heavy, and by the time I was a little beyond Soissons it was quite dark. I stopped to consult *Michelin* for a place to stay. The Hotel du Lion Rouge in Soissons listed still Champagnes as a specialty. I had never had one, since they are not exported, but I had read about them in Longfellow's often-quoted verse and elsewhere. There was no doubt as to where I would stay that night even if it meant a bit of backtracking. I studied the wine list first (I always do) and ordered a half bottle each of white Mesnil and red Bouzy. On the menu specialties were listed in block letters. There was ANDOUILLETTE SOISSONNAISE, a smoked sausage of various things not calculated to please everybody. When I ordered it the head-waiter exclaimed, "Oh, sir, it's not for you! It is made from the insides of pigs!" If it was a local specialty it was for me, whatever it was made from. I persisted, and it was good. Then I saw they had *vin de paille,* the famous and rare dessert wine made from partially dried grapes in the Jura, so I had to try that, too. When I ordered coffee it occurred to me that they might have a *marc de Champagne.* I was not sure that I had even heard of such a thing, but we were near the Champagne country, and it was reasonable to expect that there, as in most wine districts, they would make a brandy from the grape skins. They did. Another first! Next morning I drove off in the rain and gloom feeling it had been a very successful stop.

———

If I were starting a cellar today it would be rather different from the one began twenty years ago. The great wines of Bordeaux, Burgundy, and Germany would still be there, but in much smaller numbers. So would the Cabernets of California. In Bordeaux and Burgundy I would buy mostly '61s and '62s, a few '59s, and a few older vintages if they could be found at tolerable prices. I would include some of the light, pleasing clarets of 1960 for immediate use, and a considerable variety of the less famous and less costly wines of France, Germany, and California—wines like Beaujolais, Pouilly-Fuissé, Pouilly Fumé, and others not so well known. Nor would I ignore Italy, Spain, and Portugal. And there are often good values in the well-known wines of "off" years, the years that get low numbers on the vintage charts. With modern techniques of disease control in the vineyard and improved winemaking, genuinely bad vintages are almost a thing of the past. An "off" year is more of an opportunity for the careful buyer than a misfortune.

My cellar is slowly moving in exactly this direction. I use the great wines sparingly. Replacement by younger vintages is not quite so rapid as use. At the same time, lesser wines are increasing. A few years ago it would hardly have been possible to follow this policy because the lesser wines were not widely available except as doubtful bargains. Now that prices on the great wines have gone so high, merchants find it profitable to search out good lesser wines their customers can afford to enjoy regularly. One London firm has founded a very successful business on an exclusive specialization in the less known but delightful wines of the Loire, Provence, Bergerac, and of the more obscure villages of Burgundy, Bordeaux, and the Rhône Valley. This is good for everybody. Consumers who are forced to save the great wines for very special occasions can still afford good wines for everyday use. Merchants who find the great wines difficult to sell are making money on the lesser ones, and producers, basking in the newfound attention, are encouraged to make better wines.

It is a change, but I, for one, do not regret that it is no longer possible to open a Château Lafite for Sunday night supper *en famille*. That little Côtes-de-Fronsac from across the way is very nice, too. In California wines Cabernet Sauvignon does not appear on the table so often as it did, but there are plenty of less expensive Gamays, Zinfandels, Barberas, Charbonos, and even good blends from the top producers to take its place.

November 1965

DANDELION WINE

Ray Bradbury

On this one special afternoon in the great oasis of summer, the dandelions flooded the world, dripped off lawns into brick streets, tapped softly at crystal cellar windows, blew and agitated themselves so that on every side lay this green lake, dazzling and glittering with molten sun.

The boys picked the golden flowers.

"I encourage them," Grandfather said. "For two weeks, at the very heart of summer, the lawn mower is banished! Let the dandelions *run*, I say! Run amuck, like a herd of African lions in the yard. A beautiful flower. So common, however, that we have forgotten how beautiful it is. Why, look right at it and it'll burn a hole in your eye."

Plucked tenderly, one by one, the dandelions, in sacks, pots, and pans, were carried to the cellar. In great buckets of sunshine they arrived. The cellar glowed with them.

The wine press opened. A golden bushel of flowers poured in. The, press, replaced with the large rotating screw, personally twirled and twisted by Grandfather, gently squeezed upon the harvest. "There," he murmured. "So."

And before long, the golden tide, the essence of wild summer, of the good fair months, trickled and then ran and then rushed from the spout below. A clear essence, like a breath of July, the color of stars on August nights, gathered to be crocked and waited on, to be worked, to be skimmed of ferment, to be bottled in crystal and cut glass, and shelved and ranked in glittering rows in cellar gloom.

Dandelion wine.

The words were summer on the tongue. The wine was summer in a bottle. It was all the warm afternoons and the cloudless skies, stoppered tight; to be opened, said the label, on a January day with snow falling fast. To be drunk, was the intimation, when the sun had gone unseen in thirty-nine days. Then let those who seek after summer tiptoe with stealth into the dim twilight nether world of the cellar and put up a hand.

There row upon row, with the soft gleam of flowers open at morning, with the light of a June sun glowing through a faint skin of dust, lies the dandelion wine. Uncork it, hold it up, peer through it at the wintry day. The snow is melted to grass, the trees are reinhabited with bird, leaf, and blossom, like a continent of butterflies breathing on the air. The sky is colored from gray to blue.

Hold summer in your hand, pour summer in a glass, take a great sniff of the wine and change the season in your veins by the simple expedient of raising the glass to your lips and tilting summer in.

"All right, now, to the rain barrel!"

Nothing else in the world would do but the rare waters which had been summoned from the sweet lakes far away and the sweet fields of grassy dew on early mornings, lifted to the open sky, carried in laundered clusters nine hundred miles, brushed with wind, electrified with high voltage, and condensed upon cool air. This water, falling through space, gathered still more of the heavens in its crystals. Taking something of the east wind and the west wind and the north wind and the south, the water made rain and the rain would soon be well on its way to wine.

Douglas ran with the dipper. He plunged it deep in the rain barrel. This water must be carried in dipper and bucket down to the cellar, there to be ladled in freshets, in mountain streams, upon the dandelion harvest.

Even Grandma, when snow was whirling fast, dizzying the world, blinding windows, stealing breath from gasping mouths, even Grandma, one day in February, would vanish to the cellar.

Above, in the vast house, there would be coughings, sneezings, wheezings, and groans, childish fevers, throats raw as butcher's meat, noses like bottled cherries, the stealthy microbe everywhere.

Then, rising from the cellar like a June goddess, Grandma would come, something hidden but obvious under her knitted shawl. This, carried to every miserable room upstairs and down, would be dispensed with aroma and clarity into neat glasses, to be swigged neatly. The medicines of another time, the balm of sun and idle August afternoons, a wind from the Hebrides, the faintly heard sounds of ice wagons passing on brick avenues, the rush of silver skyrockets and the fountaining of lawn mowers moving through ant countries, all these, all these in a glass.

Yes, even Grandma, drawn to the cellar of winter for a June adventure, to stand alone and quietly, in secret conclave with her own soul and spirit, as did Grandfather and Father and Uncle Bert, or some of the boarders, communing with a last touch of a calendar long departed, with the picnics and the warm rains and the smell of fields of wheat and new popcorn and bending hay. Even Grandma, repeating and repeating the fine and golden words, even as they were said now in this moment when the flowers were dropped into the press, as they would be repeated every winter for all the winters in time. Saying them over and over on the lips, like a smile, like a sudden patch of sunlight in the dark.

Dandelion wine. Dandelion wine. Dandelion wine.

June 1953

Pinot Noir: A Love Story

James Rodewald

More than twenty years ago, on a busy fall night, I lost my heart for
the first time. I was behind the bar at a small restaurant in Rhinebeck,
New York, mixing drinks, opening beers, answering the phone—the
usual bartender routine. A Culinary Institute of America student had
dropped a cassette on the bar on his way in. In the year or so I'd been
tending bar there, he'd been in five or six times. He often brought his
own wine, and he always brought music to woo his date by. I didn't
know his name, but I was always glad to see him—it meant a short
respite from the usual sound track. As this particular dinner hour
wound down and the serious drinkers settled in for the long night
ahead, a waitress brought me a nearly empty wine bottle and told me
it was from "the Culinary Institute guy."

I'd been out of college a year, and wine was not high on my drinks
menu. I'd had plenty of the jug stuff, and it did what it was supposed
to do; I'd certainly tried "serious" wine, but it usually seemed unpleas-
antly sour and bitter. I was about to experience a paradigm shift.

———

My dinner break rolled around, and as I ducked under the bar, I saw
the wine bottle. In a corner of the now empty dining room I took a sip.
I was dumbfounded. It tasted like nothing I knew. The wine wasn't

bitter or sour. It wasn't sweet, exactly, at least not like the Mountain Nectar I'd gotten used to—it tasted like a mouthful of ripe fruit. The bottle said "Pinot Noir" and "Domaine Laurier." Sounded French. Why wasn't it mouth puckering and thin like the bottle of Bordeaux our busgirl had liberated from her parents' cellar? Was it because, as it also said on the label, it was from Sonoma County? The whole thing was baffling. And I had to eat my dinner and get back to work.

For months I looked for a bottle of Domaine Laurier Pinot Noir. When I finally found one and brought it home, I couldn't bring myself to open it—it seemed too special. Seven years and many thousands of miles later, I stumbled upon a reference to Laurier in a newspaper column. The story mentioned the winemaker there: Merry Edwards. I decided to open the 1979 Domaine Laurier Pinot Noir I'd carried back and forth across the country in the trunk of my car. You can guess what I found—complete and utter disappointment. There was no fruit, barely any color. I'd killed it.

As the years went by and I grew more interested in wine, I occasionally came across Edwards's name in connection with wineries other than Laurier, and so I bought wines from Olivet Lane, Pellegrini, and Nelson Estate. More recently, if I saw a Merry Edwards Pinot Noir on a restaurant wine list, I always ordered it. Her wines seemed to have finesse and elegance without sacrificing intensity or fruit. They weren't flashy and they didn't hit you over the head. They seemed to complement good food perfectly.

On a recent trip to the Russian River Valley, where Edwards has, after more than twenty-five years of making wine for others, established her own vineyards, I finally got to meet the person responsible for my love of wine. She was as intense and direct as her wine. Nothing about her operation suggested a winemaking superstar. I was particularly surprised by her personal wine cellar, which was about the size of a small walk-in closet. Although modest, it held the up-and-down road map of Edwards's career—great bottles, a few labels that had fallen victim to corporate takeovers, much critical acclaim, and plenty of struggles. Trying to sound nonchalant, I asked if there might still be a bottle of the 1979 Domaine Laurier Pinot Noir. Edwards's husband, Ken Coopersmith, looked a little puzzled but gamely poked around a bit. He pulled out a Laurier from 1990. "Um, I don't think Merry was at Laurier then."

I let it go, not wanting to seem pushy. We shared a glorious home-cooked meal, accompanied, needless to say, by a delicious bottle of Pinot Noir. The excitement of finally meeting Edwards almost obscured the nagging sense that I had apparently gotten a key fact wrong. A few days later, the afterglow had faded, but the question remained. I got on the phone, working my way back through the various winemakers at Laurier. I arrived quickly at the Merry Edwards years, 1989 to 1991. It was true, she hadn't made wine at Laurier until years after my eureka moment. My emotions ran the gamut from confusion to sadness to betrayal. Of course it wasn't her fault, but how to explain my deep attachment to the wines I had always thought she'd made? Had I been blinded by my first crush? And who, in fact, had made that wine? I kept working the phone. Eventually I found Steve Test, now the winemaker at Merryvale (no connection to my Merry). He worked at Domaine Laurier starting in February of 1980, and he bottled the 1979. Who, I asked him, made the 1979? "The original winemaker there was Terry Leighton," Test replied. "He was a professor of microbiology at Berkeley. I know he was there in 1978, and I think he was still there in 1979. Kalin Cellars is his winery now." I tracked down the number and called. This had to be it. I'd reached the end of the line. The phone rang. A machine picked up. I left a message. I waited. And while I waited, I went out and bought a bottle of the Kalin Cellars Cuvée DD Sonoma Pinot Noir 1994 (astonishingly, it was the current release). It was strange, but delicious—full of wild aromas and flavors, changing with every sip.

He never called back. Love hurts.

February 2005

CINDERELLA'S BOTTLE

Kate Coleman

When the bell rang, I was up to my elbows in mashed parsnips. It was New Year's Eve, and I'd promised to bring a dish to my sister's house. Opening the door, I was happy—and somewhat relieved—to see my friend David Tanis, then the chef of Chez Panisse. He thrust a bottle wrapped in flashy silver and black paper into my hands. "Happy New Year," he said, with a big smile.

"Oh, you're a dear. C'mon in. You can help me figure out what to do with all these parsnips." David was on his way home across the Bay to San Francisco after menu consultations at César, the tony tapas restaurant next door to Chez P. He set the gift bottle on the end of my butcher block and looked around the kitchen for inspiration, seizing immediately on a wreath of southwestern dried chiles hanging from a wire basket and a knob of fresh young ginger.

"Toast these chiles and crumble them over the top," he commanded, like the cooking guru he is. I busied myself toasting the chiles, and soon the kitchen was filled with their sweet pungency. (I love these spontaneous moments when David turns his culinary genius to my pathetic cooking attempts.)

As he started to chop the ginger, I stripped the holiday wrapping from the bottle. The label looked like old parchment. Its typography was aristocratic. I saw a number and a lot of French words.

"David, what is this?" I asked. "It looks too good!"

He spun around. "Wait a minute, lemme see that."

What? He didn't know what wine he'd just given me?

"Oh jeez!" he said, rolling his eyes. "You've got to promise me something. That you invite me over to share this with you when you open it."

I laughed. "Hey, take it back. I don't mind. So, David . . . just how good is it?"

He sounded almost funereal: "Very, very, very good."

"Like what, couple of hundred?" I wasn't a poor slum goddess for nothing.

"More."

"Five?"

"Let's just say it's very good wine indeed."

We examined the label closely. (I learned the following day from my adorable French wine importer, Sylvie Sullivan—who is Burgundian and comes by her knowledge of wine direct from the soil up to the top of her curly head—that the wine, a Burgundy, was a Musigny from Domaine Comte Georges de Vogüé, 1961, with its own reserve number: 002840.) David, who also knows his Burgundies, thought it could easily go for $1,000 at wine auction. Or more.

How had he come by such a treasure? He had been at the tapas joint, he told me, when one of the silent partners had arrived to deliver holiday gifts and bonuses. This man was something of a freak of good fortune. Not only had he won millions in the state lottery, but he'd been blessed with a dot-com entrepreneurial bonanza. He had given David the wine rather casually, and David had passed it along to me without actually looking at the label. ("Better you than the parking attendant," he said.)

We made a pact: We would organize a dinner around the consumption of the wine. David; his partner, Randal; and me. Just the three of us.

It is almost a year later, and tomorrow, Sunday, is the day of our ritual bottle opening. I am to cook a lamb shank dinner, for which I plan to shop this afternoon.

David calls. "Listen, we just went to the farmers market and we've got a ton of gorgeous food: a Hoffman chicken, beautiful vegetables. What if we cooked the dinner over here at my place tonight?"

I'm all for it. Good God, I'd be relieved of cooking for one of the great Bay Area chefs. But I worry about transporting the wine, possibly shaking up the sediment.

"Don't worry," says David. "Just carry it with great care."

I dress with great care, too, because this evening is a rare luxury for a freelance writer who, these days, with the continuing deregulation of California's energy industry, is loath even to turn on the heat. Luckily, I have my dead aunt Valerie's plush fox-fur collar and I wear it—both to accessorize the wine and for warmth.

"What a fabulous fur!" Randal exclaims, ushering me into their cozy kitchen. We are all excited as we unwrap the carefully swathed bottle.

"Shouldn't we decant it?" I ask, betraying my ignorance.

Randal, a wine snob of the best sort, demurs. "With Burgundies this old, this good, you never decant."

"Should we let it breathe?"

"No way. You open it at the precise moment you're ready to drink it. Wines like this can turn quickly once they're opened."

"Oh my goodness. Who knew you're supposed to guzzle down a thousand-dollar bottle of wine!" I exclaim.

Burgundies, Randal explains, are pure Pinot Noir and thus very unstable. It's like getting a blast of something rare . . . and then it's gone. Plain old Bordeaux from Cabernet grapes or Merlot can last almost forever, but Burgundies are the stuff of dreams. So we open something else to start. A rosé.

Randal tastes it. "Funky," he declares disdainfully.

David takes a sniff. "Ugh." And pours it down the sink. A new bottle is opened. Randal smells, grimaces, tastes. "I dunno. What do you think?" He pours a taste for David.

David inhales, sips, and pronounces this one acceptable. I am relieved, as I'm afraid this might start a pattern of tossing wines down the sink.

Both Randal and David have warned me not to get my hopes up about the ultimate bottle. "It could very well be vinegar by now. It happens," cautions Randal. "Musigny's Comte Georges de Vogüé is known for great, perfect wines, but you never know how it has been transported or stored."

The homey, organic, free-range chicken in David's pot-au-feu begins to offer up its own tantalizing scent. First we eat bright radishes, their decorative stems attached, along with olives and salami from David's favorite charcuterie in Paris (where he and Randal had vacationed just the week before). Randal shows me pictures from their trip, mainly of their dog, an Asta look-alike that must have wowed the Parisian pooches. David chops parsley and watercress for a sauce for the leeks, carrots, celery root, and greens.

Finally the big moment arrives. We are seated at the table. David has served each of us portions of chicken and vegetables, ladling golden broth over the top. And now, at last, it's time.

Randal gently peels off the bottle's leaded top. Gingerly he inserts the corkscrew and begins to twist. The cork plops down into the bottle. "Uh-oh. Not good," he says. David and I, watching, are nervous. Randal quickly pours a small taste into David's wineglass and hands it to him. I detect the aroma of the wine filtering into the room. His nose over the glass's edge, David inhales deeply. "Aaaahhhh."

He sips.

"Oh God," he wails, as if stricken. Oh heck, I think, sensing disaster. "Aaaahhhh. It's delicious. It's fabulous. Incredible!"

We laugh with joy and relief.

Randal pours again, with infinite care, for each of us.

We toast the generosity of David's Chez Panisse partner, the wine itself, and each other. As I raise my glass, my nose is filled with attar and the scent of all things darkly and deliciously mysterious. The bouquet is transporting. The taste is complicated, earthy, a texture of velvet—or butter. Like licorice one minute, like truffle the next. It is the smoothest, most wonderful wine I have ever drunk. And it is different with each sip, teasing the senses with ephemeral, heavenly tastes . . . and a hint of sex.

———

We can hardly bear to put our glasses down. But we do. As we eat our peasant fare, we sip a king's ransom in wine, and I know with each gulp that I shall never imbibe its like again.

But I don't want to gulp. I want this moment and this wine to last. Randal pours us each another glass of our beautiful Burgundy. This one tastes even better, if that's possible. (Sylvie confirms that I have been the Cinderella drinker of the night, for the wine served mid-bottle of this vintage treasure is, indeed, the best of all.)

But all too soon the wine is breaking down. David, reaching the sediment first, reports the change. I quickly quaff my glass for fear the magic will disappear.

Droplets are left in David's glass.

"It's going . . . going . . . gone," he says sadly.

"What does it taste like now?" I ask. He dips in his tongue, a hummingbird's taste.

"Now it's down to prunes and mothballs . . . "

I quote the Bard: "O, what a falling-off was there." But I know, sitting comfortably in the parlor after dinner, that I have safely sealed and corked the memory of this extraordinary bottle—to be decanted pleasurably at leisure for the rest of my life.

February 2003

A WORLD OF WINE

THE WINES OF NAPLES

Frank Schoonmaker

Nineteen centuries ago, before the destruction of Pompeii, and during the Golden Age of Rome, the most famous wine in the world was produced, not in Burgundy or Bordeaux or the Champagne country, not on the banks of the Rhine or by the storied isles of Greece. It came from a great hill a little to the north of what is now Naples, and it was called Falernum.

Many of those who served with the American Fifth Army (particularly with the British Tenth Corps and the American Sixth) will remember the hill, though probably without affection. It rises out of the coastal plain between the Volturno and the Garigliano rivers, not far from Formia, and it is called Monte Massico. Its vineyards, ravaged by wars without number, still yield a few fairly respectable wines (both red and white) called, even today, Falerno. These, like most of the wines of the province of Campania, are agreeable and interesting but short-lived, and surely have little or nothing in common with their illustrious Roman ancestor.

For, to judge from the evidence that has come down to us, the Falernum of the ancients must have been something altogether extraordinary. The poet Martial called it "immortal," and Pliny writes of having tasted, in A.D. 71, a Falernian wine of the famous Opimian vintage (named after the Roman consul of that year) which was then 192 years old. It was made from a special variety of grape which could not be successfully cultivated elsewhere and which is unknown, or at least cannot be identified, today. There were three distinct *crus,* or vineyard districts, the most celebrated being around what is now the village of Falciano. The wine, mentioned by almost every Latin author of consequence, was described by Horace and Tibullus, by Persius, Columella, and many others, in terms which (if we all spoke Latin) we would reserve for Chambertin and Château Latour today—*indomitum, ardens, nigrum, austerum, firmum, olens,* and so on.

Alas for progress! The red Falerno of modern times is fairly full-bodied, sturdy, not unlike a sound Châteauneuf-du-Pape, certainly no better, if indeed as good; the white is clean and pale and dry, on the order of a Pouilly-Fuissé.

Fortunately, if the Romans had their villas at Pompeii and their cellars full of the best Falernum, we today have our compensations—a Vesuvius which is for the moment as tame as a volcano can be, *spaghetti con vongole* in a restaurant on the waterfront, Pompeii itself and the wonderful museum of Naples, the Amalfi Drive, and a whole collection of wines—none very great, all very gay, all at their best young and none very expensive.

This is perhaps just as well. Naples today is hardly the sort of place that would lend itself to the dignified and careful consideration of ancient bottles—it is too full of life and fun and noise; the city and the whole bay look like the backdrop for a second-rate opera, brought surprisingly to life. There is certainly no place else on earth where one can listen, with pleasure, as I have, to fifteen or twenty repetitions of "Santa Lucia" and "O Sole Mio" on a restaurant terrace. Of course this may be, and often is, due to a bottle or so of Capri, or Lacrima Christi, or Gragnano, or *vino rosato* from Ravello.

These present-day wines of Naples, unlike Falerno, no longer come from north of the city, but from the slopes of Vesuvius, from the Sorrentine peninsula and from the islands. You can see all of these from Naples itself—Ischia and Capri bounding on the north and south that incomparable bay, the long finger of hills stretching out toward Capri behind Sorrento, and Vesuvius, quiescent ever since its destructive eruption of 1944. In other words these wines are produced practically in what might be called the suburbs of a city of a million people—most of them are consumed locally, as could be expected, but for those that the Neapolitans see fit to send us we may well be grateful, since they are very good indeed.

A few wine lovers, generally those of a romantic turn of mind, will tell you that these wines "do not travel." The truth is that the wines travel very well, but the view does not. What seems wonderful on a summer evening in a little restaurant on the enchanted Island of Capri, or on a flower-hung terrace at Ravello, is inevitably less beguiling when tasted in Indianapolis or New York.

On the other hand it sometimes seems to me that these wines, so full of the aroma and the charm of the country that produced them, could be for returned travelers not unlike the little *madeleine* which, for Proust, unlocked a whole library of memories. If one can be content, for the moment, with a magnificent fragment, and not the whole picture, then surely a bottle of Capri is Capri in miniature, a bottle of Gragnano is Sorrento, and Lacrima Christi is all Naples.

Of course there are lesser wines as well, many of them nameless when they come to the table, but nevertheless good, and a few of definite origin that you will find in and around Naples although rarely if ever in America. One that could quite possibly become popular in this country is a light, pale, rather tart white wine made near Caserta and called Asprino—it was a favorite with the GIs, to whom it was known almost unavoidably as "Aspirin." Another, which I have tasted only two or three times, but found interesting and even excellent, is the red Aglianico del Vulture from near Potenza. A third is the charming *vin rosé* produced around the enchanting village of Ravello, back of Amalfi—this last is a nice little wine but in no sense a distinguished one, and almost inevitably disappointing when tasted in the United States by those who first made its acquaintance at the Hotel Caruso, which, in Ravello, commands one of the noblest and loveliest views of all Italy.

And so back to Capri, Gragnano, and Lacrima Christi.

Gragnano, which is pronounced Gran-yon-o, is certainly the best red wine made in Italy south of Rome, and to my palate it has only some six or seven rivals among the best red wines of the whole country, including those of Chianti, Valpolicella, and Piedmont. Like Beaujolais, with which it has much in common, it should be drunk fairly young, for it has an inimitable freshness and fruit, and I know of nothing better with pizza, or with the Mozzarella cheese out of which the best pizza is made. It comes from a tiny village called Gragnano, back in the range of hills which separates the Bay of Naples from the Bay of Salerno, not too far as the crow flies but a long way by road, from Sorrento and Amalfi.

Capri wine, in theory at least, comes from the Island of Capri. As might be expected of an island wine, it is at its best with fish, for it is dry, sometimes even a little tart, pale gold in color, fragrant, with a bouquet that is intriguing and could almost be described as spicy. When well iced it is wonderfully thirst-quenching and, as a good many visitors to Capri have learned, some to their sorrow, it can be treacherous if consumed in large quantities on a hot day. Since there is hardly such a thing as a level road or path on the whole island, and since the temptation to walk or climb in surroundings of such beauty is almost irresistible, and since the sun generally shines on Capri, and since, finally, the drinking water, which is mostly rainwater kept in cisterns, is far from good, the per capita consumption of Capri wine by tourists often reaches quite extraordinary proportions.

Incidentally, a small quantity of red Capri is produced, but of most of it, the less said the better.

The Island of Capri is supposed to have, and indeed has, its own special enchantments, but for sheer magic nothing can quite equal its production of "Capri" wine; the vineyards are tiny, picturesque terraces on a crowded island; the traditional thirst of the islanders themselves is matched only by that of the travelers who arrive once or twice daily by boat from Naples. And yet you will find "Capri" in copious supply not only in Naples but all over Italy, and even here in the United States.

If the truth must be told, and it should be, very little Capri wine comes from Capri, and it is not certain by any means that the best of it is not produced elsewhere, including a good deal of what is served in the better hotels and restaurants of Capri and Anacapri. This is all quite legal, according to Italian law, which defines the zone of production of Capri wine as far more extensive than the original island, just as French law permits Bordeaux wines to be made well outside the city limits of Bordeaux. As a matter of fact, Italian experts have long claimed that the best Capri came from the Island of Ischia, Capri's larger and less famous sister island to the north. The only wholly authentic Capri that I know is that served at the Hotel Caesar Augustus in Anacapri, which comes from the hotel's own vineyard. I am certainly not prepared to say that it is better than the wine shipped by Giuseppe Scala, for example, most of which, I imagine, comes from Ischia or the mainland.

Of course we do not know what wine the Emperor Tiberius, who built the modest total of twelve villas on the Island of Capri, preferred with his far from Spartan fare. Doubtless it was Falernum in the way of red wine; but under the perennial azure of Capri's sky and with the freshly caught creatures of its azure sea, it is a little hard to believe that Tiberius, even in his maddest moments, could have wished for anything except Capri Bianco. Yet even a Roman emperor, with ten thousand slaves at his beck and call, could not in those days produce a bucket of ice, and we can be reasonably sure that the Capri we drink today is a great deal more agreeable.

Lacrima Christi is one of those non-geographical, obviously contrived wine names which a good many of us have learned to regard with a certain amount of distrust. They rarely mean anything definite, as to origin or type of quality—we nevertheless have "Bull's Blood" (Egri Bikaver) from Hungary, "Blood of Judas" (Sangue di Giuda) from northern Italy, as well as "Milk of the Blessed Virgin" (Liebfraumilch) from the Rhineland, and "Tears of Christ" (Lacrima Christi), which is produced not only around Naples, but as a sparkling wine in Piedmont, in northwestern Italy, and as a rather sweet dessert wine around Malaga, in southern Spain. It may be well to add that nothing conceivably sacrilegious is either intended or implied by these names—most of them were first used as altar wines.

It is reasonably certain that the original Lacrima Christi was produced (as it still is) on the western slopes of Vesuvius. Today it is a wine, a white wine (some reds are so labeled but they are much less good) not too unlike a Capri, but softer and less austerely dry, perhaps the best Italian equivalent of a dry Graves; it is made from the *Greco della Torre* grape, grown on volcanic soil. Not by any means great, it is extremely agreeable, soft, delicate, and fine, but scarcely fabulous.

One story is that a German tourist, tasting the wine in an inn at the foot of Vesuvius, exclaimed, "Dear Lord, why did not you weep in Germany?" This may have been a unique example of Teutonic gallantry. Another story again tells us that Lucifer, or Satan, when thrown out of Heaven, somehow had the good fortune to fall in the Bay of Naples, perhaps carrying a part of Paradise with him, since this district has long been called *"un pezzo di cielo caduto in terra,"* a "piece of Heaven fallen on Earth."

Satan's influence, as we all know, is considerable, and eventually the country around Naples became known as *"un paradise abitato dei demoni,"* or "a paradise peopled by devils." Returning to earth on one occasion, the Savior saw the state of affairs, and wept. Where his tears fell, vines sprouted, and these vines, on the southern and western slopes of Vesuvius, produce Lacrima Christi.

All this is very charming and it adds, perhaps, a certain glamour to a wine which would be, even without it, very good. Whatever the opinion of Lucifer and of German tourists, genuine Lacrima Christi is part of Vesuvius and Naples and Campania, one of the charms of a paradise which, despite the proverb, is peopled by some of the gayest and most friendly human beings on the face of the globe.

June 1954

THE WINES OF ITALY

Hugh Johnson

To the perpetual student of wine, which I am happy enough to be, one of the fascinations is that for each country he has to learn a complete new discipline—a new language, a new culture, a new set of standards. He must avoid the temptation to make comparisons across frontiers. It is as pointless to compare Italian wine with French as it is to compare spaghetti with *pommes frites*. They don't set out to be the same. They don't grow on the same tree. Each is a self-contained experience well worth getting to know.

Can one say that any wine tastes Italian? I think one can. Although it seems improbable that a common thread of flavor should run through the produce of a country eight hundred miles long, and even of its offshore islands, there *is* something—it must be the culture of Italy expressed through one of its oldest artifacts—that Italy's wines have in common. Can one describe it? Only in terms of warmth and ripeness: at its best an exquisite underlying sweetness; at its worst flatness and bitterness.

It's easier, perhaps, to generalize about its function than its taste. For vital as wine is, it plays a supporting role at the Italian table. The sensuous, varied, vivid food of Italy comes unmistakably first.

Only recently have the Italians themselves started to take their wine industry seriously. In the mid-sixties Italy overtook France as the world's biggest wine producer. At about the same time, a new wine law, the start of a series that is still lengthening every month, came into being. It became clear that, to expand exports, something along the lines of the French laws of Appellation d'Origine Contrôlée was needed—some guarantee of quality and origin. Without going into technical details, it is enough for the moment to say that Denominazione di Origine Controllata (D.O.C.) was the phrase the government coined. Each established wine area had to apply for the right to use the phrase on its labels. Since it involved agreement among scores of growers and merchants, not to mention the complete mapping of the zone, it has taken a long time and is still far from finished. Absence of a D.O.C. classification, therefore, is not yet any evidence of lack of quality or probity. Sometime in the future it should be.

Noble as their names are, and long as they have been cultivated, most of even the best Italian wines are still cottage industries. True aristocratic houses cluster in the Chianti area, and around Turin the mammoth factories of Martini, Carpano, Gancia, and the rest bottle their vermouths and *spumantes* by the millions of bottles. True cooperative wineries embracing whole counties are growing more common, but the typical Italian winemaker remains an individual with traditional tastes and no knowledge of the rest of the world.

What great wines, if any, are there in Italy? It sounds harsh, but there are very few. Two or three small regions make exceptional red wine, comparable at its best with a first-class (not a superlative) Burgundy or Rhône wine. But no Italian white wine merits being called great, and there is no real equivalent to Port and Sherry, the great dessert wines of the Iberian Peninsula. "Brilliant confectionery" is a better term for the apéritifs that are truly Italy's national drink.

—

The Alps sweep around the northern provinces of Italy, embracing them in a long curve from sea to sea. Through the center of this arc runs the great river Po. The poplars of Lombardy punctuate its broad, dull plain. Around the edges, sometimes outcropping in the center, the Alps diminish into hills—fertile, hard to plow, well drained, sunny, and open to the wind—the classic land of the vine. Virgil in the *Geor-*

gics set it down in all simplicity: "Vines love an open hill." Italy has few important vineyards that don't bear this out.

I would propose three stops in the north of Italy for the gourmet who is hunting the best wine in combination with the best truly traditional food: one in Piedmont, not far from Turin and France; one in Verona; and one in Bolzano, more than halfway over the Alps in feeling, on the road to the Brenner Pass and Austria.

———

The Torinese and the Milanese crowd in cafés, make the world's best coffee, sip sticky red drinks from tiny glasses, and eat sugary buns. Theirs is an urban world. The *autostrada* gives glimpses of a rather dreary countryside, but follow the old road from town to town, and the country never seems to come. Steer south to the banks of the Tanaro River, wandering from Alba to Asti to Alessandria. Across the river the hills have a more purposeful, agricultural look. The fall is their moment of glory, when they stand in a splendor of copper and gold above the mists by the river. On their heights are the vineyards of Barolo. Just a little lower, and downstream, are those of Barbaresco. The Nebbiolo vine is here what the Pinot is in Burgundy. But these red wines are darker and deeper and considerably stronger than any Burgundy. After a good vintage they will only pause in their fermentation as winter comes; in spring the big vats will start to heave again, and the alcoholic degree will edge up to fifteen, or even beyond.

Everything about these wines is massive, even to the gigantic casks in which they stay for a minimum of three years. Tasting from the cask is not the dreamy intellectual pursuit it is in Burgundy or Bordeaux: There is no sauntering here, pince-nez in hand. Each barrel is a mountain to climb; the cellar master leans a ladder against it, and up you go, glass in hand, to peer around the great beamy chamber from a height of fifteen feet while he dips for a sample in the dark drum below. Twelve degrees—the strength of a very strong Burgundy—is the minimum for the classic Barolos and Barbarescos. Below that strength they lose their right to the name. Declassified, they are mere Nebbiolo d'Alba. Barolo, higher in the hills, is expected to make bigger and fruitier wine than Barbaresco. I have found more of a raspberry scent in the Barolo; more of a cheesy or truffly, autumnal smell in the Barbaresco. But both at their best have the rare quality of being at once powerful, almost obvious, and hauntingly elusive. Being at their best inevitably involves considerable age—more than for any other Italian wines. There is a problem here: Fine Barolos throw off a heavy sediment. I have even seen cellars in which the bottles are kept standing up for this reason.

The repertoire of Piedmontese wines should make a Californian feel at home. For apart from Barolos and Barbarescos, named, French-style, by their districts, labels are varietal. Barbera, Grignolino, Freisa, and Dolcetto are all red-wine grapes. White wine plays little part here, except for the Moscato, most delicate, palest, and prettiest of all Muscat wines, one of which is the world-famous sparkling Asti Spumante.

It is a matter for an expert to distinguish between Barbera and Grignolino, or Grignolino and Dolcetto. So much depends on the maker and how much or how little he has moved with the times. On my last visit to Asti, I was taken to meet a winemaker who considered his Barbera '40 just about ready to drink, whereas his Grignolino was a *vin de l'année* to be drunk as soon as six months after the harvest. Yet another winegrower was drinking his last year's Barbera. Insofar as one can generalize about these everyday Piedmontese wines, the Grignolino is light, often quite pale red, with a green-fruity flavor (the region of Asti has the best); the Barbera is darker, tougher, and more acidic, but still—as made by the best people today—very pleasant and singularly appetizing when it is young.

Dolcetto is less widespread in Piedmont, though it is the wine of the country down on the Ligurian coast to the south. It is far from being a reliable wine, but good examples can be found. They will be light and fruity, with a touch of bitter almonds lingering in the flavor.

Freisa is locally popular, particularly in the neighborhood of Turin. But I find its sweetness off-putting, and even worse when, as is often the case, the wine is made sparkling.

The Moscato is probably the most widely grown grape of all, but the bulk of it is used in the vermouth factories and to make *spumante*. A natural still Moscato is a rarity, and not easily made: The degree of alcohol is kept very low indeed, as low as 5½ degrees, and the wine is filtered to remove yeast that might keep it fermenting. If I couldn't persuade a young girl to sip crème de menthe frappé with me in the Palm Court of the Plaza, I might try her on the Moscato. It's that sort of girlish but insidious stuff.

There is a perfectly respectable dry white wine called Cortese, which could really come from anywhere in northern Italy. Without being in any way sweet, it somehow feels ripe, and round, as good Italian wines do. No one makes much fuss about it, though. The emphasis is on the red. Much local pride centers around the district's Nebbiolo, its crack wine. A little to the north, in the country around Novara, which is associated more with rice than wine, the same grape is called the Spana. The Vino Spana of Gattinara and Ghemme and one or two other places, though in tiny supply, is really often as good as good Barolo.

One talks about good wine, or good examples of each type, because in Italy there are—How shall I put it?—others. My own list of reliable suppliers in the Asti-Alba area cannot be comprehensive, but for what it's worth, Fontanafredda, Franco Fiorina, Pio Cesare, Contratto, Bersano, Damilano, Marchese di Barolo, and Borgogno are some of the biggest table wine firms.

I was also given the names of two outstanding small firms, Giulio Mascarello in Barolo and Francesco Rinaldi in Alba. Both are said to make particularly good Barolo. But this is, I admit, hearsay.

Alba is the town to stay in. Its restaurant under the arcades in the town square, run by Signor Morra, is an important center for the extraordinary white truffles that seem to lend their savor to the whole of Piedmont in the fall. Asti has a big new hotel just out of town that may sound tempting, but I would advise against it on gastronomic grounds. The restaurant in Asti, if it really is traditional food and not just lyrical outbursts of typical atmosphere you are interested in, is the Falcone. It is the sort of address one gives away with misgivings, for such unspoiled seriousness is fragile.

———

It would be good to linger and cross Italy by stages, investigating every corner, for each has its wine and is proud of it. One would certainly stop in the fringes of Lombardy and look at the estate that produces the very good red and white Frecciarossa, a brand name that has gained the status of a classical wine name through what is not the most Italian of qualities—consistency. The Frecciarossa label always amuses me. It claims to be château-bottled vintage claret. More in an excess of enthusiasm than with the slightest intent to deceive.

Another stop I would certainly make would be much farther north, right under the tilt of the mountains that constitute the Swiss border, where the Adda River carves the narrow Valtellina westward through the rocky landscape. The north side of the valley is covered with steep vineyards giving red wine with a variety of names—Sassella, Grumello, and Inferno are the best known—but really only one taste. They are rather hard, dark wines that are uninviting until they have been three years in cask and at least another three in bottle. Eventually their bouquet builds up to something exceptional. I was astonished by one bottle I kept at home for six years, but this is hardly a general recommendation. Nor are these wines widely available.

One pause on the journey I would certainly make is near Modena, in rather flat and dull country, at the cooperative of the little town of Sorbara. Lambrusco, the local specialty, will always remain rather a joke with me: I find it impossible to take fizzy red wine seriously. Yet if one is going to have fizzy red wine, this is the way it should be: dark, fruity, reminiscent of black currants, a bit sweet, and very easy to enjoy. Again, however, this must not be read as an endorsement for every bottle that bears the name Lambrusco. There are some horrors to be had. If you approach Italian wine hopefully rather than confidently, and above all remember not to be too serious, you will laugh at the bad bottles and thank God for the good ones instead of cursing your way through and grudgingly admitting at the end that you had one or two that weren't too bad.

Verona is one place where you can allow yourself a certain confidence. As you penetrate the narrow streets in the center, where nothing of the twentieth century more frightening than a coffee machine has been installed; as you emerge into the most perfect market in Italy, the Piazza delle Erbe, to see the countrywomen sitting under their umbrellas, mechanically plucking thousands of little songbirds for the pot; as you count the voluptuous variety of mushrooms, watch the trickle of the fountain, see the big-bellied stone balconies sailing overhead, gaze at the fruit and vegetables and quarries of cheese, you will expect to find a gentle, a civilized, an altogether perfected wine to go with such a place. And you'll not be disappointed.

The Adige is Verona's river. It flows south from the Alps, parallel with Lake Garda, and just before Verona it turns to the east to head for the Adriatic. North of the city it skirts a range of hills, not high but abrupt and distinct. For centuries these hills have been terraced, gardened, loved, and tended. Their fertility is proverbial, and some of their villas—big country houses at the end of miles of cypress-lined drives—are very grand, and very private.

The two wines of this region, the red and the white, seem to me to echo the character of this lovely place. The white is Soave—possibly Italy's best white wine. The red is not a great wine, not even a very fine one: It is simply, to my mind, the world's most marvelous, easy, and enjoyable drink. Its name is Valpolicella.

Soave is a village, surrounded by hills, just east of Verona. The center of its industry is the Cantina Sociale or cooperative winery, said to be Europe's biggest. There is Soave and Soave Classico, the latter coming from a smaller and more strictly limited area around the village and having, perhaps, a shade more character and flavor. But both are dry, pale gold wines, without sharpness but without a trace of heaviness either. To my mind they are best very young, younger than they are often sold, when there is a really fresh, bunch-of-grapes liveliness about them. Maybe the best adjective for Soave is smooth. The narrow green Soave bottle announces a thoroughly civilized experience. There is supreme seafood in Venice, and the two are perfectly matched.

Valpolicella is a bigger area. Even its *classico* heart contains half a dozen villages that all make wine of similar quality. No guarantee goes with the name: There is some pale and bitter wine legally entitled to it. But the signs are that winegrowers are understanding more about the essential nature of their product, which is to be fresh and fruity. They are learning not to leave it in barrels where it will dry out and lose its charm. Some are even keeping it in glass containers from the start to prevent it from maturing. The perfect Valpolicella is bright, cherry red, warmly and gently scented, round and mouth-filling, but still distinctly delicate, with plenty of natural sweetness that fades away in the mouth to leave a little hint of what tastes like quinine. The bitter aftertaste is something one grows to love in this part of Italy, even more so farther north in the Tyrol. It is the mark of the country, and nothing could be more appetizing.

Valpolicella growers have a taste I find hard to get enthusiastic about. As well as making their marvelous light wine, they insist on drying grapes to make a heavier style. Most farmhouses have airy lofts where good bunches of black grapes are carefully laid out in trays to dry. By about Christmas they have desiccated to raisin size; their juice is enormously concentrated. Wine made from these grapes is called Recioto. It is darker and stronger, very often sweet but sometimes fully fermented and full of brown and black flavors. Recioto makes the great bottle for the special occasion or the honored guest. I have sat by a farmer's fireside, eating heartily in mid-afternoon the blackened, spicy, homemade sausage and liver his wife was grilling on the embers. At the same time I have furtively sipped from a glass of lovely, cool Valpolicella while pretending to appreciate the splendors of his dark brown pride and joy.

Winemakers at the southern end of Lake Garda, which is just down the road, produce several wines that are comparable to Valpolicella. On the near side there is Bardolino, grown in a big area around the resort town of that name. On the other, there is Chiaretto del Garda, grown around Saló and best around the little fortified village of Moniga. Both of these wines approach a *vin rosé*—there is little depth of redness in either their color or flavor. But comparing them to rosés, much can be said for them. I can imagine Chiaretto, in particular, finding a very good market in this country.

Before we make our third stop, up in the Alto Adige, there is a good deal of investigating to be done in Friuli–Venezia Giulia, the provinces north and east of Venice, right up to the Yugoslav border at Trieste. I have not seen as much of this country or its wine as I would like. Wine growing is becoming very important there, and farmers are tending to abandon traditional local grapes for the Merlots and Cabernets and Rieslings, which are becoming international currency.

Such local names as Piccolit, Tocai, Verduzzo, and Prosecco die hard, but I suspect more internationally known names will take over in the end. When they do, we can expect well made, standard wines at the very least.

The real export traffic at the moment is in the busy valley of the Adige, from below Trento right up to Merano, where for fifty miles or so the narrow river plain, hemmed in with granite walls of hills, literally brims over with vines.

Austrian influence is very strong here, and most of the wine is shipped north over the Alps to Austria and Germany. Here excellent research establishments and very high standards are combined, for once, with very reasonable prices.

For such a restricted area there is an absurd number of different names and types of wine. The brain grows weary of endless unfamiliar names for things that are, when all is said and done, so similar that it makes no difference. I would pick out the Teroldego of the Trentino, the province of Trento, a good standard light red wine, reliable if not exciting; the Riesling of the same province; and certainly the dry, sparkling wine made by the Trento firm of Ferrari.

A certain jealousy exists between the Trentino and the Alto Adige, the province of Bolzano. My own view is that Bolzano has the better wine. It is a fascinating center for a short stay, an Italian Alpine town, arcaded and snug in its solid stone buildings, with Tyrolean-style wine taverns, rather heavy food of splendid savor, and distant glimpses of snow on the peaks.

One memorable visit I made there was to the monastery of Muri-Gries. It was a scene from some Gothic opera. A deep bass bell tolled above the pitch-dark courtyard as the door creaked open. Long mossy flights of stairs led down into the cellars. In the dim light Father Gregor, the cellar master, giggled like an old religious squirrel over his casks.

The specialty of the monastery is one of the local red-wine grapes, the Lagrein. The monks make two types of wine from it: Kretzer, which is very light in color, and Dunkel, which is nearer red Bordeaux both in its color and its good, rather tannic, balance. I particularly liked the Kretzer, a really pretty, gentle wine that became more distinctive as one swallowed, and its characteristic, bitter aftertaste lingered.

The Schiava, the other local red grape, is more widespread and makes the two best-known wines of the valley: Lago di Caldaro (often labeled in German as Kalterersee) and Santa Maddalena. The latter, from the hill above Bolzano, is reputed the better; there is less of it and the price is higher. Lago di Caldaro is produced in large quantities. Both, at their best when young, are light red wines with an attractive softness about them.

Some of the better growers are experimenting with classical grape varieties here as well. The big firm of Kettmeier has made excellent Cabernet Sauvignon, good enough to bear comparison with some of the better ones of the Napa Valley. The same people have also started making sparkling wine with real success.

If anything, I felt even more enthusiasm for the white wines of Bolzano. The Traminer, which makes such spicy wine in Alsace, is supposed to have originated here; the Riesling flourishes; the Sauvignon Blanc and the Pinot Blanc do very well. The village of Terlano is best known for white wine. Terlaners of many different grapes and mixtures of grapes are made, but all have a thoroughly lively, attractive quality not far from that of fresh fruit. A Terlaner Sauvignon Blanc again, like the Cabernet, reminded me of California's contribution to this genre. I'm beginning to prefer this style to the better-known French versions of the same thing made at Sancerre and Pouilly.

So far, oddly enough, this vital and prosperous wine region has hardly become involved with the new D.O.C. laws. They are more concerned with defining the important traditional areas, whereas here, as in California, it is not the exact location but the grape variety and, above all, the winemaker that matter.

February 1972

THE TWO FACES OF CHIANTI

Gerald Asher

My favorite small restaurant in Florence is hardly a guitar strum from the Ponte Vecchio, but, fortunately, its unprepossessing entrance is enough to deter those who would misunderstand its simplicity. It's just a crowded cellar, down six precipitous steps from an already obscure, arched alley. But there one eats real Tuscan country food—fresh and abundant. With it, naturally, the proprietor serves pitchers of young Chianti: zesty, sprightly, fruity, exuberant, and eminently quaffable Chianti.

When I think of Chianti I tend to wax nostalgic about my little Florentine *taverna* rather than the fine estates I have visited because, like everyone else. I suppose, I have enjoyed Chianti most often in just such a carefree setting, and without ceremony. This popular image of Chianti causes problems, however, for the growers, even while winning them friends, because there is more to Chianti than checkered tablecloths. Young Chianti in its romantic *fiasco* might have been the greatest impediment to our discovering the fine, mature wines of the region, and the winegrowers of Tuscany are now engaged in a careful reassessment of what they want Chianti to mean.

The areas that produce Chianti are not extensive, yet they are diverse. Each one, tucked in a valley or fold of the Tuscan hills, claims a style of its own quite apart from the distinction, jealously maintained, between *classico* and the rest. But one division runs through all of them. On the one hand are Chianti wines made deliberately to be drunk young and traditionally bottled in the straw-covered *fiasco*, the very symbol of Chianti. On the other are wines so different in style, let alone quality, that the distance between young Chianti and them is the distance between a simple Beaujolais and a *cru* of Moulin-à-Vent or a straightforward Côtes-du-Rhône and a first-rate Hermitage. Matured in Yugoslav oak casks, these Chiantis are aged further in bottle— not in the *fiasco*, which cannot be binned, but in the shouldered bottle usually associated with Bordeaux wines and used, in fact, wherever red wines are expected to throw a deposit when aged. (The shoulder helps catch the deposit in such wines when decanted.) Chianti made for early drinking can be released for sale in March after the vintage, but mature Chianti (known in Italy as *vecchio*) cannot be released, by law, for two years. Wines labeled *riserva* must be aged for a minimum of three before release. There are also higher minimum quality standards imposed for *vecchio* and *riserva* wines.

Though some parts of the Chianti region are better endowed than others to produce wines suitable for aging, most growers make both kinds of wine in varying proportions. Not all vintages are suitable for aging, and even within the vineyards of one estate some parcels of vines do better than others. There is a practical reason, too, why growers prefer to make some wine for rapid sale as well as some for aging. If the produce of an entire vintage were reserved in the cellars, first in wood and then in bottle, with others following in succession, there might be a stock of three or four years' production of wine held at any one time. Few growers could find the money to finance such a quantity; and, at the present time, when the finest aged Chianti fetches prices not much more than the most youthful, there is little incentive for the grower to incur the expense even if he could. With part of his crop made into wine that can be released, sold, and enjoyed at once, a grower can pay his bills, and the cost of carrying the balance for aging is easier to bear.

This raises the question of why a grower would *want* to age wine at all if it doesn't pay him to do so. Pride, the respect of his peers, personal satisfaction—all contribute more to winemaking decisions everywhere than do plain economics.

In recent years the *fiasco* has been disappearing. Countrywomen who were once content to spend their days binding the straw coverings can now find more profitable work. Chianti producers have turned to an alternative, elegantly shaped bottle, restricted to Tuscany. They know that part of the charm is lost, but they hope that if attention is focused on the contents instead of the container, the finer wines of Chianti will at last receive more attention.

———

A grower decides for himself which of his wines will be sold young and which aged. Wine for aging is made from more rigorously selected grapes, perhaps from older vines on sections of a vineyard known to produce consistently high quality. But the condition of each batch at the time of actual picking dictates the best course for the grower to take. Fortunately the regulations allow some flexibility, and by varying the proportions of the different varietals that he uses to make Chianti and by adapting his method of fermentation, he can either hasten a wine to early drinkability or reinforce those qualities that are necessary for long, even development in bottle. For example, all Chianti, no matter from which zone it comes and no matter whether *classico* or not, must have at least fifty percent of its volume from the Sangiovese grape: This brings body and aroma to the wine. According to the regulations, there must also be at least ten percent Canaiolo, a red grape that softens the effect of the Sangiovese, and at least ten percent of a mixture of Malvasia and Trebbiano, white grapes that lighten the wine and give additional flavor. More Sangiovese, and the wine will be darker, stouter, more tannic for aging; more Canaiolo, and the wine will be softer; more Trebbiano or Malvasia, and the wine will be lighter and ready for market sooner.

Then, too, each grower can make up his own mind about the *governo*, a practice traditional to Tuscany whereby the scarcely finished young wine, weeks after the vintage, is provoked into a second fermentation by introducing the juice of grapes held back from the original crush and dried in order to concentrate their sugar. The warmth and activity generated by the new fermentation encourage what we call malolactic fermentation as well. Naturally and effectively, malic acid (the acid, present in young wines in large doses, that makes green apples taste green) is transformed into lactic acid (associated with milk). After the *governo* a young wine tastes less harsh, and because the fermentation leaves a slight "bead" in the wine, preserved when bottling as far as possible, it adds that sprightliness, felt on the tongue rather than seen, that is so characteristic of young Chianti.

The differences among the seven zones of Chianti production are plainer, obviously, in wines that have been kept for aging. These are generally the best of the crop of each grower and are therefore more likely to show individual character and style; the aging itself develops qualities and characteristics that are only hinted at when a wine is young.

———

Foremost among the zones, inevitably, is the region officially described as Chianti Classico. It lies between Florence and Siena and includes the towns of Greve, Castellina in Chianti, Radda, and Gaiole, as well as parts of a number of other towns and villages. Here, on gravelly, sandy vineyards, is the ancient heart of Chianti. *Noblesse oblige;* Chianti Classico must conform to minimum standards slightly more stringent than those for other Chianti districts. An association of growers agreed on regulations to control standards of Chianti Classico before the Denominazione di Origine Controllata laws were instituted in 1967, using the symbol of a black cockerel to identify the products of their members.

Following Chianti Classico, the zones of most importance are those of the Sienese hills (to the south) and the Florentine hills (to the north), Chianti Colli Senesi and Chianti Colli Fiorentini as they are known in Italian. But neither these names nor the names Chianti Colline Pisane (near Pisa), Chianti Colli Aretini (around Arezzo), or Chianti Montalbano (near Pistoia) are often found on wine labels. Unlike Chianti Rufina, the seventh zone, in the extreme northeast of the Chianti area, the wines are generally sold just as "Chianti," even when they are estate bottled. Chianti Rufina has a special reputation for its full-bodied wines, and growers there like to lay claim to their *denominazione.*

Yet another association of growers, who became known as the Consorzio del Chianti Putto after the putto or cherub that they used as their distinguishing symbol, did not have a geographic basis as did that of the Chianti Classico. Founded by growers of the Colli Fiorentini, they too established quality standards for their members before the *denominazione* regulations were written, but they extended membership to *all* Chianti growers of *all* zones who were prepared to accept the criteria of quality that they applied. Today neither putto nor black cockerel has the significance it once did as a guarantee of quality because the laws since 1967 impose on all what were once voluntary standards accepted only by the few.

The growers' associations continue now principally to promote Chianti and the wines of their memberships. The use or nonuse of the symbols can be confusing to buyers, however, who sometimes wonder whether absence of the black cockerel from a Chianti Classico means that the wine is "less *classico*" than another. In fact, membership in the associations and use of their symbols is discretionary.

Without the *fiasco,* sales of young Chianti to export markets have slowed down, whereas sales of the finer wines, though growing steadily over the years, have not increased fast enough to take their place. Tuscany pulses with fiercely held opinions on the direction growers should take. Some want to see Chianti follow the success of California and of certain northern Italian wine regions by marketing their young wines in liter-and-a-half jugs. Others insist that Chianti has already suffered for too long from the "quaffing wine" image of the *fiasco* and want to avoid its replacement by a container that would aggravate the situation. They urge less emphasis on the sale of young wine, especially in containers that do nothing to promote the distinctiveness of Chianti, and more concentration on Chianti for aging. They press for revision of the Chianti regulations to reduce the present maximum of thirty percent white grapes in the blends to fifteen percent and to lower the minimum requirement of ten percent white grapes to five percent. Without actually saying so, they would obviously prefer to see quaffing Chianti eliminated altogether. That is not

likely to happen though, both because of the financial strain on growers and because everyone knows there are large quantities of Chianti
that are *better* for being drunk young, and there always will be.

———

Fewer white grapes used in the production of Chianti red wine would,
of course, release more for the making of white wine in Tuscany. Cur-
rently the *denominazione* Chianti does not provide for other than red
wine, and most white wine is without an official *appellation.* One of the
finest white wines of Tuscany, for example, produced on the Pomino
estate of the Frescobaldi family, is entitled to no *denominazione* at all,
save that of plain "Tuscan white wine." Surprisingly, the first recorded
use of the name Chianti was for *white* wine made from Trebbiano and
Malvasia grapes: Red wine grown in the area was referred to simply as
vermiglio. Such was the case at least until the fourteenth century. How
the red grapes infiltrated the white and took over the name is not certain. Today so little white wine is produced in Tuscany, compared
with the large output of red, and so small is the proportion of it entitled to a *denominazione,* that statistics are scant and reveal little.

Bianco Vergine della Valdichiana is the white *denominazione* most
frequently seen. Roughly seven or eight million bottles of it are produced each year from vineyards around Arezzo. With a pale straw
color and crisp, not too assertive taste, it is especially good with Tuscan ham and the local herbed sausage. Vernaccia di San Gimignano,
better known, though of more limited production, is also a dry wine,
but more ample. Its fullness, in fact, makes it an admirable accompaniment to pasta. Sometimes a Vernaccia has a pungent aroma and flavor reminiscent of certain Sauvignon Blanc wines. Last summer, in
Castellina in Chianti, I drank a 1976 Vernaccia from La Quercia with
gnocchi in a sauce of Gorgonzola and Parmesan cheese and cream.
Both the wine and the dish individually had seemed to me to be perfect, but each brought out something more in the other.

Supporters of the view that Chianti needs fewer white grapes in
the blend are paying an unspoken compliment to the Brunello wines
of Montalcino, within the Chianti region, south of Siena, but defiantly
sold with a *denominazione* of their own. At about the time, a hundred
years ago, that Baron Ricasoli was carrying out his varietal experiments

at Brolio, which led to the classic grape combination of Sangiovese-Canaiolo-Malvasia-Trebbiano for Chianti, Ferruccio Biondi-Santi of Montalcino was experimenting with wine made solely from a clone of the Sangiovese, known locally as the Brunello. As one might expect, given the characteristics of the Sangiovese, it is heavier and longer lived than traditional Chianti made from a combination of grapes. Today there are more than seventy growers producing Brunello di Montalcino, including Biondi-Santi's grandson. The wine has become something of a cult, older vintages fetching prices within Italy that exceed anything paid for comparable vintages of the classed growths of Bordeaux; for as they age, Brunello wines seem to fill out and develop in an extraordinary way. Recently I had the good fortune to taste a series of vintages ranging from 1973 to 1945, all in the course of a leisurely luncheon in the Biondi-Santis' kitchen at Montalcino. We tasted examples of each of the successful vintages during that span of almost thirty years, and it must have been more than the chance style of each year that made them show better as each wine succeeded a younger one. The 1945, with its deep, lively color, was richly full-bodied, its bouquet and flavor giving delicate hints of cherries and vanilla.

The success of the growers of Montalcino has disconcerted the other growers of Chianti, for the former have followed not only their own winemaking ideas but their own name, eschewing the *denominazione* Chianti to which they are entitled. Nor is Brunello di Montalcino the only wine within Chianti to follow its own course. Vino Nobile di Montepulciano has a history longer than that of Brunello—in fact, it is as old as Chianti itself—yet its reputation has remained largely local. A mixture of red and white grapes is used, as in traditional Chianti, to produce a wine of elegance and velvety softness. I have not tasted Montepulciano wines with more than ten years of aging, so I do not know if they continue to develop beyond that, but I remember a 1969 that accompanied a roast pigeon in a *taverna* of the town a year or two ago that was as near perfect a wine as any I have had. Here, too, the growers emphasize aged rather than young wines.

While the growers of Chianti debate their future, they continue to produce wines of uncommon grace. The *riservas* of the 1975 vintage, one of the best of this century, were released recently and lend weight to arguments in support of more wine of this style and quality. Despite inflation, unpredictable currency exchange rates, and the host of other woes that combine to deprive us of so many classic wines, these *riservas* are priced modestly and must be the most undervalued fine wines in the world today. If we do not take advantage of our good fortune, how shall we answer our grandchildren when they ask: "Where were you when the 1975 Chiantis were practically given away?"

February 1979

HINTS OF GRAND THINGS TO COME

Gerald Asher

I remember well the hard frosts of early 1956. That winter I was learning to ski in Austria, and throughout February all of western Europe was in the grip of intense cold. Frau Schmidt, my landlady, would wake me with hot coffee every morning and tell me what a *wunderbar* day it was outside. But even the bright sun could not raise the temperature, and all day there were frequent stops for hot tea and rum, *Glühwein,* or bouillon. Even in Provence it was so cold that entire hillsides of olive trees were destroyed, and one of the sad sights of the following summer was the twisted, leafless, and blackened groves.

In Bordeaux the damage was severe, and particularly so because the cold had been preceded by a mild spell that had started the sap rising. The summer that followed was rather a mockery, too, and the vintage was one of the worst on record. It was a small yield—perhaps a third of a normal Bordeaux crop—and at that it consisted only of thin, sharp little wines. The following two years, 1957 and 1958, hardly made up for the disappointment of 1956, and when 1959 showed above average promise it is not surprising that there was an overreaction. Perhaps embarrassed at the clamor, the growers and merchants tended to play down 1960 even more than was warranted, and they were still restrained in their first appraisal of the 1961 wines. Bad weather during the flowering of the vine in June of 1961 had prevented the fruit from setting well, but from then on the summer was fine, with a good balance of sun and rain. The vines seemed to do well with reduced bunches to nourish, and in a quiet way growers and merchants looked forward to a small but delectable vintage.

When first tasted seriously by the trade in the spring of 1962, the wines were balanced, their color was good, and there was a firm quality to them that augured well. Shy of announcing a second "vintage of the century" so soon after 1959, the trade at least allowed themselves to murmur that the 1961s appeared to be superior to the 1959s and would probably last much longer. Indeed, one thing the 1961 Bordeaux wines seemed to have in common was a tight-shut quality that promised a long wait. There were one or two exceptions—the most notable being Château La Lagune, which matured so quickly because of the high proportion of young Merlot vines in the vineyard at the time of its growth that by 1966 I found the wine quite ready for drinking. It was an extraordinary wine with a bouquet and flavor that can be described only as voluptuous. I recommended drinking it within two or three years, and as it has been impossible to find any since 1970 I do not know whether my advice was necessary or not. The other 1961s remained *princesses lointaines*—fine, elegant, but austere—not in the least comforting or even approachable.

The longer the wines remained closed, however, the more their reputation grew—not an unknown phenomenon. Subsequent vintages, 1962, 1964, 1966, and 1967, were all compared to the yardstick of 1961; and when the 1970 vintage appeared—truly one of the most successful vintages since World War II—that, too, had to submit to the legend. There were few who dared to say that *perhaps* it could be considered equal to 1961 in its way, and no one dared to suggest that it might be better.

The fine 1961s remained closed for the most part. There were hints of grand things to come—a deep bouquet of freshly crushed black currants from Lynch-Bages and a delicate floweriness from Léoville-Las-Cases like scent caught through gauze. But generally in the last decade when I have tasted 1961 wines it has been without pleasure, and I began to wonder if they would ever come round. Even those wines with developed bouquet and flavor seemed bony—not the youthful hardness of tannin, but a much more relentless and unyielding bedrock hardness deep in the wine. It was as though behind the protective screen of young tannin there never had been the soft couch of glycerin, which carries a ripe wine triumphantly through its mature years.

———

Since there was little reason for me to taste them professionally, and for pleasure I preferred the 1962 and 1964 wines, I had neglected the 1961s for the past two or three years. I was especially curious, therefore, when three 1961 wines were served together at a Colorado Springs dinner this past spring. A small group of local business and professional men meet there once a month to share a few good bottles, and I was lucky enough to be included. The three 1961s were Château Beychevelle, Château Mouton-Rothschild, and Château Latour. Of the three I much preferred the Château Beychevelle. It seemed to present the logical outcome of all my earlier tastings of fine 1961 wines. It was a well-balanced wine of medium weight, elegant and stylish; and the bouquet and flavor were fruity, at once delicate and persistent. It had developed a gentle authority. The Château Mouton-Rothschild, on the other hand, was less captivating. The color was good, and the bouquet was delicious—not with the heavy, penetrating aroma of Pauillac, but very subtle and yet strong at the same time. The disappointment—and it was a disappointment after the promise of such a nose—was on the palate. The wine had a dry, ungenerous finish like a flower that has withered before it ever really bloomed. The Château Latour was richer and more typical of Pauillac, but the acidity was high and there seemed to be insufficient fullness in the wine to balance it.

The very next evening, on returning to New York, I was asked to choose the wine for dinner in one of the city's restaurants. I had been so intrigued by the differences the previous evening, that I hesitated only for a moment before choosing yet another 1961. It was Château Gruaud-Larose. The waiter decanted it for us—rather clumsily, I thought—but the splashing might have contributed to the quite remarkable treat we had. The wine was magnificent: big, full, and with the indefinable flavor of Saint-Julien that seems to combine cedar-wood, tarragon, and mulberries.

My hosts at Colorado Springs had used the three 1961 wines as curtain raisers, even though most of us would have felt sufficiently spoiled to have had the opportunity to taste just those three. Their plan was to present the three 1961s in contrast to the outstanding year of each of the two previous decades. The 1961s were followed by two 1959 wines, drawn from Pauillac and Saint-Julien, as had been the first three. We tasted Château Latour and Château Pichon-Baron. My first impression of both wines was that each had less breed, less raciness, and less stamp of distinguished origin than the 1961s. The Château Latour was far more generous than its 1961 counterpart, but although the balance was better, the qualities did not seem to be very well integrated, and there was a disordered, shapeless taste. Château Pichon-Baron was a lighter wine, quite elegant, especially for a 1959, but it too lacked distinction. Both had been easier to enjoy than the 1961 Latour and Mouton-Rothschild, though neither was as agreeable as the Beychevelle. But even in enjoying them, one was conscious of settling for less than the best just because they offered less resistance than the 1961 wines.

Finally, we had two 1949s, and for these we moved away from Pauillac and Saint-Julien. First of the pair was Château Cos d'Estournel, a Saint-Estèphe, and second was Château Margaux. The Château Cos d'Estournel was decanted minutes before we drank it, but even so the bouquet was very attenuated. The color was good, and the wine, delicate and silky soft, enchanted us all. The wine was still quite lively," and I could not understand why the bouquet was so withdrawn. In fact more flavor developed in the glass, but having been opened to the air for a while the wine also roughened slightly and acquired a rasping finish that had not been there when it was first tasted. We concluded with the Margaux. It had a fresh, bright color and a flowery bouquet, and though it too was beginning to dry very slightly, it was exquisitely soft and delicate.

———

How did I feel, in the end, about the 1961 vintage in relation to the earlier ones? I had difficulty in deciding. In Colorado Springs I had given my highest rating to the Château Margaux '49, and since I was tasting on the simple basis of what the wines could offer at the time, rather than speculating on their future or their past, the Château Margaux was without doubt the outstanding wine of the evening. It was followed closely by the Château Beychevelle '61, and although I was not impressed by the wine, I placed the Château Latour '59 third in order of pleasurable drinking; the Château Latour '61 and Château Cos d'Estournel '49 followed next in my private order, and the Château Pichon-Baron '59, though more than agreeable, took last place. Had we tasted the Château Gruaud-Larose '61 with the others, I would have set it very close behind the Château Margaux '49.

One should be wary of making sweeping judgments on the evidence of only a few wines, but our opinions are formed and re-formed all the time on the basis of just such encounters. Despite the fact that the two leading 1961 growths came out less well in my estimation than the Beychevelle and Gruaud-Larose, overall the 1961s seemed to be at least the equal of the two earlier great years. Perhaps we were right about them after all. They *are* haughty wines, but at last they are beginning to smile at us.

August 1973

On Sherry

Hugh Johnson

It is only in the last few years that the real meaning of Sherry has begun to come home to people. The name of the wine has so long been taken in vain by such a variety of imitators that not so long ago it seemed as though the true meaning and significance of Sherry would never float to the top again. There is still the strong, brown, heavy wine-and-spirit blend, the product of cooking white wine that would be none too good to drink raw. But there is also the delicate, unforced, quite astonishingly appealing wine of one little area in the south of Spain.

Just to think of Jerez de la Frontera gives me an appetite. It is not particularly famous for its cooking, but it is the mecca of the *tapa*, the essential accompaniment to the day-long drinking of little *copitas* of pale gold Sherry. The two are inseparable. To drink Sherry without an olive at the very least—but better with crumbled white cheese, with prawns, with ham, with fried fish, with tiny squid—is unthinkable, for the very good reason that it is the world's most hunger-making wine, the liquid embodiment of the dinner gong.

The Jerezanos have come to terms with their appetites in a way I never can. The last time I was in Jerez we were invited to dinner in the gardens of one of the great wine-shipping houses. We were on parade at eleven o'clock sharp—in fact, the sharpest thing for miles was my appetite. About midnight, or nearer half past, a trickle of other guests began to arrive. At one-thirty the gardens began to fill up. By two we were finding our places around a table on which the dew was making the glass gleam. Lorries rumbled into the dawn carrying the half bottles I had emptied in that Andalusian vigil. Always half bottles in Jerez—not so much a gesture of gentility as a way to preserve the fine freshness of the wine up to the very last minute.

This special freshness is the thing that needs definition. It is the very quintessence of wine, wood, and age. Yet in the wine that the Spanish prize most, there is no great age involved. Like all great wines, Sherry is the result of a unique combination of soil and climate brought out in a way the natives have perfected over centuries. Certain of its characteristics are susceptible to imitation. Many of the imitations are well made and good in their own way. But none of them recaptures the astonishing finesse of true Sherry—a quality, to my mind, as distinctive and unique as the quality of great Champagne.

The word "finesse" is a good deal bandied about in talking about wine. It is a term used in most cases to convey the final polish of inspired professionalism—the performance of an opera singer, for example. Finesse is the inevitable word for good Sherry, but not in quite the same way. *Fino* is the Spanish word for the best class of Sherry, and fine it precisely means: not as in "fine fellow" or "fine product," but as in fine needlework. Fino Sherry is, or can be, delicate, pure, limpid, fresh—all the cool, clear things—and yet brilliantly vivid in flavor and unmistakably powerful. Have I just described the perfect dry Martini? There are moments when words let one down.

The factors that make Sherry so good are, strange to say, very much the same ones that make Champagne *hors concours.* At the two extremes of wine-growing Europe, the two districts echo each other in almost every way, except climate. Both make their best wine on soil that is nearly pure chalk. Both demand a vital white grape for which no substitute is possible. Both involve enormous capital in their "elaboration," as the Spanish so graphically put it. And both have made their producers considerable fortunes, which are reflected in the whole style of the business. Jerez and Reims are both, in their subdued ways, millionaire towns.

My introduction to Jerez came at the time of the annual *feria,* the fiesta that coincides with the start of the grape picking. I daydream about it as though the girls were always astride the horses, the gardens were full of candles, and the patios were decked with flowers. There must be moments when the air is not full of white doves above the belfry, the bullring is not blazing with pageantry, and the people do not dine and dance until dawn. Yet the daydreams persist. They were born in days of inexhaustible splendor, when such an electric charge went through me, when energy and joy so overflowed, that one day drifted into another, all friends were lovers, and all lovers, friends.

Most magic of all, so extraordinary that I wonder whether I was dreaming indeed, were the gardens of Jerez on those warm early-September nights. From dusk no vehicle but horse or carriage could enter the alleyways among the trees. The black sky was velvet behind a million lanterns. Here there were cafés and stalls—a whole fairground of noisy hucksterdom, bursting with people who would stamp and swing into a dance at a handful of notes from a passing guitar. There, cheek-by-jowl with the crowds, were pavilions of exclusive luxury, peopled with uniforms, starch, and satin, dazzlingly lighted from canopies of glass and delicate ironwork—the scene of suppers and coquetry, waltzing and the territorial conversations of grandees. Jerez, to me, is quintessential Spain.

That was about ten years ago. In those days the vintage scene was still like something out of an Egyptian tomb painting. By day during the *feria* one would go out into the vineyards, which were hidden away on low hills out of sight of the town, with a sense of going to a play. In the unreal light of the sun on stark white soil, reflecting upward even under the eaves of the white buildings so that shadow was banished utterly, brown men in white trousers stooped among vines of an almost lurid green. How, under that sun, the vine leaves were not toasted by midsummer is one of the mysteries of Sherry making. In their shelter the amber grapes were hanging in clusters that were already warm to the touch. The baskets of wicker and esparto grass; the primevally simple, short, curved blade of the knife, unchanged for two thousand years; the nodding donkeys panniered up with hundreds of pounds of grapes—no modern anachronisms broke the spell.

As the grapes were brought to the press house they were laid out on round grass mats in the sun. In the low white house the ritual of treading was unaccompanied by music. Six or seven men in white trudged unceasingly around the *lagar* (wooden trough) in which the grapes were piled, grinding them down with their hobnailed boots into a pulp from which a steady stream of liquid ran. In another *lagar* where the treading was finished, workmen strained on a capstan, wringing the last drop out of a mound of pulp by winding a strip of grass matting around it. In another room in the press house the men ate their bread and fish and drank water cooled in clay pitchers. It was one of those scenes in which simplicity is beauty.

—

There are those who will be relieved, and those who will be disappointed, to hear that most of this process has changed today. I don't believe the wine is either better or worse for the fact that big hydraulic presses have superseded boots, that the wine is usually made in the central *bodega* of the shipper, or that the floor is more likely to be of white tiles than bare earth.

What is more crucial in the making of Sherry—the long-drawn-out rearing of the wine—remains almost exactly as it always was. It also remains, to my mind, the greatest spectacle in the whole, cheerful, eccentric world of wine.

Whereas most wine spends its early life in caves or tunnels, Sherry lives in a church. Or, rather, that is the impression its lofty home indelibly makes on the mind. *Bodega* is the word for almost any premises connected with wine in Spain—be they bars, cellars, wineshops, or, *bodega* of *bodegas,* these soaring storerooms in which thousands of broad-chested butts stand in stacks often five barrels high and as much as a hundred yards long. Over them, lighted with the shifting spotlights of clerestory windows, attenuated viaducts of white arches support the roof. There is an air of long-settled dust, of long-woven cobwebs; the deep gray-brown of seasoned oak has penetrated the very air. A faint chill strikes up from the earth floor, even on a day when the palm trees outside have drooped with heat exhaustion. The heavy presence of the wine seems to absorb all sounds—of workmen with ropes and levers manhandling half-ton barrels as easily and gently as eggs, of a little party, led by the *capataz* of the *bodega*, moving from butt to butt, tasting and mumbling and spitting the wine into the dust.

At first the wine goes into a nursery *bodega*, a *criadero*. At this early stage in the life of the wine the skill of the *capataz* lies in classifying each barrel, not only for quality but for style. Barrels with identical backgrounds can turn out to be surprisingly different as they settle down: one showing, let us say, a marvelous vitality and cleanness of flavor; another, a rounder and fuller taste with less scent.

Three completely distinct categories of Sherry arise naturally in this way. There must be gray areas where they shade into each other, but the distinctions are clear enough for the experienced taster to classify them confidently.

Of the two I have just mentioned, the first, all brightness and freshness, would almost certainly turn out to be a Fino. Finos are the Sherries that, even at a year old, seem invitingly ready to drink. Their qualities are vividness and cleanness of flavor and, above all, balance. They are precarious qualities: Never has a Fino from a bottle tasted quite so scintillating as it did from the butt in the *bodega*. The wine trade has learned that it needs the prop of a small dose of alcohol—perhaps only one percent—to keep it in good condition for shipping overseas; and even this small addition seems to take the edge off its perfection. But of all the experiences in the world of wine that make one catch his breath in wonder, make one go back to the glass in his hand with all his concentration to try to unravel the subtleties and complexities it offers, there is perhaps nothing like a great *solera* Fino.

What gives it this mysterious quality, beyond anything a normal white wine—say a white Burgundy—can achieve? The answer is a local form of yeast that takes over after the normal yeasts of fermentation have finished their work and lives on the surface of the wine, polishing off the last traces of the sugar remaining in it. To encourage the *flor*—to the fanciful this white foam on the wine looks like flowers—the butt is never filled to the top. Nine inches of air space are left for the *flor* to grow in. The contact with the air would turn any normal wine into vinegar, but Fino, already relatively strong and protected by the *flor,* only grows more concentrated in flavor.

The *capataz* of the *bodega* has a characteristically stylish way of producing samples for tasting. He carries a four-foot wand of whalebone, to the end of which is attached a slim silver beaker. Removing the bung from the barrel top, he plunges his *venencia* through the layer of *flor* into the cool body of the wine. His *pièce de résistance* is the way he pours it out: holding the glasses at arm's length and letting the thin stream of gold arc through the air from the *venencia,* held high, straight into the mouth of the narrow glass. I have seen a *capataz* fill four glasses this way without pausing and without spilling a drop. It is not only showmanship, however; that fleeting contact with the air, that splashing into the glass just before one sips, is the best way of releasing all the perfumes in the wine. And when one comes to sniff it, there is more than he ever expected: To me there is always an elusive reminder of the fragrant smell of new-baked bread about it, a teasing saltiness, an almost dusty dryness, an expanding mouthful of the flavor of grapes but without any suggestion of sugar.

———

Among Finos there is a separate class in which the finesse, the lightness, and the saltiness are even more pronounced. It is known by the name of Manzanilla. Manzanillas tend to come from the westernmost of the Sherry vineyards, which cluster around the little fishing town of Sanlúcar de Barrameda on the mouth of the river Guadalquivir. Sanlúcar has its own *bodegas:* As far as anyone can tell, it is in these *bodegas* rather than in the vineyards that the special Manzanilla qualities arise. Curiously, the Manzanilla Finos that are taken to *bodegas* in Jerez, only fifteen miles away, become just good plain Finos. Conversely, good Jerez Finos reared in a Sanlúcar *bodega* often take on the Manzanilla character. Linking the saltiness with the presence of the sea, most people believe that it is somehow the sea air that makes a Manzanilla. I would hazard a guess that the strain of *flor* yeast in Sanlúcar is slightly different—again, possibly, a question of having lived by the seaside for centuries. Whatever the reason, Manzanillas can be the most delicate and racy of all Finos.

There is one place on earth to learn in an unforgettable way the character of this rare and exquisite wine. On the beach at Sanlúcar stands a ramshackle restaurant, the Casa Juan, only a shrimp's throw from the sea and the boats. There one eats shrimps, grilled on charcoal, and then red mullet with herbs. One learns he can drink two or three half bottles of Sherry with his lunch.

If a butt of Sherry is not a Fino, it is probably either an Amontillado or an Oloroso. Or rather it *will* be an Amontillado, for this style of Sherry takes time to develop. Wines that could be Finos, yet whose balance suggests to the *capataz* that they will improve with age, are set aside in an Amontillado nursery. Instead of the two or three years it takes a Fino to mature, an Amontillado can be nursed for six or seven years, or indeed for sixteen or seventeen.

As the term is commonly used, it signifies barely more than medium Sherry—neither very sweet nor very dry. Yet a natural Amontillado—and there are a few sold—is very different. It has depths of flavor that make it a total assault on the sense of taste.

I would not claim that everyone is going to experience such a revelation of new beauties. A black thread of bitterness can underlie the huge pungent buttery body of a wine of this sort. I remember once taking a few bottles of Valdespino's Amontillado Tio Diego directly from Spain to some friends in Italy—whose drink, of course, was not Sherry but vermouth. They felt perfectly at home with it, assuming that its complex of flavors was achieved with quinine and wormwood and all the alchemical trickery of the vermouth factory, whereas, of course, wine, oak, and age unaided make this formidable mouthful of flavor.

The terminology of Sherry is far from being an exact science, alas. Most wines labeled Amontillado are blends of young and aged wine, colored with caramel to achieve the look of age and sweetened to an innocuous neutrality of taste. It is only the natural, and therefore dry, Amontillados that have the real distinction I am talking about. As Sherry takes its place on discerning tables in America, Amontillados will become more familiar. Already one importer in Sacramento, California, has built up a collection that a Spaniard would be proud of.

—

All the really sweet dessert Sherries—the creams and the milks—are blends based on an Oloroso. Oloroso is the description for the kind of Sherry that is opposite to a Fino: a wine of more body, less finesse, and less thrilling but fuller flavor. A young Oloroso has less scent and seems, in fact, a duller wine.

Even a greater scale of flavors, however, is lying in wait in a great Oloroso than in a Fino. Time is the essence here. In an old unsweetened Oloroso there is a deep, warm nuttiness, a hint of tar, and an enveloping scent. Among dry wines it becomes almost the opposite number of a great vintage Port. Like vintage Port, however, its relevance seems limited to winter weather. We have a Sunday morning ritual in England of walking back from church across the park to a glass of Oloroso in front of the fire. It tastes best on days when the ground is still hard with frost though the sun is flooding into the house, burnishing the polished oak and vases of flowers.

The best sweet Sherries keep all the subtlety of the natural Oloroso and add to it only the smooth creamy sweetness of an old sweetening wine. These wines for sweetening, undrinkable on their own, are made from a special grape, the Pedro Ximénez, dried in the sun to concentrate its sugar. *Vinos de color,* as black as ink, are similarly made and kept for the blending vat.

Once it is established in what category a barrel belongs, its description is chalked in traditional hieroglyphics on its end. Barrels of each kind are kept in their separate nurseries. They include wines of no special merit, classed as *rayas,* which will be used only for making the cheaper blends.

The wine lover wants to know, naturally enough, how to find the very best Sherry. Finding the best wine is made relatively simple in France. But in Jerez there are no First Growths to lead the rich and greedy straight to the point. It is almost axiomatic with Sherry that the best wines are not the best known. For the world's most famous Sherries are the ones blended specifically for a mass market, whereas the world's best are precisely the opposite.

Sherry and Champagne differ completely here. Each Champagne shipper makes his standard wine at a level of quality he can maintain year after year. In good years, in addition, he makes a smaller quantity of better-than-average "vintage" wine, bearing the individual style of the year in question. In Jerez the shipper makes a dozen or more styles of wine simultaneously and continuously; no "vintage" wine is kept apart.

The whole system is aimed at achieving continuity—at whatever level of quality the customer is prepared to pay for. And the shipper's system to achieve this is to operate what is known as a *solera* for each style of wine he sells.

Imagine a row of, say, five barrels, all full of the best Fino Sherry the shipper can find: The wine in barrel five is five years old; in barrel four, four, and so on. The shipper draws off half the wine in barrel five to sell it. He tops up barrel five from barrel four, four from three, and so on up the line. New wine is constantly coming in at one end of the *solera,* and mature wine is being bottled from the other. But in most cases the *solera* in question has been operating in this fashion for years and years: In each barrel there must be traces of wine from way back—even an infinitesimal amount of the original wine from the time the *solera* was inaugurated.

Not all *soleras* start with new wine. There are rare and valuable *soleras* that consist of old, older, and oldest, kept, in this case, for blending purposes. Really old Sherry, kept for thirty or forty years in cask, achieves a concentration of flavor that makes it almost unpleasant to drink on its own, yet makes its influence in a blend—even in the smallest measure—quite extraordinarily telling.

Thus the character of any Sherry is passed on in a sort of hereditary process. It is not the vineyard, not the vintage, but the *solera* that establishes its individuality. On the other hand, for most Sherries the *solera* is only the halfway point in their upbringing, for very few *solera* wines are offered for sale in their virgin state. The best are almost too valuable to sell, but, more important, time has shown that they are not what the public wants.

At this stage all Sherry is totally lacking in sugar—as dry as a drink can be. All Sherry starts life in this way: with its fermentation allowed to use up all the natural grape sugar in making alcohol. Such completely natural Sherry is an acquired taste: Whether it is light and pale and delicate, or old and deep and almost bitter, it is the most austere wine in the world. In most people's terms it is a wine to sip and respect, before turning with relief to something easier to drink.

In view of this preference, virtually all Sherry is offered to the public in a more or less sweetened state. But it is not only sweetened. Between the wine in the *solera* and the bottle one buys is a whole department of art known as blending. To match a brand consistently, staying at the same price whatever the fortunes of the seasons and never letting color or flavor or sweetness vary perceptibly, is to perform a difficult task. As a Sherry shipper described the process to me, the blender uses his *solera* wines as a painter uses the colors on his palette. If he mixes too many, the result is brown. And so it is with Sherry: A good blend is very far from just an averaging-out process. It must create a vivid new character out of as small a number of old ones as possible.

The Sherries one sees advertised—the Bristol Creams, Dry Sacks, and La Inas—are all products of this process. Most blended Sherries stick fairly closely to one of the classical styles in which *soleras* are classified. In other words, despite blending, they remain recognizably Finos, Olorosos, or Amontillados.

But some adopt more descriptive names—Cream, Milk, Golden, Brown, Amoroso, or just Medium. Blends like these are often made to order by one of the large shippers of Jerez for a big-trade customer who has no *bodegas* of his own. Until recently even the famous Bristol Cream was ghosted for Harvey's by famous Spanish houses.

The English influence in Jerez is obvious in the names of many of the biggest shipping firms, although today the Spanish share of the business is growing. Williams & Humbert recently has been bought by a Spanish company. But Duff Gordon, Sandeman, Osborne, and Wisdom & Warter are all names that tell the same story as the great Port names: Croft, Taylor, and, again, Sandeman. Gonzalez, Byass & Co. and Pedro Domecq are among the biggest and best of the Spanish houses. Among the other very distinguished *bodegas* whose wines one should look out for are some of my favorites: Valdespino, La Riva, Garvey, Bobadilla, and Emilio Lustau.

Each of these houses ships a full range of dry, medium, and sweet Sherries. The word "dry," however, has so many connotations and is used so freely that it is wise to look for the exact term "Fino" if a pale dry Sherry is what one wants. Gonzalez, Byass & Co.'s Tio Pepe, Pedro Domecq's La Ina, Garvey's San Patricio, and Williams & Humbert's Pando are probably the best known of all Finos. But I would try any Spanish-bottled Fino that was recommended to me, as long as I thought it was freshly in stock and had not been waiting on a shelf for months, a fate that all too many suffer. The same applies to Manzanillas but even more emphatically: Their special quality is a perishable commodity.

It used to be the fate of Sherry in England to sit around on sideboards in dusty decanters until all its life and flavor had drained away. As it did not actually turn to vinegar, nobody noticed how flat it had become. The wine trade knew this and fortified its wine accordingly, making it strong and dull but at least relatively stable.

Today we are beginning to understand that Sherry is as sensitive as any other great wine. We chill it, as a white wine should be chilled, and we drink it up as we would a bottle of Rhine wine or Burgundy. The result is that less highly fortified, more delicate Sherries are within our grasp. There is no wine so stimulating to the appetite, as I began by saying. With the greatest respect to the dry Martini, I must say it is outclassed by Sherry before any meal at which wine is to be drunk. And as we enter the Golden Age of Gastronomy, at what meal isn't it?

June 1972

Adrift on a Sea of Vines

Gerald Asher

There is a point on Route Nationale 7 between Avignon and Aix-en-Provence where a slight rise leads through a cutting. Especially on a summer evening it is here that a traveler on the road from Paris first breathes in, along with the mingled perfume of wild thyme and pine, the air of the Mediterranean. When I drive through that gap I have a special sense of release, of entering a world that is at the same time more languid and more intensely ardent than any other, more elegant and more sensuous, more intelligent and more frivolous, with priorities ranged in good-humored perspective.

The car windows are always opened wide to let in the flood of memories: Familiar hilltop villages, buffeted by the years and bleached by the sun, fade into visions of herb and lemon stalls in the Toulon street market; images of fishing boats at Sanary-sur-Mer unloading their catch for sale under the manicured palms that surround, at a respectful distance, the very proper town bandstand are replaced by remembrances of lazy afternoons on the beach at Les Lecques, shared, of course, with half the population of Marseilles; and even stronger is the memory of fresh-caught sardines grilled on a fire of vine cuttings at the kitchen door of the Peyraud house. Yes, I think, above all, the Mediterranean means to me the joyful atmosphere of the Peyraud house, comfortably adrift on a sea of vines, the most loving and serene of ships; a welcoming Noah's Ark for people. Plain and gray, like many another Provençal *mas,* it has the air of containing the secret of life's happiness, apparent less in signs of mellowness—the patina of crumbled stucco and faded window shutters—than in the message of the child's worn swing that hangs from a lopsided cherry tree; the umbrella pine that doubles as an outdoor family salon, protecting an old millstone table and a clutter of dusty wooden chairs from the late afternoon sun; the ancient vine that curls over the west front of the house and covers the uneven brick terrace with a shady green canopy; and the wide front door with its fist-size key always on the outside—day and night.

One evening late last May I took the familiar turn off the main road at Le Canet, through the hills to Le Beausset, and then followed the narrow, high-banked road that leads to Le Plan-du-Castellet and the Domaine Tempier of the Peyraud family. It had been a long drive from Paris, and it was almost nine o'clock when the noise of the engine and the barking of the dogs brought the family out to greet me. There were Lucie and Lucien Peyraud (it is strange that two such names should come together, like a shepherd and a shepherdess in an early Mozart opera); their sons, Francois and Jean-Marie; their sons' wives, Catherine and Paule; Véronique, the last daughter to remain at home; and, in the background shyly, some sleepy grandchildren. With a glass of Champagne we crossed the year that had elapsed since we had last seen each other, and by the time we went into the dining room it was as if I had left them only yesterday.

Lucie Tempier Peyraud has roots at Le Plan. Descended from a line of Marseilles merchants, she inherited this country *mas,* orginally built for her great-great-grandmother. The vineyards around it, mostly spilling down narrow, terraced ledges that the labor of centuries created, were destroyed by phylloxera about a hundred years ago, and their replanting and regeneration has been an act of faith and courage. Lucien Peyraud's attachment to the Tempier vineyards is almost mystical, as if in marrying Lucie he had also married these few scattered acres that remain attached to their steep hillsides only through the will of God and backbreaking work on the supporting terrace walls. Some of the ledges, rarely more than thirty or forty yards long, are so narrow that they can hold only a row or two of vines each, and most of the cultivation must be done by hand. His face and hands roughened by sun and wind, Lucien Peyraud is a down-to-earth man if ever there was one, yet he is as proud and tender in his regard for his vines as any father for his child. No other vineyard I know is nourished by such passion as his.

———

The wine region of Bandol is one of the oldest in France. We can be certain that the Greeks, whose settlements led to the founding of the cities of Marseilles and Nice, brought vines and planted them where they seemed most likely to flourish. They undoubtedly saw, as we still can see today, that the hills above the bay of Bandol, quite close to Marseilles, form an arena protected by the mountains behind them. Here, vine-covered slopes face south and benefit from the clear sunlight reflected off the sea, as well as from the tempering effect of the water.

There is evidence of trading in Bandol wines as far back as Roman times. Wine jars, or fragments of them, continually turn up in the nets of local fishermen, and in a geography of Provence, published in 1787, the region was lauded for its red wines "of first quality . . . mostly highly prized. They sum up quite simply the real virtues of the Provençal soil and its products: honesty, finesse and ardour." By the mid-nineteenth century, wines from all the villages that surround the port were being shipped to markets as far away as Brazil and India. Just as Bordeaux—on a much grander scale, of course—gave its name to the whole region that shipped from its quays, so Bandol gave its name to the wines of La Cadière-d'Azur, Le Plan-du-Castellet, Le Castellet, Le Beausset, Saint-Cyr-sur-Mer, Sanary-sur-Mer, Ollioules, Le Brulat, and Sainte-Anne-d'Evenos. It is impossible to say whether the million gallons of wine exported each year by the close of the Second Empire were all Bandol in the sense that the *appellation* is defined today, but the region, if fully planted, is capable of producing that much wine. In 1941, when a decree officially granted Bandol growers their own Appellation Contrôlée, annual production of wine from the entire area had dropped to barely thirty thousand cases. Production is now about 150,000 cases of red, rosé, and white wines a year, from the vineyards of some two hundred small growers—a fragmented, but very personal, wine region.

I first became interested in the wines of Bandol in the late fifties. There was, and is, very little white. In that climate it is difficult to produce the crispness that one would most want in a white wine. Clairette and Ugni Blanc grapes are used, primarily for wines to be consumed by the grower's family. Oddly enough, the fishing village of Cassis, only a few miles away, manages to produce a quite passable white wine from the same grapes; but then the *calanques* (deep creeks), which bring the cool sea air well into the hillsides there, probably help. The best white wine of Bandol that I remember was from Château Millière, near Sanary, a vineyard now threatened with extinction by the spread of grotesque little villas. Monsieur Roethlisberger, a Swiss winegrower, had brought his light touch with white wines from his native Alpine vineyards and until his death produced wines of extraordinary delicacy and flavor.

The rosés, found in every good restaurant from Marseilles to Nice, had more character than most others and were much superior to the general run of Provence rosés. Ranging from the heavy, tannic wines of Château Pradeaux at Saint-Cyr to the racy, elegant wines of Lucien Peyraud at the Domaine Tempier, the reds were obviously in a class with wines from far more distinguished regions. Over the years that I shipped them regularly to London—where they met with some success—I found that the rosés, though delicious when young, aged unusually well, developing an aroma of ripe pears. The reds, especially those from Pradeaux and Tempier, needed to be aged.

Grenache vines are common throughout this region of the Rhône delta: They are as important in Bandol as they are at nearby Châteauneuf-du-Pape and Gigondas. Important, too, is the Cinsault vine, thought, because of its country name of *le romain,* to have been brought to the region in the knapsack of some wandering centurion. These two varieties are the basis of the rosé wines of Bandol, but small patches of the uncommon Tibouren or the local Pécoui-Touar are to be found here and there, adding a more subtle strain of flavor.

The special quality of the reds is due entirely to the Mourvèdre and its adaptation to the particular conditions of Bandol. It is a variety of vine that spread through southern France from the Mediterranean coast of Spain during the Middle Ages. In most areas its popularity was short-lived. Though vigorous in growth, it is low in yield; and the wine, deep colored and tannic, has an intense personality that needs careful aging to give of its best. There are still a few Mourvèdre vines at Châteauneuf-du-Pape and even as far away as Cognac in the Charentes, where the variety has the inexplicable name of Balzac Noir. It seems to have found its natural home in the band of chalk and silica that runs through the Bandol hills. In most cases I have found that the quality of any red wine of Bandol can be directly related to the proportion of Mourvèdre in the vineyard. The *appellation* law has established that, of the vine varieties permitted, a minimum of ten percent must be Mourvèdre; and although a wine made entirely from Mourvèdre grapes might be overwhelming in scale even when mature, I am certain that the basis of Lucien Peyraud's quality is the sacrifice he makes to maintain such a high proportion of these vines, difficult and ungenerous though he knows them to be.

Altitude also affects the quality of the wine, but whether this is a result of the greater exposure to sunlight, the cooling effect of the breezes, or the more arid, spare soils one finds on the hilltops, I wouldn't like to say—probably a combination of all three. Lucien ferments separately the grapes from each small lot of vines. Eventually he blends them to produce a uniform wine for each vintage, but checking the young wines with him, noting the differences of character and style that mark each one, is an exciting experience. At a tasting the next morning a colleague traveling with me, a man whose training and experience had been in the wider acres of California, was astounded at the family's care to preserve every nuance of their wines and at their familiarity with the shading of taste that each lot brings.

———

At table that night we began with a neighbor's white wine because Lucien doesn't produce one. We drank it with the typical hors d'oeuvres of Provence: cold spinach omelet, purée of eggplant, *tapenade* of olive and anchovy. The hors d'oeuvres were followed by a superb *mérou*, a Mediterranean fish related to the grouper, gently poached and served simply with a little lemon and a fruity olive oil as sauce. With it Lucien produced a rosé in an unfamiliar bottle. It was from Bellet, a village a few miles above Nice possessing one of the few other Appellations Contrôlées in the south of France. It was at least fifteen years since I had last tasted one, on a visit to that very village, at the personal vineyard of a prosperous Nice wine merchant. Standing at the roadside near his house I had seen how the suburbs of Nice were poised to engulf his vines. The wine, as I remember it, artfully packaged in a dumpy bottle with gold thread around it, was among the less distinguished wines that I have ever tasted; and though it might seem uncharitable, I was able to contemplate its possible end without feeling much distress.

But here was a wine from Bellet from a grower I hadn't known of, a wine that showed why this tiny enclave of vines had been recognized with an *appellation* of its own in the first place. It was delicately fruity, crisply dry, and with a fresh, lingering aftertaste. It was lighter than most of the Bandol rosés, which, though not particularly alcoholic, seem to have a richness of glycerin that gives them a muscular, full-bodied style.

Lucien followed the rosé with both the 1969 and 1970 reds of the Domaine Tempier while Lucie produced a leg of lamb, fragrant with garlic and the pungent herbs of the *garrigue* to accompany them. The 1969, with which I was already very familiar thanks to a small stock at home in San Francisco, is one of Lucien's most elegant wines. It is dark, with a bouquet that I find, perhaps fancifully, to have an echo of the thyme and pine perfume of those hills. Well balanced, it is soft enough to enjoy and zesty enough to promise pleasure for quite some time. The 1970, which I had previously tasted only in wood, is a bigger wine. It is heavier than the 1969, is less revealing in bouquet and flavor, and its youthful tannin is still quite bold. We preferred first the pleasure of one, then the promise of the other, and then weren't sure, and went on tasting and talking and nibbling at the fresh little Banon cheeses that had appeared on the table—and nobody noticed how late it was getting to be.

November 1975

Upstarts Down Under

Gerald Asher

For weeks I had been telling friends that, no, I wasn't going to visit *Australia,* I was going to visit *wineries in Australia,* not realizing how much more I would see than those who only get to gawp at the Great Barrier Reef, Ayers Rock, and the Sydney Opera House.

For a start, and particularly in Victoria and South Australia, I was astonished to see a countryside lifted straight from eighteenth-century canvases. With immense grass borders for herding animals, gravel and sand roads wind past mannered trees—gracefully inclined and just smudged here and there with a suggestion of painterly foliage—under which perfect rent-a-flock sheep peacefully graze. Most of the time I seemed to be driving through a series of picture frames, and I half expected John Constable to jump out from behind a hedge waving his brush and palette.

And then I was unprepared for the charm of Australia's small towns. At Mudgee, for example, in the hills of New South Wales, the municipal buildings and railway station were designed and built, even at that remote edge of empire, from the same plans and drawing boards as town halls and railway stations all over Victorian England. The clock turned back a hundred years for me, and I saw the firm hand of the Colonial Office. In Victoria the town of Bendigo, once a gold rush metropolis, is decorated with a profusion of cast-iron frippery that makes New Orleans' French Quarter look chaste. And, if Australian moviemakers have back lots, I am sure a replica of the main street of Rutherglen is on one of them.

Australia's vineyards are spread through all six states, but mostly they are in New South Wales, Victoria, and South Australia. For comparison's sake, at the last count, in 1985, California had 728,000 acres of vineyard, including, as do Australia's 160,000 acres, vines producing grapes for raisins and table use as well as for wine.

Though the first Australian attempt to plant vines—in 1788 in what is now called Sydney—was unsuccessful, by 1822 an Australian red wine shipped to London had earned a silver medal from the Royal Society of Arts. The medal was awarded by way of encouragement (the wine was "by no means of superior quality," the Society's archives record), but that could hardly have been true of the gold medal awarded the same grower for a wine shipped six years later.

By then, however, the settlers in general and the medal-winning grower, Gregory Blaxland, in particular had had the benefit of James Busby's *A Treatise on the Culture of the Vine and the Art of Making Wine,* published in Sydney in 1825. Busby, son of the colony's newly arrived water engineer, had studied viticulture in France before accompanying his father to Australia, and the *Treatise* drew on what he had learned there as well as on the published works of others. After teaching viticulture for a while to boys at an orphans' farm school near Sydney, Busby left in 1831 to travel through Spain and France, reviewing techniques there while collecting vine varieties that he hoped would flourish in Australia. The carefully packed cuttings of the more than a hundred varieties shipped back were propagated to provide a basic stock from which many of Australia's early vineyards sprang.

Though Busby himself moved to New Zealand in 1832 to take up a government appointment and remained there until he died some forty years later, his book and the cuttings had a lasting effect on viticulture in Australia. Certain rare French varieties thought to be relics of Busby's collection (the Crouchen, for example) are planted commercially in Australia but no longer exist in France; and a preferred clone of Chardonnay now spreading through Australia from the small and viticulturally isolated wine region around Mudgee is believed to be directly descended from cuttings taken by Busby from vines within Clos Vougeot more than 150 years ago. Above all, he is credited with the introduction of the Shiraz grape, sometimes known as Hermitage from the name of the Rhône Valley hill where, under the synonym Syrah, it gives its most famous wine. (I had first carelessly written "its best wine," but memories of too many superb Australian Shiraz came crowding in to rebuke me.)

After their initial flourish, both interrupted and sustained by a rush to the gold fields, Australia's vineyards lapsed into mediocrity from the turn of the century until the end of World War II. Australians at that time ate and drank with no particular interest in either food or wine. Overseas the United Kingdom, Australia's principal market, had a structure of Imperial duty preference that favored high-strength Australian red wine sold there as Invalid Port (labels promised cures for everything from liver troubles to loss of willpower) or blended with thinner stuff to create a cheap flagon wine called Australian Burgundy. In short neither home nor export markets offered much encouragement to Australian vintners to produce anything but alcoholic red wine and high-strength white suitable as a base for Sherry.

There had always been exceptions, of course, to serve as reminders of what was possible. But a renaissance started when Max Schubert, winemaker at Penfolds in South Australia, returned in 1950 from a visit to Bordeaux. Working with Shiraz rather than Cabernet Sauvignon, Bordeaux's key grape variety, and with more obstruction than support from the Penfolds board, he translated what he had seen in France into a wine now considered an Australian classic—Penfolds' Grange Hermitage.

Inspired in part by his success (which took some years to be recognized as such) and in part by the ideas that had influenced him, others followed. Changes initiated during the sixties and gathering momentum in the seventies have led to a worldwide respect for Australian wine, magnified perhaps by present interest in Australia but by no means merely a consequence of it. It is food for thought that a group of competent London professionals, recently sitting in blind judgment on the quality of wines served by major airlines to Business Class passengers on their international services, gave first place to Qantas for a Tyrrell Cabernet-Merlot from Hunter Valley, in New South Wales, and moved British Airways from nineteenth place last year to third this as a result of the airline's switch to a Pirramimma Cabernet Sauvignon from South Australia's McLaren Vale. It is significant, too, that an Australian has recently been invited to head the University of California's Department of Viticulture and Enology at Davis, the principal teaching and research institution for wine in the United States.

———

Max Schubert's urge to do better would not have been enough to change the tide had there not been strong complementary currents. Since the war, new immigrants to Australia (until then most immigrants were from the British Isles) had arrived from Italy, Greece, Yugoslavia, and other parts of Mediterranean Europe. Increasing numbers were arriving from Asia. By the 1960s Australia was changing. And, because almost ninety percent of Australians live in twelve major cities, the changing produce markets and restaurants rapidly affected the eating habits of *all* Australians. (It is ironic that the country many Americans perceive as a wild new frontier should have the most urban population in the world.) *Souvlaki* bought from a Greek butcher would appear on the barbecue along with the customary chops; marinated chicken wings and stuffed quail, Indonesian *satés,* and grilled bell peppers became part of the regular family backyard menu. Neighbors talked about food. And drank wine.

Demand created by those used to drinking simple red wine with their meals could not have come at a more opportune time, because it was clear the United Kingdom outlet for Australian high-strength blending wines would disappear with the loss of preferential rates of duty accompanying Britain's entry into the Common Market.

Australia had, for decades, selected warm sites, chosen vine varieties appropriate for them, and used winemaking techniques directed at producing wines valued in the United Kingdom for their bulk and their alcohol. At first the vintners were obliged to combine ingenuity with what they already had in order to transform these same grapes into new-style wines with the required freshness, flavor, and zest for table-wine consumption. Gradually equipment caught up with the winemakers' changed needs, and vineyards spread into cooler areas, especially at higher elevations. Hill-Smith, for example, a veteran wine-growing family in Barossa Valley, elected to plant its new Heggies vineyard at fifteen hundred feet; David Wynn, the man credited with reviving Coonawarra as a region for Cabernet Sauvignon, has now developed eighty acres of vineyard at two thousand feet on what was virgin pastureland; and Brian Croser of Petaluma winery has created a series of temperate vineyards from a slice of the steep Adelaide Hills, once given over to foggy market gardens. New acreage of previously scarce varietals—Cabernet Sauvignon, Pinot Noir, Sauvignon Blanc, and Traminer—advances as fast as Grenache and Palomino retreat. Whereas there were fewer than a hundred acres of Chardonnay in all Australia just ten years ago, there are now close to seven thousand.

These European varieties, familiar to us, will grow in all of Australia's wine regions. But in each region some do better than others. Even Shiraz, a grape that adapts to conditions just about everywhere, gives a completely different *style* of wine from region to region. The taste of Shiraz from Hunter Valley, for example, especially a Tyrrel or a McWilliam's, with full-throated flavor and a typical tarry, leathery bouquet that hangs in the air (known to local connoisseurs as "sweaty saddle"), hardly resembles the rich, concentrated fruit of a Mudgee Shiraz from Huntington Estate, Miramar, or Botobolar, let alone the elegant, scented versions produced in central Victoria at Mount Avoca and at Chateau Tahbilk (my idea of how the Garden of Eden must have been), the intensely berry-flavored wine produced by Kay Brothers Amery Winery from McLaren Vale Shiraz vines planted in 1892.

To help Australian vintners establish new priorities in making this transition from fortified wines, where errors were more easily accommodated, to light, crisp table wines, where they are not, the Riverina College of Advanced Education at Wagga Wagga introduced courses in the early seventies with a highly structured approach to winemaking. ("Wagga Wagga" is aboriginal for something like "place where many crows screech together," not entirely inappropriate for a College of Advanced Education.) Inevitably the highly technical Wagga methods, relying heavily on an appropriate installation, left little room for rule of thumb and seemed, on the face of it, opposed to the pragmatic approach of several generations of Roseworthy Agricultural College graduates, who still made wine from the vineyard up rather than forward from a computer console.

Roseworthy graduates still pretend to be a little scornful of their Wagga peers, who are unnerved, say the former, if placed in a winery without every conceivable electronic aid; and Wagga graduates are quick to identify as flaws what their Roseworthy colleagues treasure in their wines as idiosyncratic characteristics. In fact, though everyone has some kind of ax to grind, by asking each winemaker to explain, step by step, what he actually did to make his wine, I found a greater uniformity of view than either side admits. Theoretically, for example, the Wagga school believes in cleaning white grape juice by mechanical means—filter or centrifuge—before fermenting it, whereas Roseworthy allows the juice to stand so that grape solids can fall and leave the juice (more or less) bright. Wagga worries about such things as stuck fermentation in its nice, clean juice, but Roseworthy says: "What do you expect when you take all the yeast's nutrients away?" In practice, however, Roseworthy graduates are as eager as anyone else to benefit from the latest filters and bladder presses; and some Wagga graduates, on the other hand, are happy to leave young Chardonnay wallowing on its yeast-lees for months after fermentation.

—

Brian Croser, who set up the Wagga courses after graduating from the University of California at Davis, says he wanted to give positive instruction instead of taking what he felt was California's remedial approach. An influential guru to those he has taught, Croser describes sound winemaking as "causing least aberration to fruit received from the vineyard." Though others would differ, at least in degree, he refers to the options of winemaking as condiments and maintains that a wine's structure, as well as the length and style of its flavor, are established in the vineyard. "The rest is spice, and, if it is allowed to dominate, it is because the fruit wasn't good enough."

In reaching back to the vineyard, Croser demonstrates that, though he and others might place emphasis differently and even hold divergent opinions on everything from the width of vine rows to the aeration of grape juice, all sides of the Australian industry accept that fermentation and aging are steps in a winemaking process begun when a vine is planted. In Australia it is the vineyard rather than the winery that presently absorbs most attention.

Croser's vines are labor intensive, requiring careful control of the leaf canopy to advance grape maturity and retain an appropriate bite of acidity. But vineyard labor in Australia is expensive and not always available. Not only is there greater reliance on mechanical picking, proportionately, than seems to be the case in California, but pruning, too, is often mechanical, carried out with equipment resembling monster hedge cutters. Mechanical pruning leads to growth at the head of the vine as dense and as convoluted as the coils on Medusa's head, and sometimes as dangerous. Though small bunches held within the tangle present no problem to mechanical pickers, which shake the vine vigorously to cause ripe grapes to fall onto receiving track belts, they are difficult to reach with protective sprays during the growing season and therefore become subject to molds and rot.

To resolve this, in 1973 Australia's official Commonwealth Scientific and Industrial Research Organization (CSIRO) initiated trials with vines pruned so minimally that for all practical viticultural purposes they could be considered not pruned at all. Contrary to the hedge-pruned vines, grown in upon themselves, these vines—left virtually untouched for years except for something resembling a haircut along the bottom each year after the fruit had set, just to keep the aisles clear from trailing growth—form for themselves an arbor of old wood as a supporting trellis, just as an unpruned rosebush would. Bunches close to the surface ripen evenly with better sugar and better acid than do those on either mechanically or conventionally pruned vines.

These studies are highly controversial. They destroy traditional bearings (in my mind I saw woodcut images of hundreds of generations of little men, from Noah on, all with secateur in hand and all about to be proved wrong), and there are winemakers who suggest that the very qualities claimed for the fruit of such vines (more but smaller bunches, meaning more skin for flavor and color relative to juice) would be detrimental to fine wine because of the greater measure of harsh tannins they would also contribute. On the other hand, though comparative taste tests among Coonawarra Cabernet Sauvignon wines made from the test block of vines and from neighboring vineyards pruned normally can be no more than sketchy indicators due to the limited nature of the experiment, wine made from the minimally pruned vines gave the best result. (The CSIRO block is part of the Coonawarra Rouge Homme vineyard owned by Lindemans.)

———

Coonawarra, a thin layer of red clay over a freak bed of limestone a mile wide and about eight miles long, has five thousand acres of potential vineyard land, of which four thousand are already planted. It is always described as fertile, but with my own eyes I saw vines producing more prolifically on the black earth at its perimeter. Coonawarra shares, however, with the Médoc and Napa Valley an affinity for Cabernet Sauvignon and produces from it wines with tightly focused flavor. As a result more Cabernet Sauvignon is planted here than anywhere else in Australia.

Because of the prestige of Cabernet Sauvignon, and the variety's concentration in Coonawarra, most major wineries own vineyards or buy grapes there. Seppelt, of Barossa, and Petaluma grow Cabernet Sauvignon in Coonawarra; Orlando uses Coonawarra grapes for its St. Hugo Cabernet Sauvignon; and even Rosemount and Hungerford Hill grow grapes in Coonawarra and then lug them, chilled, all the way to their home wineries in New South Wales. Some wineries own satellite or subsidiary establishments in Coonawarra. Lindemans, also of New South Wales, owns the Rouge Homme vineyard and winery, where its St. George Vineyard Cabernet Sauvignon is produced, and Penfolds owns Wynns, which makes the outstanding John Riddoch cuvées of Cabernet Sauvignon.

Not all Coonawarra wineries and vineyards have far-flung connections, however. Among other wineries offering excellent Cabernet Sauvignon, with the vintages I most liked when I visited, are Hollick's Wines (1985), Bowen Estate (1982), and Katnook Estate (1984). Mildara's winemaker, Gavin Hogg, has made a sensational 1985 (called, rather prosaically, Alexander's Dry Red Blend) in which he has combined Cabernet Sauvignon with Cabernet Franc and Malbec, a combination that is more common in Saint-Emilion than in the Médoc. It is a beautiful wine, scented and with backbone.

———

Apart from its success in Coonawarra, Cabernet Sauvignon also does well elsewhere in South Australia. In McLaren Vale south of Adelaide it is firmer (Wirra Wirra, Pirramimma, and Daringa produce good examples of the local style). In Clare, best known for its Rhine Riesling (as Johannisberg Riesling is known in Australia), it is lighter. Clare has a cool climate, despite its location to the north of Coonawarra; Australia is topsy-turvy, remember. Cabernet Sauvignons produced there by Grosset, Knappstein, and Mitchell wineries in particular are Bordeaux-like in the way they combine depth of flavor and grace of structure. Tim Knappstein, listening patiently when I told him so, observed: "I don't think we try to make Bordeaux copies, but we do strive for classic dimensions."

In central Victoria, Cabernet Sauvignon has a firm and, to my taste, even severe style, the best example of which is produced at Taltarni. At Chateau Remy, a few miles away, this style is broadened by the addition of Shiraz and Merlot for the Blue Pyrenees Estate red wine.

Combinations of Cabernet Sauvignon and Shiraz are common in Australia, and, though they might seem bizarre, they have an honorable antecedent in the blending of Syrah-based Hermitage wine from the Rhône with the Cabernet-Merlot wines of Bordeaux in the nineteenth century. Writing in his *Journal of a Tour Through Some of the Vineyards of Spain and France,* a record of his 1831 trip, James Busby wrote: "The finest Clarets of Bourdeaux [*sic*] are mixed with a portion of the finest red wine of Hermitage, and four-fifths of the quantity of the latter which is produced are thus employed." The best, and most expensive, red wines of Bordeaux at that time, including the first growths, were those improved in this way and listed as *Hermitagé.*

I found the combination works especially well in Hunter Valley (where the Cabernet Sauvignon is softer and tames the boisterousness of Shiraz without greatly changing it) and in Coonawarra, in Lindemans' Limestone Ridge Vineyard blend and in Penfolds' Coonawarra Cabernet-Shiraz blend—particularly its recent Bin 620, a 1982 vintage. There, when Cabernet Sauvignon character becomes too aggressive, Shiraz mellows in.

New South Wales has been less successful than either South Australia or Victoria with Cabernet Sauvignon (honorably excepting the elegant Cabernet Sauvignon from Lake's Folly—Max Lake plays Bach to encourage the yeast in its work—and the outstanding wines made at high elevation by Mudgee wineries such as Montrose and Huntington Estate), but it produces Chardonnay and Sémillon of a scale unmatched elsewhere. Phillip Shaw, winemaker at Rosemount Estate, makes internationally acclaimed Chardonnays in a voluptuously complex style, and Davie Lowe, winemaker at The Rothbury Estate, produces big, intense Sémillons that age magnificently. Petersons is also known for the scale of its Chardonnay, and there are others, less assertive perhaps, produced at Brokenwood, McWilliam's, and Wyndham Estate. The Robson Vineyard's fine, spare Chardonnay is quite distinct from others in the region.

If South Australia has Cabernet Sauvignon and Riesling as its specialties, and New South Wales its Shiraz, Chardonnay, and Sémillon, Victoria's climate (or climates) makes possible an even wider range of wines. Near Rutherglen, in the northeast, are rich, aged Muscat wines with the dense flavor of hazelnut praline. Victoria is where the best examples of Pinot Noir can be found, at Balgownie winery in the center of the state (Stuart Anderson, Balgownie's winemaker, produces a well-bred Cabernet Sauvignon, too) and at Yeringberg, Yarra Yering, and Diamond Valley Vineyards, all in Yarra Valley, northeast of Melbourne. Yarra Valley suffered severe setbacks earlier in the century, when prohibitionist sentiments in Victoria did much to damage the state's wine industry. It is, however, rapidly recovering and producing outstandingly balanced Chardonnays at Coldstream Hills and Yarra Burn and deliciously forthright Cabernet Sauvignons at Mount Mary and Seville Estate.

———

Many wineries were kind enough to show me treasures: an 1886 Port at Seppelt, aged in barrel for a century so that it had become less like a vintage Port and more like a rich, very old Oloroso Sherry; fine old

Liqueur Muscats at the Morris and Campbells wineries at Rutherglen; and luscious old Tokays at Baileys. I was introduced to wines I had not seen before: flowery whites made at Lindemans, Hungerford Hill, and Hardy's from the Verdelho grape of Madeira; pure Marsanne (in France it is usually blended with Roussanne) at Mitchelton and Chateau Tahbilk; and Tarrango, a cross of Tarrigo and Thompson used at Brown Brothers to produce a dry white wine with raspberry-like aroma.

What impressed me particularly, however, was to find some of the best wines of all within the facilities of the largest wineries. Orlando, Penfolds, Mildara, Wynns Coonawarra, McWilliam's, and Seppelt are far from anyone's idea of boutique wineries. Robin Day, senior winemaker at Orlando, where I tasted one of the most perfect Traminers in years, said that small wineries are snobbish about the volume of bag-in-box wines turned out by the major wineries.

"Apart from the fact that bag-in-box wines have made Australia a wine-drinking country, their success means we have the resources as well as the will to run small wineries where premium wines are made within our large wineries." What he said held true even for the giant Berri Estates cooperative in the Riverland of South Australia, which clunk-clunks its way through the largest production of any winery in Australia but manages to produce Chardonnay and Shiraz that would be the envy of many hands-on winemakers.

Small wineries in Australia are more idiosyncratic than ours in California and are less likely to bulge with expensive equipment. ("A small winery doesn't have to be like a large winery reduced in scale," one small-winery owner explained with irrefutable logic.) Ian Macrae, whose 1985 Mudgee Chardonnay was among the finest I tasted, has surrounded his winery with what I can only describe as an acre of existential junkyard so that he can design and make his own equipment to get his wine the way he wants it.

Others successfully adapt simple domestic appliances and equipment or learn, appropriately, to think small. One grower overcame the cost of installing sealed steel tanks for carbonic maceration (to keep grapes in an atmosphere of carbon dioxide generated by their own fermentation) by picking the bunches off the vines and putting them directly into huge, tough plastic bags. The maceration takes place as the sealed bags sit between the rows of vines. Tipping the contents into the winery's crusher later is a lot easier than transferring the mass of grapes from a tank.

A "waste not, want not" attitude applies to Australian wine-region food, too. In country restaurants I could usually order the bits that don't go to market—kidneys, lamb brains, tongue—all imaginatively and well cooked. I also had hot smoked leg of young lamb at the Knappsteins', and I remember with special pleasure barbecued fillets of kangaroo at Coldstream Hills.

A few days before I came home I lunched with the owner of a small Clare winery and his wife. We were drinking a bottle of his Cabernet Sauvignon with stuffed quail straight off the grill in a small restaurant—more a glassed-in lean-to, really—set in a thicket of aromatic trees off one of those unpaved roads. We were eating late, and there were no other customers, and so the cook, a quite young woman, put a Mozart aria on her record player in the kitchen. I can't remember now who the singer was or what she was singing, but I remember thinking that, for all we hear about Australia, no one ever bothers to say how poetic the place is.

August 1987

Chile's New Golden Age

Gerald Asher

Earlier this year, on a ship cruising the coasts of Greece and southern Italy—a part of the world where the local wines flow as easily and almost as cheaply as water—one of the red wines offered at dinner every night was a Cabernet Sauvignon from distant Chile. The English, the Japanese, and the Scandinavians are all drinking Chilean Chardonnay; and Chile, after Italy and France, is now the third most important supplier of imported wine to the United States. Last year Chile shipped over fifteen million cases of wine to more than eighty countries around the globe, up from twelve million cases the previous year and nine million the year before that. The most remarkable thing is that just twenty years ago Chile exported next to no wine at all.

Spain's sixteenth-century conquistadors brought the first vine cuttings to Chile. They were mostly País, a simple black grape, rather like the Mission in California, that crops abundantly but makes dull wine. According to family records, Gregorio Ossa, founder of Viña La Rosa in the Cachapoal Valley, ninety miles south of Santiago, brought cuttings of French vines to Chile as early as 1824. What they were is not clear; Cabernet Sauvignon and other specifically Bordeaux varieties are thought to have been introduced only in 1851 by Silvestre Ochagavia, who planted them on his family estate at Talagante, about thirty miles from Santiago. In 1856 the influential Cousiño family—at various times its industrial empire has reached into every aspect of economic activity in Chile—acquired the Macul hacienda, and some years later replanted its vineyards, renowned since colonial times, with French vines. Other growers, too, began to plant French vines, culminating in a great surge of new vineyards in the 1870s and 1880s, about the time Chile went to war with Peru and Bolivia to gain sole possession of the nitrates and copper in a disputed desert on their common border.

Chile's subsequent dominance of the Pacific coast of South America (Chilean troops had actually occupied Lima from 1881 to 1883) brought enormous wealth to the country's governing families. For them it was a golden age. The specific impetus to plant vineyards at this time was probably the outbreak of phylloxera in France; there was widespread speculation that French wine production would never recover from it. But the appearance of so many handsome new wineries attached to elegant residences—all of them within a carriage ride of the capital—was clearly intended to display more than an interest in agricultural pursuits.

But the golden age didn't last. The nitrate boom ended when German scientists discovered, under the exigencies of World War I, how to fabricate nitrates industrially. And then Chile put a spoke in its own viticultural wheel. An anti-alcohol law of 1938, intended to curb the production of cheap País wine sold by small farmers in the impoverished south, imposed draconian controls nationwide that made any extension of the area under vines virtually impossible (a move not entirely unwelcome among the families with extensive vineyard holdings). It also fixed a ceiling on the annual national wine production at sixty liters a head. Over the next forty years, however, Chile's population doubled and wine production was allowed, within the limits of the 1938 law, to follow suit. But the area under vines remained the same. The predictable decline in quality was made worse by import controls imposed at the start of World War II. These blocked the acquisition of winemaking equipment and, for decades, effectively cut Chile off from the technical advances made elsewhere. Fermented in concrete tanks at high temperatures and then aged for excessively long periods in wooden vats that had seen better days, most of the wines were increasingly dull, oxidized, or both.

"It wasn't that the producers *wanted* to keep their wines so long in wood," Arturo Cousiño, of Cousiño-Macul, explained to me when I was in Chile last March. "Bottle supplies were totally inadequate and deliveries were irregular and unpredictable. We had to scrounge for old bottles and reuse them. To have hoped to keep stocks of wine in bottle would have been to dream of an unattainable luxury."

Not surprisingly, Chileans turned away from wine to the fresher, cleaner taste of bottled beers and soft drinks, newly available in the 1970s. And they increased substantially their consumption of *pisco,* a young white brandy usually taken with lemon juice—an ironic consequence given that the 1938 law had been designed to promote sobriety. Through that decade and the next, Chile's annual consumption of wine dropped steadily from sixty liters a head to fifteen. The prices paid for grapes collapsed, and many growers left crops unharvested. Between 1980 and 1985 more than a third of the country's vineyards were ripped out and replaced by fruit orchards, and by the end of the 1980s all but two of the family-owned wineries—founded with such pride more than a century before—had been sold for cash.

In 1979, in the midst of this period of decline, Miguel Torres, of the well-known Spanish wine family, came to Chile and bought at auction an abandoned vineyard near Curicó, some 110 miles south of Santiago. "Curicó is cooler than Maipo, and I saw possibilities," he told me when I met with him at his winery. "The vines were in poor shape. It took two or three years to bring them back. In the meantime I bought grapes to make wine and released my first—a light, fruity Sauvignon Blanc of the 1980 vintage—as soon as it was bottled."

That wine took Santiago by surprise. Compared with the clumsy, throat-grabbing white wines the city had by then become used to, it seemed indecently frivolous. "They called it a ladies' wine," Torres told me. "I told them it was a wine for discriminating drinkers—men or women. But whatever they said, they all wanted to taste it. The enologists flocked to Curicó." What they found were stainless-steel tanks, a refrigeration plant that allowed Torres to control fermentation temperatures, new French oak barrels, and, most important of all, a meticulous approach to winemaking.

"They were particularly impressed by the low temperatures my equipment made possible. But the winery owners were reluctant to spend money. And there were still restrictions—permits, high duties—which made it difficult for them to import the equipment they needed, even had they wanted to. But local reaction was not important to me, really. My efforts were export-directed, and in England, especially, our wines sold well. Other wineries paid attention. They understood what I was doing, and by the late 1980s many of them were making an effort to improve the wines they were hoping to sell abroad."

Rafael Guilisasti, director of overseas sales at Concha y Toro, confirmed that his winery had adopted such a strategy. "When we started looking for new markets, we realized that things had to change. The wines the world was drinking were brighter and fresher than those we had to offer. We needed different varieties, too. Chardonnay, for example, rather than Sauvignon Blanc; Merlot as well as Cabernet Sauvignon.

"By then there were no longer restrictions on vineyard development. The business environment had changed, too. Import duties on capital goods had fallen, allowing us to buy the equipment we needed, and corporate taxes had been lowered to encourage investment. Everything changed very quickly, not only in the wineries but also in the vineyards. Where we had used trellis systems for the vines—they allow heavier yields—we changed to wire-trained cordons for better exposure of the fruit. The lower yields we wanted called for tighter control of irrigation, difficult when our system was basically row flooding. The installation of drip irrigation meant we could move onto the hillsides—better for vines anyway—and use water to improve quality rather than just boost quantity."

In a few years, the structure of the wine industry itself evolved. Faced with the possibility of selling their crops at prices that would barely cover the cost of cultivation, if that, many growers began to build wineries of their own. At the beginning of the 1980s there had been fourteen or fifteen wineries. There were soon sixty, even seventy. Meanwhile, the family ownership of wineries founded in the golden age had dispersed over the years among cousins of the fourth or fifth generations who could not agree on how to finance the costly changes necessary for survival, and so sold their properties. Fortunately, new owners brought enthusiasm as well as money to the industry. Previously untapped areas were opened up to vineyards—the cool Casablanca Valley, for example, between Santiago and the port city of Valparaiso; new clones were introduced from both France and California; and more thought was given to which varieties should be planted where. The producers looked more closely at the differences among Chile's wine regions and started adding distant vineyards, sometimes in the face of logistical efficiency, so that each of the varieties they produced could be grown in an appropriate environment. Everything was monitored. Every vineyard in Chile became a work in progress.

Change had come with a rush that had Chile's youthful winemakers both ecstatic and confused. There was an influx of experts from California and France, most of them involved in joint or new ventures, who brought valuable experience but tended to define the personality of Chilean wines in terms of the markets they were used to. And so, at first, the renaissance was completely market driven. We are now seeing the reemergence of individual winery mannerisms and a freer expression of Chile's regional characteristics. Chile's producers realize that only by showing the distinctiveness of their wines and the nuances of their origins can they break through price barriers that would otherwise keep them forever in the bargain bins of commodity varietals.

"The variety should always be clear," Alvaro Espinoza, the energetic young winemaker at Villa Carmen, told me. "But our *reserva* wines should also reflect the valley, even the vineyard, where the fruit was grown."

He let me taste a pair of 1997 Sauvignon Blancs to illustrate his point. One of them, from moderately warm vineyards in the Rapel and Maule valleys, had a deliciously honeyed, ripe-melon character; the other, made from grapes grown in the Casablanca Valley, was crisper, brighter, and had the slightly green tones that many find attractive in this varietal. Both wines had the direct appeal typical of Espinoza's wines, yet their regional differences could not have been more obvious.

I was aware of other distinctions. For instance, I thought I could detect a difference of style between wines made from Chardonnay vines that had been around in Chile for some time and those made from clones recently introduced from California. There probably *is* such a difference, but I eventually realized that I was picking up the variance between fruit from recently—and therefore densely—planted vines, and fruit from vineyards planted earlier, at a time when there had been a vogue to copy California's wide rows. (When planted densely, the individual vines need ripen fewer bunches for the same yield per acre; but cultivation costs are higher.) I eventually met what was without question Chile's older Chardonnay clone in Santa Carolina's 1997 Reserva de Familia. Made from Chardonnay grapes grown on old vines—some of them planted a century ago—at Santa Rosa del Peral in the cool upper Maipo Valley, close to the Andes, the wine had a tender elegance that masked a firm structure. Its flavor was delicate but long. "The crop is very small," winemaker Pilar Gonzalez told me. "The vineyard's on a slope, and the soil there is thin. Years of open irrigation have eroded much of what there was."

That Maipo Chardonnay stood in startling contrast to another Chardonnay, produced at the Santa Carolina winery by Ignacio Recabarren, an enologist who has led much of the recent viticultural reform in Chile and who now pops up all over the place—as consultant here, winemaker there, special-project director somewhere else. At Santa Carolina he is charged with the production of a separate range of wines marketed under the Villa Casablanca label. His 1997 Chardonnay from the Santa Isabel vineyard in Casablanca Valley, made from vines replicated from cuttings recently brought in from Davis, California, is intense, bold, and lively. The clone, the soil (gravel and limestone), the climatic conditions of a valley completely open to the Pacific, and Recabarren himself must all have contributed something to that wine. Yet even though the valley can give quite fat Chardonnay when the conditions are right—witness the 1996 Amelia from Concha y Toro and the 1995 from Veramonte—the lively acidity and the intensity of fruit flavor at the core of that Recabarren wine are the qualities most characteristic of Casablanca Valley Chardonnays. Others I especially liked, not least for these same regional traits, included the Wild Yeast Cuvée '97 from Errázuriz and the Medalla Real '97 from Santa Rita.

"The Casablanca Valley had been ignored," Agustin Huneeus told me as we toured Veramonte, his imposing new winery overlooking the main highway to Valparaiso. Huneeus, a native of Chile, now lives in California, where he is responsible for the group of wineries associated with Franciscan Vineyards of Napa Valley. "We're beyond the reach of irrigation from the Andes here," he said, "so one is obliged to dig for water; the climate is difficult—there is a high frost risk; and because the vintage is always later here, there is always the danger of rot if the autumn rains arrive early. As a result, cultivation costs are high, and one must be content with limited yields. But when everything is right the wine is magnificent, and that is what makes the risk and the costs acceptable."

———

When Silvestre Ochagavia and his peers brought their cuttings from Bordeaux to Chile, it had been their intention to use a mix of vines of Bordeaux origin to make wines with characteristics similar to those of the Médoc. It would not have occurred to them to make a wine from any single kind of vine: Each one was valued for what it contributed, not for what it was. They were jumbled together in their vineyards, and the wines were sold as proprietary blends. In recent years, when growers needed to identify their individual vines so that cuttings could be taken to create single-variety vineyards for the production of "varietal" wines, they had great difficulty doing so. Some varieties still flourishing in Chile were never replanted in France after the devastation of phylloxera, so even the French, called in to help, couldn't do much better. Carmenère, for example, is a vine not used anymore in Bordeaux. In Chile it was at first misidentified as Merlot. As a result, many vineyards in Chile planted as Merlot are now known to contain a mix of Merlot and Carmenère, or even Carmenère alone. The vines are being sorted out and a few wineries in Chile are now making a Carmenère *cuvée*. Undurraga made an exciting one in 1997. It has a big, wild flavor.

Malbec, too, is being sold as a varietal wine. The best I tasted—more assertive than the few I've come across in California—is the 1997 made by Patricia Inostroza, the winemaker at Montes Wines. Its aroma is of violets, very pure and very intense. Cabernet Sauvignon had played a minor role in Bordeaux in the early nineteenth century, and Carmenère and Malbec quite important ones. If a Chilean producer could be persuaded to produce a wine that combined just these two varieties, we might have a chance to taste what an early nineteenth-century Médoc was really like.

In any case, it is with classic Bordeaux varieties, chiefly Cabernet Sauvignon and Merlot, that Chile has made its greatest impact. It is also among these wines that regional distinctions become clearest. Merlots, for instance, bring out the opulence of the Maipo Valley (as in the Santa Rita 1996 Reserva), the elegance of the Rapel Valley (as in the impressive Merlots from Viña La Rosa), and the lean intensity of Casablanca. There are narrower geographic comparisons, too. I'm sure, for example, that the difference between Cabernet Sauvignons from Santa Rita and those from Concha y Toro, both based in Maipo, has more to do with their vineyards than with anything that happens in the winery after the fruit is picked. Concha y Toro Cabernets have a strong eucalyptus or cassis element; Santa Rita shows in its Cabernets the chocolaty character of very ripe tannins.

In the course of a week I had a chance to taste Cabernets from all regions and from many vintages, some of them going back to the 1970s and 1960s. It would be pointless to list them all when few of the older wines, anyway, are available in the United States. It might be helpful for me to mention, though, that there are some fine 1996s and 1997s on the way from Domaine Paul Bruno, Santa Monica, Veramonte, and Miguel Torres (especially his Santa Digna). The recent vintage that made the greatest impression on me, however, was the 1995. Even allowing for differences of quality, the wines of this vintage are uniformly full, round, and harmonious. Those I remember most clearly are Don Melchor of Concha y Toro, Casa Real of Santa

Rita, Caliterra Reserva, Undurraga's Bodega de Familia, a particularly suave Colchagua Valley Cabernet Sauvignon from Viña Viu Manent, Miguel Torres's Manso de Velasco, Montes Alpha, and Don Maximiano of Errázuriz.

A 1995 blend, excluded from that short list because it is not a pure Cabernet Sauvignon, was nevertheless one of the most memorable wines I tasted in Chile. Cousiño-Macul's Finis Terrae, a *cuvée* first produced in 1992, combines roughly sixty percent Cabernet Sauvignon with forty percent Merlot. A deep-colored wine, it has a distinction beyond the sum of its component varieties and a lithe power that owes nothing to mere technique.

Arturo Cousiño thanked me when I complimented him on it. "You know," he said, "my family has been making wines from our Macul vineyards for nearly 150 years. They are an expression of this place. We don't buy grapes from others and we don't concern ourselves with the latest winemaking fad. We have a tradition and a style of our own. This is Chile."

September 1998

SPAIN'S BIG SECRET

Gerald Asher

Has a totally unfamiliar white wine ever given us such a jolt? Such pleasure? Albariño from Rías Baixas, in northwest Spain, is still no more than an eddy in a puddle compared to the ocean of Chardonnay we consume every year. But in the United States, sales of this seductively aromatic wine have bounded from just 2,000 cases in 1992 to 22,000 in 1998. If production could have supported it, sales would have risen even faster.

In Spain, the wines from this small corner of the province of Galicia have won praise on all sides—they are now on the list of every serious restaurant from Seville to San Sebastián—and for at least the past decade, they have had a place at the royal table.

Albariño is actually part of a much larger secret. In summer, when northern Europe invades Spain's Mediterranean beaches, the Spanish themselves disappear to Galicia, a private green refuge tucked between Portugal's northern border and the Atlantic. Santiago de Compostela, the region's capital, ranks with Rome and Jerusalem as a place of pilgrimage for the world's Catholics, of course. But for most Americans it's usually just a stop on a wider European tour. Having paid their respects to the cathedral—its altar ablaze with gold and silver—and allowed themselves to be beguiled for a day or two by the medieval charm of narrow, winding streets that open abruptly onto vast plazas of an austere splendor, they are on their way. Rarely do they venture the short distance to the coast, with its countless bays and inlets—the *rías*—or discover, farther inland, the rivers that long ago carved out deep canyons in Galicia's ancient mountains (now mostly protected as natural parks), or walk in woods where paths are banked with creamy rockroses and clearings edged with beds of tiny scarlet wild strawberries.

Galicia is hardly the Spain of popular imagination: of strumming guitars, stamping heels, and carnations between the teeth. The Moors never established themselves here, so Galicia dances in slippers to the Celtic drum and bagpipe, and its pilgrims walk in sneakers and parkas (but still with cockleshells pinned to their hats) on roads punctuated by tall crucifixes directing them to the tomb of St. James. For curious travelers there are mysterious cave drawings and prehistoric dolmens, feudal castles and Romanesque churches, Roman bridges (still in daily use) and monasteries built near remote passes where pilgrims in centuries past could find a night's shelter and protection from brigands unimpressed by their piety. Elsewhere are sober, seventeenth-century stone *pazos*—manor houses presiding over villages that still live on what they can wrest from a wild land and an even wilder sea. Like Brittany and the west coast of Ireland, Galicia is a place of sudden storms and drowned fishermen, of lighthouses, ghost stories, wee folk, and things that go bump in the night.

Above all, however, it's a place where one eats and drinks well. There are mussel and oyster beds in the *rías,* and every village up and down the coast has its own line of fishing boats. Only Japan consumes more fish per capita than Spain, and in this region, which boasts two of Europe's most important fishing ports—Vigo and La Coruña—meat is rarely more than a footnote on the menu. Even the scruffiest of the bars and taverns that line Santiago's twisting Rua do Franco serve just-caught fish of unimaginable variety cooked with a confidence that would put any restaurant in Paris or New York on the defensive.

No one knows when the vine was introduced to this part of Spain. It can be assumed that the Romans, who settled in the area two thousand years ago to mine the hills near Orense for precious metals, would have provided for themselves somehow. The first reliable record we have that links past to present, however, is of vineyards planted in the twelfth century by Cistercian monks at Armenteira in the Salnés Valley near the fishing port of Cambados. (According to local legend, Albariño is descended from cuttings of Riesling brought from Kloster Eberbach in the Rheingau by some of these Cistercians. It's a pretty story, but recent DNA research has shown beyond a doubt that there is no such connection; the variety's origin is, therefore, still a matter of speculation.)

More vines were planted later on lands granted to the monastery of Santa María de Oia, forty or so miles south within the sharp angle formed by the estuary of the Miño—the river that establishes the frontier with Portugal—and the Atlantic. From these early beginnings evolved the vineyards of Val do Salnés to the north and those of O Rosal and Condado do Tea to the south. (A fourth defined zone roughly midway between them, Soutomaior, was created recently, but it produces such a small quantity of wine that, commercially, it has had no impact as yet.)

There are all kinds of shadings and subtleties to be explored—with wine there always are—but an explanation of the differences between Salnés on the one hand and Rosal and Condado on the other is enough to illustrate most of what one needs to know about Albariño. The vineyards of Salnés form an open bowl facing west to the ocean. From the terrace of the Martín Códax winery on Burgans Hill, above Cambados, there is a limitless view of the bay and the Atlantic beyond. The individual shelves and terraces of vines face this way and that to catch the sun, but all are exposed to whatever blows in from the sea. The vineyards of Rosal and Condado also turn about, to accommodate the rise and fall of a terrain shaped by the streams and rivulets that feed the Miño, but their broad direction is always to the south, to the river. Rosal is affected by the ocean less directly, and Condado—because it is farther upstream—even less. Their vineyards are drier and warmer than those of Salnés; they get less rain and have more hours of sun.

———

There are other differences, too. Vines in Salnés are on a fairly homogenous granitic sand, while those of Rosal and Condado also contend with crumbled schist, clay, and the rolled pebbles typical of any place where the water's flow has shifted. These differences of soil and prevailing weather do not make any one zone better than the others (though you can be sure that's not the way the growers see it), but they do impose distinct and varied characteristics on their wines. A Salnés Albariño is bolder than one from either Rosal or Condado. It has good acidity, a pungent aroma and flavor (some say of pineapple), and it gives a powerful, fleshy impression. Its focus is intensely varietal. Rosal wines—and to an even greater degree those from Condado—are more graceful and more supple. Their flavor steals across the palate and lingers there. If a Salnés wine tends to express the varietal more than the site, a Rosal or Condado wine does the opposite.

The official revival of Rías Baixas (pronounced REE-as BUY-zhas) had its start in 1980, when the local board of control recognized the distinct qualities of the Albariño wines produced in Galicia with a new *denominación de origen*. The ruling was rewritten by the Spanish legislature in 1988 to conform to European Economic Community standards that required the primary definition of an appellation to be geographic rather than varietal. The redrafted regulations formally established four zones and listed Albariño, Loureiro, Treixadura, and Caiño Blanco as the main vine varieties recommended to be grown within their boundaries.

Any Rías Baixas wine labeled Albariño is made from that variety alone, and a Salnés wine is almost always one hundred percent Albariño. The other recommended grape varieties do not grow as well in that valley: Conditions are too extreme. But that isn't the case for either Rosal or Condado, where Loureiro and Treixadura in particular have always contributed to the style of the wines. In fact, regulations require, for example, that a wine labeled Rías Baixas–O Rosal must have at least a little Loureiro to enhance its natural fragrance, and one sold as Rías Baixas–Condado do Tea is understood to have the benefit of Treixadura's finesse and structure. Using other varieties in this way reinforces long-standing distinctions among the zones of Rías Baixas, but Albariño now predominates in more than ninety percent of the vineyards, and most producers offer Rías Baixas only as an Albariño varietal wine.

The aroma and bite for which Albariño is celebrated owe much to the cooling proximity of the ocean and to the stress-free growth guaranteed by ample spring rain. In Spain, at least, these are conditions unique to the Rías Baixas. Ground humidity brings potential problems, of course, even though Albariño has a thick skin. As protection from rot, the vines are trained over high, horizontal pergolas. The hefty granite pillars used are not the most elegant supports, but they fit in with the local custom of scattering vines about in handkerchief-size plots like untidy afterthoughts. A vineyard is sometimes no more than an arbor attached to the side of a house, an arrangement of granite and wire in an awkward bend of the road, or a backyard shared with a patch of turnips or cabbages. For years, most families in Rías Baixas have had vines to make wine only for their own consumption. It was a crop grown for the household—like peppers, corn, and potatoes—that sometimes provided a surplus that could be sold.

Ironically, it was a crisis in the fishing industry that sparked Albariño's resurgence. New restrictions on fishing in European waters in the mid-1980s hit small ports like Cambados, Bayona, and La Guardia badly. The big factory ships of Vigo and La Coruña could go in search of new fishing grounds; boats from the smaller villages have a limited range, though, so these communities had to find a way to supplement what was earned from the sea. Shopkeepers, schoolteachers, and particularly the fishermen themselves—everyone with a few vines—moved from making wine for their own consumption to expanding their production and selling it. From the five hundred acres of vines existing in Rías Baixas in 1986, the acreage is now close to six thousand.

The Martín Códax winery, one of the first to come onto the scene in Salnés, was founded in 1986, funded by a group of small growers who knew they could achieve more together than if each tried to make and market wine on his own. With modern equipment—good presses, refrigeration for cool fermentation, easy-to-clean stainless-steel tanks—they were able to reveal Albariño's forgotten qualities. "And who is Martín Códax?" I asked Pablo Buján, the firm's sales manager. "The prime mover of the project? The partner with the biggest holding?"

"He was a thirteenth-century Galician poet and troubadour from this very place," Buján replied. "He drank a lot of wine."

The thirsty Códax would doubtless be pleased to know that the winery named for him is probably the most successful in Rías Baixas, producing almost 1.5 million bottles of wine in a normal year. To understand the difficulty of this feat, one must remember that the grapes are grown by more than two hundred partners who together own nearly four hundred acres of vines divided over twelve hundred separate plots.

Over the years, land in Galicia has been divided and divided again through successive inheritance. Vineyard plots on the terraced hillsides got smaller and smaller, and in the end those at a distance from the villages were hardly worth the effort needed to cultivate them. In the 1940s and 1950s, under General Franco, most were given over to stands of eucalyptus trees to provide pulp for a paper mill in Pontevedra. In the rain their drooping leaves and peeling bark lend a wistful melancholy to the landscape. But where the trees have been cleared, the original terracing can still be seen.

"Our natural trees are oak and chestnut. Eucalyptus trees give a poor return and are bad for the soil," says Javier Luca de Tena, director of Granja Fillaboa, with a dismissive wave of the hand. Angel Suárez, manager of the Lagar de Cervera (now owned by the Rioja Alta winery), endured several years of painstaking negotiations with disparate owners to put together enough land to restore a rational, workable vineyard. Often a single row of trees belongs to one family, and the next one to another. Each of four brothers will cling to his clump of half a dozen eucalyptus trees when their entire holding, taken together, makes up a block no bigger than a kitchen garden.

A program encouraging owners to swap land in order to build up the size of individual holdings has not been a great success. Apparently, the smaller the patch, the greater its mystical importance to someone unwilling to part with it. To put together an economically viable vineyard, therefore, takes a great deal of forbearance and much money. (One doesn't buy land in Galicia, one bribes the owner to part with it.)

Another Rioja winery, Bodegas Lan, now owns Santiago Ruiz in O Rosal, a small producer of such prestige in Spain that it could afford to dispense with marketing a varietal Albariño, despite the demand, and concentrate on producing a Rías Baixas–O Rosal, a superb wine in which Albariño's exuberance is tempered by Loureiro to just the right degree. La Val, another producer in Rosal, also makes, along with its particularly delicious varietal Albariño, an exquisite wine made from Loureiro and Albariño—reversing the proportions used by Santiago Ruiz.

I was not surprised when José Luis Méndez, son of the owner of Morgadío, told me that his family was trying to think of a way in which Loureiro could be brought back into the vineyard. The producers' dilemma is that they would all like to offer the more stylish wine that a proportion of Loureiro can give, but they don't want to give up the right to the magic name Albariño on the label. Both in Spain and in the United States, it gives instant recognition. While in Galicia recently, I lunched with Angel Suárez at a restaurant near the old fishing harbor of La Guardia. We chatted over a bottle of his 1998 Albariño and a dish of assorted fish—hake, turbot, and monkfish— simmered with potatoes and served in a sauce of garlic and *pimentón,* a very small pepper that is dried over a slow wood fire and then ground to a fine powder. It has a hauntingly smoky, sweet-sharp taste, and no Extremaduran or Galician kitchen is ever without it.

I enjoyed the wine, but Suárez said 1998 had been a difficult year for Rías Baixas. Spring came early: The vines sent out tender shoots in February, but the weather then turned very cold, with a predictable effect. Hailstorms in April did further damage, and rain in June meant that the fruit set poorly. As a result, the crop was barely forty percent of the previous year's and never did reach the level of quality hoped for. The 1997 vintage had been more or less normal in Rosal and Condado, though it presented some problems in Salnés. But 1994, 1995, and 1996 had been three good years for all of Rías Baixas. "After a run like that," Suárez said, "our difficulty now is to keep people happy when we have a year with so little wine for them.

"A red wine region copes with this kind of difficulty more easily," he continued. "Red wine is usually aged for a year or two, and differences of crop size from one year to another can be blurred, at least, by delaying or bringing forward the release date. Albariño is best when bottled and consumed young. We have no stocks to fall back on. Production is increasing a little every year, but at present, even when the crop is of a good size, it seems there is never quite enough to meet demand."

He poured the last of the 1998 into my glass, leaving none for himself.

September 1999

Silent Revolution

Gerald Asher

How good are organic wines? For a start, there are far more of them out there than you might suspect. They're not in some fringe niche either: They include, for instance, Château Margaux, the Médoc first growth; the wines of the Domaine Leroy in Burgundy; those of Robert Sinskey Vineyards in Napa Valley; and certain bottlings from the Penfolds vineyards in South Australia's Clare Valley.

The question, then, would seem to answer itself, but there's a catch: Wines like these rarely display the word "organic." Sometimes it's to avoid having the wine perceived as funky, or bought for what the grower believes is the wrong reason. Robert Sinskey says he doesn't want people to think first about the way he cultivates his grapes and then about the quality of the wine. "We want the customer to buy our wine because it's good. The way we nurture the vines is simply part of our effort to make it that way."

Robert Gross of Cooper Mountain Vineyards in Oregon also insists that quality is the point of the wine and that organic cultivation is simply a technique. Gross does use the words "organically grown" on his label because he knows there are people looking for it. "But it can also be a turnoff," he said. "Some wine drinkers see it and think we're being preachy."

Many producers of wine from organically grown grapes keep mum on the subject to leave their options open in the vineyard. Organizations that certify organic compliance sometimes impose parameters based on philosophically wholesome principles rather than on the practical needs of viticulture. In an extreme emergency, growers might be faced with the choice of spraying, as innocuously as possible, or losing a crop. They argue that it's better not to carry an "organic" statement at all—even when the vineyard is certified—rather than find themselves obliged to explain, in such a situation, why it had to be dropped. And then there are the many grape growers of California who ignored the chemical revolution of the 1950s and continue to do what they have always done. As bemused as Monsieur Jourdain—the character in Molière's *Le Bourgeois Gentilhomme* who discovered he'd been speaking prose all his life—they now learn that they have long been practicing organic viticulture without having once given it a thought. "They just don't make a big deal of it," Bob Blue, winemaker for the Bonterra organic wines of Fetzer Vineyards, told me. "They don't even bother to sell their grapes as 'organically grown.' But that's probably because they'd have to get involved with the maze of certifying organizations and state regulators to do it. And the fees can be heavy for a small producer."

Aside from those who had never grown grapes in any other way, the return to organic practices, both in California and in Europe, began in the early 1980s. I remember my surprise, sometime about then, when I found Ulysses Lolonis of Redwood Valley in Mendocino County dumping buckets of predator ladybugs among the vines in his family's vineyard. He says he started because of concern about the pesticides being proposed to him. "Eventually we found we didn't need them at all," he told me recently. "If we left enough grass between the rows of vines to serve as bug territory, it soon had a mixed population of insects keeping themselves busy devouring each other without bothering us.

"We've come a long way since then. Now, rather than grass, we grow a nitrogen-rich cover crop to feed the soil when we plow it under. The bugs are just as happy, and we can do without pesticides, herbicides, and fertilizers. Do these organic methods enhance the flavor or quality of our wine? Well, they don't seem to take anything away from it." (In fact, Lolonis's Zinfandel is one of the best in California.)

———

John Williams of Frog's Leap Winery in Napa Valley is more forthright. He is convinced that organic cultivation does make a difference to wine quality. "The first vineyard we purchased in 1987," he said, "had been farmed by an old-timer on what we would now call organic principles. Wanting to do things right, we retained a firm to test the vines and the soil and make recommendations to us. They found many things wrong, but fortunately were able to supply us with all the chemical supplements they said we needed. The effort was grandly expensive and soon led to a general decline in the vineyard, the quality of its fruit, and the wine we made from it.

"I was urged to talk to an organic-farming consultant. Amigo Bob [Cantisano] certainly looked the part—ponytail, shorts, and tie-dyed T-shirt. What he said made sense, and we decided to give it a try in a couple of test areas. We now have nine growers in Napa Valley producing organically grown grapes for us.

"We found that a soil rich in organic matter absorbs and holds moisture better—so we were able to go back to dry farming, the old way of growing grapes in California, instead of relying on irrigation. We discovered that plants fed by compost and cover crops, rather than chemical fertilizers, draw in nutrients in a measured way that helps control growth. Our vines are therefore strong and healthy and give balanced fruit. We've learned to think about the causes of problems rather than react with a quick fix to each one as it comes up. It's made us better farmers. In doing all this, I'm not trying to save the world. I just want to make good wine."

There are others who farm organically simply because they don't like the idea of using industrial products in the vineyard. Jean-Pierre Margan of Château La Canorgue in the Côtes de Luberon (Peter Mayle country) told me he was taught in his viticulture courses which synthetic fertilizers to use and what and when to spray. "I never liked the idea," he said. "My father and grandfather had made good wine in the traditional way, and when my wife and I started to revive her family's dormant vineyard, I decided to do the same. It wasn't an act of defiance.

"But confronting nature directly means you have to be vigilant. You must look ahead—mistakes are difficult to correct organically. You become more efficient because you have to stay on top of every detail of every vine—and perhaps that's why the wine is better.

"Though the 'organic' aspect of the vineyard is simply the way we work, I put it on the label to allow those who want wine from organically grown grapes to find us. But there should be no need for me to say anything. Organic cultivation is and should be the norm. It's those who use chemicals that should have to identify themselves.

"I'm not alone in the way I work. There has been a tremendous awakening among winegrowers in France. Usually it starts with the growers getting involved with a program of reduced reliance on synthetic sprays and fertilizers and the reintroduction of more benign techniques—but they soon see the difference in their vineyards and move increasingly toward the freedom that organic cultivation allows."

That awakening has been greatly accelerated by the work of Claude Bourguignon, whose highly influential book, *Le sol, la terre et les champs* (*The Soil, the Land and the Fields*), is now in its third edition. Almost every French winegrower I've talked to in the past several years has at some point introduced Bourguignon's name into our conversation. Now he's one of the leading French experts in soil analysis—his client list includes Domaine de la Romanée-Conti and Château Latour and reads, in fact, like an honor roll of French viticulture. Much of what he has to say comes down to the essential role of microorganic life in the soil. He expresses regret, in the introduction to his book, that the issues involved have become noisily politicized.

In the second edition of his book *Burgundy*, Anthony Hanson describes a visit to Bourguignon's laboratory, north of Dijon. Having collected a random sample of earth from a flower bed, Bourguignon shook it with water, added a coloring agent, then put it under his microscope for Hanson to look at. "I shall never forget the sight," Hanson writes. "Tiny specks of solid particles (clays and other inanimate matter) were bathed in liquid which teemed with swimming, turning, thrashing, pulsing little organisms—bacteria, yeasts, microbes of all sorts."

In an ounce or two of healthy soil, Bourguignon will tell you, there are billions of such microorganisms. They transform mineral elements in the soil to make them available to plants that could not otherwise assimilate them. They attach iron to acetic acid, for example, forming the iron acetate that a plant can absorb. This symbiotic relationship allows a plant to function properly, to capture the energy in sunlight. That's where the energy-into-matter-and-matter-into-energy food chain starts. Soil bacteria need no human presence to flourish and do their work. It's sobering to be reminded that our lives depend on them.

—

Biodynamic farming takes organic cultivation one step further by paying special attention to soil bacteria and to harnessing the rest of the energy in the cosmos in ways that strengthen the vine. It has developed from theories expounded by Rudolph Steiner, the Austrian social philosopher, in the 1920s. Those who practice it are used to the skepticism, even the mockery, of others—there's an air of both New Age mysticism and Old Age witchcraft about it. But it works.

Robert Sinskey, who is heading toward biodynamic certification for all his vineyards, got interested because of a specific problem with one vineyard in particular. "The soil was as hard as rock," he told me. "It was dead. It was planted with Chardonnay, and the wine from those vines was always green and lean. We put in a cover crop and began using biodynamic sprays to encourage the development of microorganisms in the soil. Gradually we brought that vineyard around, and the wine is now so appealing and distinctive that we will soon be bottling it with a special designation."

Robert Gross, a physician whose interests include alternative medicine, is also moving toward biodynamic certification for his vineyards at Cooper Mountain. "It brings the vines into harmony with their environment," he told me.

Two of the biodynamic sprays—500, a very dilute solution of cow manure that has been aged in a cow horn placed underground through the winter and then stirred into blood-warm water with a motion calculated to maximize its effect; and 501, a similarly dilute solution of powdered silica—are basic to the system. Other sprays, mostly homeopathic teas of herbs and flowers, are used by some and not by others. Working in accordance with phases of the moon and reserving certain days for spraying, pruning, or planting to take advantage of propitious movements of the planets are ideas that some accept and others reserve judgment on.

Farming with due provision for the gravitational pull of the moon is ancient wisdom. Jim Fetzer—who started the program of wines made from organic grapes at Fetzer and is now owner of the Ceago Vinegarden, a fully accredited biodynamic vineyard estate in Mendocino County—said he never has to explain any of this to his Mexican workers. "They're used to the idea that various aspects of agricultural work should coincide with the phases of the moon," he said. "It makes sense: If the changes in atmospheric pressure associated with the moon's waxing and waning can affect the rise and fall of oceans, you can be sure it affects the position of the sap in the vines." As for the special days, Alan York, Ceago Vinegarden's biodynamics consultant (and consultant to Joseph Phelps and Benziger, among others), put it to me this way: "We don't know why or how the plant responds to the changing positions of the planets. It's like surfing. There's this force and you try to ride it."

There is much more to biodynamics than homeopathy and "root" days. A key element is the systematic introduction of other plants among the principal crop. There is a rich diversity of them growing among the vines at Ceago Vinegarden, including olive trees, lavender, and buckwheat—habitat to tiny wasps that lay their eggs inside the eggs of leafhoppers and stop that problem before it starts. When I was young, I took it for granted that most vines in Italy and France had peach trees and even a line or two of corn planted among them. I thought it was to make full use of the land, but now I know better.

"Biodynamics is neither a recipe nor even a specific technique," says Nicolas Joly, owner of Coulée de Serrant, the white-wine jewel of Loire Valley vineyards. "It can't be applied mechanically. It demands a complete understanding of what is happening in the life cycle of a plant and the formation of its fruit so that the functions can be enhanced."

Joly, an articulate advocate and proselytizer, condemns completely what he sees as the sins of modern viticulture. "Herbicides and pesticides annihilate the microbial life peculiar to any particular soil, and synthetic fertilizers then standardize the vines' nourishment and thus the character of the fruit. What is the point of talking about *terroir* in such circumstances?"

———

There is a wide gap between biodynamics and conventional viticulture, and a considerable one even between standard and organic practices. Part of that difference is cost. The abuse of pesticides, herbicides, and synthetic fertilizers can create an imbalance ever more expensive to address. But the considerable handwork involved in organic viticulture is also costly—and justified economically only if higher quality attracts a better price for the wine.

In the detailed report on its experiment of organically cultivating roughly 125 acres of vineyard on its Clare Valley estate over the past ten or twenty years, Penfolds (owned by Southcorp Wines) shows that the cost of cultivating those blocks of vines was as much as 50 percent higher than that of cultivating similar neighboring blocks by conventional methods. Australia has high labor costs, and that accounts to some extent for this startling difference; but, when expressed as cost per ton because of the smaller yields when compared with conventional viticulture, the cost of Penfolds's organically grown grapes becomes 100 percent higher.

In the face of such numbers, we can't ignore the fact that whatever satisfaction growers may get from the quality of their products and from their stewardship of the land, they accept the risk inherent in growing a crop as fragile as grapes in order to make a fair return.

———

In most parts of the winemaking world, particularly in California, there are programs designed and supported by growers' associations to help members wean themselves from dependence on synthetic chemical treatments and to combine organic farming principles with a sound and limited use of environmentally safe products in a cost-effective manner. The program run by the Lodi-Woodbridge Wine-grape Commission, financed by an assessment on grape production voted by the growers themselves, includes a step-by-step workbook that encourages growers to meet regularly in small groups for mutual support and the exchange of information and to constantly survey every aspect of their work. They evaluate their progress in sowing cover crops, for example, and installing nesting boxes near their vine-yards for predator barn owls. There are similar programs organized by the Central Coast Vineyard Team, and still more are being developed on a smaller scale in Amador and Lake counties.

These programs encourage growers to check their vines closely and, by thinking ahead, to discover new options for dealing with problems. They lead them to a system of fully sustainable agriculture—or beyond—and at the same time help them steadily improve the quality of their wines.

Paul Pontallier, manager of Château Margaux—where herbicides, pesticides, and synthetic fertilizers are rarely used—commented to me recently that there's much to be said for organic farming and for biodynamic viticulture, whatever the circumstance, so long as the approach is always practical. "The danger comes," he said, "when some particular way of doing things is turned into an ideology."

September 2000

A Nose for Quality

Chandler Burr

There is a small, largely unknown area in southwest France called Jurançon. Sitting up against the wall of the silvery, daggerlike Pyrenees that line the Spanish border, and blessed with a dry, clean Atlantic climate, Jurançon is beautiful, rather Edenic actually, and it produces a golden wine that would have been perfectly at home in the first garden. The Jurançon *moelleux*.

Years ago, I met a man, a sensory wizard, and he had, once, tasted a Jurançon *moelleux*, and he wanted to taste more of them, and now it is morning, and I am driving with him down the highway from Toulouse's airport. This man—he's Italian, Argentine, and French, and sort of English—is a genius of smells and tastes. He loves them. I asked him: "Why?" He thought, and then answered with wine: "I suppose because I'm French, and France is a country of smells. There's something called *pourriture noble*, 'noble rot.' It's the fungus botrytis. It grows on grapes, draws the water out, concentrates the juice wonderfully, adds its own fungal flavor, and then you make wines like the sweet Sauternes. Paradise. From rotten grapes." He rolled his eyes. "In America they'd hand out antibiotics to exterminate half the food in France."

Luca Turin is a biophysicist. He has created a new theory that may have solved a baffling scientific mystery: how we are able to smell. And he was led into the theory through his love of perfume. Turin is the author of the bestselling perfume guide in France, *Parfums: Le Guide.*

Of Gucci's Rush, he writes: "This thing smells like a person. In fact, due to its milky lactone molecule, it smells like an infant's breath mixed with his mother's hair spray." Perfume is his smell passion. His taste passion is wine. "In 1982," he told me, "a scientist colleague brought to the lab the first good Sauternes I'd ever tasted, a Château Lamothe-Despujols 1981. I bought a case of that stuff, and every time I had a glass it was a religious experience. The guy showed us a photo of the fungus attacking the grape; that, of course, got me seriously into Sauternes, which is, believe me, an expensive habit to acquire. These things have been famous since the 1750s, commanding huge prices forever.

"Years later, when I sold my flat" (Turin lives with his wife and two young children in London), "I bought a 1959 Rieussec—a hundred and ten pounds. Some friends and I wolfed it down in the lab. Utterly sensational. A honeyed, summery exterior covering a late November liquid. There are three elements—a beeswax, a woody, and a floral banana—with a perfect balance between extreme acidity and huge, heavy, oily sweetness, like a blend of jasmine and musk. The '59, in a bottle for forty years, comes out the way James Bond emerges from a wet suit in a perfect tuxedo and murmurs, 'What kept you?'"

But one day he stumbled onto a bottle of sweet wine he'd never heard of that astounded him. "I was in Saint-Emilion, and they had a very interesting wine store. I noticed a bottle that looked like a Sauternes—clear glass bottle, gold lettering on a white label. But it was from Jurançon." (If Jurançon whites are undiscovered in the United States, astonishingly they also remain little known in France itself.) "The woman said, 'It's Clos Thou. Eighty euros.' I said, 'A Jurançon for eighty euros? It'd better be good.' She said, 'Try it.' It was incredible. Probably the best sweet wine I've ever had. I thought, 'Who *are* these guys? Why aren't they famous?'"

And that is why we are driving away from the Toulouse airport in pursuit.

These wines are made in vineyards that lie east of Biarritz on the

Atlantic coast just north of Spain. As we move south the land transforms, greener, lusher, the air fresher; the land rolls gently, and suddenly, "Jesus!" says Turin. It is as if the Pyrenees have materialized before you, a mass of astonishing peaks against crystalline and cobalt skies, stretching across the horizon. The car dips down below some hills, then swoops up again, and their imposing, steely beauty is breathtaking.

Late in the afternoon, under silken sunlight, we pull into our hotel in Pau, a Le Fer à Cheval. It is an old *relais* with fruit trees—pear, cherry, apple, peach—and a barn, whose slight dilapidation and big, adorable Labrador make it all the more lovely.

—

The next morning, Turin and I set off for Domaine Castéra, in the town of Monein. With its manicured gardens and Basque architecture it looks like a pristine, idealized-medieval movie set. Christian Lihour, whose grandfather bought the place in 1895, shows us around with pride, pointing out some huge photos of the grapes (the Jurançon appellation has the right to use five varieties, but almost everyone plants only Petit Manseng and Gros Manseng) over-ripening beautifully on the vines, just like Sauternes. Lovely dark spots, shriveled and sweet and almost rotting. The flavor practically drips off the photo. But Lihour says firmly, "We try never to have botrytis."

In the Sauternes region, he explains, they are able to use botrytis to shrivel the grapes because the climate is drier, so the fungus doesn't hang around in the soil to rot the roots. "Here," he said, "we use *vendange tardive,* late harvest, leaving this grape variety all spring, summer, and fall to ripen and sweeten."

The tasting room is filled with oak barrels and the rush of the marvelous yeast smell. By law the Jurançon appellation may make only whites, but they can be either dry or sweet. Domaine Castéra's Jurançon (unless there's a *sec* in its name, a Jurançon wine is always a *moelleux,* "sweet") is seven euros per bottle (Turin murmurs, with raised eyebrows, "These prices are ridiculously low"), 100 percent Gros Manseng, and aged entirely in stainless steel.

"Lovely," says Turin, and it is: not truly a sweet yet not a dry, hovering delightfully somewhere in between, bright as summer. (As we walk out, Turin muses darkly to me about his beloved Sauternes: "I'll say this against Sauternes, they are profoundly saturnine wines, wintry. It's like, if you listen to Jascha Heifetz play the violin and you're a little stoned, you realize that it's actually extremely melancholy.")

Lihour, with a collegiality that impresses Turin, has directed us down the road to Domaine Bordenave, where Gisèle Bordenave gets out several bottles. The Harmonie is a 2001. "Not interesting," says Turin, emptying his glass. But he stands inhaling the 1999 Cuvée des Dames and a 1999 Cuvée Savin. "That's fabulous. Wonderful!" he says to Madame Bordenave. She just looks back, stoically. "The Savin is the more brutal of the two," says Turin.

At one o'clock we finally find what seems like the one restaurant in Monein. Small French towns at lunchtime are the most deserted places on earth, but inside, L'Estaminet is packed, blue berets everywhere.

As we tuck into huge portions of *garbure* (a delicious Basque bean soup) and roast duck on the front terrace, Turin's mind is still on the wine. "Absurdly," he says, "people drink sweet whites with foie gras. A dreadful and very petit bourgeois tradition of having all the expensive things together. It's a very naïve idea of luxury. In fact, foie gras goes well with Jack Daniel's. One should have expensive things as often as one can afford them, but preferably separately so you can actually taste them, and also so you don't drop dead from a heart attack." He sips a glass of wine and adds, "Another mistake: drinking *moelleux* as dessert wines. At the end of a meal your nose is shot to hell anyway. This includes for perfumes."

—

I note that Turin, author of the legendary perfume guide, perfume critic par excellence, never once critiques these wines as he does perfumes ("Like an infant's breath mixed with his mother's hair spray"). "Never thought about it," he says. He mulls it over for a moment. "I couldn't. Perfumes are made by humans. They are works of art, and art is communication between humans. These wines are made, ultimately, by nature, and you can't critique nature."

He sips from his glass, a local *moelleux* we've ordered, and has another thought. "But," he says, "it is becoming quite clear to me that there is a cognate in perfumery for the Jurançons. It comes from their unusual *crème de marron* note, a signature they all share. What makes the great Caron perfume—I'm thinking of the old ones, Nuit de Noël and En Avion—quintessentially Caron is an interesting creamy *marron glacé* fragrance that the perfumer Daltroff invented in the 1930s and used in every Caron fragrance. It's the equivalent of Guerlain's house recipe, a vanillic, powdery scent that Jacques Guerlain created in the same era and carefully kept secret.

"In a way, Sauternes is Guerlain and Jurançon is Caron. The great Sauternes do this delicious, fruity, big *bouquet de fleurs* thing, the style of Guerlain. These Jurançons, on the other hand, really do belong to a different school of perfumery. Caron's signature was a chypre base with a soft, creamy sandalwood that gave you *marron glacé*, a smell lying between the slightly sour note of fresh cream and the warm note of burnt dark sugar. Rum and cream together. That is the note I find in these Jurançons. I absolutely smell that."

That night, we dine happily under the grapevines in the Fer à Cheval's exquisite garden restaurant. I'm having perfectly prepared lamb chops and local vegetables.

As we taste the wine (a Jurançon dry), Turin surprises me by saying, "The best place in the world to buy wine for sheer range and value is America. The choice is incredible and the quality is fantastic. The only thing I'd complain about concerning the United States is flavored coffee. May they rot in hell. This 'hazelnut'—just a bunch of thiazines and pyrazines." He rolls his eyes.

———

The next morning we're off again. All at once Turin exclaims, "Clos Thou!" The wine by which he discovered Jurançon. He's excited. Everything we've had thus far is quite good, but will this kick it up a level?

The inevitable dog barks up to the car in the dusty drive. The owner's father, an elderly, delightful Frenchman named Raoul, leads us into a stone building to taste. He and the son tell us about the fabled year of 1995, when the weather was heavenly and the grapes were Bacchus's morsels, and they made a *moelleux* that was suddenly as good as anything the $200-a-bottle guys were putting out. *"Un accident de nature,"* says Raoul.

Turin sips. Whoa. Yep, we've risen to another floor. They're just getting better. He buys a case. You breathe stale cigarette smell every time one of the cheerful Frenchmen walks by. The dogs bark in the hot yellow sun under the azure sky.

Next stop is Clos Lapeyre, and the barking dog leads to a flower-filled garden. Jean-Bernard Larrieu, a third-generation winemaker, looks like a Berkeley dude in his baggy T-shirt and shorts, and talks an astonishing southern French: *"Les ans"* is *"lez ankhs"* and *"la main"* is *"la maéin."* He opens his most expensive *moelleux* for us, the very smoky Vent Balaguèr. We're now at six times the prices we started with. Turin sips. *"Crème brûlée* plus woody," says Turin. ("Worth the price?" I murmur at him. "Oh, yeah!" says Turin. "Damn!")

We have one last vineyard: Domaine Cauhapé. The late afternoon light is becoming increasingly golden. There is still snow on some of the Pyrenees peaks. I drive through a centuries-old arch into a perfectly kept courtyard. I park out of the sun and we wander into the large, spotless tasting room. Bottle upon beautiful bottle. "Everything is perfect," whispers Turin, "Whoever the owner is, he's a maniac." He means this in the French sense: crazy for quality.

Henri Ramonteu, the owner-maniac, arrives, fifty-five years old, fit, good-looking. Intense. Shakes our hands. The least expensive *moelleux* is Symphonie de Novembre 2001, 14 percent alcohol. Lovely. We taste a Noblesse du Temps 2000 and a 1995, prices going up rapidly. Turin is walking around the tasting room, murmuring into his glass. I watch his reverie as Ramonteu says, "I absolutely agree, you should drink *moelleux* before and with a meal, but not with dessert."

He pours a liquid so golden it looks like honey. Sets down the bottle: Quintessence du Petit Manseng 1998. Fifteen percent alcohol. And 138 euros. He hands us the glasses.

Turin: "I have to sit down." He staggers outside and sits. "Gesù, Maria, e Giuseppe," he says. "This is beyond good. And it damn well better be; you're getting to where one plant gives you maybe two glasses. I mean ..." Sips. Thinks. Decides definitively: "This is as good as any Sauternes. Apricot and apple, flowers, rich honey, utterly perfect balance, all the harmonies. You taste how optimistic that is?" He's grinning.

Ramonteu puts us in the back of his truck and we grumble up an almost vertical slope to stop under three huge oaks. The sun, pouring in from Spain like the ocean, runs down the perfectly manicured green plants as we look out over the vineyard, the emerald valley below it, the Pyrenees beyond them. We're high from the Quintessence du Petit Manseng.

May 2004

VINTAGE YEARS

Washington State Comes of Age

Gerald Asher

Trinket sellers attach themselves to Seattle's Pike Place Market like barnacles, but nothing can detract from the grand profusion of its fruits and vegetables, flowers and mushrooms, pots of honey, and fish in never-ending variety fresh from boats below. Crowds surge there every day to find the best of what is locally available.

And in Washington State "the best" extends beyond the largesse of woods, fields, and waters. No one doubts that interest in the state's own wines, part of local food bounty, has taken per capita wine consumption in Washington to fourth highest in the nation. While United States wine consumption lagged, Washington State consumed 22 percent more wine in 1986 than in 1983. In those three years the number of Washington wineries expanded from 28 to 62, and wine production went from 1.6 to 2.7 million gallons.

Washington's climate—too wet, too dry, or too cold—hampered early development of the state's potential to grow fine wines. Dividing the state roughly in two, the Cascade Mountains impose on the west both its own ample rainfall and that intended for the east, where, while guaranteeing bright, dry summers, the mountain divide, blocking any possible tempering effect from the Pacific, ensures winters of brass monkey severity.

Hudson's Bay Company settlers had brought *labrusca* grapes native to the eastern United States to Fort Vancouver, in what is now southwestern Washington State, as early as 1825, but it was not until fifty years later that Lambert Evans, a Civil War veteran, planted a vineyard of any consequence on Stretch Island in Puget Sound. But the *labrusca* vines he had brought with him fared poorly. So in 1890 he sold half his 160-acre homestead to Adam Eckert, a native of New York's Finger Lakes region, who experimented with a number of alternative varieties before choosing Island Belle, a *labrusca* hybrid with the economic advantage of allowing production of table grapes and grape juice in addition to wine.

East of the Cascades, in what was then little more than desert, the introduction of irrigation began the transformation of Yakima Valley quite early in this century. Along with a multitude of agricultural crops that still dominate Yakima's landscape and economy, newly irrigated lands were planted extensively with *labrusca* vineyards for the production of grape juice. At first Eckert's Island Belle (now known as Campbell's Early) was brought in from Puget Sound, but gradually it was replaced by Concord vines arriving from the eastern United States at about that time.

There had been attempts to plant European *vinifera* vines, the varieties from which we receive most of the fine wines familiar to us, even before irrigation systems had brought Cascades water to Yakima. The political and social climates of the time were hardly propitious to the idea of wine grapes, however, with or without irrigation. Only in the 1930s, when Prohibition was almost over, could William Bridgman, a pioneer of irrigated agriculture in the Yakima Valley, plant *vinifera* vines there and, later, build himself a winery. Though Bridgman was unlucky in his choice of winemaker and the wines of his Upland Winery, commercially unsuccessful, were eventually withdrawn from sale, small quantities of his varietal grapes continued to be harvested. Unfortunately as fast as they were picked they disappeared into the vats of fortified and generic blends then fostered by the monolith of Washington's state system of distribution.

In the 1960s Bridgman's vineyards in the Yakima Valley were

acquired by American Wine Growers, a company that could claim tenuous and indirect descent from the original Evans and Eckert vineyards and until then producing mainly fruit and *labrusca* wines. It had recently been purchased by a partnership of new investors just as another group—an association of academics turned amateur winemakers—took a further turn by also acquiring proprietorship of a Yakima *vinifera* vineyard and emerging professionally as Associated Vintners. These two groups, American Wine Growers, now Chateau Ste. Michelle, and Associated Vintners, now Columbia Winery, founded the modern wine industry of Washington State.

———

Scattered vineyards and wineries on and around Puget Sound, a handful of wineries deliberately established near concentrations of their customers in Seattle and Spokane rather than close to their grape sources, and one, Salishan, a gloriously distracted tumble of vines and orchard that seems somehow to have strayed north from Oregon across the Columbia River, far from the Willamette Valley where so obviously it belongs, confuse anyone trying to make sense of the state's viticultural geography. For the most part, however, Washington vineyards and wineries are on the far side of the Cascades in the Yakima and Columbia valleys and in south central and southeastern areas of the state close to their confluence. And it is in all those places, of course, that winter temperatures determine which vine varieties can be grown in Washington. They must, when all is said and done, be hardy enough to survive.

Yakima Valley farmers—attracted to *vinifera* wine grapes by the expected growth of the wine companies—took advice from the extension service of Washington State University and planted Johannisberg (White) Riesling for its known resistance to winter cold. In Washington it had positive advantage, too. Compared with California, Washington State has mild summer temperatures but long daylight hours. Light builds grape sugars while tempered warmth simultaneously protects acids, so that Washington wines, above all, are distinguished for their crisp, compelling flavor. Basic to all Washington wines, it is a quality nowhere seen to greater advantage than in Washington Johannisberg Rieslings. Known and appreciated by all in its home state, where Johannisberg Riesling sells well, it is a quality often unrecognized, alas, elsewhere. Having often been disappointed by flabby and mawkish Riesling variants, few of which are based on Johannisberg Riesling anyway, many are wary of the name.

The resistance has dampened enthusiasm for Johannisberg Riesling in Washington State, unfortunately, despite its advantages and success there. Just before the last harvest, I noticed Riesling "special offers" at most tasting-room retail outlets and heard much talk of lower grape prices likely—even of the conversion of Johannisberg Riesling vineyards on marginal sites to other crops. The pity is that the problem lies with a name that fails to inspire consumer confidence, not with the wine. Perhaps growers and wineries will yet get together and develop another name, unique to the state and therefore protected from goings-on elsewhere. It is what any corporation would do if the wrong brand name were causing problems for the right product. I wonder how much Châteauneuf-du-Pape would get sold if the growers insisted on sending it off to market labeled "Grenache, etc."

For the present, though, Washington growers and wineries are turning their attention from Johannisberg Riesling to Chardonnay, a *vinifera* variety that shares its winter hardiness, and Cabernet Sauvignon, which does not. To say they are doing so to meet the demand created by popular recognition of these two varietal names would be only partly true. There is also their inarticulated hope that success with one or the other of these varieties, both associated with the world's most prestigious white and red wines, will make any prejudice against a particular variety irrelevant.

In theory Washington's growers and wineries are on firm ground with Chardonnay. The variety is as winter-hardy as Johannisberg Riesling and, needing less cellaring than Cabernet Sauvignon, has distinct cash-flow advantages for a new industry. In retaining acidity and boosting varietal flavor, however, Washington's climate is not an unmixed blessing to Chardonnay, which like Cabernet Sauvignon lends itself to winemaker enhancement. That, essentially, is what gives both varieties their prestige, after all. Beyond the all-important preservation of his grapes' inherent quality there are three things a winemaker can do, if appropriate. He (or she) can ferment Chardonnay in oak barrels instead of stainless steel and can choose to do that completely or partially. (Or, alternatively, age a steel-fermented wine for a while in oak barrels or vats.) He can allow the fermented wine to remain in contact with the lees of fermentation for a longer or shorter period—or not at all. He can allow, or provoke, a bacterial fermentation that transforms biting, and sometimes bitter, malic acid—the acid of green apples, always present to some extent in wine—into lactic acid, a softer acid associated, as the name suggests, with milk.

Each of these choices and the degree to which it is exercised will modify the "crisp, compelling flavor" basic to Washington style. The decision on how best to proceed is made more (or perhaps less) difficult for some because the use of French oak barrels, whether for fermentation or aging, and the warmth that must be generated in wintry Washington cellars to allow malolactic conversion cost money that is not always available. Prudence holds back others from changes that, once started in a wine, cannot be reversed. Many Washington winemakers, I suspect, rationalize aesthetically to justify economic decisions.

———

Because "she makes house calls," as Ronald and Glenda Holden put it in their book *Northwest Wine Country,* and is winemaking consultant on retainer with at least half a dozen local wineries, Kay Simon, a former winemaker at Chateau Ste. Michelle, has influence well beyond the tiny Chinook Winery she runs with her husband, Clay Mackey. And she has no enthusiasm for malolactic fermentation. "We don't put our [Chinook] Chardonnay through malolactic," she explains, "because we want the fruit flavors to come forward. We sell our wines around Puget Sound, where the clean style of our wine goes well with seafood."

Simon does give her white wines a short time in either French oak barrels or small oak vats, however, without allowing what she calls "oak smells and flavors" to dominate their varietal character. So successful is Ms. Simon in her restraint that, from tasting it, I would not have imagined her dryly etched and steely clean 1984 Chardonnay to have spent even a day in oak. Others who share her pared-to-essentials style of making Chardonnay include two of the state's most respected winemakers: Joel Klein of Snoqualmie, also a Chateau Ste. Michelle alumnus, and Wayne Marcil of Covey Run, whose 1984 Chardonnay, to my taste, is so lean that the oak aging of one cuvée simply honed its austerity.

Left alone, as if it were Johannisberg Riesling, Washington Chardonnay has a not unappealing appley, sometimes pineappley, aroma. But the wine is mordant when young and ages without charm. Washington winemakers, used to the style of their Chardonnays, defend them, claiming their tart edge to be "like Chablis." They insist that subjecting Chardonnay grown under Washington conditions to malolactic fermentation ages them too quickly. Perhaps they are right: But what they perceive as "aging too quickly" is often the loss of raw bite and the mutation of overly simple grape characteristics that some of us prefer in mature wine.

A growing number of winemakers are giving their Chardonnay a few weeks in oak barrels, both to soften the wine and to allow oak's vanilla flavor to lend an illusion, at least, of complexity. Though I didn't detect this effect in the Chinook Chardonnay, I did elsewhere: in Columbia Winery's 1984 Chardonnay, Quarry Lake's 1985 Chardonnay, and Arbor Crest's 1983 Reserve Chardonnay, for instance. Low-profile but elegantly structured wines, all have their innate tartness partially veiled and interest added to what otherwise would be rather simple wines. On the other hand, oak can aggravate a wine's lack of balance, of course, as in the Covey Run 1984 and Bookwalter Winery's 1983 Chardonnay, a rawboned wine much praised by others but that I find overwhelmed rather than sustained by its time in oak.

Some winemakers, however, are already beyond tentative barrel-aging and are flirting, hesitantly, with barrel fermentation, malolactic conversion, and lees-aging. A little of one, two, or all three seems to make a fundamental difference. Partial barrel fermentation alone after a start in steel tanks might be responsible for the lasting, delicate flavor of Chateau Ste. Michelle's 1983 Chateau Reserve Chardonnay, for example; for certain it will have contributed to the wine's firm texture.

I, too, may be guilty of rationalizing only to justify a personal preference, and so I shall say only that I find most to my taste two Washington Chardonnays that had been subjected to a measure of all three. Rob Griffin, winemaker at The Hogue Cellars, said "some people didn't understand" the supple style and many-layered flavor of his 1985 Reserve Chardonnay, barrel fermented, aged on the lees, and partially subjected to malolactic conversion. It presented no problem to me. Neither did Mike Januik's 1985 Chardonnay from Stewart Vineyards, in which roughly 20 percent of the blend had been barrel fermented, aged a while on its lees, and subjected to malolactic conversion. Compared with Januik's tight and angular (but multi-gold-medal-winning) 1984 Chardonnay, made without any of these modifications, its stylish quality might go far to persuade others.

———

Other than by name, it is now frivolous to distinguish between Sauvignon Blanc labeled and sold as Sauvignon Blanc and Sauvignon Blanc labeled and sold as Fumé Blanc, because no two wineries in the United States agree on the definition by which they distinguish one from the other. Washington's inherent "crisp, compelling flavor" could present its greatest challenge to a variety so popular among Washington winemakers that it now commands the highest grape price per ton in the state. In California and elsewhere the flavor of Sauvignon Blanc, when intense, is disagreeably stalky. "Grassy" and "herbaceous," words often used, only partly convey a pungent taste reminiscent of the grapes' own stems. Perhaps because specially on guard, winemakers in Washington have learned to handle the variety with skill and sensibility. Particularly successful and representative of what the state can offer are Chateau Ste. Michelle's (Fumé Blanc) '84, Staton Hills' '85, The Hogue Cellars' '84, and Arbor Crest's '82. The Arbor Crest, aged for a time in oak, shows how satisfactorily Washington Sauvignon Blanc can acquire mature bouquet and flavor without loss of freshness.

In Washington—as in California and Bordeaux—Sauvignon Blanc is also often used in tandem with Sémillon in varying proportions. Sémillon is more attractive than Sauvignon Blanc to Washington grape growers because it is more resistant to winter frost damage. The acreage of each is now roughly equal. (In California the proportion is roughly one acre of Sémillon for every five of Sauvignon Blanc.)

At Chinook Winery, for example, Kay Simon used Sémillon to brighten her 1983 Sauvignon Blanc, giving a delicious impression of crisp Sancerre. On the other hand, in a 1984 proprietary wine, Topaz, she uses predominantly Sémillon and only 40 percent Sauvignon Blanc. The result is rather neutral, even though Washington Sémillons often show more flavor than Sauvignon Blancs.

Sémillons come in styles ranging from Columbia's and Snoqualmie's 1985s, both fresh, crisp, and lightly fruity—precise, Washington-style renderings of the variety, one might say—to Chateau Ste. Michelle's 1982, a wine aged in French oak and, like the Arbor Crest 1982 Sauvignon Blanc, both fresh and mature, and Woodward Canyon's 1985, a wine of honeyed nose and rich flavor. (I can't explain the honeyed nose unless the grapes were shriveled by botrytis. But I know for sure that the wine had the benefit of malolactic fermentation and oak aging. I shall say no more or appear to be obsessed with the subject.) Latah Creek's 1985 Sémillon, an attractively clean, gently herbaceous wine modified by a hint of oak, is typical of the style of those holding the middle ground.

Gewürztraminer has been successfully grown and produced. But it was planted to meet the growers' need of winter-hardy varieties rather than any known market demand. It has not sold well. "In New York they love our Gewürztraminer," said one perplexed winemaker, probably meaning New York–based wine writers rather than the millions who live there, "but they don't buy it." There seemed little point in explaining that delicious rose-scented escapades are all very well, but most of us, when choices must be made, go home sensibly to a familiar spouse.

Plantings of Chenin Blanc have expanded more dramatically than any other white variety in the state. Washington wineries pay almost double the top price paid for this grape in California. Usually Washington winemakers leave a balancing zip of residual sugar in their Chenin Blanc, but that element of "crisp, compelling flavor" keeps it polished and invitingly fragrant. It remains to be seen whether Washington wineries will be able to command prices for its Chenin Blanc that justify the grape prices paid.

—

Cabernet Sauvignon had first gripped the imagination of the expanding industry in the sixties, but as vineyard expansion gathered momentum after 1978, involving not only wineries putting in vineyards but fruit farmers seeing cash benefits in an alternate crop, the acreage of climatically safer Johannisberg Riesling rapidly overtook Cabernet Sauvignon. In 1984 there were 2,679 acres of Johannisberg Riesling in Washington for 882 acres of Cabernet Sauvignon vines, compared, for perspective, with California's 10,046 acres of Johannisberg Riesling for 22,617 acres of Cabernet Sauvignon.

Cabernet Sauvignon's popularity in the national market apart, wines already available from Washington wineries demonstrate amply how well the variety can do there. Outstanding among the wines I have tasted (and obviously there are many I haven't) are those of Quilceda Creek, a small, neat winery in the extended garage behind the house of Alex Golitzin, nephew of André Tchelistcheff—especially a 1982 made of grapes from Kiona and Otis vineyards; all the impeccably crafted Cabernet Sauvignons of Columbia Winery (they, too, include some made from Otis Vineyard grapes); the 1981 Cabernet Sauvignon from Woodward Canyon in the Walla Walla Valley; and a 1983 Cabernet Sauvignon from Paul Thomas Wines, which I drank with prime rib of moose on my recent visit. (You see what I mean about local bounty.)

These successful Washington Cabernet Sauvignons—though in general leaner than those of California—lack neither flavor nor intensity. There are others still entrenched at the extremes of being either high-funk or high-tech, boringly cleaned-up and softened-down. Each extreme might be as much an extension of physical plant as the result of winemaking philosophy. Washington wineries themselves tend toward high-tech sterility or exuberant high-funk. On the other hand it wouldn't surprise me to learn that each style had polarized in reaction to the other.

Growers like Merlot because it is less capricious than Cabernet

Sauvignon, and wineries like it because the wine is forward and can be sold and enjoyed sooner. So the acreage is expanding at a rate that will soon bring it level with Cabernet Sauvignon. Covey Run's 1984 Merlot, aged in American oak for richer flavor, is a prime example of how attractive Washington Merlot can be. There is little interest in the state in Pinot Noir or the various Gamays, despite Washington's rueful glances at the recent notoriety Pinot Noir has brought Oregon. The one winery producing good Pinot Noir with reasonable consistency is Salishan, and a glance at a map will reveal that, regardless of political boundaries, its location is more within the range of Oregon's Willamette Valley than within any of Washington's viticultural areas.

Lemberger (sometimes spelled Limberger), a black variety that arrived in Washington in the 1930s by way of Canada, has been supported in Yakima Valley by Walter Clore, an emeritus faculty member of Washington State University referred to as Washington's Mr. Grape for his extensive and lifelong viticultural work. A winter-hardy variety known under various synonyms in central Europe, Lemberger gives fruity, dark red wine. Without staying power, it is attractive in the way that a young Beaujolais would be attractive if it had more color. The name is not its strongest selling point, and at present there are barely fifty acres in the state. Covey Run's 1984 Lemberger is an example of how good it can be.

To write a progress report on the Washington State wine industry while ignoring its salient feature—the fact that one single grower, winery, and marketing company produces (depending on who is telling you about what) from 70 to 80 percent of the state's wine— would give an impermissible distortion of perspective. Such a giant could easily inhibit competition, depress prices, hold growers for ransom, and choke the enthusiasm of young independents. It was refreshing to hear Washington wineries acknowledge that without the locomotive of Chateau Ste. Michelle, they themselves would still be explaining to the public that Washington wines were not grown on the banks of the Potomac. They credit their friendly local giant with establishing Washington wines nationally in a price segment that allows other wineries, large and small, to compete and succeed. They say the professional enthusiasm of the technical staff at Chateau Ste.

Michelle—in both their vineyards and their wineries—sets a healthy tone for the Washington wine industry, and the quality of the wines they produce, though neither always the best nor always the most interesting, is of a standard that has helped win acceptance for all Washington wines and that provides every other winery with a consistent measuring stick.

April 1987

CELEBRATING OREGON'S
PINOT NOIR

Gerald Asher

Of all the festivals, fairs, fetes, and other wine gatherings my work takes me to (yes, it's a hard life), the one I most enjoy is the International Pinot Noir Celebration, held every year since 1987 in McMinnville, Oregon, on the last full weekend of July. The setting—a redbrick college on a tree-shaded campus at the edge of a small rural town— is idyllic, of course, but it's the gaiety of the event and its lack of pretension that I find especially appealing. The basic message at McMinnville is that one drinks wine (and Pinot Noir in particular) for pleasure.

The celebrants, as I suppose one must call them, their numbers limited to a manageable 550, are usually a knowledgeable and jolly lot. They are wine drinkers rather than collectors and include a high proportion of literally down-to-earth growers from Europe and Australasia as well as the United States. The Swiss and the New Zealanders are not as thick on the ground as the French and the Californians, but the *international* in the event's title is not vainglory. Places are much in demand, and the organizers begin each year's roster of guests with the waiting list from the year before.

One might think there has to be a limit to what can be said or learned about one grape variety, but every year changes of focus give a fresh perspective on the familiar and provide a look at something new. The tastings are, in any case, always instructive and enjoyable, the presentations well prepared and enlightening, and the prevailing shirtsleeve informality inclusive of all. There is ample opportunity to get to know the men and women who make the wines; everyone participates and has a good time.

At the heart of this unabashedly hedonistic retreat are the memorable meals, which offer proof enough, if any be needed, that wine really does gladden the heart, loosen the tongue, and bring people together. Nick Peirano, whose Nick's Italian Café put McMinnville on the gastronomic map, and Michael Wild of The Bay Wolf in Oakland, California, supply continuity in the kitchen from one year to another. They are usually responsible for the opening Friday lunch and help to organize the other meals.

On Saturday night there is always a salmon roast under a grove of ancient, lantern-lit trees. Spitted on stakes, Northwest Indian–style, the fish cook over a great fire pit and are served with a cornucopia of Oregon's bounty: shellfish, fruit, corn, and salads of all kinds. In its simple, delicious abundance, the salmon roast sets a tough standard for the chefs who come from all over the United States and France to prepare the other meals. This past year, Greg Higgins of Portland's Heathman Hotel met the challenge with a Friday night dinner of chilled soup based on toasted almonds and roasted garlic; a terrine of pork *rillettes* and *shiitake* wrapped in grape leaves and served with a *focaccia* of caramelized onions; grilled spiced leg of Oregon lamb with a local version of *ratatouille; chipotle rémoulade* and blue cornmeal anadama bread; and, finally, sweet polenta fritters accompanied by a fruit compote and cinnamon ice cream.

Saturday's lunch was cooked by Thierry Guillot, of the Michelin-starred Côte d'Or restaurant in Nuits-Saint-Georges, who kept to much-loved French dishes, all impeccably prepared: *jambon persillé au Chardonnay,* the classic Burgundian dish of pressed ham set in white-wine jelly; fillets of Atlantic red mullet on a potato purée whipped with a thread of olive oil and a touch of garlic (as far removed from traditional mashed potatoes as is the Eiffel Tower from the Washington Monument); and a Burgundian *coq au vin.* He ended the meal with meltingly fine shortbread pastry shells filled with *sorbets* and Oregon berries. No one goes hungry at the International Pinot Noir Celebration.

Wines are not matched to specific dishes. Any group of eight (seating is casually where-you-will) finds ready at the table up to a dozen bottles of assorted red and white wines from wineries in Oregon, France, California, Australia—or from wherever else Pinot Noir and Chardonnay might grow. The wines are there to be tasted, to be drunk, or to be swapped for wines at other tables. No two tables have quite the same selection, and it's amazing how quickly word gets around that "the table over there" has a superb Pommard Epenots, say, or that one is enjoying a Saintsbury Pinot Noir, and how soon suitors appear with appealing bottles to swap for one's coveted Wild Horse Pinot Noir or Henry Estate Chardonnay. "What if I give you both of these for that one?" is a common negotiating ploy. It's illuminating to see how quickly a market of relative values establishes itself.

—

Demand for the wines of "hot" Oregon producers is a reminder of the speed with which the state's growers have placed themselves center stage in the world of Pinot Noir. When Richard Sommer, an agronomy graduate of the University of California at Davis, established a Riesling vineyard in Oregon's Umpqua Valley in 1961, to be followed five years later by David Lett, a graduate of the Department of Viticulture and Enology at Davis, who pushed farther north to the Willamette Valley to plant Pinot Noir, they were regarded less as pioneers than as madmen. Lett, in particular, was warned by his professor Maynard Amerine that he would be frosted out every spring and rained out every autumn, and that he would get athlete's foot up to his knees.

But Sommer and Lett would certainly have known that wine grapes had been grown successfully in Oregon in the last century and that their risks were therefore to some extent limited. In fact, the first vine planted in the Willamette Valley was an Isabella, a *labrusca* originally from the eastern United States, brought to Oregon in 1847 by Seth Lewelling, a settler from Iowa.

According to Thomas Pinney in his *History of Wine in America*, European *vinifera* vines were planted in the Willamette Valley in the 1860s, probably having spread there by way of the Umpqua Valley from the Rogue Valley, just north of the California border, where Peter Britt, a Swiss immigrant, had planted them in the 1850s. A *vinifera* vineyard established by the Doerner family in the Umpqua Valley in 1878 still exists (though probably not with the original vines); its grapes are now sold to neighboring wineries, the family having closed its own winemaking facility as recently as 1965. But the first Doerner winemakers were not alone. By the 1870s there were so many wine-grape growers in the state that prizes for wine made from both "American" and "foreign" varieties were offered regularly at the Oregon State Fair.

Prohibition most likely gave the Oregon wine industry its *coup de grâce,* but it had been in decline and all but vanished long before that. The strongest markets for Oregon wines were the gold-mining settlements in the southwest of the state, and, once the miners began to fade away, the vineyards faded with them. Jacksonville, a gold town in the Rogue Valley now protected in its entirety as a national living monument, has a population today of only a thousand or two, but at the turn of the century it supported fifteen thousand—as well as Peter Britt's Valley View Winery.

Unfortunately, when towns like Jacksonville lost their free-spending miners, Portland offered the growers scant alternative for the sale of their wines. Portland's timber and fishing industries had attracted northern European settlers, especially Scandinavians, who felt more comfortable with their own particular mix of hard liquor and piety. In Oregon, the sale of spirits is still limited to state-controlled stores, just as in Norway and Sweden, and the rural population, especially, is less than enthusiastic about wine's renaissance in the state, despite the economic benefits it has brought to their counties. In McMinnville, an economically moribund town that is now—thanks to wine— flourishing, the police department raised objections when the town council voted to include a bunch of grapes in the municipal emblem.

———

Without some acquaintance with this viticultural past, it is tempting to shrug off Oregon's recent success as a passing phase, an accident of nature. But neither Richard Sommer nor David Lett was mad. The success of Lett's Eyrie Vineyards Pinot Noir '75 in the now notorious Gault Millau competitive tasting in Paris in 1979, repeated in more rigorous conditions in Beaune in 1980 by a skeptical Robert Drouhin, was not a fluke.

Drouhin, dismayed that The Eyrie Vineyards Pinot Noir '75 had placed third in Paris among a range of wines that included several distinguished Burgundies, insisted that the result would have been quite otherwise had the competing Burgundies been of appropriate quality and the tasting conducted in a more closely controlled atmosphere. On January 8, 1980, a jury composed of European professionals, assembled by Drouhin in the thousand-year-old Hall of Justice of the former dukes of Burgundy, tasted blind a dozen wines, including The Eyrie Vineyards Pinot Noir '75, six Drouhin burgundies—among them a 1961 Chambertin Clos de Bèze, a 1978 Beaune Clos des Mouches, and a 1959 Chambolle-Musigny—and assorted Pinot Noirs from other countries. It was assumed that this tasting, meticulously conducted, would reverse the findings of that in Paris. But, although the wine with the highest combined score of 70.0 was Drouhin's 1959 Chambolle-Musigny, in second place by only two tenths of a point was The Eyrie Vineyards Pinot Noir '75. The third wine, Drouhin's 1961 Chambertin Clos de Bèze, trailed well behind at third place with a combined score of only 66.5.

Today, one need only taste the Pinot Noir wines of Rex Hill, Domaine Drouhin (after the events of 1979 and 1980, Drouhin took to heart the old aphorism "If you can't beat them, join them"), Ponzi Vineyards, Adelsheim, Yamhill Valley, Amity, Cameron, Henry Estate, Girardet, Callahan Ridge, Bridgeview, Knudsen Erath, Cooper Mountain, St. Innocent, and at least a dozen more to see that Oregon Pinot Noir does not have to be judged by standards different from those by which one would judge Pinot Noir produced anywhere else.

Which is not to say that Oregon Pinot Noir could, or should, pass for Burgundy. Though taking Burgundy's wines as their criterion, Oregon's winegrowers have consistently affirmed that their Pinot Noirs do not have to taste like, or be mistaken for, those of Burgundy to be legitimate. Nor is it to say that every Pinot Noir produced in

Oregon is even worthy of comment. As production has increased, so the range of quality has widened.

And production has increased dramatically. The rush to plant Pinot Noir in Oregon after Lett's initial success in Paris and Beaune accelerated when Drouhin bought land in the Dundee Hills and announced plans for a winery there; it came close to a fever pitch when Brian Croser of South Australia's distinguished Petaluma Winery announced plans for a sparkling-wine facility at Newberg in the Willamette Valley with a partner no less renowned than the Champagne house of Bollinger. Between 1979 and 1991, the acreage of Pinot Noir in the state grew from 212 acres to 2,131. Whereas ten years ago, annual sales of Oregon wines were 260,000 gallons, they have now increased to some 900,000, and in that same span of time what was a mere handful of wineries has blossomed into almost ninety.

This growth has been accompanied by much change. For a start, Oregon's wine reputation is now bankable. New wineries have had less difficulty in attracting money; rarely are they so acutely and obviously underfinanced as those that went before. Money alone doesn't guarantee quality, but it helps provide space appropriate to the work; equipment to give the best possible technical support; and more, better, and newer barrels. Formerly, the rule was always make shift and make do, but now there is everything a winemaker could reasonably want and a discreet elegance besides.

The Rex Hill winery, converted from the buildings of a hazelnut farm, has a charmingly bricked courtyard surrounded by an extensive rambling garden. Its reception area, complete with fine old rugs, has the odd piece or two of eighteenth-century English furniture. Argyle, Brian Croser's facility for making sparkling wine from Pinot Noir and Chardonnay by the classic Champagne method, uses the nineteenth-century frame house that once was Newberg's city hall as a decoratively picture-perfect setting for its tasting and reception rooms. And Domaine Drouhin—which expects to spend another five million dollars on top of the seven million already invested in its vineyard and winery—brought from France eight sea containers of specially made tiles for the roof of a winery planned as much by the supervising landscape designer as the architect.

Other changes, in the vineyards and in the approach to winemaking, are sometimes simply the result of time passing but have profound consequences anyway. For example, now that vines planted in the 1970s and 1980s have matured, their grapes have a more concentrated flavor; vines planted in the last three or four years, though hardly yet bearing fruit, have included Pinot Noir clones brought in by Oregon State University from the French government experimental station at Dijon.

These new clones supplement the three on which most growers were previously obliged to rely. One of the three came from the Swiss viticultural station at Wädenswil near Zurich and was valued for the structure and delicacy it gave to wine. Another, drawn from the University of California's program at Davis, was originally brought to California from Pommard in Burgundy and was appreciated for the body and color it could contribute. The third is the Pinot Noir clone known in California—confusingly—as Gamay-Beaujolais, because of the fragrant wines it gives. For balance, most Oregon winemakers have tried to have access to all three of these clones, and they have done well with them. The clones newly introduced from France extend their options further, however, and should help them produce wines of even greater depth in the future.

If research has shown that a mix of clones gives the best result for Pinot Noir, many believe that a variety of yeast strains for the fermentation makes a similarly significant contribution. Some Oregon producers are experimenting with combinations of two and three different strains of selected yeasts, but others—including Drouhin, whose newly released wines are outstanding—rely on wild yeasts to get their fermentation going. "Wild yeasts are always a mix of many," says John Paul, the winemaker at Cameron Vineyard. "I encourage them along with two or three selected yeasts to add yet another layer to my wine."

Oregon growers have also had to concern themselves with cultivation techniques, though that has been the case from the very beginning of the present resurgence of grape growing. Those first growers soon realized that the state's climate wouldn't allow them to rely entirely on either French or California experience. As Dick Ponzi puts it: "In those early days, we were forever in seminars teaching each other as we learned—the importance of training our vines vertically, for instance, the better to expose the leaves to sunlight, as opposed to what they were doing in California, where leaf canopy gave shade to both plant and fruit. We have now learned that, like the Europeans, we must plant our vines more densely. We then need fewer bunches on each vine to get the same yields, and that allows us more leaves working for each grape."

All new vineyards in Oregon are being planted almost to the standard European density. Domaine Drouhin, for example, one of the largest of recent plantings, has a density of 3,000 vines to the acre against California's usual 650. Those who can't start over again have inserted vines between existing ones. Along with density, Oregon's growers have experimented with trellising to increase leaf area, and their innovations are now influencing the way wine grapes are grown elsewhere in the world. After all, what is of crucial importance in Oregon, close to the northern limit within which wine grapes will ripen, is usually at least beneficial to any vine, no matter where it is grown.

The system developed by Scott Henry of Umpqua Valley, for instance, was praised by Richard Smart of New Zealand in his book *Sunlight into Wine* (Dr. Smart is presently the international wine industry's guru on trellising) and is now being introduced in vineyards all over the world with excellent results. Henry divides the vine's shoots, training some up and some down, to create for each vine a great sheet of leaf surface that acts like a solar panel.

Oregon growers are also more flexible in their expectations. The marginal climate of Oregon, and of the Willamette Valley in particular, is what makes it possible to produce great wines there. But a marginal climate has a serious drawback, too: Consistency from year to year cannot be guaranteed. Wine producers, having found that difficult to accept at first, are now much more sensitive to the style inherent in each year's fruit and are less preoccupied with forcing it to a predetermined end. Fruit from a cool year, for example, when body is sure to be light, is fermented at a low temperature likely to bring out as much fragrance as possible. In other years, fermentation can be warmer. Producers have also learned to avoid packing in tannin and extract, a practice based on the false notion that a wine unapproachable when young is sure to be better for it when aged. One need only compare the rather massive wines of 1983 and 1985, both successful vintages in Oregon, with the same wineries' elegant 1988s to see how far winemakers have come and how quickly.

—

Oregon winegrowers pay a price for their success with Pinot Noir and for their decision, taken through the Oregon Wine Advisory Board, to capitalize on it by projecting for the state a clear image that focuses on this one variety and, essentially, on the Willamette Valley. Other varieties produced in Oregon and other regions—even when they produce Pinot Noir—remain in the shadows. Pinot Gris is carried along by the success of Pinot Noir (three of the best Pinot Gris are from The Eyrie Vineyards, Ponzi, and Rex Hill), but Oregon's Chardonnays get less attention than they deserve.

Those Chardonnays are mostly lighter and silkier than California's, partly because of more restrained levels of alcohol but largely because of a higher acidity that encourages growers to rely on malolactic fermentation, the bacterial change that converts harsh malic acid into milder lactic acid. Malolactic fermentation affects more than the acidity of a wine, however; it also draws all the wine's flavor components together in a way that has been compared to that of the final wash applied to a watercolor to bring the disparate hues into harmony.

Oregon Chardonnays rely on subtle appeal rather than assertive aromas and flavors, though there are exceptions (such as Henry Estates', which are richly full-bodied). Consistently among the best of Oregon's Chardonnays are those produced by Tualatin from a vineyard tucked into an angle on a hillside that traps warm air rising from the Tualatin Valley floor. Other wineries offering good Chardonnays include Argyle, Rex Hill, Ponzi, The Eyrie Vineyards, Adelsheim (which gets such accolades for its Pinot Noir that its Chardonnay, a model for all Oregon, is often overlooked), Valley View Vineyard, Ashland, and Weisinger's. Bridgeview, at an elevated and somewhat remote location in the Siskiyou Mountains close to the California border, offers a delicious barrel-select 1990 Chardonnay with something approaching a California style as well as another, very modestly priced Chardonnay with the mild fruit, nerve, and freshness of a good French Chablis.

We hear little of the state's remarkable Gewürztraminers and Rieslings, and even less of some better-than-creditable Cabernet Sauvignons and Merlots. Tualatin's Gewürztraminer has a following because of the winery's success with Chardonnay and because of its proximity to Portland, but the intensely flavored Gewürztraminers of Foris, Bridgeview, and Weisinger's, all in the Rogue Valley, are little known—if at all—outside the state and are not very familiar to consumers even within it. The Umpqua Valley Rieslings of Richard Sommer's Hillcrest, of Henry Estates, and of Callahan Ridge, particularly, are also superb.

I shall long remember a 1987 Callahan Ridge Riesling, a wine picked in relays, overripe berry by overripe berry, and labeled *Vinum Aureolum*. I sipped it under a tree one day at the back of the winery after an alfresco lunch. As I sat there, Richard Mansfield, the man who had made it, wandered off into a strawberry patch to bring back a few sun-warmed berries to accompany it.

There are exceptional Rieslings being made at Valley View, too, in the Rogue Valley. But even more surprising are Valley View's Cabernet Sauvignons and Merlots, neither variety being as rare as one might expect in Oregon. Wines of similar, and perhaps even better, quality are also being produced at Ashland Vineyards. In fact, the 1990 Merlot from Ashland is as concentrated, as well formed, and as fine as any other American Merlot I have tasted from that vintage.

Oregon's Chardonnays, Gewürztraminers, Rieslings, Cabernets, and Merlots are at present obscured rather than illuminated by the success of its Pinot Noir. But perhaps, in time, we'll be celebrating them, too. After all, France makes a virtue of its diversity—Burgundy, Bordeaux, Alsace, and Champagne are just the beginning there—and eventually Oregon will surely find a way to do the same.

January 1993

A California Original

Gerald Asher

The table in my kitchen is small and round; no more than two, perhaps three, can eat there together comfortably, a limit that allows me to open—for what is often an impromptu meal—one of those bottles we all hoard but that could never be stretched to a dinner party. I share some of my best wines in the kitchen. Though curiosity sometimes prompts us to seek out wines we know will be difficult to appreciate, wine is never intended to be anyone's jousting partner. And, especially in the kitchen, it should comfort and be companionable, whatever its pedigree; cheer rather than challenge. Few wines show these qualities as consistently, as comprehensively, and as exuberantly as *good* Zinfandel.

The qualifier is important, because there is a mass of not very interesting Zinfandel, too. Twenty years ago it was usually simple, and often dull, red jug wine. Now it's more likely to be a simple, and often dull, white (well, pink anyway). We also had a spell of Late Harvest monsters that would have amply satisfied anyone's fancy for demanding, challenging, and intimidating wine. But during all that time, and particularly since the late sixties, there has also been a subculture of distinguished Zinfandels, almost all produced in wineries far out of the mainstream, using fruit grown on what I can only describe as California's viticultural fringes.

For years these wines were hardly known beyond the circles of those who made a cult of them. But the secret's been out for quite a while now, and, as production has slowly increased, these handcrafted Zinfandels have become available to anyone prepared to take the trouble to look for them. In price they range from as little as seven dollars a bottle, though most are from ten to fifteen, and a few of the most celebrated are now pushing toward twenty.

—

The potential for outstanding Zinfandel quality was always there, of course, even when there were few wines to provide confirmation of it. In his 1880s book, *Grape Culture & Wine Making in California*—the standard text in California until well into this century—George Husmann said he had "yet to see the red wine of any variety [that he preferred] to the best samples of Zinfandel produced in this state." Some sixty years later, in 1941, when the California wine industry was struggling to recover from the years of Prohibition, Frank Schoonmaker wrote in his classic work, *American Wines,* "[Zinfandel] deserves more respect than it generally gets . . . [it] reflects so obviously, in the quality of its wine, the soil on which it was grown. . . ."

When Schoonmaker wrote that, few Americans gave much thought to the idea of a wine reflecting the soil on which it was grown. Accustomed to using the same name for a grape and for the wine made from it, Americans expected no more than that one should reflect the other. It was left to Europeans, who name their wines geographically rather than varietally, to concern themselves with a soil, with the climate that goes with it, and with a pattern of winemaking intended to resolve incompatibilities between the two.

However, leaving aside such idiosyncrasies as White Zinfandel and Zinfandel Nouveau (no matter how successful commercially, they could hardly have been what Schoonmaker had had in mind), most California winemakers working seriously with Zinfandel would agree with Husmann that, when grown on appropriate sites and handled with the care given other varieties in California, Zinfandel can give red wine at least as fine as any in the state. They would also accept Schoonmaker's view that Zinfandel reflects its physical environment in ways that impose distinct variations on the wine from one region of California to another.

———

Tasting my way recently through almost 150 California Zinfandels, almost all of them of the 1990 and 1991 vintages, I began grouping the wines by style to get an easier grasp of what I had before me. It quickly became clear that by doing so I was in fact also sorting them into regions of origin—wines from Dry Creek Valley here, Sonoma Valley there—though that had not been my intention.

In California much is made of geography (witness the American Viticultural Areas, the officially delimited wine regions like Carneros or Stags Leap District or Sonoma Valley) when it suits a marketing strategy. Otherwise, little more than lip service is paid to the differences of style and taste imposed by location. Producers who buy grapes from various parts of the state know very well what these differences are—they base their buying decisions on them. But too often they then allow regional distinctions to disappear in the blending vat. Some of the Zinfandels on my tasting table had clearly been made that way. Though not necessarily less attractive than the others, they were less focused, less collected.

Most of the wines, however, were clearly defined by the regions from which they came. For example, the Zinfandels from Sonoma Valley were the hardest, the most tannic, and the most astringent. Those with a bright, crisp style—an edge of acidity, rather than tannin, that was coupled with the clear, forward berry-fruit aroma and flavor we most associate with California Zinfandel—were likely to be from Dry Creek Valley, Russian River Valley, or the Lytton Springs region, where the previous two areas meet. Wines from the upper part of Dry Creek Valley or from Alexander Valley, across a watershed, were more mellow, had a more complex—or at least a deeper—flavor, and were generally more plump.

Though no less bold, the fruit of Zinfandels from Amador County in the Sierra Foothills comes across as plum rather than berry and sometimes as dried fruit rather than fresh, with hints of apricot and prune. Zinfandel grapes, known for their tendency to ripen irregularly within the bunch (some berries have already become raisins while others are barely ripe), accumulate sugar in a rush just before picking. So their alcohol, most often in the 13 and 14 percent range, is usually higher than the average for table wine in California. In Amador County Zinfandels, the alcohol can be particularly generous, and it is the headiness of these wines, combined with their spicy, dusky aromas and flavors, that makes them so richly and so appealingly exotic.

Napa Valley Zinfandels are the opposite: well-structured, well-bred, and impeccably straight-backed. Though vigorous, they have perfect balance and show a patrician restraint. Nothing is to excess. Their aromas and flavors, while at times quite powerful, have finesse and delicacy. Sometimes one can detect in them a touch of the cassis one associates with Cabernet Sauvignon. But, then, it's not unknown for the producers of Napa Zinfandels to add a little Cabernet Sauvignon to the blend, in proportions that the law allows, to give exactly this effect.

Zinfandels from hillside vineyards above Napa Valley—from Howell Mountain, Stags Leap, and Atlas Peak on the east side of the valley and Spring Mountain and Mount Veeder on the west—have characteristically tighter flavors. Closed when the wine is young and then, as it develops, opening to an unexpected (sometimes even medicinal) intensity, the flavors are nevertheless all of a piece with the wines' lean and forthright hillside style.

———

Such differences within a single region are not at all uncommon with Zinfandel; they are further confirmation of the way this variety adapts to and reflects every changed circumstance of growth. In Mendocino there's an equally wide divide between the tense and concentrated Zinfandels produced from old vines planted by turn-of-the-century Italian immigrants who settled the exposed, high ridges between Anderson Valley and the Pacific and the subtly urbane wines from vineyards almost as old but planted in milder and better-protected sites around Ukiah and in the adjacent McDowell and Redwood valleys.

Jed Steele of Steele Wines, a man who knows the vineyards on the Mendocino ridges better than anyone, says of them, "The vines there have never been irrigated and they yield very little. Even when the fruit is really ripe, the acid is always good. There is never a hint of the raisining common in late-picked Zinfandel elsewhere. That's why the flavor is so pure and seems to be etched into the wines despite their opulence." To see the difference between the two styles of Mendocino Zinfandel, one need only compare the inherently wild qualities of a wine from the ridge with the supremely civilized Private Reserve Zinfandel from Lolonis Vineyard in Redwood Valley.

I found the Zinfandels from around Paso Robles, in San Luis Obispo County, the hardest to pin down. They were all supple and agreeable (except when too much oak had been dumped on them), but in the end I recognized them more for what they weren't than for any particular characteristics they shared. They were amiable rather than assertive and seemed to vary more in response to winemaking technique than anything else. Charm made up for their low profile, and Paul Draper, Ridge Vineyards' winemaker, told me that their very reticence was a quality readily accepted in many markets. As far as his own wines were concerned, he said, Europeans in particular preferred the relative quiescence of Ridge Vineyards' Paso Robles Zinfandel (a wine I nevertheless found more concentrated and more muscular than other Paso Robles Zinfandels) to the high vivacity of his Lytton Springs wine.

Zinfandels from the Arroyo Grande Valley at the opposite end of San Luis Obispo County (I know only of those from Saucelito Canyon Winery and Santa Barbara Winery) are remarkably engaging and sweetly harmonious—they've not a note out of place. In some ways they come close to the bright-berry style of Dry Creek Valley, but they are both more tightly woven and more supple. The intense fruitiness of these wines makes them irresistibly delicious.

—

Zinfandel is California's own grape, but it's also California's mystery. Its history, both before and after its arrival in the state in the 1850s, has been continually revised in the light of both serious research and enlightened speculation. There seems little doubt that Zinfandel's name has come to us from the Zierfahnler grape by way of its Czech-language variant, *cinifadl.* The name was used for both white and black grapes grown in the nineteenth century in the vineyards of a region that spilled across what until recently was the Austrian-Hungarian-Czechoslovakian border. The black version—Blauer Zierfahnler—is thought to have been either the Kadarka grape or the Kékfrankos, both of Hungary. But that doesn't necessarily tell us anything much about California's Zinfandel because there is no certainty that its connection with the Blauer Zierfahnler goes further than the name.

Zinfandel came to California from nurseries in New England where vines of that name (or slight variants of it) were already being grown and offered for sale in the 1830s. But either there, or after its arrival in California, Zinfandel could have become confused with Black St. Peter's, a vine of similar appearance bearing similar grapes, developed from seed in eighteenth-century England (it's mentioned in William Speechly's *Treatise on the Culture of the Vine*, published in 1789). Black St. Peter's was introduced to California from East Coast nurseries at the same time as Zinfandel, and its wines started winning awards in California as soon as the first vines came into production. We know that cuttings of both Zinfandel and Black St. Peter's were sent in the late 1850s to General Mariano Guadalupe Vallejo, the last military commandant of what had been Mexican northern California, for his vineyard near the old Sonoma mission—a vineyard that was itself the source of cuttings for the establishment of many vineyards elsewhere in the county.

But no matter whether today's California Zinfandel is still the variety that arrived as such in the state or is Black St. Peter's with a change of name, we know from genetic fingerprinting that it's related to the Primitivo di Gioia, a black grape grown in Apulia, the heel of Italy. For a while, after the Primitivo connection had been established, it was assumed that Zinfandel's mystery was solved and that one must have come from the other. But Primitivo was introduced into Italy only in the late nineteenth century, when the vines indigenous to Apulia had been destroyed by the vine pest phylloxera. That was long after Zinfandel had been brought to California. All that can be said with certainty is that Zinfandel and Primitivo are related and that they have a common connection, possibly a common ancestor, in the Plavać Mali, a grape grown on the Adriatic coast of Croatia. Croatia, of course, was part of the Austro-Hungarian Empire until 1918. And that, perhaps, brings us back full circle to the Zierfahnler.

—

The revival of California Zinfandel as a serious varietal wine began with the rediscovery of forgotten patches of old vines such as those on the Mendocino Ridge, most of them tucked away among hillside orchards. ("Rediscovery" might not be the appropriate word: When I used it once to Ken Deaver, a Zinfandel grower in Amador County, he stared at me and said, "We didn't know we'd been lost.") These old vineyards were always small because there was no point then in a man's planting more vines than he could cultivate alone by hand. In any case, those who had planted vines had done so mostly to nourish their families. Wine was as intrinsic to the diet of most immigrants settling on the land at that time as it had been in Europe, and they sold, more or less haphazardly, only the wine that was surplus to their needs. (In a recorded oral history of the Mendocino coast, Joe Scaramella, a former mayor of Point Arena, describes how, as a boy, he was given Zinfandel every day to take to school to moisten the otherwise dry bread that served as his lunch.)

Age gives a Zinfandel vine many important advantages. Once established, the vine's extensive root system protects it from climatic adversity; rarely, if ever, does it need to be irrigated. It is always head-pruned—an old system of shaping and training a vine low to the ground in the form of a fistful of spread fingers with the support of neither stakes nor wires—with leaves and fruit open to sun and air to help the grapes ripen more easily. "It's interesting if you look at what they [the growers] are doing today with leaf trimming, opening up the center of the vine to let light onto the fruit," Michael Martini of the Louis M. Martini Winery recently told *Wines & Vines,* a trade publication. "That's exactly what happens with a head-prune vine naturally."

The yield of old, head-pruned vines is limited—partly because of the age of the vines but also because it's more difficult to over-crop head-pruned vines than vines supported on wires. For that very reason the regulations for some French controlled appellations stipulate that vines must be head-pruned and their shoots left unsupported.

Perhaps the most significant advantage of all, however, is that California's old Zinfandel vines are of a type giving small bunches of small berries that can be relied on to produce wine with character. Though cuttings from these old vines are once again being used for the propagation of new—anyone with an old vineyard is trying to extend, duplicate, or preserve it—most of the Zinfandel vineyards established in recent years were planted with a clone selected and developed by the Department of Viticulture and Enology of the University of California at Davis. It's a clone that gives generous crops of large bunches of big berries—appropriate, perhaps, for White Zinfandel but for little else.

Old vineyards have something more in their favor: a generous sprinkling of other black varieties, most commonly Petite Sirah, Carignane, and Grenache, that the "little old winegrower" of yesteryear planted at random in his vineyard to add interest to his finished wine and, more importantly, to compensate for any possible lack of color, alcohol, or finesse. A few years ago Ridge Vineyards went through the vines it leases from the Trentadue family at Geyserville and found that the proportion of Zinfandel there was actually less than two thirds (the balance was made up of roughly even proportions of equally ancient Petite Sirah and Carignane vines). Having made successful wines from the vineyard exactly as planted for almost thirty years, Ridge Vineyards has chosen to continue as before, but it now sells the wine simply as Geyserville, with no varietal designation. The 1990 Geyserville is so remarkable that it lent considerable excitement to the California Grill at Bordeaux's Vinexpo last June.

—

A few of the old vineyards had been abandoned, but most were still being cultivated for fruit to be used by the owners or sold to home winemakers or to the large producers who could always accept another ton or two for their big-volume blends. Jed Steele had started to make wine from old Mendocino Ridge Zinfandel vines at the Edmeades Vineyard & Winery in Anderson Valley in the early 1970s, but David Bennion and his partners at Ridge Vineyards had stumbled onto the possibilities of old Zinfandel vines almost ten years earlier. The founders of Ridge Vineyards, colleagues at the Stanford Research Institute, had bought their mature Cabernet Sauvignon vineyard on

Monte Bello Ridge in the Santa Cruz Mountains, south of San Francisco, in 1958. On their drives up and down the mountain they'd often stopped to buy Zinfandel made by their neighbors the Picchetti family. (The Picchettis had been making wine from their Zinfandel vineyard since 1877, selling it mostly at the winery gate.)

In his book *Angels' Visits,* an inquiry into California Zinfandel published in 1991, David Darlington describes what happened next. Darlington has a keen eye for the telling detail (and, although not evident in the excerpt below, a wicked skill in allowing the characters in his saga to skewer themselves on their own offhand remarks). His book is one of the most entertaining (and honestly informative) on wine to have appeared for many years. This is what he has to say:

> In October 1964 the [Ridge Vineyards] families were nearly finished with the Monte Bello harvest when they learned that the Picchettis were giving up the wine business—ordered by the county health officials to put in a concrete floor, the younger generation, insufficiently enamored with winemaking to comply, abandoned plans to pick their grapes. The '64 Monte Bello Cabernet crop had been short, so the Ridge owners leaped into the lurch. They harvested the Picchettis' Zinfandel (at twenty-four degrees Brix, a sugar level that the owners considered overripe) and fermented it according to their traditional methods. "It was so good right from the beginning," Dave Bennion recalled, "that when we needed a wine for dinner, I'd just go get some from the barrel and put it in a flask. Our Cabernet couldn't be quaffed that way. I saw right then that Zinfandel could be our bread and butter."

The next year Bennion arranged to buy more Zinfandel grapes from old vines in a Paso Robles vineyard that still supplies Ridge Vineyards to this day. He also agreed to help finance the restoration of the badly neglected Zinfandel vines in the Jimsomare vineyard, another property on Monte Bello Ridge. In 1966, Bennion contracted to purchase grapes from old Zinfandel vines in the Trentadue vineyard that is now the source of the winery's Geyserville *cuvée* mentioned above. All those early Ridge Vineyards Zinfandels were provocatively different from other wines then being made in California. Sometimes they were overbearingly clumsy, but they were always impressive. Ironically, by the time Ridge Vineyards had left that more or less experimental stage of their winemaking behind them, others seemed to be taking Ridge's early wines as models for their own.

———

Those others did not include the late Joe Swan, a Western Airlines pilot who had made a hobby of wine for years before a transfer from Los Angeles to San Francisco allowed him to buy a vineyard near the Russian River planted in the old-timers' classic mix of Zinfandel, Petite Sirah, and Carignane. He made his first Zinfandel in 1968, and the wines his Joseph Swan Vineyards continued to produce through the 1970s and 1980s are as much a part of California legend as the man himself.

Joel Peterson of Ravenswood—now perhaps the leader in California Zinfandel—served an apprenticeship of sorts with Joe Swan in the mid-1970s. Peterson had been raised with a broad knowledge of wine (he sat in at his father's distinguished twice-weekly tasting group from the age of nine) and brought to winemaking a sophisticated palate, a scientific training as a biochemist, and a confident insouciance.

Acknowledging his debt to Swan, he told David Darlington, "[Swan] tended his fermenting wine as if it were a newborn child. He was so meticulous. He smelled every barrel in the winery, made sure everything was clean to his nose; he never rushed, never did anything unconsciously."

Peterson made his own first Zinfandel with Swan's equipment in 1976. His Zinfandels from the Dickerson Vineyard in Napa Valley and Old Hill Vineyard in Sonoma Valley are now among the finest wines—regardless of variety—produced in California; few, at any price, are as thrilling as they. (On the day after my big Zinfandel tasting I passed up a chance to drink Léoville-Las-Cases '70 with my lunch, preferring to take a glass from the opened bottle of Dickerson Vineyard '91 instead.)

Peterson follows Swan's precepts: He chooses fruit from old, head-pruned vines with low yields and ferments it with its natural, indigenous yeast in old open redwood fermenters that are wide rather than high—the mass of skins and pips that floats on the surface is then more shallow and easier to punch down for flavor and color extraction. "We let the fermentation get quite warm," he told me, "and, depending on the fruit and the year, we let the skins macerate when fermentation is finished for anything from three to five weeks. For the size of our operation, we have a large cellar staff. That's important, too. You need to stay close to the wines. You mustn't let them get away from you."

——

Ridge, Ravenswood, and Rosenblum Cellars—the last a winery in Alameda, across the bay from San Francisco, founded and run by Kent Rosenblum as a sideline to his veterinary practice—are known among enthusiasts as the big *R*'s of Zinfandel. Of the three, Ridge Vineyards' Zinfandels have classic measure, Ravenswood's are flowingly romantic, and Rosenblum's are gorgeously, dramatically florid. If Ridge Vineyards is the Bach of the Zinfandel world, Ravenswood is the Brahms and Rosenblum the Strauss—Johann, of course, not Richard.

February 1994

THE SON ALSO RISES

James Rodewald

Like nine-year-old kids all over America, Geoffrey Gruet has a world of opportunity in front of him. But his world is a little larger than most. Sure, he could be president of the United States, or a fireman, or an astronaut, but there is at least one unique path open to him—he can be a third-generation producer of world-class sparkling wine. In New Mexico.

His family legacy, after all, is a history of making great wine in un-expected locations. "In 1950, all the great Champagne was from Éper-nay," explains Geoffrey's dad, Laurent, who makes highly regarded wines in the impossible-to-miss brick-faced building that stands prominently alongside I-25, the main route from Albuquerque to Santa Fe. "At the time, anything from outside Épernay was considered worthless."

But not by Laurent's father, Gilbert, who in 1952 planted vineyards in the Côte de Sézanne, a region of Champagne that had been ignored by vintners, mostly because of its distance from Épernay and Reims, the centers of Champagne production. Gilbert, who was twenty-one at the time, saw the potential there (and the lower real-estate prices), started small, and grew slowly. Other winemakers took note of the quality of his grapes and the wine he was making and followed his lead. Today, the area's Chardonnay is particularly valued for its ripeness and low acidity, and some of the top Champagne houses—Laurent-Perrier, Pommery, Moët & Chandon—blend grapes from Sézanne into their wines.

In the early 1980s, the Gruet family, faced with rising land prices in France and looking for ways to expand their business, came to the United States. "We didn't want to have all our eggs in one basket in Champagne," Laurent says. "So we visited California, Texas, and New Mexico. California was great, but it was already well established—big companies like Chandon were already there. We saw New Mexico as a challenge; we wanted to prove great wine could be made here."

Contrary to its cactus-and-tumbleweed image, New Mexico has a long viticultural history. In the seventeenth century, missionary priests were making sacramental wine, and in 1880 the state produced nearly a million gallons of wine. Twenty years later, root rot took its toll, and in 1943 a devastating flood all but destroyed the industry. The climate is harsh—late frosts are common, summer days can be hot, and the monsoon season often brings dramatic and potentially damaging rain and hail. On the other hand, the soil can be quite good, and even on the hottest days the temperature drops drastically after the sun goes down (warm, sunny days help ripen the grapes, while the cool nights allow acids to develop, leading to well-balanced fruit). Stress may not be healthy for humans, but the best wines are made from grapes that have struggled a bit.

———

At the time of the family's New World scouting trip, Laurent was just seventeen, but his father went back to France to run the parent company, leaving him and his older sister and her husband to establish the family's North American outpost. They bought grapes from around the state to pinpoint the best areas for vineyards, built the winery—Laurent calls the building "a big billboard"—and began making sparkling wine using the traditional techniques of Champagne.

The grapes they liked best came from a site 150 miles away that was controlled by a German wine company. By 1984, the Germans were ready to give up on New Mexico, and the Gruets were ready to grow their own grapes. The location is remote—near the Jornada del Muerto, a desolate stretch of the route taken by the first Spanish colonizers of the area—but it was clear it would be worth the long drive from Albuquerque. The vineyards are high enough that late spring frosts are less problematic than in the nearby river valleys (cold air sinks), and the soil is high in gypsum, which isn't exactly the same as the famous limestone of Champagne, but Laurent feels there are similarities. "Champagne is unique because of the *terroir*," he says, "but also because of the techniques used there. We follow the rules as they are in Champagne." In fact, they go well beyond the rules. Like many of the top producers in France, where at least fifteen months of aging on the lees before bottling is mandatory for nonvintage Champagne, Gruet ages its nonvintage sparkling wines for two years. "We want to be almost as good as Champagne," says Laurent. "Champagne is the best sparkling wine in the world."

As he moves quickly from the new press to the stainless-steel tanks where the Chardonnay juice is flowing and then to the barrels where special wines are aging, it's easy to see the badges of the profession the six-foot-four Frenchman has earned. A two-inch scar runs down his forehead; he has another on his right cheek, a few on his chin, a couple around his eyebrows. "This year I got cut twice by exploding bottles," he says. The flawed glass that leads to such high-pressure mishaps is very unusual, but this news has me edging away from the bottle-lined walls of the winery.

"I'm thirty-eight years old," Laurent says. "But I have twenty-two years of experience. When I was sixteen, I was supposed to go to wine school in Avize. I went for one year before my dad said, 'You're going to go to *my* wine school.' I learned winemaking from him, but I also learned the wine business." Now, says Laurent, he wants to pass his knowledge on. "I want to teach somebody what I know," he says. "But I only want to do it once. For example, the smell in the tank after you pump out the wine is the same smell the wine will have two years later. That's a lesson that takes time to understand. Teaching will take at least five years, which is why I want it to be someone from the family."

Laurent's lessons will not be limited to sparkling wine. "I love Pinot Noir," he says. "I made my first Pinot in 1998. My dad joked about it. Then he tasted the wine and he was really surprised. The 1999 was even better. That was the year my father got sick. I brought a barrel sample with me when I went back to France to see him. It was his last glass of wine."

December 2003

Generation Next

William Hamilton

In 1952, Elias Fernandez's father left Michoacán, Mexico, and traveled to Stockton, California. A few years later, he and his wife moved to St. Helena, picking walnuts, plums, and grapes. Like many other children of migrant laborers, Elias started throwing fruit and nuts into buckets and boxes as soon as his hands were big enough.

Fernandez still picks fruit, but now he's evaluating grapes for Shafer Vineyards, which makes one of California's most sought-after wines, the Hillside Select Cabernet Sauvignon. And he's their winemaker.

"When I was little my dad used to run the machine that shook the trees," Fernandez says. "Then I remember sitting up with him on tractors, hauling those old fruit and nut trees away. Everything was getting pulled up for vineyards." By the time he was nine, his father was working for a vineyard management company, and young Elias knew how to drive the tractor.

———

The change in what was being grown in places like the Napa Valley was soon followed by a shift in the kinds of people buying land there. In 1972, John Shafer, a visiting Chicago executive, fell madly in love with the area, acquired an old paisano-style vineyard, moved his family out, and took a job teaching high school to provide some cash flow while he replanted his predecessor's mix of Charbono, Grenache, Syrah, Zinfandel—and obscurer ingredients of an old home-barreled red-wine recipe—with Cabernet Sauvignon. This vineyard turned out to be in exactly the right place, the Stags' Leap area, at exactly the right time—just before the most consequential blind tasting of wine in history, the 1976 debacle, in which French experts, to their national chagrin, chose a Stags' Leap Cabernet over Bordeaux's grandest marques.

It's safe to assume that the hallways of St. Helena High were not ringing with talk of that tasting. Fernandez, in fact, was much more focused on the trumpet at the time, and when he graduated he was awarded a Fulbright scholarship for music. He entered the University of Nevada, Reno, but in a city built on the lure of beating the odds, Fernandez soon realized just how much of a long shot a career as a musician would be.

"I didn't know what I wanted to do with my life," he says. "I had grown up here in the Valley, and after high school I just wanted to get away. But I kept coming home and that's when you really see how beautiful this place is: every time you come back. So after a year in Reno I transferred to UC Davis, and there were basically three things you could study: construction, real estate, or wine. And I thought, 'Wine sounds good. I've done that vineyard stuff.'"

While Elias Fernandez would undoubtedly have been a success at real estate or construction, the admiration I felt for the Shafer Hillside Select Cabernet Sauvignon I was drinking (you have to be on the mailing list to buy it, and then you have to fork over $150 a bottle) as I listened to his Horatio Alger story made me gladder and gladder that he had chosen the most salubrious and humane of his three college study possibilities.

"One of the advantages I think I have is that I know the vineyard. I grew up in it. And the people that work there are all Hispanic. I know the culture. I know them. They respect me because of where I have come from and they do things how I think they should be done to make great wine. It starts in the vineyards—we sort bunches, we sort the berries. That's why it's so important that the workers know exactly what you want and do the job you want."

Despite the renown of the Hillside Select and the high quality of Shafer's other wines, Fernandez is not a household name among wine connoisseurs. He is, however, well respected in the winemaking community both for the excellence of his wines and the way he goes about making them.

"He's one of the few winemakers I know who personally inspects each barrel both visually and by smelling," barrel merchant Bayard Fox told the prestigious *Quarterly Review of Wines,* which selected Fernandez as California Winemaker of the Year in 2002. "He's so conscientious he's practically a nuisance." His bosses have provided the most succinct tribute to Fernandez's character by naming the winery's latest bottling, a Syrah launched in 2002, for him. It's called Relentless.

February 2004

Notes on Contributors

GERALD ASHER has been contributing articles about wine to *Gourmet* for thirty years. His books include *The Pleasures of Wine* and *Vineyard Tales: Reflections on Wine.*

JAMES BEARD wrote more than twenty books on food and cooking, including *Delights and Prejudices* and *The New James Beard.*

HILAIRE BELLOC was a prolific writer, publishing more than 150 books on a wide range of subjects including poetry, fiction, social commentary, and biography.

RAY BRADBURY has written more than fifty books, including *The Martian Chronicles, The Illustrated Man,* and *Fahrenheit 451.*

ROY BRADY was the chairman of the Alta California Wine and Food Society from 1965 to 1983 and wrote for *Saveur, Wine World, Coast,* and *Architectural World* in addition to *Gourmet.*

ILES BRODY was the author of the books *The Colony: Portrait of a Restaurant and Its Famous Recipes, Gone with the Windsors,* and *On the Tip of My Tongue.*

CHANDLER BURR is a journalist and the author of *Emperor of Scent: A Story of Perfume, Obsession, and the Last Mystery of the Senses* and *A Separate Creation: The Search for the Biological Origins of Sexual Orientation.*

NARDI REEDER CAMPION is author of the memoir *Everyday Matters: A Love Story.*

KATE COLEMAN is a veteran investigative reporter and author. Her most recent book is *The Secret Wars of Judi Bari: A Car Bomb, the Fight for the Redwoods, and the End of Earth First.*

WILLIAM HAMILTON, a cartoonist and writer, has contributed frequently to *Gourmet* since the 1980s.

HUGH JOHNSON has written several celebrated books about wine, including *Vintage: The Story of Wine* and *The World Atlas of Wine.*

LILLIAN LANGSETH-CHRISTENSEN was a travel writer and author of several books, including *How to Present and Serve Food Attractively* and *The Instant Epicure.*

JAMES RODEWALD is the editor of *Gourmet*'s "Drinks" section.

FRANK SCHOONMAKER wrote about wine for *The New Yorker* before covering the topic for *Gourmet.* He was the author of *Encyclopedia of Wine.*

ANDRÉ L. SIMON was born in France but lived most of his life in London, where he was a champagne merchant as well as an editor and author of more than a hundred books on gastronomy and wine.

FREDERICK S. WILDMAN, JR., was a wine importer and writer. He also wrote *Wine Tour of France.*

EVERETT WOOD was an airline pilot based in Germany during the 1950s. His articles appeared in *Gourmet, Gray's Sporting Journal,* and *Field & Stream.*

RUTH REICHL, former restaurant critic of *New West* magazine, *California* magazine, the *Los Angeles Times,* and *The New York Times,* is now editor in chief of *Gourmet* magazine. She is also the author of the bestselling memoirs *Tender at the Bone, Comfort Me with Apples,* and *Garlic and Sapphires.* Reichl lives in Manhattan with her husband, her son, and two cats.

A Note on the Type

The principal text of this Modern Library edition
was set in a digitized version of Janson, a typeface that
dates from about 1690 and was cut by Nicholas Kis,
a Hungarian working in Amsterdam. The original matrices have
survived and are held by the Stempel foundry in Germany.
Hermann Zapf redesigned some of the weights and sizes for
Stempel, basing his revisions on the original design.